MIDWEST AND GREAT PLAINS

Walter Havighurst, Editor

The cover shows a combine harvesting wheat.
This machine cuts the wheat stalks and separates the grain from the husks and stems. The
grain is blown through the spout into the truck.

LIBRARY OF CONGRESS CATALOG CARD NUMBER: 67-17399

CONTRIBUTORS

WALTER HAVIGHURST
Research Professor of English
Miami University
Oxford, Ohio

JOHN FRASER HART
Professor of Geography
University of Minnesota
Minneapolis, Minnesota

J. R. T. HUGHES
Professor of Economics
Northwestern University
Evanston, Illinois

CHARLES P. LOOMIS
Professor of Sociology
Michigan State University
East Lansing, Michigan

ASHLEY MONTAGU
Anthropologist
Princeton, New Jersey

PENROD MOSS
Curriculum Consultant
Dixie School District
San Rafael, California

WALTER T. K. NUGENT
Associate Professor of History
Indiana University
Bloomington, Indiana

CATHERINE COLE
Manuscript Editor

JAMES G. EKWALL
Manuscript Editor

RAYMOND E. FIDELER
Editor and President

RUTH E. FIDELER
Design Editor

MARGARET FISHER HERTEL
Staff Writer

JERRY E. JENNINGS
Staff Writer

PAULINE J. KELTON
Picture Editor

JOYCE KORTES
Manuscript Editor

WAYNE M. McDOWELL
Senior Editor

MARY MITUS
Map Editor

CONNIE J. NEGARAN
Manuscript Editor

BETTY O'CONNOR
Staff Writer

T. J. O'CONNOR
Staff Writer

CAROL S. PRESCOTT
Staff Writer

DOROTHY M. ROGERS
Senior Manuscript Editor

BARB M. ROYS
Design Editor

JUANITA G. SEIFER
Senior Manuscript Editor

JERRY D. SMITH
Manuscript Editor

MARION H. SMITH
Staff Writer

MARY B. SPANOS
Manuscript Editor

DAWN A. VANDERVEEN
Manuscript Editor

FRANCES D. WAER
Manuscript Editor

Chicago, Illinois, is the largest city in the Midwest and Great Plains. The picture on the opposite page shows skyscrapers along the Chicago River, which flows through the heart of the city.

MIDWEST AND GREAT PLAINS

Walter Havighurst, Editor

CALIFORNIA STATE SERIES

PUBLISHED BY CALIFORNIA STATE DEPARTMENT OF EDUCATION
SACRAMENTO, 1967

CONTENTS

Part 6   Great Plains States

Maps, Charts, and Special Studies

EDITORIAL AND MAP ACKNOWLEDGMENTS

Grateful acknowledgment is made to Scott, Foresman and Company for the pronunciation system used in this book, which is taken from the Thorndike-Barnhart Dictionary Series. Grateful acknowledgment is made to the following for permission to use cartographic data in this book: Creative Arts: Pages 50, 51, 75, and top maps on page 359; Base maps courtesy of the Nystrom Raised Relief Map Company, Chicago 60618: Pages 21, 28, 29, and bottom map on page 359; Panoramic Studios: Page 16; Rand McNally & Company: Pages 18 and 19; United States Department of Commerce, Bureau of the Census: Pages 117, 155, and 157.

PICTURE ACKNOWLEDGMENTS

Grateful acknowledgment is made to the following for permission to use the illustrations found in this book:

Allis-Chalmers Manufacturing Company: Pages 199 and 271
Alpha Photo Associates: Page 41
Aluminum Company of America: Page 224
American Airlines: Page 183
American Museum of Natural History: Pages 70 and 71
American Oil Company: Page 314
American Telephone and Telegraph Company: Page 110
Art Institute of Chicago: Page 119
Authenticated News International: Page 121
Bell Helicopter Company: Page 200
Black Star: Pages 43, 123, and 337
Bob Taylor: Pages 316, 318, and 319
Bureau of Public Roads: Page 68
Burlington Railroad: Page 179
Camerique: Page 321
Caterpillar Tractor Company: Pages 145 (lower) and 212
Celotex Corporation: Page 232
Chesapeake and Ohio Railway: Page 193
Chicago Association of Commerce and Industry: Page 214
Chicago Department of Development and Planning: Page 124 (both)
Chicago Historical Society: Page 120
Cincinnati Chamber of Commerce: Page 282
Cincinnati Milling Machine Company: Page 196
Cleveland Chamber of Commerce: Page 171
Colorado State Historical Society: Page 73

Columbus Area Chamber of Commerce: Page 23
Cosden Oil and Chemical Company: Page 197
Dallas Chamber of Commerce: Page 343
Dallas Morning News: Page 139
Deere and Company: Page 211
Des Moines Chamber of Commerce: Page 235
Detroit Department Report and Information Committee: Page 114
Devaney: Pages 35, 105, 134, 218, 221, 258, and 344
Dow Chemical Company: Page 246
Dresser Industries, Inc.: Page 163
Eleanor Kalafsky: Page 87
Firestone Tire and Rubber Company: Page 279
Ford Foundation: Page 132
Ford Motor Company: Pages 188, 189, 191, 198, and 245
Frank Fulkersin: Page 250
Frederick Way, Jr.: Page 67
Freelance Photographers Guild: Pages 3, 53, and 342
Galloway: Pages 74, 90, 118, 161, 165, 171, 181, 220, 228, 259, 297, 300, 302, and 328
Gendreau: Page 65
General Mills, Inc.: Page 201
General Steel Industries, Inc.: Page 267
Grand Rapids Press: Page 249 by Ralph Truax
Harnischfeger Company: Page 289
Hibbing Chamber of Commerce: Page 168
Honeywell, Inc.: Page 257
Houston Chamber of Commerce: Page 339

TO THE STUDENT

Why the social studies are important to you. During the next few years, you will make an important choice. You will choose whether or not you will direct your own life. Many people are never aware of making this choice. They drift through life, never really trying to understand what is going on around them or why things turn out the way they do. Without knowing it, these people have chosen not to direct their own lives. As a result, they miss many enriching experiences. Other people make a serious effort to choose a way of life that will bring them satisfaction. The chances are that you will have a more challenging life if you decide to live by choice instead of by chance.

You will need three types of knowledge to live by choice successfully. Living by choice will demand a great deal from you. You will have to keep growing in three different types of learnings — understandings, attitudes, and skills. As the chart below shows, the type of learning we call understandings includes the kinds of information you need in order to understand yourself, your country, and your world. The type of learning we call attitudes deals with the way you feel toward yourself and your world. The third type of learning includes the different kinds of skills you need to use in gaining understandings and developing constructive attitudes. Among these skills are knowing how to locate and organize information, how to read with understanding, and how to work effectively with others.

The social studies can help you grow in the three types of learnings. Your social studies class is one of the best places in which you can explore the three types of learnings. Here you can obtain much of the information you need for understanding yourself and your world. You can practice many important skills. Through many experiences, you can begin to evaluate what in life is worthwhile to you.

The problem-solving method will help you achieve success in social studies. Since the social studies are of such great importance, you want to use the best possible study method. Of course, you could just read a textbook and memorize answers for a test. If you did so, however, you would forget much of the information soon after the test was over. Your attitudes would not develop, and you would not have the opportunity to use many important skills. We suggest that you use a better way of studying. This is the problem-solving method. To use this method in learning about the Midwest and Great Plains, you will need to follow these steps:

1. Do some general background reading about the Midwest and Great Plains or about one of the states in the Midwest and Great Plains in which you are most interested.

2. Choose an important, interesting problem that you would like to solve.

Three Types of Learnings

Understandings	Attitudes	Skills
A. Concepts*	A. Values*	A. Obtaining knowledge
B. Generalizations*	B. Appreciations*	B. Handling knowledge
C. Facts	C. Ideals	C. Working with others

*See **Four Words To Understand**, page 10.

Write it down so that you will have clearly in mind what it is you want to find out. (Look at the sample problems on page 10.) If there are small problems that need to be solved in order to solve your big problem, list them, too.

3. Consider all possible solutions to your problem and list the ones that seem most likely to be true. These possible solutions are called "educated guesses," or hypotheses. You will try to solve your problem by proving that these hypotheses are true or false. Some will be partly true and partly false.

4. Find out which hypotheses are correct, or partly correct, by doing research. This book provides you with four main sources of information about the Midwest and Great Plains. These are the text, the pictures, the maps, and the Glossary. To locate the information you need, you may use the Table of Contents and the Index. The sugges-tions on pages 346-350 will help you locate and evaluate other sources of information.

As you do your research, make notes of all the information you find that will help you prove or disprove your hypotheses. You may discover that information obtained from one source disagrees with information from another. If this should happen, check still further and try to decide which facts are correct.

5. Summarize what you have learned. Have you proved or disproved your hypotheses? What new facts have you learned? Do you need to do further research?

You may want to write a report about the problem and the solution or solutions that you believe to be correct. To help other people share the ideas that you have come to understand, you may decide to illustrate your research project with maps, pictures, or your own

Gavins Point Dam, on the South Dakota–Nebraska border. The people of the Midwest and Great Plains need to make better use of their water resources. A study of geography will help you to understand why this is true.

drawings. You will find helpful suggestions for writing a good report on pages 350 and 351.

You can use the problem-solving method throughout your life. In addition to helping you to achieve success in the social studies, the problem-solving method can help you in another way. By using it, you will learn a way of dealing with problems that will be valuable to you throughout your life. Many successful scientists, businessmen, and government leaders use this method to solve problems.

Sample problems to solve. You may wish to investigate problems about the Midwest and Great Plains as a whole or about one state in this part of our country. The following sample problems are about the Midwest and Great Plains as a whole:

1. **The standard of living in the Midwest and Great Plains today is much higher than it was one hundred years ago. Why is this so?** In order to solve this problem, you will need to make several hypotheses. In forming hypotheses, consider how each of the following has contributed to a higher standard of living in this part of our country:
   a. changes in the way resources are used
   b. changes in the way goods are produced
   c. changes in farming methods
   d. the migration of people from farms to cities
2. **Some parts of the Midwest and Great Plains are densely populated while other parts have very few people. Why is this so?** To solve this problem, you will need to consider facts about each of the following:
   a. the land features and climate in different parts of the Midwest and Great Plains
   b. job opportunities in different parts of the Midwest and Great Plains

Four Words To Understand

1. **A concept** is a big, main idea that is based on smaller ideas and facts. An example of a concept is the idea of "trade." Many kinds of exchange are included in this idea. Two boys who exchange marbles on the playground are carrying on trade. A woman who pays money to the grocer for a loaf of bread is also carrying on trade; so is a factory that buys raw materials from other countries and sells its manufactured products overseas. Only as you come to see the various things that the word "trade" includes do you grow to understand this concept. Another example of a concept is the idea of "climate." Still another is the idea of "standard of living."

2. **A generalization** is a statement that shows how two or more concepts are meaningfully related to each other. "Through trade, all people on the earth can have a better living," is one example of a generalization. There are four concepts in this statement: "trade," "all people," "the earth," and "a better living." These four have been put together like pieces of a puzzle to make a bigger picture that gives you a better understanding of the world in which you live. The many thousands of facts you read, hear, and experience will make much more sense if you can think of them as parts of concepts which can be combined to form meaningful generalizations.

   Keep one important warning in mind when you make, hear, or read a generalization, however. If a generalization is based on wrong facts or is carelessly thought out, it may give a very wrong picture. Make certain that you understand the different concepts that are being combined in a generalization, and judge carefully whether or not you think it is true.

3. **Values** are ideas or standards that a person considers to be worthwhile. A person's values influence the way he behaves. For instance, a person who believes that every individual is important will treat everyone he meets with consideration.

4. **Appreciation** is the understanding or awareness of the worth of something. For example, you may develop an appreciation for art or music. You may also develop an appreciation for the accomplishments of people of other cultures.

| States of the Midwest |
| Great Plains States |
| Great Plains Section |
| — State Boundaries |

Scale of Miles
0   200   400

Land and Climate

What is the Midwest and Great Plains? This book provides information about the land, the climate, and the people in a vast area of the United States called the Midwest and Great Plains. This area stretches across the central part of our country from Canada on the north to Mexico on the south. It includes fourteen of our states. (See map on this page.)

What is the Midwest? As you study the map on this page, you will see that the Midwest is made up of eight states in the northeastern part of the Midwest and Great Plains. These states are Illinois, Indiana, Iowa, Michigan, Minnesota, Missouri, Ohio, and Wisconsin.

What are the Great Plains states? The remainder of the Midwest and Great Plains is made up of six states. We call these the Great Plains states. They include Kansas, Nebraska, North Dakota, Oklahoma, South Dakota, and Texas.

What do we mean by the Great Plains? In this book, we use the term Great Plains to refer to a section of generally flat land in the Interior Plains region of our country. The map on pages 28 and 29 shows different land regions of our country and the sections into which these regions are divided. The map on this page shows that each of the Great Plains states includes part of the Great Plains land section.

11

Watching a sunrise in space. The sun, which is the center of our solar* system, is a star. The sun and all of the stars we see in the night sky are part of an enormous star system, or galaxy, called the Milky Way. The Milky Way is one of billions of galaxies scattered through the vast space of the universe.

1 A Global View

A Study Guide

As you study this chapter, look for answers to the following questions:

1. What is a galaxy?
2. What is the Milky Way?
3. Where in the Milky Way is our solar system located?
4. What makes up our solar system?
5. What is the average distance of the earth from the sun?
6. Why is the earth's atmosphere important to us?
7. On which continent is most of the United States located?
8. What is the conterminous United States?
9. Where in the United States is the Midwest and Great Plains located?
10. Which states are in this part of our country?

*See Glossary

Our Solar System Is in the Milky Way

Our sun is a star in the Milky Way. Our sun, like other stars in the universe, is a huge, whirling ball of burning gases. It is the center of our solar* system, and is much closer to us than any other star. During the daytime, the light of the sun is so bright that we cannot see any other stars. When we look at the sky on a clear night, however, we see hundreds of stars glittering against the blackness of space.

The sun and all of the stars we see in the night sky are part of an enormous star system, or galaxy, called the Milky Way. The Milky Way is one of billions of separate galaxies scattered through the vast, nearly empty space of the universe. Each one of these separate galaxies is made up of billions of stars and other heavenly bodies.

The Milky Way is a spiral galaxy. As the painting on this page shows, the Milky Way has a spiral shape like that of a pinwheel. In one arm of the pinwheel is our own special star, the sun, together with the earth and the other heavenly bodies included in our solar system.

The Milky Way is shaped like a pinwheel. Our solar system, which is made up of the sun and the heavenly bodies that revolve around it, is located in an arm of the pinwheel.

Our Solar System

Our solar system includes nine main planets. Some of these main planets, such as our earth, have one or more moons. The solar system also includes thousands of small planets, called asteroids, that circle the sun between Mars and Jupiter.

Exploring Our Solar System

The earth is a planet in the solar system. The earth is one of the solar system's nine main planets. These are balls of fairly solid material that revolve around the sun. The solar system also includes thousands of small planets, called asteroids. (See illustration above.) Some of the main planets, including the earth, have one or more moons.

Learning about our neighbors in the solar system. During the last few years, we have begun to explore some parts of the solar system with space probes.

MAIN PLANETS		
Planet	**Diameter in Miles**	**Average Distance From Sun in Miles**
Mercury	3,010	36 Million
Venus	7,610	67 Million
Earth	7,918	93 Million
Mars	4,216	142 Million
Jupiter	88,700	483 Million
Saturn	75,100	886 Million
Uranus	30,900	1,783 Million
Neptune	27,700	2,797 Million
Pluto	3,600	3,671 Million

These are unmanned spacecraft carrying cameras and other instruments. By sending out space probes we have gained much new scientific information. In 1965, an American spacecraft called Mariner IV sent close-up photographs of Mars back to earth. These were the first such photographs ever taken of another planet. Other spacecraft, such as Surveyor I, have landed on the moon and sent back photographs of its surface.

Observing Our Earth

Looking at the earth from space. We have also learned much about our own planet through observations made from space. Astronauts have taken many photographs of the earth from high above its surface. For example, the photograph below was taken from the spacecraft Gemini 11. In this picture and others taken by astronauts, the surface of the earth is partly hidden by fluffy white clouds. These clouds are part of the atmosphere, the envelope of air that surrounds our earth. The atmosphere is our planet's greatest treasure. It provides the air we breathe. It holds the moisture that brings life-giving rain to the earth. The atmosphere also protects us by night from the bleak cold of outer space, and by day from the burning rays of the sun.

The earth as viewed from the spacecraft Gemini II. This photograph was taken from more than five hundred miles above the earth's surface. The white patches in the picture are clouds.

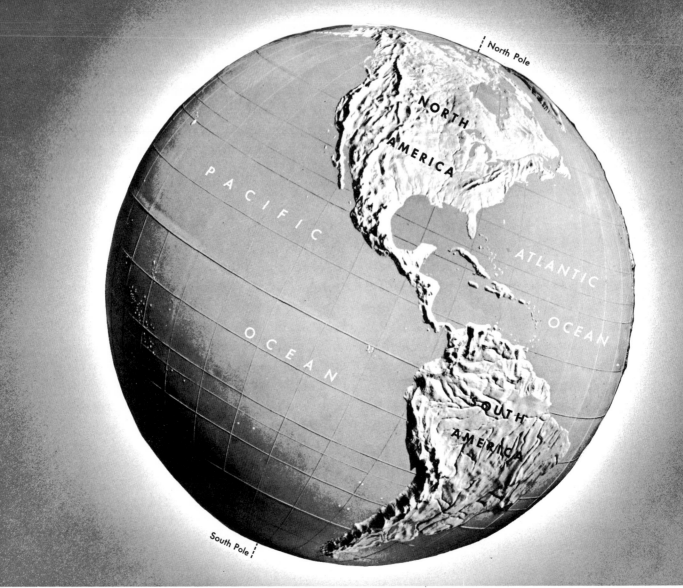

North Pole

NORTH AMERICA

PACIFIC

ATLANTIC

OCEAN

OCEAN

SOUTH AMERICA

South Pole

Our earth. The surface of our earth is made up partly of land and partly of water. The largest masses of land are called continents, and the largest bodies of water are called oceans.

The earth's surface is made up of oceans and continents. As astronauts orbit the earth high above its surface, they often catch sight of the sparkling blue waters of the earth's great oceans. These waters make up about three fourths of the earth's surface. The largest land-masses on the earth are called continents. Our earth's six continents, together with many islands, make up about one fourth of the surface of our planet. The chart at right shows the approximate size of the earth's continents and oceans.

MAJOR LAND AND WATER AREAS	
Continents and Oceans	Area in Square Miles
CONTINENTS	
Africa	11,685,000
Antarctica	5,100,000
Australia	2,971,000
Eurasia	
Europe	3,825,000
Asia	17,085,000
North America	9,420,000
South America	6,870,000
OCEANS	
Arctic	5,427,000
Atlantic	31,744,000
Indian	28,371,000
Pacific	63,855,000

ALASKA
U.S.A.

C A N A D A

U N I T E D   S T A T E S

MEXICO

CANAL ZONE
(U.S.A.)

North America. Most of our country, the United States, is on this continent. The countries of Canada and Mexico are our neighbors.

95°   90°   85°   80°   75°   70°   65°

A   A   D   A

45°

Winnipeg

Red River of the North

Fargo

Duluth

Lake Superior

Sault Ste. Marie

MICHIGAN

Lake Huron

Quebec

St. Lawrence River

MAINE

Augusta

Montreal

Montpelier

Lewiston

MINNESOTA

St. Paul

Minneapolis

Mississippi

WISCONSIN

Lake Michigan

Grand Rapids

Saginaw

Flint

Ottawa

VT. N.H.

Portland

Concord

Sioux Falls

Sioux City

Madison

Lansing

Toronto

Lake Ontario

Rochester

NEW YORK

Albany

MASS.

Boston

40°

Milwaukee

River

Chicago

Buffalo

MOUN

Hartford

CONN. R.I.

Providence

IOWA

Omaha

River

Davenport

Des Moines

Gary

Detroit

Lake Erie

Cleveland

Akron

PENNSYLVANIA

Pittsburgh

Harrisburg

Trenton

N.J. New York

Philadelphia

Peoria

Toledo

Lincoln

ILLINOIS

OHIO

Columbus

Baltimore

Dover

MD. DEL.

Annapolis

35°

Topeka

Springfield

Indianapolis

Cincinnati

WEST VIRGINIA

Washington D.C.

Kansas City

INDIANA

Kansas City

St. Louis

Louisville

River

Charleston

VIRGINIA

Norfolk

A S

Jefferson City

Frankfort

Lexington

Richmond

Wichita

MISSOURI

OZARK

KENTUCKY

Ohio

NORTH

Raleigh

PLATEAU

River

TENNESSEE

Nashville

Charlotte

CAROLINA

Tulsa

River

APPALACHIAN

Ft. Smith

ARKANSAS

Memphis

SOUTH

Columbia

HOMA

Little Rock

Mississippi

Birmingham

Atlanta

CAROLINA

30°

S

Dallas

ALABAMA

Macon

GEORGIA

Charleston

MISSISSIPPI

Jackson

Savannah

Shreveport

Montgomery

Beaumont

LOUISIANA

Baton Rouge

Mobile

Pensacola

Tallahassee

Jacksonville

FLORIDA

Houston

New Orleans

A T L A N T I C   O C E A N

NORTH LATITUDE

Galveston

90°

Tampa

St. Petersburg

25°

Miami

O U N T A I N S

STRAITS OF FLORIDA

TROPIC OF CANCER

WEST LONGITUDE

95°   90°   85°   80°   75°

Havana

UNITED STATES

Scale of Miles

0   100   200   300

⊗ National Capitals   ☆ State Capitals   ● Other Cities

Shading from green through yellow, brown, and red indicates increase in altitude. Figures show approximate altitude in feet for corresponding color.

10,000 ft.

5,000 ft.

2,000 ft.

1,000 ft.

500 ft.

COPYRIGHT BY RAND McNALLY & CO. MADE IN U.S.A.

Exploring Our Country

Our country is made up of fifty states. Two of these, Alaska and Hawaii, are separated from the others. The part of our country that is made up of the remaining forty-eight states is called the conterminous United States. (Compare the map below with the map on pages 18 and 19.)

In addition to the fifty states, our country also includes the District of Columbia. This is a small section in the eastern part of the conterminous United States. It covers the same area as the city of Washington, which is our national capital.

Over the years, the United States has gained control of various areas. One of these is the island of Puerto Rico, in the West Indies.* Today, Puerto Rico is a self-governing commonwealth associated with the United States. Another American possession in the West Indies is an island group called the Virgin Islands of the United States. Various islands and island groups in the Pacific Ocean also belong to us. Among these are Guam, Wake, and American Samoa. In addition, the United States controls the Panama Canal Zone.

The United States. Our country is made up of fifty states. Two of these, Alaska and Hawaii, are separated from the other forty-eight. The part of our country where the forty-eight states are located is called the conterminous United States. Since this map is drawn on a Mercator* projection, Alaska appears much larger than it really is. (Compare this map with a globe.)

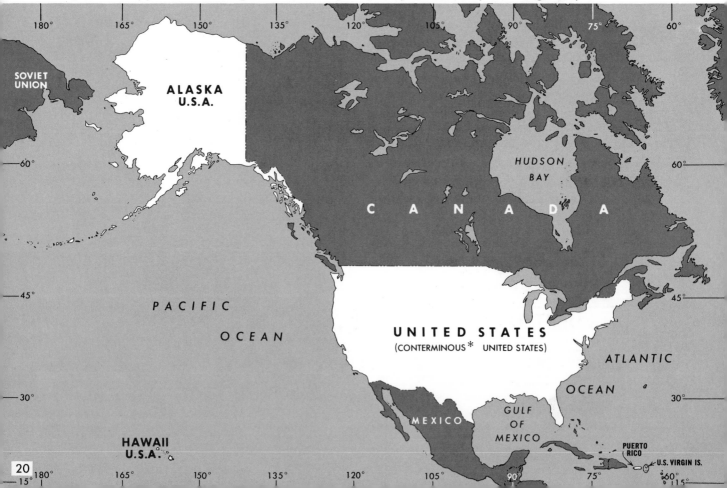

United States

(CONTERMINOUS UNITED STATES)

Main groups of states. The states in the conterminous United States may be divided into groups. The following table lists the states in each of these groups. The District of Columbia* is included in the Northeast. (Compare the map above with the map on pages 18 and 19.) Not all geography books group the states in this way. Can you think of any other ways of grouping them?

The West	The Midwest and Great Plains		The South	The Northeast	
	The Midwest	**Great Plains States**			
Arizona	Illinois	Kansas	Alabama	Connecticut	New Jersey
California	Indiana	Nebraska	Arkansas	Delaware	New York
Colorado	Iowa	North Dakota	Florida	District of	Pennsylvania
Idaho	Michigan	Oklahoma	Georgia	Columbia	Rhode Island
Montana	Minnesota	South Dakota	Kentucky	Maine	Vermont
Nevada	Missouri	Texas	Louisiana	Maryland	West Virginia
New Mexico	Ohio		Mississippi	Massachusetts	
Oregon	Wisconsin		North Carolina	New Hampshire	
Utah			South Carolina		
Washington			Tennessee		
Wyoming			Virginia		

The Midwest and Great Plains

An important part of our country. The Midwest and Great Plains lies in the vast central part of the United States. (See map on page 21.) At the time our country was founded, this area was a wilderness of forests and prairies. Indians roamed over the land, hunting buffalo and other wild animals. Today, about 67 million people live in the Midwest and Great Plains.

Much of our country's most productive farmland is in the Midwest and Great Plains. This area also includes many of our leading industrial cities,

A view of the Midwest from five hundred miles out in space. This photograph was taken by the weather satellite Tiros IV, in 1962. At left you can see the curve of the earth. The white patches are clouds. The dark patches are the Great Lakes: Lake Superior, Lake Michigan, Lake Huron, Lake Erie, and Lake Ontario. (Compare this photograph with the map on page 19.)

The Midwest and Great Plains is an important part of the United States. This huge area includes many of our country's leading manufacturing cities, such as Columbus, Ohio, which is shown above. Much of our country's best farmland is also found here. An excellent transportation system connects the Midwest and Great Plains with other parts of the United States and with foreign countries.

such as Chicago and Detroit. A network of highways, railroads, airways, and waterways connects the Midwest and Great Plains with other parts of our country and the world.

In this book you will learn about the land, the climate, and the history of the Midwest and Great Plains. You will also learn about the people here and how they live.

Learn With Maps, Charts, and Pictures

Use the maps, charts, and pictures in this chapter to answer the following questions.

1. In what part of the Milky Way is our solar system located?
2. What two main planets are closest to the earth?
3. Name the six continents on the earth.
4. Name the four oceans on the earth.
5. What states are included in the Midwest? Name the Great Plains states.

Our Sun—A Life-giving Star

Although our sun is only one of billions of stars in the universe, it is by far the most important star to us. Without it, life on earth could not exist. Do research about the sun and then prepare an oral report to share with your class. Your report should answer questions such as the following:

1. How far away is the sun?
2. What is the sun made of?
3. How do plants use the sun's energy to manufacture food?
4. What would the earth be like if there were no sun?

Pages 346-352 contain helpful suggestions for locating information and organizing it into an interesting report.

Level farmland in Minnesota. More than three fourths of the Midwest and Great Plains lies in a vast region of the United States called the Interior Plains. Most of the land in this region is flat or gently rolling. The Interior Plains may be divided into two sections—the Central Lowland and the Great Plains.

2 Land

A Problem To Solve

How do the land features of the Midwest and Great Plains affect the people who live here? In order to solve this problem, you will need to make hypotheses about how the land features of this part of our country affect:

a. where the people live
b. how the people earn their living
c. transportation

Chapters 7, 9, 11, and 12 contain additional information that will be useful in solving this problem.

See TO THE STUDENT, pages 8-10.

If you were to ask an expert in geography to tell you four important facts about the Midwest and Great Plains, he might list the following:

1. These fourteen states lie in the central part of North America.

2. Most of the land in the Midwest and Great Plains is flat or gently rolling.

3. Only a few parts of the Midwest and Great Plains rise high above sea level.

4. Four of the five Great Lakes border or lie in the Midwest. These are among the largest lakes in the world.

Most of the Midwest and Great Plains lies in one region of our country. The geography expert might show you a map like the one on pages 28 and 29. On this map you will see that more than three fourths of the Midwest and Great Plains lies in a vast region of the United States called the Interior Plains. The Interior Plains may be divided into two sections. One section is called the Central Lowland. Here most of the land is low and gently rolling. To the west of the Central Lowland are the Great Plains. These plains are generally flat, but they are higher in elevation than the Central Lowland. The states of North Dakota, South Dakota, Nebraska, Kansas, Oklahoma, and Texas lie partly in the Great Plains section. This is why they are called the Great Plains states.

Some parts of the Midwest and Great Plains lie in another great lowland region of the United States. This is the Coastal Plain. It extends along most of our country's Atlantic coast, and also forms a broad, irregular band along the Gulf of Mexico.

As you study the map on pages 28 and 29, you will see only four small highland areas in the Midwest and Great Plains. One of these is part of the Appalachian Plateau. Another lies in the

A helicopter trip over the Midwest and Great Plains. During this trip, we will fly over some of the main land features in this part of our country. We will see flat plains and rugged mountains, sparkling lakes and slow-moving rivers, fertile farmlands and great cities.

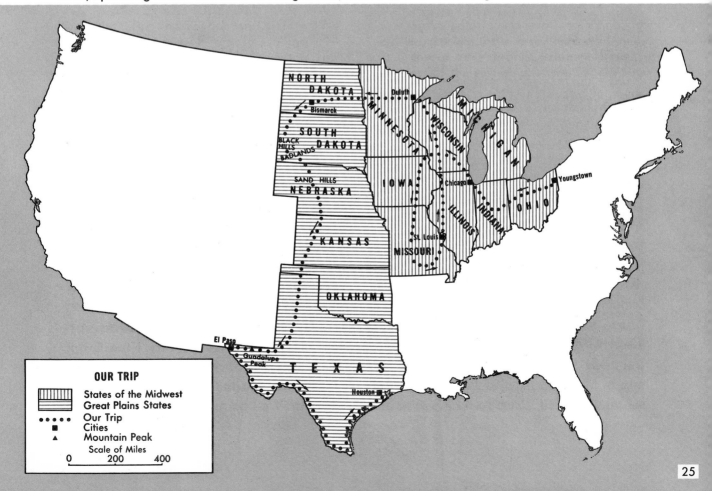

Interior Highlands. The third is part of the Superior Upland, and the fourth is in the Basin and Range Country.

To learn more about the land features of the Midwest and Great Plains, we will take a trip by helicopter over this part of our country. The route that we will follow is shown on the map on page 25. It is also shown on the map on pages 28 and 29.

The Appalachian Plateau

A small part of the Midwest lies in the Appalachian Plateau. Our trip will begin in the Appalachian Plateau, which covers most of eastern Ohio. We board our helicopter at the important manufacturing city of Youngstown. (See map on page 25.) As we take our seats, our guide tells us about the Appalachian Plateau. He says it is a large highland area that extends from the central part of New York State southwestward into Alabama. However, the Appalachian Plateau makes up only a small part of the Midwest.

Our helicopter is rising into the air now. Soon we are high enough to see for many miles in every direction. We notice that most of the land around Youngstown is hilly or gently rolling. In some places, dairy cattle are grazing on hillside pastures. In much of the Appalachian Plateau section of the Midwest, the land is too hilly or the soil is too thin and stony for growing crops. Under the surface, however, there are large deposits of coal and limestone. These are valuable mineral resources that are used by many industries. We learn from our guide that there are several important industrial cities besides Youngstown in the Appalachian Plateau section of the Midwest.

The Central Lowland

Entering the Central Lowland. Now our helicopter heads westward from Youngstown. As we fly across Ohio, the land gradually becomes flatter. Our guide tells us that we are now in the Central Lowland. (See map on pages 28 and 29.) This large section covers more than three fourths of the Midwest. It also extends westward into Texas, Oklahoma, and the other Great Plains states.

We learn that the Central Lowland contains some of the best farmland in the United States. Here are many fields of corn, hay, and other crops. In some places, there are pastures for dairy cattle. Farms in this section produce large numbers of beef cattle and hogs.

The corn belt is a huge area of fertile farmland that stretches through the heart of the Midwest into the Great Plains states. More food is produced in the corn belt than in any other area of the same size in the world.

Our guide shows us a map like the one on page 140. When we compare this map with the one on pages 28 and 29, we see that a number of large cities are located in the Central Lowland. Among these are Cleveland, Detroit, Chicago, Minneapolis, St. Louis, and Oklahoma City.

As we look down from our helicopter, we notice that the land is crossed by many highways and railroad tracks. Because the Central Lowland is gener-

ally level, it has been easy to build roads and railroads here. Excellent transportation facilities have aided the development of farming and industry in the Midwest.

What is the corn belt? The land that we now see below us resembles a patchwork quilt. It is marked off in neat squares of green and tan. These squares are fields of corn, oats, and other crops. Our guide tells us that we are flying over the corn belt. This is a huge area

Build Your Vocabulary

Interior Plains   Central Lowland   Interior Highlands   Superior Upland

Appalachian Plateau   Ozark Plateau   Great Lakes   glacier   Midwest

corn belt   dairy belt   tributary   Mississippi River system   sea level

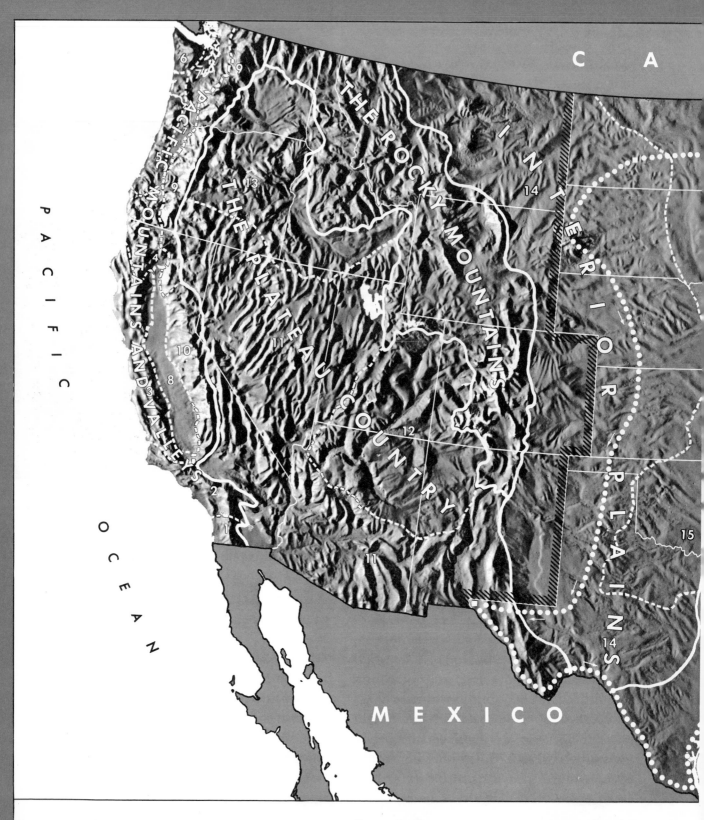

THE ROCKY MOUNTAINS

INTERIOR PLAINS

PACIFIC OCEAN

PACIFIC MOUNTAINS AND VALLEYS

THE PLATEAU COUNTRY

CANADA

MEXICO

LAND REGIONS

PACIFIC MOUNTAINS AND VALLEYS

1 San Diego Ranges
2 Los Angeles Ranges
3 California Coast Ranges
4 Klamath Mountains

5 Oregon Coast Range
6 Olympic Mountains
7 Puget-Willamette Lowland
8 Central Valley
9 Cascade Range
10 Sierra Nevada

THE PLATEAU COUNTRY

11 Basin and Range Country

12 Colorado Plateau
13 Columbia Plateau

THE ROCKY MOUNTAINS

INTERIOR PLAINS

14 Great Plains
15 Central Lowland

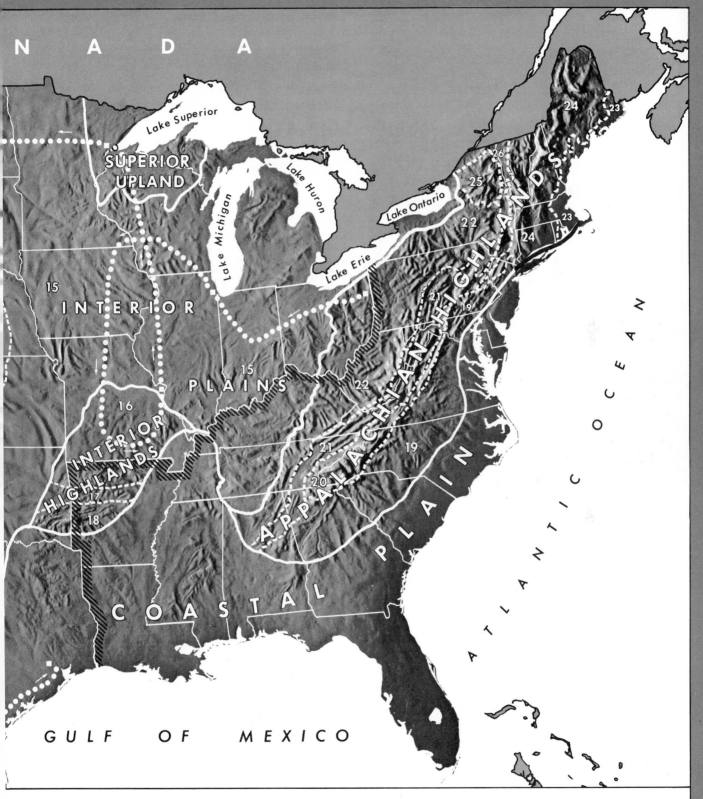

N A D A

Lake Superior

SUPERIOR
UPLAND

Lake Huron

Lake Michigan

Lake Ontario

Lake Erie

24

23

26

25

22

23

24

INTERIOR

15

2

19

PLAINS

15

22

16

INTERIOR

HIGHLANDS

21

19

17

20

18

APPALACHIAN HIGHLANDS

COASTAL

PLAIN

A T L A N T I C   O C E A N

GULF   OF   MEXICO

SUPERIOR UPLAND	21 Appalachian Ridges and Valleys	●●●● Our Trip
INTERIOR HIGHLANDS	22 Appalachian Plateau	■ Cities
16 Ozark Plateau	23 New England Lowlands	▨ States of the Midwest
17 Arkansas Valley	24 New England Highlands	and Great Plains
18 Ouachita Mountains	25 Adirondack Mountains	
	26 St. Lawrence Valley	Scale of Miles
APPALACHIAN HIGHLANDS		
19 The Piedmont Plateau	**COASTAL PLAIN**	0 150 300
20 Blue Ridge		

Chicago, Illinois, spreads for many miles along the southwestern shore of Lake Michigan. This great city has a larger population than any other city in our nation except New York. More than seven million people live in Chicago and its neighboring communities.

of fertile farmland that stretches through the heart of the Midwest into the Great Plains states. (See map on page 153.)

We learn that more food is produced in the corn belt than in any other area of the same size in the world. There are several reasons for this. First, most parts of the corn belt are covered with rich, dark soil. Summers here are warm, and rainfall is plentiful. These conditions are just right for growing corn, which is the main crop in the corn belt. Soybeans and many other crops also grow well here. Because most parts of the corn belt are level, farmers find it easy to use tractors and other farm machines to cultivate their land.

We ask our guide to tell us what is done with all the corn that is grown in the corn belt. He tells us that most of this corn is not the kind we eat as a vegetable. Instead, it is a type of corn that is fed to cattle and hogs to fatten them for market. For this reason, people often say that corn grown in the corn belt "travels to market on four legs." A small part of the corn grown here is used in manufacturing breakfast cereal, corn syrup, and other products.

The second largest city in the United States. When we reach the central part of Indiana, our helicopter turns northwestward. Soon we see before us a great expanse of silvery-blue water.

Our guide tells us that this is Lake Michigan, one of the five Great Lakes. Later in our trip, we will learn more about the Great Lakes and how they were formed.

Along the shore of Lake Michigan, we see what appears to be a single great city spreading out for many miles across the plains. We are approaching Chicago, Illinois. (See map on page 25.) This city has a larger population than any other city in the United States except New York. Chicago and its neighboring communities have grown so close together that we cannot tell one city from another. More than seven million people live in the Chicago metropolitan* area.

As our helicopter flies closer, we can distinguish different kinds of buildings. We see houses, stores, schools, and churches. We also see the smokestacks of steel mills and other factories. In the distance are tall hotels and office buildings. Railroad tracks and broad highways form a crisscross pattern like the threads in a spider's web. Now we are approaching a small airport along the shore of Lake Michigan. We will land here so that our helicopter can be refueled.

The dairy belt. After a short wait, we are ready to resume our journey. Our helicopter heads northwestward from Chicago, and we are soon flying over the state of Wisconsin. Below us we see rolling hills covered with green pastures, where herds of dairy cattle are grazing.

Our guide tells us that we are now in the dairy belt of the Midwest. This area includes most of Wisconsin, Michigan, and Minnesota. (See map on page

*See Glossary

153.) The land here is generally more hilly and less fertile than in the corn belt. In many parts of the dairy belt, summers are too cool and the growing season is too short for corn to ripen fully. However, this kind of climate is excellent for raising grass, which can be cut for hay or used as pasture for cattle. There are many fine dairy farms in this area. On pages 152 and 153, you can learn more about the dairy belt.

Crossing the Mississippi River. Our helicopter turns westward now. Before long, we are crossing the broad, winding Mississippi River. Trace the route of the Mississippi River on the map below. You will see that it begins in the northern part of Minnesota and flows southward into the Gulf of Mexico.

Most of the other large rivers in the Midwest and Great Plains flow into the Mississippi. A river that empties into a larger river is called a tributary. The largest tributaries of the Mississippi are the Ohio River and the Missouri

MISSISSIPPI RIVER SYSTEM

The Mississippi River, together with its tributaries, drains a vast area in the central part of our country. This area includes most of the Midwest and Great Plains. The Mississippi begins in northern Minnesota and flows southward into the Gulf of Mexico. The Ohio and the Missouri rivers are the Mississippi's chief tributaries.

31

River. Together, the Mississippi and its tributaries form the Mississippi River system. This is one of the largest river systems in the world.

Why is the Mississippi River important? Our guide tells us that the Mississippi River and its tributaries played an important part in the history of the United States. In the early days of our country, there were few roads and no railroads. Waterways were a very important means of transportation. Pioneer families on their way to establish new homes in the wilderness journeyed by flatboat down the Ohio and other rivers. These people often settled near the rivers, which they used to transport their prod-

ucts to market. Flatboats loaded with furs, lumber, and farm products were floated down the Mississippi River to the port of New Orleans. (See map on pages 18 and 19.) From New Orleans, these goods were sent by ship to cities in the eastern part of the United States and to Europe.

Gradually the flatboats were replaced by steamboats, which could travel much faster. Another advantage of steamboats was that they could go upstream as well as downstream. By the middle of the 1800's, there were hundreds of steamboats carrying passengers and goods up and down the Mississippi River.

A towboat pushing barges on the Mississippi River. The great Mississippi River begins in northern Minnesota and flows southward into the Gulf of Mexico. This river is an important transportation route for bulky products such as grain and oil.

Many port towns were established along the Mississippi and its tributaries. Some of these towns have grown into important cities. Among them are Minneapolis, St. Paul, St. Louis, Kansas City, and Cincinnati.

Today, few people travel by boat on the Mississippi River. However, the river is still an important transportation route for certain types of cargo. Large amounts of grain, oil, and other bulky products are carried by barges on the Mississippi. These products can be transported more cheaply by boat than by train or truck.

Our guide says that the rivers in the Mississippi River system can be harmful as well as helpful to the people living nearby. In the spring, melting snow or heavy rains sometimes cause a river to overflow its banks. The rising water may destroy millions of dollars' worth of property and leave thousands of people homeless. Sometimes many people are drowned.

Dams have been built on the Mississippi River and some of its tributaries to control the flow of water and prevent floods. The water stored behind some of these dams is used by power plants to produce electricity. (See page 172.) In dry areas dams are also used to store water for irrigating farmland.

The richest farming state in the Midwest. After crossing the Mississippi River, our helicopter turns southward. We are now flying over Iowa. Nearly all of Iowa lies in the corn belt. Our guide says that most of the corn grown in this state is fed to livestock. Iowa leads the nation in the production of hogs and beef cattle. Farmers here earn more money from their products than farmers in any other state of the Midwest.

The Interior Highlands

There are forest-covered hills and low mountains in the Interior Highlands region. Our helicopter continues southward, and we fly over the fertile farmlands of northern Missouri. After we cross the broad, muddy Missouri River, we notice that the land becomes rougher. We are now in the Interior Highlands region. (See map on pages 28 and 29.) Below us is the Ozark Plateau, which forms the northern section of this region.

As we fly over the Ozark Plateau, we see many steep-sided hills covered with thick forests. There are small farms scattered throughout this section, but most of the land is too rugged for growing crops.

The scenery in much of the Ozark Plateau is very beautiful. Rushing streams flow between wooded hills. In some places there are clear blue lakes. Each summer, thousands of people come to the Ozark Plateau to spend their vacations.

The map on pages 28 and 29 shows that there are two other sections of the Interior Highlands. South of the Ozark Plateau is the fertile valley of the

The Ozark Plateau of Missouri lies in the Interior Highlands region. Here, rushing streams flow between wooded hills. There are small farms scattered throughout the Ozark Plateau, but most of the land here is too rugged for growing crops.

Arkansas River. Still farther south are the Ouachita Mountains. These mountains are low but quite rugged. Most of their slopes are covered with dense forests of pine and hardwood trees. Lumbering is an important industry in this area.

As we leave the Interior Highlands, we see before us a large city that extends for miles along the western bank of the Mississippi River. This is St. Louis, Missouri. We will spend the night here before continuing our journey through the Midwest and Great Plains.

The Superior Upland

Most of the Superior Upland is hilly and wooded. From St. Louis we fly far to the north until we reach the Superior Upland. Parts of Minnesota, Wisconsin, and Michigan lie in this region. Here

we see rolling hills and low mountains with gentle slopes. The highest point in the Midwest lies in the Superior Upland in Minnesota. It is about 2,300 feet above sea level.

We notice that much of the land below us is covered with dense forests. In only a few places do we see towns or farms. Our guide says that most of the soil in the Superior Upland is poor for farming. In addition, summers are too cool for growing many kinds of crops. Little manufacturing is carried on in this region. However, there are sawmills and paper mills that use wood from nearby forests.

Our guide tells us that many large iron mines are located in the Superior Upland. About three fourths of all the iron ore mined in the United States each year comes from deposits in this region.

To learn more about iron mining in the Superior Upland, see pages 167 and 168.

Although the Superior Upland region is thinly populated, it attracts large numbers of tourists each year. In this region are wooded hills, swift-flowing rivers, and thousands of sparkling lakes. Lake Superior, one of the Great Lakes, extends into the Superior Upland.

How the Great Lakes were formed. Ahead of us we see the dark blue waters of Lake Superior. This is the largest of the five Great Lakes. We ask our guide how these huge bodies of water were formed.

In the Superior Upland. Parts of Minnesota, Wisconsin, and Michigan lie in this highland region. Little farming or manufacturing is carried on here. However, about three fourths of the iron ore mined in our country each year comes from deposits in this region.

The Story of Glaciers

North America. The map above shows the part of North America that was covered by glaciers at one time or another during the Great Ice Age.

The Great Ice Age. About one million years ago, the climate of the earth was colder than it is today. Great quantities of snow fell in and near Arctic regions of the world. In some places more snow fell in winter than melted in summer. The snow piled higher and higher each year, and the bottom layers gradually turned to ice. Finally, the enormous weight of the snow on top caused the ice below to spread out in all directions. A mass of moving ice formed in this way is called a glacier.

As the centuries passed, glaciers spread over large areas in Europe, Asia, and North America. In some places, they were almost two miles thick. As glaciers moved across the land, they carried away soil and rocks, scooped out deep hollows, and rounded off the jagged tops of mountains.

Gradually, the climate of the earth became warmer. The glaciers began to melt. As they melted, they left behind the soil, rocks, and other material they had carried. Some of the hollows that had been made by the glaciers were filled with water from the melting ice. In this way, many lakes and ponds were formed.

Three more times during the Great Ice Age the earth's climate cooled and then became warmer again. Each time, glaciers spread over large areas of the earth's surface and then melted. The last of these ice sheets retreated only about 18,000 years ago. Scientists are not completely certain why these great changes in climate took place.

How glaciers affected the Midwest and Great Plains. During the Great Ice Age, glaciers spread over much of the Midwest and Great Plains. (See map on this page.) They scooped out thousands of hollows in the earth. Later, water from the melting glaciers filled many of these hollows, forming the Great Lakes and thousands of smaller lakes. The melting glaciers also left a thick layer of sand, clay, and finely ground rock over large areas of land. In many parts of the Midwest and Great Plains, these materials helped to form very fertile soil. Some of the world's best farmland is found today in parts of the Midwest and Great Plains that were once covered with glaciers.

Present-day glaciers. Glaciers are still being formed in some parts of the world. They are found mainly in cold, mountainous areas that receive abundant snowfall. For example, the island of Greenland and the continent of Antarctica are almost completely covered by huge glaciers.

Glacial lakes in Minnesota. In some places, glaciers scooped out hollows in the earth, which later became lakes. In other places, glaciers left thick deposits of sand, clay, and finely ground rock.

Our guide tells us that many thousands of years ago, great ice sheets called glaciers developed in northern Canada. (See feature on page 36.) As the glaciers moved southward, they gouged large hollows in the earth. Later, the climate became warmer and the glaciers slowly melted. Water from the melting ice filled the hollows dug by the glaciers, forming the Great Lakes.

A great inland waterway. Our helicopter turns westward. Now we are flying over Duluth, a port city at the western end of Lake Superior. In the harbor of Duluth, we see many long lake freighters. Some of these boats are carrying iron ore. Others are loaded with grain or coal. We also see freighters carrying automobiles and other manufactured products. Our guide says that Lake Superior is part of the most important inland waterway in the world, the Great Lakes–St. Lawrence Waterway. (See feature on pages 184 and 185.)

We learn that the Great Lakes are important for reasons other than transportation. For one thing, they provide an abundant supply of fresh water to homes and factories in nearby cities. Also, thousands of people spend their vacations at cottages or resorts along the Great Lakes. Here they can enjoy swimming, boating, and other water sports. Commercial fishermen take large quantities of fish from the Great Lakes every year. In addition, as Chapter 3 explains, the Great Lakes have an important effect on the climate of many areas along their shores.

A fertile river valley. We have nearly completed our flight over the Midwest. (See map on page 25.) Now we are ready to visit the Great Plains states. As we fly westward from Lake Superior, the land becomes flatter, and the forests give way to large, prosperous farms. Before long, our guide tells us that we are flying over the fertile valley of the Red River of the North. This river, which flows northward into Canada, forms the boundary between Minnesota and North Dakota.

The Great Plains

The Great Plains are generally flat. Soon after leaving the Red River Valley, we are flying over the Great Plains. This section forms a wide band extending from Canada in the north to Mexico in the south. (See map on page 28.) The eastern edge of the Great Plains is less than two thousand feet above sea level. From here the land slopes gently upward toward the west until it meets the Rocky Mountains. Near the western edge of the Great Plains, some places are more than a mile above sea level.

Most of the land in the Great Plains appears to be nearly as flat as a tabletop. In some places, however, steep hills called buttes rise like skyscrapers above the plains. Rivers flowing eastward across the plains have carved deep valleys in the level surface of the land.

The Great Plains form a wide band extending from Canada in the north to Mexico in the south. In the Great Plains, the land slopes gently upward from east to west. Most of the land here appears to be nearly as flat as a tabletop. In some areas, however, mountains and steep hills rise above the plains.

During our trip over the Great Plains we will not see many forests. One reason why there are few forests in the Great Plains is the lack of rainfall here. Much of this section receives less than twenty inches of rainfall a year. (Compare maps on pages 28 and 49.)

Wheat fields cover vast areas of land on the Great Plains. As we continue across North Dakota, we notice that the land below us is marked off into long, narrow strips. Some of the strips are light green, and others are dark brown. We ask our guide what causes this interesting pattern. He says that the green strips are fields of unripened wheat, while the brown strips are patches of earth on which no crops are being grown. To conserve moisture in this land of little rainfall, farmers grow crops on only part of their land at one time. (See page 151.)

Build Your Vocabulary

Great Plains   Basin and Range Country   Black Hills   Coastal Plain

Sand Hills   gorge   Badlands   erosion   butte   Great Plains states

Our guide tells us that more wheat is grown on the Great Plains than in any other part of the United States. The soil here is fertile, and the dry, sunny climate is well suited to growing wheat. Most of the land is level enough to be cultivated with large machines. Wheat grown on the Great Plains is shipped to many parts of the United States and to foreign countries, where it is used in making flour and other products.

A bare land. After spending the night at Bismarck, North Dakota, we resume our helicopter trip over the Great Plains. Soon we are flying over the western part of South Dakota. Here much of the land is too dry for growing crops. We travel for many miles without seeing any towns or cultivated fields. The plains below us are covered with short, brown grass on which herds of cattle are grazing. Our guide tells us that cattle ranches on the Great Plains are usually very large, because many acres of grassland are needed to provide enough food for a herd of cattle. Now and then we fly over a lonely ranch with a tall windmill used to pump water for livestock.

The Black Hills are rugged and wooded. Ahead of us we see a group of mountains rising from the plains. From a distance, these mountains appear black. As we come closer, however, we can see that they are covered with forests of dark-green pine trees. These are the Black Hills. Some of the peaks in this

The forest-covered Black Hills in western South Dakota. Some of the peaks in these mountains rise more than seven thousand feet above sea level. Mining and lumbering are important occupations in the Black Hills. This scenic area also attracts many tourists in summer.

area rise more than seven thousand feet above sea level. Between the mountains are rushing streams and sparkling lakes.

We ask our guide how the Black Hills were formed. He says that millions of years ago, movements deep within the earth raised the surface of the land to form a huge dome about fifty miles in diameter. As the centuries passed, rainwater wore away some of the dome to form a number of rugged peaks and sharp pinnacles. The wearing away of rock and soil by water, wind, and other natural forces is called erosion.

Our guide tells us more about the Black Hills. He says they contain rich deposits of gold and other minerals. The forests on their slopes provide much wood for lumber. In the summer, thousands of people come to the Black Hills to enjoy the beautiful mountain scenery.

Erosion created the Badlands. From the Black Hills we fly eastward until we reach the Badlands of South Dakota.

The jagged peaks in the Badlands of South Dakota were sculptured by rainwater over a period of millions of years. The layers of rock in these peaks are tinted every color of the rainbow.

Our guide tells us that millions of years ago this area was a high, level plain. Rainfall was very light here, but occasionally there were severe rainstorms that washed deep gullies in the dry, bare earth. As time passed, rainwater carried away still more soil and rock, forming many jagged peaks like the ones shown in the picture on this page. When we fly over the Badlands, we see that they are strangely beautiful. The layers of rock in these eroded peaks are tinted every color of the rainbow.

We learn that the Badlands were given their name many years ago because the land here could not be used for farming, and traveling across this area was difficult. Also, hostile Indians sometimes hid among the peaks and gullies. Today the name "badlands" is used for any area that has been eroded like this one. There are badlands in North Dakota, Nebraska, and other states.

The Sand Hills of Nebraska are used mainly for grazing. Now our helicopter turns southward again. Before long we are flying over rolling hills covered with a thick carpet of light-green grass. These are the Sand Hills of Nebraska. They are made up of sand that was piled here centuries ago by strong winds blowing across the Great Plains. It is almost impossible to grow crops in the sandy soil of this area, but the grassy hillsides provide excellent pasture for cattle.

Our nation's "breadbasket." After crossing the wide, muddy Platte River, we take another look at our map. It shows us that we are about to fly over the state of Kansas. Our guide says that Kansas produces more wheat than any

Combines harvesting a field of golden wheat in Kansas. More wheat is produced in Kansas than in any other state. For this reason, Kansas is sometimes known as our nation's "breadbasket."

other state. For this reason, it is sometimes known as the "breadbasket" of the United States.

Now we see wheat fields stretching out to the horizon like a sea of shining gold. We ask our guide why the fields here are gold instead of green, as they were in North Dakota. He explains that the wheat we saw in North Dakota was planted just this spring, and it is not yet ripe. The wheat that we see below us now was planted last fall, so it is ripe and ready to harvest.

From our helicopter, we see objects that resemble giant bugs moving slowly over the wheat fields. These are machines called combines, which cut, thresh,* and clean the wheat. Trucks carry the wheat to tall buildings called elevators, which are located near railroad tracks. The wheat is stored in the elevators until it can be loaded onto trains that will carry it to flour mills in the cities. As we continue our flight over Kansas, we see many grain elevators rising like watchtowers over the rolling prairies.

Two panhandles. From Kansas we fly over the Panhandle of Oklahoma. This is a long, narrow strip of territory that extends westward from the rest of Oklahoma like the handle of a frying pan. (See map on pages 18 and 19.)

Now we are entering Texas, which is the largest state in our country except for Alaska. The northernmost part of Texas is also known as the Panhandle. Here we see large wheat fields and cattle ranches. Under the surface of the Texas Panhandle are rich deposits of petroleum and natural gas.

Irrigated cotton fields stretch across the Great Plains in Texas. As we continue southward, we notice that some of the land below us is covered with neat squares of bright green. Our guide tells us that these are cotton fields. He says that Texas produces more cotton than any other state. The reasons why so much cotton is grown in Texas are explained in Chapter 9. Because rainfall is light on the Great Plains, cotton farmers here must irrigate their fields with water from wells and streams. Many irrigation ditches have been dug to transport water to the thirsty cotton plants.

Large herds of cattle graze on the Texas plains. Gradually we leave the cotton fields behind and fly over dry plains where few crops are grown. Here most of the land is covered with tufts of brown grass or with low, thorny shrubs. We see a cloud of dust formed by a large herd of cattle moving across the plains. The cattle are being driven by a group of cowboys on horseback. Our guide tells us that Texas is a leading producer of beef cattle.

The Basin and Range Country

The Basin and Range Country is dry and mountainous. Our helicopter is turning westward now. Soon we are flying over ranges of rugged mountains separated by wide, level basins.* Our guide tells us that we are now in the Basin and Range Country. This is part of a great region called the Plateau Country, which covers much of the western United States. (See map on pages 28 and 29.)

From our helicopter, the land below us looks dusty-gray or tan. Most of the land in the Basin and Range Country is so dry that it can be used only for grazing. The basins are dotted with mesquite* and other plants that can live without much water. Now we are flying over Guadalupe Peak, the highest point in the Great Plains states. This lofty peak rises more than eight thousand feet above sea level.

Night is falling over the mountains now. Ahead of us we see the lights of a large city. This is El Paso, in the western tip of Texas. It is located along a river called the Rio Grande, which forms the boundary between Texas and Mexico. We will spend the night at El Paso before completing our journey.

Following the Rio Grande. As we leave El Paso the next morning, our guide tells us that we will follow the Rio Grande all the way to its mouth. During our flight, we can observe a variety of land features. Near El Paso, the Rio Grande is bordered by a green ribbon of irrigated farmland. Farther downstream, the river flows through deep gorges that it has carved in the rugged surface of the land. Some of the land in this area has been set aside by the federal government as a national park.

The Basin and Range Country extends across southwestern Texas. In this area are many rugged mountain ranges separated by basins. Most of the land here is so dry that it can be used only for grazing. The basins are dotted with mesquite and other plants that do not need much water.

The Coastal Plain

There are farms, forests, oil fields, and busy cities on the Coastal Plain. The land below us is gradually becoming more level. Our guide says that we will soon enter the great region of our country known as the Coastal Plain. This region covers most of eastern Texas and a small part of Oklahoma. It also reaches into the southern part of the Midwest. (Compare the map on pages 18 and 19 with the map on pages 28 and 29.) Near the Gulf of Mexico, the Coastal Plain is very low and flat. Farther inland, it is somewhat higher and more rolling. However, hardly any point on the Coastal Plain rises more than one thousand feet above sea level.

Our guide tells us that the Coastal Plain is a very important part of Texas. In this region are large areas of nearly level land with soil that is good for growing peanuts, cotton, and many other crops. Under the surface of the Coastal Plain are vast deposits of petroleum and natural gas. They have helped to make Texas the leading state in the production of these minerals. Large forests in the eastern part of the state supply much wood for making lumber, paper, and other products.

Fruit orchards and truck farms. As we continue our flight along the Rio Grande, we begin to see many large orchards of orange and grapefruit trees. We also notice many small truck farms, where tomatoes, lettuce, and other vegetables are grown. Our guide tells us that the soil in the lower Rio Grande Valley is very fertile. Winters here are so mild that crops can be grown the year around. The fields and orchards must be irrigated, however. We fly over huge Falcon Dam, which has been built across the Rio Grande to store water for irrigation and to help prevent floods.

Flying along the Gulf coast. When we reach the Gulf of Mexico, our helicopter turns northward and flies along the seacoast. We notice that most of the land near the coast is low and marshy. Rice, a crop that needs much moisture, is grown in some areas. Along the coast are many large bays and inlets. Now and then we fly over a harbor crowded with fishing boats and cargo ships. A few miles off the coast, in the Gulf of

A rice field in the Coastal Plain of Texas. Most of eastern Texas lies in a vast lowland region of our country called the Coastal Plain. In Texas, this region is bordered by the Gulf of Mexico. The land in the Coastal Plain is level or gently rolling.

Mexico, are long, narrow islands made up largely of sand. Here are fine beaches where tourists come to swim and to enjoy the sunshine.

Now we are approaching a city that sprawls for many miles across the Texas plains. This is Houston. Although it is located nearly fifty miles from the coast, it is connected to the Gulf of Mexico by a channel deep enough for large, oceangoing ships. Houston is a leading seaport and a great manufacturing city. It has a larger population than any other city in the Great Plains states.

Our helicopter is preparing to land at the Houston airport now. During our trip, we have seen the main land features of the Midwest and Great Plains. We have also seen some of the ways in which these features affect the lives of people in this region.

Learn About the Central Lowland

1. Why has it been easy to build roads and railroads in the Central Lowland?
2. What is the corn belt? Why is it an important farming area?
3. Where is the dairy belt located? Why is this area well suited to raising dairy cattle?
4. What are the two main tributaries of the Mississippi River?
5. Why has the Mississippi River system been important in the history of our country?

Explore the Great Plains

1. What is the land like in most of the Great Plains?
2. Give one reason why few forests grow in the Great Plains.
3. Why are the Great Plains well suited for raising wheat?
4. Explain why cattle ranches on the Great Plains are usually very large.
5. How were the Black Hills formed?
6. Explain how the Badlands were created.

Practice Your Writing Skills

Most of the Midwest and Great Plains lies in the vast Interior Plains region of our country. However, several other regions and sections extend into the Midwest and Great Plains. These are listed below.

Appalachian Plateau   Coastal Plain
Interior Highlands   Superior Upland
Basin and Range Country

Do research and write a brief paragraph about each, describing what you would see on a trip through each region or section. Use words that will create vivid images in the mind of the listener. (See page 351.) When you have finished your paragraphs, read them to your class. Ask your classmates to decide if you have created accurate images of the places you have described.

Investigate the Great Ice Age

During the Great Ice Age, glaciers moved over much of the Midwest and Great Plains. Read about the Great Ice Age, and prepare an oral report for your class. The questions below will guide your research and help you decide what should be included in your report.

1. When did the Great Ice Age begin, and approximately how long did it last?
2. What caused glaciers to form during the Great Ice Age?
3. What parts of the Midwest and Great Plains were covered by glaciers?
4. What changes did glaciers make in the land features of the Midwest and Great Plains?

You will find much useful information for your report in the feature on page 36 and in the Land sections of some of the chapters in Parts 5 and 6 of this book. The suggestions on pages 350-352 will help you prepare your report and present it to the class.

An Iowa cornfield in July. In most parts of the Midwest and Great Plains, there are extreme differences in temperature between summer and winter. This is partly because the Midwest and Great Plains lies far north of the equator. Also, most of this part of our country is far from large bodies of water, which help to moderate temperatures.

3 Climate

A Problem To Solve

Temperatures differ greatly from season to season in the Midwest and Great Plains. Why is this so? The following questions suggest some hypotheses that will be helpful in solving this problem.

a. How does distance from the equator affect temperatures in the Midwest and Great Plains?

b. How does distance from the ocean affect temperatures here?

c. What effects do winds have on temperatures in the Midwest and Great Plains?

See TO THE STUDENT, pages 8-10.

A CONTINENTAL CLIMATE

A summer day in Iowa. It is a sunny afternoon in July, and we are standing in an Iowa cornfield. The temperature is 101 degrees. Not a breeze is stirring, but the hot, moist air seems to shimmer above the green rows of corn. We are perspiring freely. The farmer, who has been cultivating his corn, stops to talk with us. He is wearing a large hat to shade his head from the glaring sun. The farmer says that rain is expected this evening, but that it will probably not cool the air very much. Here in Iowa, summer nights are usually warm and humid.

We remark that the weather makes us feel very uncomfortable. The farmer agrees, but he adds, "I like it just the same. This is wonderful weather for raising corn. On a quiet summer night, you can actually hear the corn growing." The farmer tells us that hot, humid summer weather has helped to make Iowa one of our country's leading corn-producing states.

Iowa in the wintertime. Six months later, we visit the farm again. We can hardly believe that we are in the same place. The weather now is bitterly cold. According to the latest weather report, the temperature is only three degrees above zero. The sky is dark and cloudy, and the wind is blowing hard. Snow is whipping across the bare fields and piling into drifts against barns and fences. The farmer's wife tells us that people are being warned to stay at home because the drifting snow may soon block all roads. She says that cold, snowy weather like this is common in Iowa during the winter months.

In the Midwest and Great Plains, temperatures change greatly from season to season. On our visits to the farm in Iowa, we found two different kinds of weather. It was very warm in July and very cold in January. In most other parts of the Midwest and Great Plains, just as in Iowa, there are extreme differences in temperature between summer and winter.

The feature on pages 50 and 51 helps explain why temperatures differ from season to season in the Midwest and Great Plains. This part of our country, like the rest of the conterminous* United States, lies far north of the equator. The weather near the equator is hot all year long, except in the mountains. In lands that are far away from the equator, there are noticeable differences in temperature between summer and winter.

You might expect that all places located the same distance from the equator would have the same kind of climate. This is not true, however. In Seattle, Washington, for example, the average temperature in July is about sixty-six degrees and the average temperature in January is about forty-two degrees. Bismarck, North Dakota, lies at about the same latitude as Seattle. However, Bismarck's average July temperature is nearly seventy-two degrees and its average January temperature is only ten degrees. In most of the Midwest and Great Plains, summers are warmer and winters are colder than they are in other areas at the same latitude.

*See Glossary

Build Your Vocabulary

continental climate	humid	latitude	cyclonic rainfall
growing season	tornado	blizzard	Indian summer
drought	convectional rainfall	thunderstorm	rain shadow

Distance from the ocean affects the climate of the Midwest and Great Plains. The map on pages 18 and 19 will help you understand why there is such a great difference between summer and winter weather in most parts of the Midwest and Great Plains. When you study the map, you will see that most parts of the Midwest and Great Plains lie far from any ocean. Large bodies of water, such as the oceans, gain or lose heat more slowly than the land does. Therefore, the water is warmer than the land in winter and cooler than the land in summer. Winds blowing from the oceans bring mild weather to lands along the coast. Only a small part of the land in the Midwest and Great Plains is cooled in summer or warmed in winter by ocean breezes. As a result, temperature extremes in most of the Midwest and Great Plains are greater than they are along our coasts. The kind of climate found in most of the Midwest and Great Plains, as well as in other areas far from any ocean, is known as a continental climate.

WINDS AND RAINFALL

Winds from the north and the south help to cause great changes in temperature. The winds that sweep across the Midwest and Great Plains help to cause

A street in Chicago after a January blizzard. The winds that sweep across the Midwest and Great Plains help to cause changeable weather here. In the wintertime these winds often come from Canada, bringing snow and bitterly cold weather. In summer, winds from the Gulf of Mexico bring hot, humid weather to much of the Midwest and Great Plains.

AVERAGE ANNUAL RAINFALL

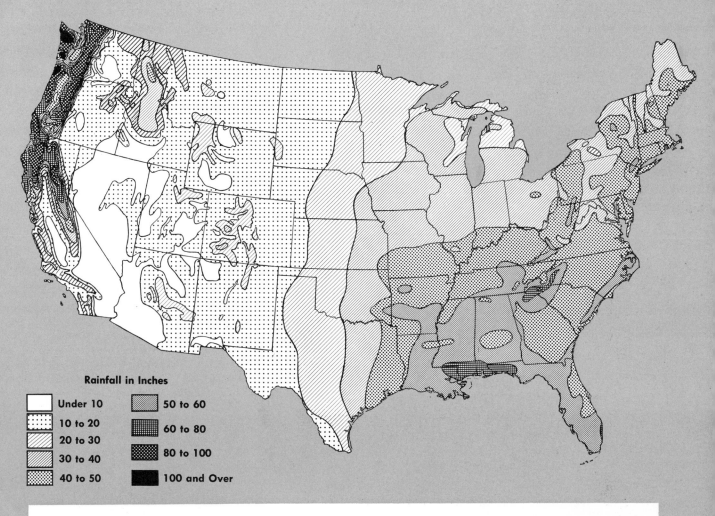

Rainfall in Inches

- Under 10
- 10 to 20
- 20 to 30
- 30 to 40
- 40 to 50
- 50 to 60
- 60 to 80
- 80 to 100
- 100 and Over

The map above shows the average yearly rainfall in different parts of the conterminous* United States. As used here, the term "rainfall" includes not only the amount of water that falls as rain, but also the amount that falls as snow and other forms of precipitation. It may take from six to thirty inches of snow to equal one inch of rain.

Rainfall is plentiful in the Midwest and along the eastern edge of the Great Plains states. Much of the rain that falls here is brought by moist winds from the Gulf of Mexico. These winds seldom reach the western part of the Great Plains states. Also, this area lies in the rain* shadow of the Rocky Mountains. As a result, the climate here is dry.

changeable weather here. Like other parts of our country, the Midwest and Great Plains lies in a belt of westerly winds. These winds sweep across the United States from west to east. However, they are joined or interrupted by winds blowing from other directions.

In the wintertime, the winds that pass over the Midwest and Great Plains are often from the north. These winds, which come from northern Canada, are cold and dry. They bring bitterly cold weather to much of the Midwest and Great Plains.

THE SEASONS

The year is divided into four natural periods, or seasons, which we call summer, autumn, winter, and spring. Each season is marked by changes in the length of day and night and by changes in temperature.

The seasons are caused by the tilt of the earth's axis and the revolution of the earth around the sun. It takes one year for the earth to revolve around the sun. On this trip, the earth remains tilted at the same angle to the path along which it travels. The chart below shows how this causes the Northern Hemisphere to be tilted toward the sun on June 21 and away from the sun on December 22. On March 21 and September 22, the Northern Hemisphere is tilted neither toward the sun nor away from it.

The chart on the left shows that on June 21 the sun shines directly on the Tropic of Cancer.* This is the northernmost point ever reached by the sun's direct rays. In the Northern Hemisphere, June 21 is the first day of summer and the longest day of the year.

The chart on the right shows that on December 22 the sun shines directly on the Tropic of Capricorn.* This is the southernmost point ever reached by the sun's direct

A large area around the
North Pole is lighted.

The axis of the earth
is tilted toward the sun.

North Pole

Arctic Circle

Tropic of Cancer

Equator

DIRECT RAYS
OF THE SUN

Tropic of Capricorn

South Pole

A large area around the
South Pole is in darkness.

SUMMER IN THE NORTHERN HEMISPHERE

The chart above shows how the earth is lighted by the sun at noon on June 21, the first day of summer in the Northern Hemisphere.

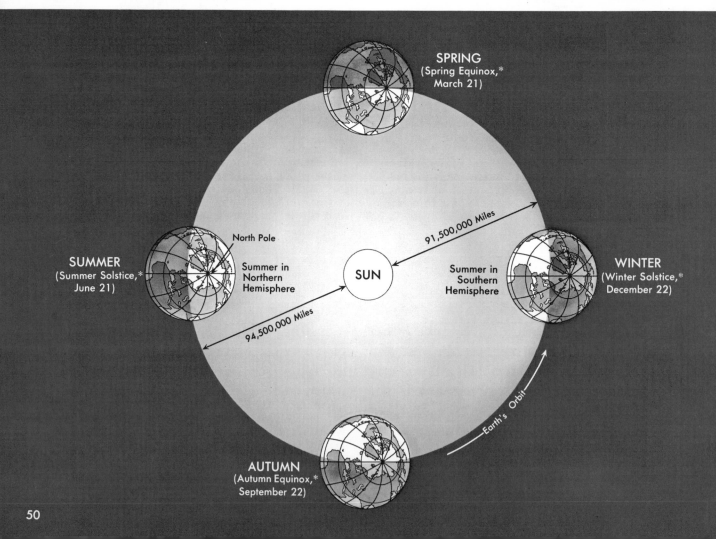

SPRING
(Spring Equinox,*
March 21)

91,500,000 Miles

SUMMER
(Summer Solstice,*
June 21)

North Pole

Summer in
Northern
Hemisphere

SUN

Summer in
Southern
Hemisphere

WINTER
(Winter Solstice,*
December 22)

94,500,000 Miles

Earth's Orbit

AUTUMN
(Autumn Equinox,*
September 22)

OF THE YEAR

rays. In the Northern Hemisphere, December 22 is the first day of winter and the shortest day of the year.

When one hemisphere is tilted toward the sun, the other is tilted away from the sun. For this reason, the seasons in the Southern Hemisphere are just the opposite of those in the Northern Hemisphere. Summer in the Southern Hemisphere begins on December 22, and winter begins on June 21.

Temperatures are affected by the slant of the sun's rays as they strike the surface of the earth. Study the chart below, and the picture of Tulsa, Oklahoma, to help you understand why this is true.

Near the equator, the sun is almost directly overhead throughout the year. For this reason, the weather near the equator is always hot, except in the mountains. In areas farther away from the equator, the sun's rays are more slanted. Therefore, the weather is usually cooler.

The southern part of the United States is closer to the equator than the northern part of our country. This explains why the weather is generally warmer in the south than it is in the north.

*See Glossary

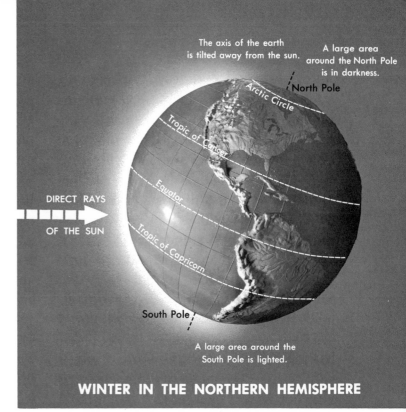

WINTER IN THE NORTHERN HEMISPHERE

The chart above shows how the earth is lighted by the sun at noon on December 22, the first day of winter in the Northern Hemisphere.

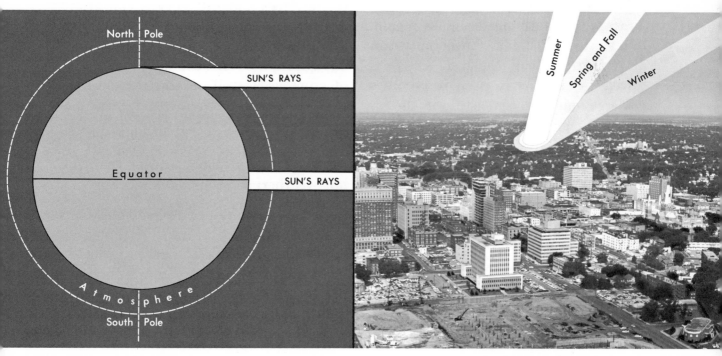

The chart above shows that when the sun's rays strike the earth at a slant, they must travel through more atmosphere than when they strike it directly. This affects temperatures because the atmosphere absorbs heat from the sun's rays. The more atmosphere the rays must pass through, the less heat they retain to warm the earth. This is one reason why temperatures are higher if the sun is directly overhead than they are if the sun is low in the sky.

This picture also helps to explain how changes in temperature are caused by the different angles at which the sun's rays strike the surface of the earth. During the summer, the noonday sun is high in the sky. The rays of the sun are concentrated into narrow areas. As a result, they produce much heat. During the winter, the noonday sun is low in the sky. The slanting rays of the sun are spread over much wider areas, so they produce less heat.

51

The warm winds that sweep across the Midwest and Great Plains in the summertime come mainly from the south. Some of these winds contain large amounts of moisture that has evaporated from the Gulf of Mexico. These moist winds bring hot, humid weather to the areas over which they move.

In the Midwest and Great Plains, the weather often changes rapidly from day to day. There are no high mountain ranges in this part of our country, so winds from the north and the south can move swiftly over the level land, bringing sudden changes in temperature.

Winds also affect rainfall in the Midwest and Great Plains. The winds that pass over the Midwest and Great Plains not only cause changes in temperature, but they also bring rain. Much of this rain occurs when a mass of warm, moist air from the south meets a mass of cold, dry air from Canada. Since the warm air is lighter than the cold air, it is forced to rise. As it rises, it becomes cooler. Some of the moisture in the air condenses and falls to earth as rain or snow. The kind of rainfall that results from the meeting of warm and cold air masses is known as cyclonic rainfall.

On hot summer days, rainfall is sometimes produced in a different way. As warm, moist air from the Gulf of Mexico moves northward over the land, it is heated still more. This hot, moist air rises very rapidly. As it rises, it becomes cool. Some of the moisture in the air condenses, bringing heavy summer rains. The kind of rainfall that is formed in this way is called convectional rainfall. It is often accompanied by thunder and lightning. (See feature on page 54.)

The Midwest receives plentiful rainfall. In the Midwest, rainfall is usually plentiful the year around. This part of our country lies directly in the path of the moist winds that move northward from the Gulf of Mexico. Rainfall is heaviest in the southernmost part of the Midwest, which lies nearest to the Gulf. Some places here receive about fifty inches of rainfall a year. (See map on page 49.) Less rain falls in the northern part of the Midwest. In some areas, the average annual rainfall is less than thirty inches.

Rainfall has helped determine the kinds of plants that grow in the Midwest. Before this part of our country was settled, dense, green forests covered most of the land. Tall grasses grew in many areas that were not forested. Trees and tall grasses can grow only where there is plenty of rainfall.

Throughout the Midwest, there is enough rainfall for farming. Most kinds of crops grow well on thirty inches of rainfall a year. Even less rainfall is needed in places where summers are not too warm. Less water is evaporated from the soil in cool weather than in hot weather, so crops have more moisture to use. Long periods of dry weather, known as droughts, do not occur very often in the Midwest. When they do, they seldom last long enough to cause severe damage. Abundant rainfall has helped farmers in the Midwest to produce large quantities of crops.

Because rainfall is plentiful in the Midwest, people here usually have enough water to supply all their needs. There are many lakes and rivers in this part of our country, as well as a large supply of groundwater.* As a result,

In the Midwest, rainfall is usually plentiful the year around. There is enough rainfall for farming throughout this part of our country. In the Great Plains states, rainfall decreases from east to west. In the western part of these states, the average rainfall is less than twenty inches a year. This is not enough moisture for growing most crops.

most communities can get the water they need for homes and industries. Pages 170 and 171 provide more information about the Midwest's water resources.

In the Great Plains states, rainfall decreases from east to west. The map on page 49 shows that there are considerable differences in rainfall within the Great Plains states. Rainfall is heaviest along the eastern border of these states, especially in Texas and Oklahoma. Some places here receive about fifty inches of rainfall a year. As you go westward across the Great Plains states, the amount of rainfall decreases steadily. In the western part of these states, the average rainfall is less than twenty inches a year. Most kinds of farm crops

do not grow well on this amount of rainfall. There is also too little rainfall for trees to grow.

A comparison of the maps on pages 20 and 49 will help you understand why rainfall is so light in the western part of the Great Plains states. The western part of these states does not lie in the path of the moist air that moves northward from the Gulf of Mexico. Usually this air drifts eastward toward the Atlantic Ocean.

Another reason why this area receives so little rainfall is that it lies in the rain* shadow of the Rocky Mountains. Throughout the year, moist winds from the Pacific Ocean blow toward the western coast of the United States. When

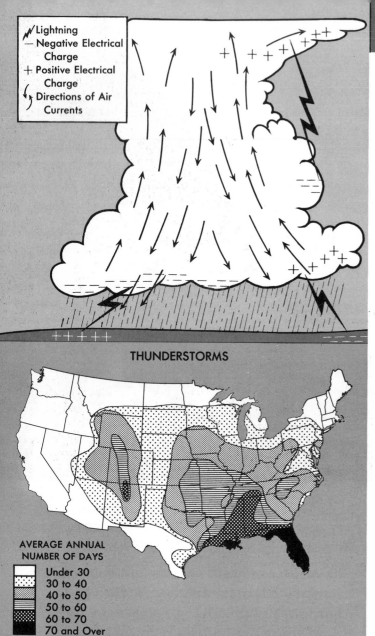

THUNDERSTORMS

AVERAGE ANNUAL
NUMBER OF DAYS

Under 30
30 to 40
40 to 50
50 to 60
60 to 70
70 and Over

Thunderstorms

A thunderstorm is a heavy shower of rain accompanied by gusty winds, thunder, lightning, and sometimes hail. The map on this page shows which parts of the United States receive the most thunderstorms each year. Few such storms occur beyond 60° north or south latitude.

Practically all rain is formed by the rising and cooling of moist air. As the air cools, moisture condenses into tiny droplets of water. If there are enough droplets, a rain cloud forms. Then the droplets combine as raindrops, and a shower results. One raindrop may contain as many as 8 million cloud droplets.

A thunderstorm may occur when a warm land surface heats moist air very rapidly. This heating creates strong currents of rising air. When rain clouds form, the rising air currents sweep them upward, several miles above the earth's surface. Falling raindrops are broken up into fine particles by the rising air. These particles develop electrical charges, some negative (-) and some positive (+). Particles with the same charge collect in different parts of a cloud, or form new raindrops that fall to earth. When the difference in charge becomes great enough, electricity may be discharged between parts of one cloud, between two clouds, or between a cloud and the ground. This discharge, or flash of lightning, heats the air through which it passes. The heated air expands violently, creating the sound waves that we call thunder. Since it takes about five seconds for a sound wave to travel a mile, a person can tell how far away a storm is by counting the seconds between a flash of lightning and the thunder that follows.

these winds reach the mountains in the western part of our country, they are forced to rise. As they rise, they become cooler and lose most of their moisture in the form of rain or snow. By the time these westerly winds have finally crossed the Rocky Mountains, they are very dry. As they move down the eastern slopes of the mountains, the winds become warmer. Instead of giving off moisture, they take up moisture from the land. This helps explain why the climate is so dry in the western part of the Great Plains states.

In this area, rainfall is not only light, but it is very uncertain. The amount varies greatly from year to year. In some years, there is enough rain for growing good crops of wheat. In other years, so little rain falls that crops wither and die. Sometimes, droughts in the western part of the Great Plains states last for a long time, bringing great hardship to farmers.

The Changing Seasons

This chapter has explained why there are great differences in temperature between summer and winter in the Midwest and Great Plains. It has also shown why rainfall varies from place to place in this part of our country. To learn more about the climate of the Midwest and Great Plains, let us see what the weather is like during each of the four seasons of the year.

WINTER

Winters are cold in the northern part of the Midwest and Great Plains. The left-hand map on page 56 shows average temperatures in North America during January. You will notice that the average January temperature in the northern part of the Midwest and Great Plains is below thirty-two degrees. Since thirty-two degrees is the temperature at which water freezes, you can see that winters are cold in this area. Winters are especially cold in far northern states such as North Dakota and Minnesota, which lie directly in the path of icy winds from Canada. In these states, the temperature often drops below zero on frosty winter nights.

In the northern part of the Midwest and Great Plains, snow may blanket the ground for months at a time. Snowfall is especially heavy along the eastern and southern shores of the Great Lakes. As cold winds from the north and west blow across the lakes, they become warmer and take up much moisture. In winter, they drop this moisture over the cold land in the form of snow. Along the southern shore of Lake Superior, over eight feet of snow may fall each winter.

Snowfall is lighter in the Great Plains states, because the climate here is generally drier. Sometimes, however, the strong winds that blow across the plains pick up large quantities of fine, powdery snow and send it whirling through the air. A snowstorm of this type is called a blizzard. People or animals who are caught outdoors in a blizzard may lose their way in the blinding snow. They may even freeze to death if they cannot find shelter.

The people who live in the northern part of the Midwest and Great Plains have learned to prepare for cold winter weather. Their homes and other buildings are heated with furnaces that burn gas, oil, or coal. Houses in this area are built to keep out the cold. When people go outdoors in the wintertime, they wear heavy clothing to keep themselves warm.

Cold, snowy weather sometimes hinders transportation in the northern part of the Midwest and Great Plains. Cars often become stuck in snowdrifts, and icy roads make driving dangerous. Buses and trains may be delayed by a heavy snowfall. Snowplows are used to clear the streets and highways so that traffic can move. For about three or four months each winter, ice covers parts of the Great Lakes. Ships cannot travel from one port to another unless special boats called icebreakers clear a path through the ice for them.

Farmers in the northern part of the Midwest and Great Plains do not work in their fields during the winter, for the ground is frozen and covered with snow. The farmers must care for their livestock, however. They have to provide warm barns and plenty of food for their animals during the wintertime.

Many people in this area look forward to the winter months, when they can enjoy skiing, ice-skating, and other winter sports. There are many ski resorts in Michigan, Wisconsin, and Minnesota.

Average January and July temperatures in North America. Winters are colder in the northern part of the Midwest and Great Plains than in the southern part. Except for a small area along our country's northern border, summers are warm or hot throughout the Midwest and Great Plains.

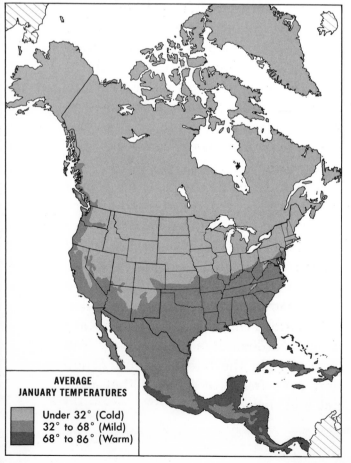

AVERAGE
JANUARY TEMPERATURES

Under 32° (Cold)
32° to 68° (Mild)
68° to 86° (Warm)

AVERAGE
JULY TEMPERATURES

Under 32° (Cold)
32° to 68° (Mild)
68° to 86° (Warm)
86° and Over (Hot)

Skaters on a pond in Wisconsin. In the northern part of the Midwest and Great Plains, snow may blanket the ground for months at a time during the winter. Many people here enjoy ice-skating, skiing, and other winter sports. Along the Gulf coast of Texas, winter weather is mild enough for people to go swimming and boating.

In the southern part of the Midwest and Great Plains, winters are milder. If you were to travel southward through the Midwest and Great Plains during the wintertime, you would find the weather gradually becoming warmer. Winters are mild in the southern part of the Midwest and Great Plains. The reasons for this are explained in the feature on pages 50 and 51.

Winters are especially mild along the Gulf coast of Texas. As you learned earlier, large bodies of water such as the Gulf of Mexico are warmer than the land in winter. Warm winds from the Gulf bring mild weather to the lands along the coast. In Houston, for example, the average January temperature is fifty-five degrees.

Occasionally during the winter, cold winds from the north sweep southward all the way across Texas. Temperatures may fall below the freezing point, but it rarely snows in the southern part of the state. When snow does fall, it seldom stays on the ground more than a few days at a time.

People who live where winters are very mild can work and play comfortably outdoors all year long. They do not have to wear heavy clothing or heat houses with large furnaces. During the

57

winter months, they can sometimes enjoy swimming, boating, and other outdoor sports. In the lower Rio Grande Valley of Texas, farmers grow fruits and vegetables during the winter months to sell to people in the cold northern part of our country. Some of these crops, such as oranges and grapefruit, cannot be grown at all in areas where winters are colder.

SPRING

Spring is a season of changeable weather. In the Midwest and Great Plains, spring weather is usually very changeable. One day the weather may be sunny and pleasant, with temperatures so warm that people can go outdoors without wearing coats. The next day, the temperature may drop below freezing, and snow may fall. These sudden changes in the weather are caused by cold winds from the north and warm winds from the south that blow across the level land.

Spring is a stormy time of year in the Midwest and Great Plains. The clashing of cold and warm air masses often results in windstorms and heavy rainfall. Violent storms known as tornadoes sometimes develop in spring or early summer. (See feature on opposite page.) More tornadoes strike the Midwest and Great Plains than any other part of our country.

Springtime is a season of changeable weather in the Midwest and Great Plains. Sudden changes in temperature are caused by cold winds from the north and warm winds from the south that blow across the land. The clashing of warm and cold air masses often results in severe storms.

Tornadoes

The black funnel cloud of a tornado moves slowly across the plains of Kansas.

We are visiting a small town in the eastern part of Kansas. It is a warm, humid afternoon in early May. The air is unusually still. In the distance, we can hear the low rumble of thunder. Large, black storm clouds are gathering on the western horizon. The people we are visiting have turned on a radio in order to hear the latest weather report. They know that this is the kind of weather that sometimes produces destructive windstorms called tornadoes.

Suddenly we hear the loud whine of a warning siren. We rush to the window and look out. In the distance, we can see a black, twisting cloud shaped somewhat like a funnel, which reaches all the way down to the ground. (See picture above.) This is the funnel cloud of a tornado.

As the tornado moves toward the town, we hurry to the basement. There we will be safer if the house should blow off its foundation. It is raining very hard now, and lightning flashes across the sky almost continually. When the tornado strikes the town, the noise is like the roaring of a hundred freight trains. Buildings in the path of the tornado suddenly explode. Trees are

ripped from the ground, and cars are tossed into the air like toys. Soon the tornado has passed, leaving a path of wreckage about a hundred yards wide. It will take many months to repair the damage that the tornado caused in less than a minute.

A tornado is one of nature's most violent storms. It is made up of very strong winds that whirl rapidly in a circle. Scientists believe that the whirling winds in a tornado may sometimes blow at speeds of more than three hundred miles an hour. The storm itself, however, travels forward rather slowly. Its average speed is only about thirty-five miles an hour.

The exact way in which tornadoes are formed is not yet known. However, they seem to occur when a mass of warm, moist air and a mass of cold, dry air come together in a certain way. In the Midwest and Great Plains, this usually happens in spring or early summer, when cold air from Canada meets warm air from the Gulf of Mexico.

More tornadoes occur in the Midwest and Great Plains than anywhere else in the world. Each year they destroy millions of dollars' worth of property. Sometimes many people are killed. In recent years, however, scientists have developed better methods of predicting tornadoes and of warning people when one of these storms is approaching. These measures have undoubtedly helped to save many lives.

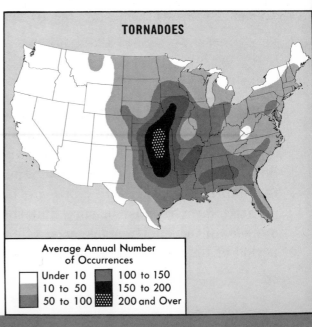

TORNADOES

Average Annual Number of Occurrences

Under 10	100 to 150
10 to 50	150 to 200
50 to 100	200 and Over

AVERAGE LENGTH OF GROWING SEASON

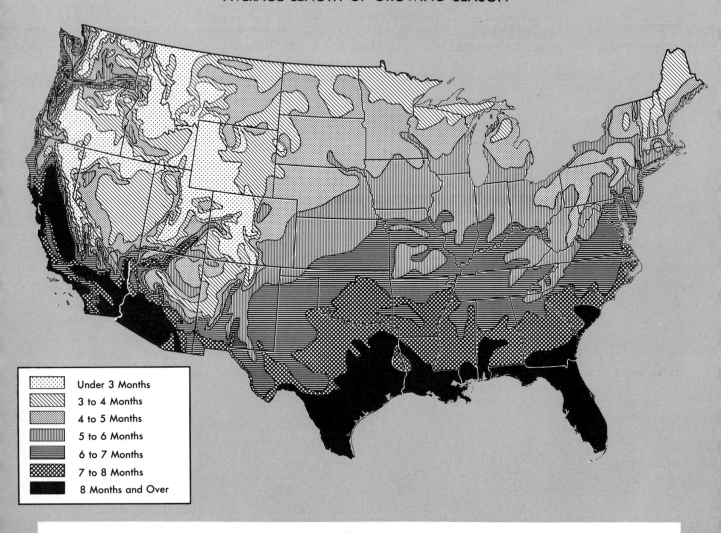

▦	Under 3 Months
▨	3 to 4 Months
▦	4 to 5 Months
▥	5 to 6 Months
▤	6 to 7 Months
▦	7 to 8 Months
■	8 Months and Over

The growing season is the period of time during which crops can be grown outdoors without being killed by frost.

As the map above shows, the growing season in most parts of the Midwest and Great Plains lasts from four to seven months. We can say that these areas have a moderate growing season. In much of Texas and Oklahoma, the growing season lasts for more than seven months. Some areas in the northern part of the Midwest and Great Plains have a growing season that is only three to four months long.

The growing season differs from place to place. During the springtime, farmers in the Midwest and Great Plains are busy plowing the land in preparation for planting crops. Before crops can be planted, farmers must be sure that the danger of severe frost is past. The period of time when crops can be grown outdoors without being killed by frost is known as the growing season.

The map above shows the average length of the growing season in different parts of the United States. When you study the map, you can see that the length of the growing season varies greatly in the Midwest and Great Plains.

Some areas in the northern part of the Midwest and Great Plains have a growing season that is less than four months long. Farmers in these areas must grow crops such as hay, potatoes, and barley, which do not take a long time to ripen.

In much of the Midwest and Great Plains, the growing season is between four and seven months long. (See map on page 60.) Here the period without frost is long enough for growing corn, soybeans, and many other crops. The fertile farming area known as the corn belt lies entirely within this part of the Midwest and Great Plains.

The map on page 60 also shows that in parts of Texas and Oklahoma the growing season is more than seven months long. A long growing season is helpful to farmers here. They can grow cotton and other crops that need many months to ripen. In addition, they are able to plant their crops earlier in the year than farmers in the northern part of our country. As a result, they can harvest their crops and send them to market earlier. In this way, they are likely to get a better price.

The Great Lakes affect the growing season near their shores. The growing season in some parts of the Midwest is

A grapefruit grove in the lower Rio Grande Valley of Texas. The growing season lasts more than seven months in parts of Texas and Oklahoma. Farmers in the lower Rio Grande Valley can grow crops outdoors the year around. Grapefruit and oranges, which cannot be grown where winters are colder, are important crops in this part of Texas.

Campers at a lake in Missouri. During July and August, daytime temperatures in the Midwest and Great Plains often rise above eighty degrees. To escape the hot weather, many people spend weekends and summer vacations at nearby lakes.

affected by the Great Lakes. Like other large bodies of water, these lakes gain and lose heat more slowly than the land does. In the spring, winds from the north and west are cooled as they blow across the lakes. The cool winds help keep fruit trees from budding until the danger of frost is past. In the fall, the Great Lakes are warmer than the land. Warm winds from the lakes help to protect fruit from the danger of early frost. Because the climate is so favorable for growing fruit, there are many large orchards and vineyards along the eastern shore of Lake Michigan and the southern shore of Lake Erie.

SUMMER

Summers are very warm in most parts of the Midwest and Great Plains. The right-hand map on page 56 shows average temperatures in North America during July. Notice that summers are warm or hot throughout the Midwest and Great Plains except for a small area along the northern border of our country. During July and August, daytime temperatures in the Midwest and Great Plains often rise above eighty degrees. Occasionally winds from the north bring cooler weather, but this does not usually last long.

In the Midwest, summers are not only warm but humid. The warm air that drifts northward from the Gulf of Mexico during the summertime is very moist. Moisture in the air makes people feel warmer and more uncomfortable than they would if the air were dry. Although many people do not like warm, humid weather, it is excellent for growing many kinds of crops. Rainfall is plentiful in the Midwest during the summer months. Much of it comes during thunderstorms. (See page 54.)

In the Great Plains states, summers are often warmer than they are in the Midwest. In North Dakota, for example, daytime temperatures sometimes rise above one hundred degrees. However, people usually do not mind the heat so much because the air is drier. In the western part of the Great Plains states, droughts may occur during the summer months. Hot, dry winds from the southwestern part of our country often blow across the plains, causing crops to wither.

The people of the Midwest and Great Plains have learned how to stay comfortable during the heat of summer. They dress in light summer clothing. Ice cream and cool drinks are popular during the summer months. Many people have air conditioners in their homes, cars, and offices. These devices keep the air cool and pleasant on even the hottest days. To escape hot weather at home, many people in the Midwest and Great Plains spend weekends and summer vacations at nearby lakes. Here they can enjoy swimming and other water sports.

Summers are milder in the far north. In the northernmost part of the Midwest and Great Plains, summers are milder than they are farther south. (See the right-hand map on page 56.) Summer weather is especially pleasant near the Great Lakes. In the summertime, these lakes are cooler than the land nearby. Breezes from the Great Lakes help to keep the weather in the northernmost part of the Midwest from becoming very hot. During the summer months, millions of people come to the northern parts of Minnesota, Wisconsin, and Michigan to spend their vacations.

AUTUMN

Autumn weather is cool and pleasant. Autumn is a favorite time of year for many people in the Midwest and Great Plains. During this season, masses of cool, dry air from Canada often drift

Autumn is a favorite time of year for many people in the Midwest and Great Plains. This is a season of cool, refreshing weather and clear, blue skies.

Autumn is harvesttime in the Midwest and Great Plains. Farmers are busy harvesting corn and other crops before winter comes.

southward over the United States. They bring cool, refreshing weather and clear, blue skies. The leaves of oaks, maples, and other hardwood trees turn brilliant shades of gold, orange, and scarlet. In the morning, the ground is covered with a silvery layer of frost.

Autumn is harvesttime in the Midwest and Great Plains. Corn and many other kinds of crops have ripened and are ready to be picked. Tender crops, such as tomatoes, cucumbers, and certain kinds of fruit, must be harvested before the first killing frost of autumn.

Late in autumn, people in the northern part of the Midwest and Great Plains often enjoy a period of fine weather known as "Indian summer." Days are warm and sunny, and the air is sometimes hazy with the smoke from burning leaves. Before long, however, the sky turns gray and a cold wind blows down from the north. Autumn is almost over, and winter is on its way.

Build Your Vocabulary

As you learn about the climate of the Midwest and Great Plains, be alert for the words and terms listed below. The suggestions on page 353 will help you find the meanings of those that are new to you. Test your understanding of these words and terms by writing a brief definition of each.

latitude	growing season
drought	blizzard
tornado	humid

Questions To Guide Your Reading

1. How has rainfall helped determine the kinds of plants that grow in the Midwest?
2. How do the Rocky Mountains affect rainfall in the Great Plains states?
3. What causes sudden weather changes in springtime in the Midwest and Great Plains?

Learn By Sharing Ideas

As a class, discuss the following question:

How does the climate of the Midwest and Great Plains affect the people here?

To prepare for your discussion, you will need to read about the climate of the Midwest and Great Plains and the ways in which the climate affects the people who live in this part of our country. Take notes, so you will be able to contribute to the discussion. As you read, look for ways in which climate affects each of the following:

a. the clothing that people wear
b. the kinds of homes people live in
c. transportation
d. sports and recreation

You may also wish to consider some of the ways in which climate affects your life.

The statue "Pioneer Mother" stands in a park in Kansas City, Missouri.

SHALL BE MY PEOPLE AND THY GOD MY GOD

Part 2
History

For thousands of years, the Midwest and Great Plains has been a good place for man to live. Until the early 1500's, only the Indians lived here. Then people from Europe began to explore this land. However, these Europeans did little to tame the wilderness. In the late 1700's, hardy pioneers from other parts of the United States began coming to the Midwest and Great Plains to make their homes.

These pioneers and the people who followed them used the rich resources they found here. They changed the Midwest and Great Plains from a vast wilderness into a land of prosperous farms and great industrial cities. The three chapters in this unit tell about these people — their ideas, their courage, and the work they did to make the Midwest and Great Plains an important part of our nation.

THINK AND READ AS HISTORIANS DO

Make your study of history an exciting adventure. In the next three chapters, you will be studying the history of the Midwest and Great Plains. If you think and read the way historians do, this journey into the past will be an exciting adventure.

How do historians think and read? Historians know they can never learn about everything that has happened in our world. Of the millions of events that have taken place since ancient times, only a small number have ever been recorded. Even so, there are more historical records than any person could possibly study in a lifetime. There are even too many records about certain subjects, such as the American Revolution, for any one person to study.

Since it is usually impossible for an historian to examine all the records about the subject he is studying, he has to decide which records to examine. He also has to decide which of the thousands of people, events, and ideas described in these records are important, and why. To make these decisions, the historian uses much the same method as the one described in "To the Student," which begins on page 8.

1. He reads historical records that give general background information about his subject.

2. He chooses some important questions for which he would like to find answers.

3. He makes educated guesses, or hypotheses, about what the answers to these questions might be.

4. He selects the records that will be most likely to help him prove whether these hypotheses are true, partly true, or false. As he studies these records, he looks for information about people, events, and ideas that relate to his hypotheses.

As you can see, the historian does not simply try to memorize as many facts about the past as possible. He has a much more important purpose for studying history. He is trying to discover the meaning of what has happened in the past.

Ask yourself questions as you read about the past. When you use the historian's method, you look for meaning in what you read. Instead of just remembering, you try to see which of the people, ideas, and events you read about are important, and why. To do this, you need to ask yourself questions as you read.

Let us think about some of the questions you can ask yourself as you read these chapters about the history of the Midwest and Great Plains. For thousands of years, this part of our country was a wilderness where scattered tribes of Indians hunted buffalo and other wild animals. Then great changes began to take place here. Most of the changes that created the Midwest and Great Plains we know today have taken place only in the last one hundred years. Why didn't these changes take place sooner? What people lived here during the thousands of years when so few changes took place? What people brought about the changes? What ideas and tools helped them to make these changes? If you ask yourself questions such as these, your study of the history of the Midwest and Great Plains will be much more challenging.

Make hypotheses about the past. The next step in making your study of history an adventure is to think what the answers to your questions might be. Why do **you** think the Midwest and Great Plains remained almost unchanged for so long? What ideas and inventions do **you** think may have helped to create the Midwest and Great Plains we know today? Use your imagination and try to think of all the possible answers. Then decide which hypotheses seem most reasonable.

Find information to test your hypotheses. To test your hypotheses, you need to find reliable sources of information about the subject you are studying. As you search these sources for facts to use in testing your hypotheses, your study of history becomes really exciting. You find that you can never read enough.

Each time you prove or disprove your hypotheses, a new question comes to your mind and you form new hypotheses to test. No matter how deeply you dig into the past, you will never come to the end of exciting discoveries.

Become a critical and independent thinker. The historian's method of studying the past will help you to become a critical and independent thinker. As you know, our knowledge of the past is very incomplete. History books only present their authors' ideas of the past and the facts they have assembled to support these ideas. Most of these authors are scholars who have studied the past carefully and tried to be as honest as possible. However, if you use the historian's method, you may sometimes disagree with an author's conclusions, or you may have questions that are not answered.

When you read a history chapter or book, think of the author as a person like yourself or your teacher. Try to see how his mind worked to reach the conclusions he presents in his book. In your mind, talk to him as you read. When something he has written seems vague, only partly true, or untrue, imagine that you are telling him so. List the facts that support your ideas. As you do so, you will find that your ability to think independently and to support your ideas with facts is greatly strengthened. You will also find that history comes vividly alive.

A river steamboat, photographed in the 1800's. When you study history as historians do, you must use many kinds of information, such as historical pictures, maps, and documents.

The Midwest and Great Plains is a rich and beautiful land. Man has lived here for thousands of years. Indians were the first people to inhabit this area. About four hundred years ago, people from Europe began coming to the Midwest and Great Plains. (The picture above shows Indians and fur traders in Michigan.)

4 Adventures in the Wilderness

As You Read,
Ask Yourself Questions

1. What makes the Midwest and Great Plains a good place in which to live?
2. What different groups of people have lived here through the years?

A rich and beautiful land. For thousands of years, the Midwest and Great Plains has been a good place for man to live. This is a land of great beauty. Green fields, sparkling lakes, and forests of tall trees cover much of the countryside in the Midwest. In the Great Plains states, vast grasslands and broad fields of golden wheat stretch for many miles under the blue summer sky.

The Midwest and Great Plains is also a land of rich resources. The soil in this part of our country is generally fertile. In many places, summers are long and warm, and enough rain falls for crops to grow. Beneath the soil are rich deposits of coal, iron ore, and petroleum.

Who has lived in the Midwest and Great Plains? It is not surprising that a land as rich and beautiful as the Midwest and Great Plains has been inhabited by man for thousands of years. The time line on page 80 lists the main groups of people who have lived in this part of our country. As you read about these different groups of people, you will learn how they have helped to shape the Midwest and Great Plains that we know today.

Indians of the Midwest and Great Plains

The people who have lived longest in the Midwest and Great Plains are the Indians. Where did these dark-haired, copper-skinned people come from? Did they make any important changes in this part of our country?

Where did the Indians come from? No one knows for certain where the ancestors of the American Indians came from. However, two clues lead scholars to think their homes originally were in Asia. First, the Indians look much like the Mongolian people of Asia. Second, as you can see on a globe, Asia and North America are separated by only a narrow strip of water in the far north. In prehistoric times, a land bridge may have connected the two continents here. People could have traveled from one continent to the other across this land bridge.

The newcomers from Asia probably began coming to North America about twenty thousand years ago. They may have been fleeing from enemies or searching for food. We do not know. As the years passed, the Indians gradually moved into many parts of North and South America. Here they lived for thousands of years, isolated from the rest of the world.

How did the Indians use the resources of the land in which they lived? Scholars think that the first people who came to North America were primitive stone-age hunters. As time went on, their descendants learned to raise crops. In some parts of North America, farming became the main way of obtaining food. In other parts, such as the Midwest and Great Plains, the Indians continued to meet their needs mainly by hunting. Neither the hunters nor the farmers learned to make tools and weapons of iron. The Indians left untouched the vast deposits of coal, iron ore, and oil that lay beneath the ground.

We do not know exactly why the Indians had not advanced further by the time Europeans arrived in America. The fact that they were isolated from the rest of the world may have held them back, for they could not take advantage of the ideas of people in other lands. Also, until the Europeans came, the Indians had no large animals such as oxen and horses that they could tame to help them with their work.

The Indians in North America were divided into many tribes that spoke different languages. The way these groups lived was shaped by the climate, the plants, and the animals around them. We will see how greatly environment shaped their lives when we compare the Indians of the midwestern forests with the Indians of the Great Plains.

Indians of the midwestern forests. In Indian times, vast forests covered much of the Midwest. The Indians in these forests obtained their food mainly by hunting wild animals. The men of the tribe were the hunters. Women added to the family food supply by raising corn and other vegetables in little garden plots. They also gathered wild roots, berries, and fruits. Near the Great Lakes, the women and girls harvested wild rice.

The Indians of the Midwest needed warm clothing, for winters in this part of the country are long and cold. The women made the clothing their families wore. Using stone and bone tools, they cut and sewed the skins of deer and other animals to make skirts, robes, moccasins, and leggings.

These Indians also needed warm houses. The most common type of house was a round or oval-shaped hut called

Indians of the midwestern forests lived in huts called wigwams, which were made by covering a frame of poles with sheets of bark. These Indians obtained their food mainly by hunting wild animals. The men of the tribe were the hunters. The women raised corn and other vegetables in little garden plots. They also made clothing from the skins of deer and other animals.

a wigwam. To make a wigwam, an Indian woman stuck poles in the ground, bent them over, and tied them together to make a frame. Then she covered this frame with sheets of bark. Inside the wigwam, she placed mats along the wall for the family to sit and sleep on. In the middle of the floor, she built a fire. The smoke from the fire escaped through a hole in the roof.

Indians of the plains. The Plains Indians lived very differently from the Indians of the forests. In the plains, trees grew mainly along the banks of streams. The rest of the land was covered with waving grass. Great herds of buffalo grazed on this grass. The Plains Indians depended on the buffalo for food, shelter, and clothing.

Most of the Plains Indians lived in tent villages, which they moved from place to place as they followed the herds. Their cone-shaped tents, called tepees, were made of poles covered with buffalo skins. The women of the village took these tents down and put them up again each time the tribe moved.

Hunting buffalo was the men's work. Before Europeans brought horses to America, the Plains Indians had to hunt on foot. Sometimes they disguised themselves in wolf or coyote skins and crept close enough to the herd to shoot the buffalo with bows and arrows. At other times, they drove the herd of buffalo to the edge of a high cliff. As the frightened herd pushed forward, hundreds of

Indians of the plains depended on the buffalo for food, clothing, and shelter. Most of these Indians lived in tent villages, which they moved from place to place as they followed buffalo herds.

animals fell helplessly over the cliff and were killed. In winter, when the snow drifted across the plains, the Indians hunted in snowshoes. The heavy buffalo, wallowing in the snow, were easy targets at that time.

Like the Indians of the forests, the Plains Indians made their clothing from the animal skins the hunters brought home. Both men and women wore robes, leggings, and moccasins. These garments were often decorated with designs made of porcupine quills.

Build Your Vocabulary

explorer   treaty   Coronado   fur trapper   wilderness   pioneer

Louisiana   La Salle   buffalo   missionaries   Marquette and Joliet

The influence of the Indians. Although Indians lived in the Midwest and Great Plains for thousands of years, they did little to change this part of our country. The number of Indians who lived here was very small. It is believed that the population of Detroit today is larger than the entire Indian population of Canada and the United States in Indian times. Also, the kind of life the Indians lived did not make it necessary for them to change the land. Since they met their needs mainly by hunting, they did not need to plow the grasslands or cut down the forests. They built no great cities, and they did not mine the rich deposits of iron ore and other minerals.

We have important reminders that the Midwest and Great Plains was once the land of the Indians, however. The names of many places here, such as Michigan, Ohio, and Milwaukee, are Indian names. One of the main crops grown here, corn, was first planted by the Indians. In addition, many people in the Midwest and Great Plains are Indians, or are of mixed Indian and European descent.

Europeans Come to the Midwest and Great Plains

As You Read,
Ask Yourself Questions

1. When did Europeans begin coming to the Midwest and Great Plains?
2. How did these Europeans differ from the Indians?
3. Why did the Europeans come?
4. From what countries in Europe did they come?
5. What changes did the Europeans bring to the land?

In the summer of 1541, the Plains Indians in the land we now call Texas saw a strange sight. An army was marching across the plains. The soldiers in this army wore armor made of hard, shiny material, and carried sticks that shot "fire and thunder." Their supplies were packed on the backs of large animals. No Indian war party had ever been equipped like this.

The army that crossed the Texas plains that summer was led by a Spanish explorer named Coronado. Coronado and his men hoped to find silver and gold. They were among the first Europeans to come to what is now the Midwest and Great Plains. In the years that followed, many other Europeans were to come to this part of our country.

What were the Europeans like? The Europeans who came to the Midwest and Great Plains differed in several important ways from the Indians who were living there. Europeans had not been isolated from the rest of the world as the Indians had been. By trading with people in Asia, they had learned about such useful inventions as gunpowder and the compass. These inventions gave the Europeans a great advantage over the Indians.

The Europeans had another advantage over the Indians of the Midwest and Great Plains. Within these Indian tribes, the only division of labor was between men and women. The men hunted. The women did nearly all the other work. Almost everything the tribe needed was produced by its own people. In a European community, however, the men did different kinds of work. For example, some were farmers, some were blacksmiths, and some were shoemakers. Merchants helped people within the community to exchange the goods they produced and trade with other communities. This type of economic system allowed Europeans to have a larger quantity and greater variety of goods.

The Europeans differed from the Indians in still another way. Most of the Indians in the Midwest and Great Plains belonged to small tribes. In Europe, however, kings had established nations, such as Spain, France, and England. Each of these nations had a much larger population, and was therefore much more powerful, than any Indian tribe.

Why did Europeans come to the Midwest and Great Plains? The story of Europeans in America has its beginning in the desire of Europe's people for trade. Some of the goods that people in Europe wanted most were spices produced in Asia. In the 1400's, European explorers began to search for an all-water route to the spice lands.

Coronado and his army crossed the Texas plains in the summer of 1541. They hoped to find treasures of gold and silver for Spain. Coronado was only one of many Europeans who came to America after 1500. Some of these people came to find treasure. Others wanted to find a water route to Asia or to bring Christianity to the Indians.

One of these explorers was Columbus. During his search for an all-water route to Asia, he accidentally discovered America. After Columbus returned to Europe and told about the lands he had found, many other Europeans sailed to America. Some hoped to find a water passage through this new land that would lead to Asia. Others came to find treasure or to bring Christianity to the Indians. Still others came to find freedom and a better way of life.

Spain

Spaniards were the first Europeans to come to the part of our country we call the Great Plains states. The early Spanish explorers who had followed Columbus to the New World had conquered the great cities of the Aztec and Inca Indians in Mexico and Peru. These conquests had brought Spain a vast fortune in gold and silver. Hoping to find more riches and also to discover a water passage to Asia, other Spanish explorers traveled northward from Mexico and the West Indies to the land that is now the United States.

The map on page 75 shows the routes some of the Spanish explorers followed.

A Spanish mission in San Antonio, Texas. Spaniards were the first Europeans to come to the part of our country we call the Great Plains states. Their explorations made it possible for Spain to claim Texas. Today, many cities in Texas have a colorful Spanish atmosphere.

Spanish Explorations

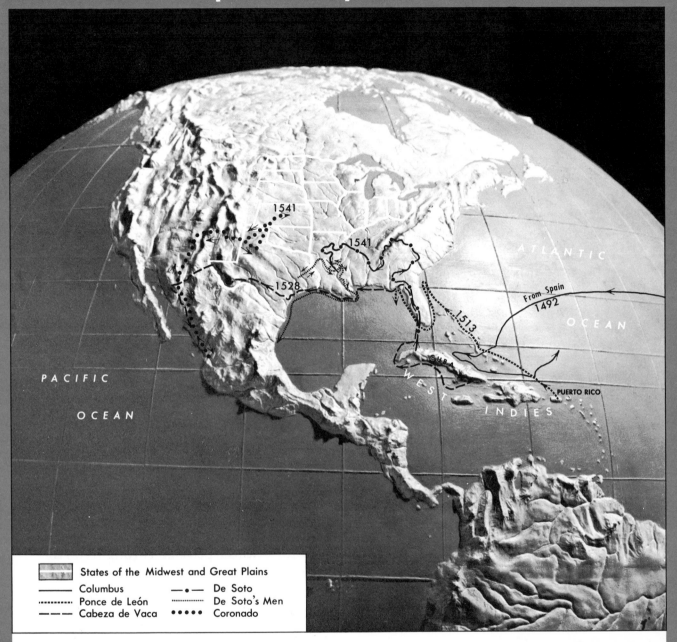

States of the Midwest and Great Plains
——— Columbus   —•— De Soto
·········· Ponce de León   ·········· De Soto's Men
— — — Cabeza de Vaca   ••••• Coronado

Columbus discovers America. In August, 1492, Christopher Columbus sailed westward from Spain in search of an all-water route to Asia. Many weeks later, he reached the islands now called the West Indies. (See map above.) He explored there for three months and then returned to Spain. Columbus made three more trips to America, but he never realized he had found a new part of the world instead of Asia.

Other explorers come to America from Spain. Columbus' discoveries brought many more explorers from Spain to the New World. Among them were Juan Ponce de León, Álvar Núñez Cabeza de Vaca, Hernando de Soto, and Francisco Coronado. (See map above.) Their explorations gave Spain a claim to large areas of land in what is now the United States.

Ponce de León sailed northwestward from Puerto Rico in 1513. During his voyage, he discovered and named Florida. Ponce de León was the first European to reach the part of our country we now call the South.

Cabeza de Vaca was shipwrecked off the coast of Texas in 1528. With three other men, he wandered across Texas and into Mexico. Finally, in 1536, they reached a Spanish settlement in northwestern Mexico.

De Soto and his men sailed from Cuba to Florida in 1539. From there, they traveled through much of the South. De Soto discovered the Mississippi River in 1541. He died a year later, but his men continued to explore. They traveled into Texas before going to Mexico.

Coronado left Mexico in 1540. His expedition traveled northward into what is now Kansas. Coronado was seeking vast treasures of gold and silver, but his search was unsuccessful. In 1542, he returned to Mexico.

As you can see, none of these men went as far north as the Midwest. However, some of the explorers named on this map traveled through the southern part of the Great Plains states.

The influence of the Spaniards. To their disappointment, the Spaniards found no riches in the land we now call the Great Plains states. However, their explorations here made it possible for Spain to claim Texas. As we will read in the next chapter, Texas was a part of the Spanish colony of Mexico for many years. It remained a part of Mexico for fifteen years after the Mexicans won their independence from Spain. The names of cities and rivers, such as San Antonio and the Rio Grande, remind us of this period in the history of Texas.

The Spaniards influenced the Great Plains states in another way. They brought horses and cattle. Many of these animals escaped or were allowed to run wild over the plains. Plains Indians tamed wild horses and used them in hunting. As Chapter 5 explains, American settlers later used wild cattle in making the Great Plains the cattle kingdom of America.

France

About one hundred years after the Spaniards came to the Great Plains states in search of treasure, explorers from the country of France began to

A French missionary meeting Indians. In the early 1600's, people from the country of France began traveling into the Midwest. Among these people were explorers, missionaries, and fur traders.

travel into the Midwest. These were not the first Frenchmen to come to North America. Many years earlier, French fishermen and fur traders had begun coming to the New World. Explorers had followed them to look for treasure and for a water passage through North America to Asia. These explorers had traveled through much of the eastern part of the land we now call Canada.

Champlain encouraged other Frenchmen to explore the Great Lakes area of the Midwest. The man who was responsible for sending French explorers from Canada to the Midwest was Champlain. This great French explorer became known as the Father of New France for the important part he played in helping France to build an empire in North America. Like other explorers of his time, Champlain hoped to find a water passage to Asia. In his search for this passage, he discovered the Great Lakes.

Routes of French Explorers

On a May morning in 1673, Father Jacques Marquette and Louis Joliet set out from the mission* of St. Ignace in search of a water passage to Asia. They paddled their canoes along the northern shore of Lake Michigan until they reached Green Bay. (Compare map at right with map on page 285.) After traveling up the Fox River, they carried their canoes across a narrow plain to the Wisconsin River. The explorers paddled down this river until they reached the broad waters of the Mississippi. For many days they traveled down the Mississippi River, hoping it would lead them to the Pacific Ocean. Finally, however, they learned from the Indians that the Mississippi flows into the Gulf of Mexico. When Marquette and Joliet reached the mouth of the Arkansas River, they decided to turn back. Following the route shown on the map, they reached Green Bay less than five months after their journey began.

A young French nobleman known as the Sieur de la Salle wanted to explore the Mississippi River all the way to the Gulf of Mexico. La Salle left Ft. Frontenac, on the St. Lawrence River, in 1679. In a ship called the *Griffin,* he and his men sailed all the way from the eastern end of Lake Erie to Green Bay. While the *Griffin* went back for supplies, La Salle traveled by canoe to the southern end of Lake Michigan. There he built Ft. Miami and waited for the *Griffin.* However, the ship was never heard from again. Lacking needed supplies, La Salle finally had to return to Ft. Frontenac. After many delays and hardships, La Salle and some of his men reached the Mississippi River in 1682. They paddled down the great river for many days until they reached its mouth. There La Salle claimed for the King of France all the land drained by the Mississippi River.

In 1731 a French-Canadian fur trader, the Sieur de la Vérendrye, set out with his sons to explore the lands west of Lake Superior. He traveled to Lake of the Woods and then to Lake Winnipeg, in Canada, building a chain of forts along his route. (See map at right.) Although La Vérendrye and his sons faced many dangers and hardships, they continued westward. Finally, in 1738, they reached some Mandan Indian villages along the Missouri River in what is now North Dakota. La Vérendrye later returned to Canada. In 1742 he sent his sons on a journey in search of the Pacific Ocean. The explorers were unsuccessful in reaching their goal, but they visited the Black Hills and traveled across much of South Dakota.

*See Glossary

◻ Midwest and Great Plains

MARQUETTE AND JOLIET: 1673

LA SALLE: 1679-1682

LA VÉRENDRYE AND SONS: 1731-1743

Champlain explored only a small part of the Great Lakes area, but he encouraged other Frenchmen to go beyond where he had been. Some of the Frenchmen who followed him were fur traders and trappers. Others were explorers. Still others were soldiers, sent to protect the territory the explorers had claimed for France. Catholic missionaries also came to this territory to try to convert the Indians to Christianity. All of these people helped to strengthen France's claim to the Great Lakes area.

Marquette, Joliet, and La Salle give France a claim to the Mississippi Valley. In the late 1600's, Frenchmen began to move from the Great Lakes area deeper into the Midwest. Two of the best known of these men were a priest named Father Marquette and an explorer named Joliet. Father Marquette had heard from the Indians about a "great water" that flowed into a still greater water. In 1673, he and Joliet set out together to find this waterway, hoping that it would be a passage to Asia.

The map on page 77 shows the route Marquette and Joliet followed. As you can see, the "great water" that they had heard about was the Mississippi River. After traveling hundreds of miles down this river, Marquette and Joliet learned that it flowed into the Gulf of Mexico. Therefore, it was not the passage they were seeking. Disappointed, they returned to the Great Lakes.

While Joliet was on his way to Canada to report the results of his trip down

Father Marquette and a French explorer named Joliet traveled down the Mississippi River to the mouth of the Arkansas River in 1673. A few years later, the French explorer La Salle journeyed down the Mississippi to the Gulf of Mexico. The explorations of these three men gave France a claim to the Mississippi Valley.

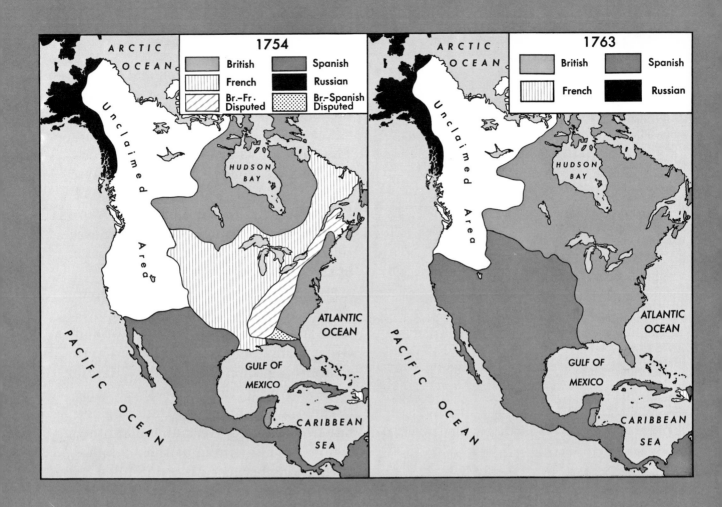

Before and after the French and Indian War. This war was fought mainly over conflicting claims to territory in the New World. As a result of the war, France lost its empire in North America. (Compare the maps above.) Great Britain gained vast areas of land on this continent. Spain, an ally of France, lost Florida but received French territory west of the Mississippi River.

the Mississippi, he met another French explorer, named La Salle. Unlike Joliet, La Salle was not particularly interested in finding a water passage to Asia. Instead, he dreamed of a vast French empire in the New World. In 1682, La Salle traveled down the Mississippi River to its mouth. He claimed the valley of this mighty river for his king, Louis XIV, and named it Louisiana in his honor.

Frenchmen travel on to what are now the Great Plains states. Frenchmen also journeyed westward into what are now the Great Plains states. A French-Canadian fur trader named La Vérendrye

led an expedition into North Dakota. Later, two of his sons explored part of South Dakota while returning from a journey in search of the Pacific Ocean. French fur trappers and explorers also traveled into Nebraska, Kansas, Texas, and Oklahoma. All these men helped to strengthen French claims to much of the interior of North America.

The French made little use of the resources of the Midwest and Great Plains. By the middle of the 1700's, most of the Midwest and Great Plains had been claimed by France. (Compare the map on pages 18 and 19 with the map at the left above.) The French made little use

10,000 YEARS IN THE MIDWEST AND GREAT PLAINS

The Indians. Indians lived in the Midwest and Great Plains for thousands of years before Europeans came. They met their needs mainly by hunting and did little to change the land.

The Spaniards. In the 1500's, Spanish explorers came to the land we now call the Great Plains states. Spain claimed the land now known as Texas, but few Spaniards settled there.

The French. In the 1600's and 1700's, most of the Midwest and Great Plains was claimed by France. The French built forts and started a profitable fur trade. They did little to change the land, however. In 1763, France lost its empire in North America. (See maps on page 79.)

American settlers. During the century following the Revolutionary War, many settlers came to the Midwest and Great Plains. They cleared the land for farms.

Century of Progress. In the middle of the 1800's, great changes began to take place in the Midwest and Great Plains. Mines and factories were started, new farming methods were developed, and great cities grew up. This century of progress created the Midwest and Great Plains we know today.

8,000 B.C.

INDIANS

A.D. 1500

1600

SPANISH

FRENCH

1700

1800

AMERICAN SETTLERS

1900

CENTURY OF PROGRESS

of the resources of this rich and beautiful land, however. Almost the only Frenchmen here were a few soldiers, missionaries, fur traders, and trappers. The soldiers, missionaries, and traders lived in forts along the main waterways. These forts had been built to protect France's claim to the land. The trappers roamed through the wilderness, returning to the forts to sell the pelts of the animals they had trapped.

France loses its empire in America. At the time that French fur trappers were traveling across the Midwest and Great Plains, people from England were establishing colonies along the Atlantic coast of North America. Settlers came to these colonies not only from England but from Ireland, Germany, and other countries. They brought their families with them because they intended to stay in America. These hardworking pioneers cleared the land for farming and built many towns.

During the years when the English colonies were growing in population, France and Great Britain* began to quarrel with one another. The left-hand map on page 79 will help you understand one reason for their quarrel. Both nations claimed land that lay between the Mississippi River and the English colonies. This conflict helped cause the French and Indian War, which began in 1754. The war was won by the British, partly because there were many more people in the British colonies than in the French colonies. Also, the British colonists had made better use of their resources. Their farms and workshops supplied the British troops in America with large amounts of food, clothing, and weapons.

*See Glossary

Under the treaty of peace signed in 1763, France lost its empire in North America. The maps on page 79 show that part of the land France had claimed in the Midwest and Great Plains was given to Britain and the rest was given to Spain.

The influence of the French. There are few reminders of the French in the Midwest and Great Plains today other than place names, such as Detroit and St. Louis. Only a small number of Frenchmen ever lived in the Midwest and Great Plains. Their way of life did not make it necessary for them to clear the land. When the territory that had been claimed by France was taken over by the British and Spanish, it looked much the same as it had when European explorers first came to America.

Explore the Early History of the Midwest and Great Plains

1. What group of people has lived longest in the Midwest and Great Plains? From where did these people probably come?
2. In what ways did the Indians of the midwestern forests live differently from the Indians of the plains?
3. What reminders of Indian times are there today in the Midwest and Great Plains?
4. What advantages did the Europeans who came to the Midwest and Great Plains have over the Indians?
5. What were some of the results of the explorations made by Spain in the Great Plains states?
6. How did France lose its empire in America?

Learn More About the Indians

Form a group with other members of your class to learn more about the Indians of the midwestern forests or the Indians of the plains. Then choose one of the following projects to work on together.

1. Make a model of an Indian village for your classroom.
2. Make a mural showing scenes from the everyday life of the Indians.

Refer to pages 346-348 for help in locating information. In working together, follow the guidelines on page 353. Your group should be prepared to answer questions from the rest of the class about the project.

Use Your Imagination

Imagine that you are one of these explorers.

La Vérendrye

Joliet   Coronado   La Salle

Father Marquette

Write a story about your explorations in what is now the Midwest and Great Plains. You will find information for this project in this chapter. To locate outside sources of information, refer to pages 346-348. In your story:

1. include some information about your early life
2. describe some of the expeditions you made
3. explain what the important results of your explorations were

In writing your story, use your imagination, but be sure that the statements you make are based on facts. Follow the guidelines for writing reports given on pages 350 and 351.

Questions for Class Discussion

1. Do you think the Europeans were justified in trying to take over the lands that were occupied by the Indians? Why, or why not?
2. Do you believe that if France had kept its vast empire in North America, it would have used the land more fully than the Indians had? Why, or why not?

Building a home on the frontier. In 1783, when the United States gained its independence from Great Britain, most of the Midwest and Great Plains was a wilderness. In the hundred years following the Revolutionary War, millions of people settled in this part of our country.

5   Coming of the Pioneers

As You Read,
Ask Yourself Questions

1. What was the Midwest and Great Plains like before American settlers moved there?

2. Why didn't American settlers move to the Midwest and Great Plains sooner than they did?

A waiting wilderness. In 1763, when France lost its empire in North America, the Midwest and Great Plains was still a wilderness. Much of this vast area of our country had not been explored. The land east of the Mississippi River belonged to Great Britain, and most of the land west of the Mississippi belonged to Spain. (Compare map on pages 18 and 19 with right-hand map on page 79.)

Many people who lived in the British colonies along the Atlantic coast wanted to move into the wilderness lands held by Great Britain. However, Britain had issued a proclamation that closed to settlers all of its territory west of the Appalachian Mountains. In this way, Britain hoped to avoid trouble with the Indians who lived in the wilderness. The colonists were angry about the proclamation. Some of them ignored the law and moved into the wilderness lands anyway, but they were few in number.

The Revolutionary War opened new lands to settlers. The colonists had not helped to make the law that closed the wilderness lands to settlers. This law, and other unpopular laws under which they lived, had been made across the ocean in Britain. The colonists resented the fact that they had to obey laws they had not helped to make. They felt that the British lawmakers did not understand the problems or needs of the colonies.

The discontent in the colonies finally led to the Revolutionary War, which began in 1775. About a year after the first shots were fired, the colonies declared their independence, and a new nation, the United States, came into being. The Revolutionary War continued for several more years. In 1783 Britain finally recognized the United States as an independent country. The treaty that was signed at this time gave to the new country the British wilderness lands east of the Mississippi River. At last this waiting wilderness could be opened to settlers.

Settlers Come to the Midwest

Two laws encouraged settlers to come to the Midwest. North of the Ohio River was a large area of land that was still very sparsely settled at the time the Revolutionary War came to an end. This land included what are now the midwestern states of Ohio, Indiana, Illinois, Michigan, and Wisconsin, as well as part of Minnesota. Because this territory lay in what was at that time the northwestern part of the United States, it became known as the Northwest. To help people settle the Northwest in an orderly manner, the government of the United States passed two important laws. These were the Ordinances of 1785 and 1787.

The Ordinance of 1785 stated how the land in the Northwest was to be divided up and sold. The land was to be divided into squares, called townships, measuring six miles on each side. Each

Build Your Vocabulary

Revolutionary War	Northwest Territory	Louisiana Purchase
steamboat War of 1812	railroad Mississippi River	reservation
Lewis and Clark cowboy	slavery plains	Homestead Act

township was to be divided into thirty-six equal sections. A settler could buy one or more sections. The government would keep a record of this sale.

The second law, the Ordinance of 1787, organized the Northwest into a territory that would someday be divided into states. This ordinance provided for orderly government in the Northwest Territory before it was divided into states. It also explained how the states were to be formed. These states would have equal rights with the original thirteen states.

The Ordinances of 1785 and 1787 took much of the risk out of moving to the wilderness. A settler who bought land here knew that his claim was protected by law. He also knew that his rights as an American citizen would be protected. He would have a voice in his government. This was an important guarantee to people who had just fought a revolution for their freedom.

The Louisiana Purchase. In 1803, an unexpected event opened for settlement vast new lands west of the Mississippi River. This event was our country's purchase of the French territory of Louisiana. The map on page 85 shows the area the United States gained through the Louisiana Purchase. This territory had been claimed by France in the late 1600's. At the end of the French and Indian War, France had given it to Spain. In 1800, however, France had forced Spain to return it.

People in the United States were not happy to see the French take over the territory of Louisiana. At this time, France was much more powerful than Spain. The Americans were afraid that France might not let the United States use the port of New Orleans, at the mouth of the Mississippi River. Farmers in the Northwest Territory and other parts of our country shipped their farm products down the Mississippi to New Orleans. Without this port, they would not have a convenient gateway for shipping their products to other parts of the United States and to foreign countries.

In 1803, President Thomas Jefferson sent a representative to France to try to buy the port of New Orleans for the United States. To his great surprise, the representative learned that France had decided it did not want to rebuild its empire in the New World. Instead of merely selling New Orleans, France was willing to sell all of Louisiana.

Soon after the United States bought Louisiana, President Jefferson sent the explorers Lewis and Clark to find out what this wilderness land was like.

Americans raising the flag in the Louisiana Territory. The United States bought this huge territory from France in 1803.

How Our Country Grew

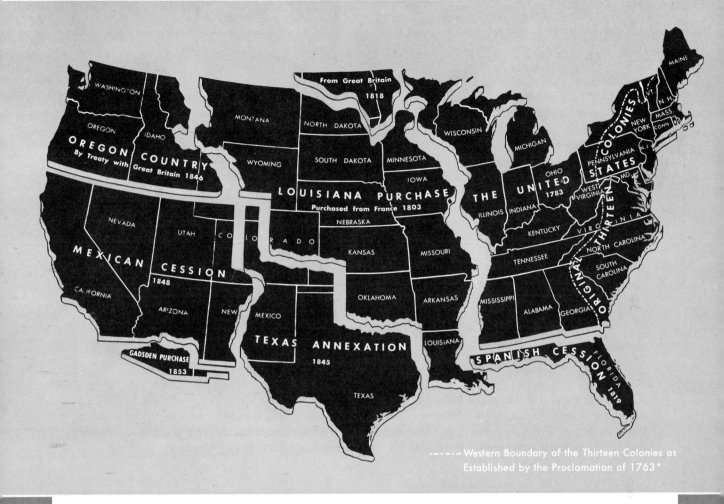

Western Boundary of the Thirteen Colonies as Established by the Proclamation of 1763*

The United States in 1783. At the end of the Revolutionary War, our country extended westward from the Atlantic Ocean to the Mississippi River, and southward from Canada to Florida.

Louisiana Purchase. To the west of the Mississippi River was a huge area called Louisiana. In 1803, the United States bought this area from France. However, the exact western boundary of the Louisiana Territory was not settled until 1819.

Treaty of 1818. In 1818, the United States signed a treaty with Great Britain, which then owned Canada. Under this treaty, the 49th parallel* became the United States-Canadian boundary from the western part of what is now Minnesota to the Rocky Mountains.

Spanish Cession. In 1763, the British gained control of Florida, which had belonged to Spain. Twenty years later, the Spanish regained Florida. In 1818, the United States sent troops here to fight Indians who had attacked American settlements. The next year, Spain signed a treaty by which the United States gained possession of Florida.

Texas Annexation. American settlers living in Texas revolted against the Mexican government and in 1836 set up an independent country. They asked the United States to annex* Texas, which it did in 1845.

Oregon Country. Both the United States and Great Britain claimed the Oregon Country, a large area west of the Rocky Mountains. In 1846, the two nations signed a treaty that gave the United States nearly all of the Oregon Country south of the 49th parallel.

Mexican Cession. Mexico was angry because the United States had annexed Texas. In 1846, the two countries went to war. The United States won the war in 1848. Mexico was forced to sell us California and other territory shown on the map above.

Gadsden Purchase. In 1853, our country bought from Mexico parts of what are now southern Arizona and New Mexico. This was known as the Gadsden Purchase.

Alaska and Hawaii. Alaska and Hawaii are shown on the map on page 18. In 1867, the United States bought Alaska from Russia. The Hawaiian Islands were annexed in 1898.

*See Glossary

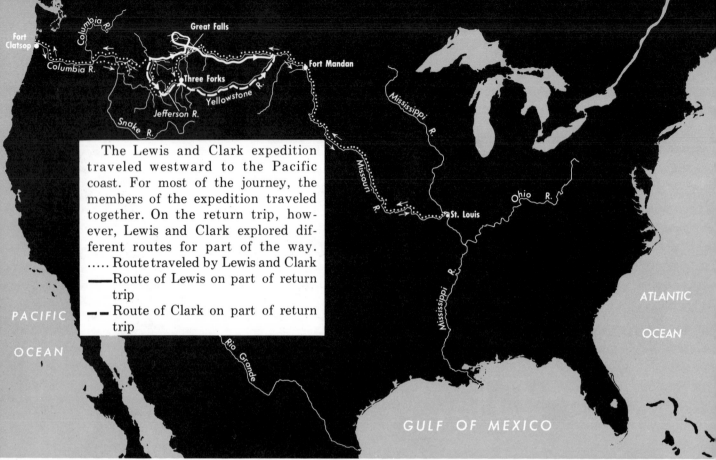

The Lewis and Clark expedition traveled westward to the Pacific coast. For most of the journey, the members of the expedition traveled together. On the return trip, however, Lewis and Clark explored different routes for part of the way.

..... Route traveled by Lewis and Clark

——— Route of Lewis on part of return trip

– – Route of Clark on part of return trip

The Lewis and Clark expedition was sent by President Thomas Jefferson to find out what the Louisiana Territory was like. The purchase and exploration of this territory opened the way for later settlement of vast lands in the western part of our country.

(See map above.) The purchase and exploration of the Louisiana Territory opened the way for the later settlement of vast western lands. Some of these lands, along the Missouri River and the upper Mississippi, were in the Midwest.

Indians attack settlements in the Midwest. The Indians who lived in the Midwest did not welcome the settlers who moved into their hunting grounds. They were determined to drive these strangers out. The Indians burned settlers' cabins and killed men, women, and children. The British in Canada, who wanted to protect their fur trade in the Midwest, did not want to see the Americans come into this area either. Some of the British encouraged the Indians to make attacks on the settlers.

Because of this British interference, many Americans in the Midwest thought we should go to war against Great Britain. At about the same time, our government was also having a disagreement with the British because they were interfering with trade we were carrying on with France. For these and other reasons, the United States and Great Britain went to war in 1812. Many Indians in the Midwest joined with the British in fighting against the Americans. Several important battles of the War of 1812 took place in this part of our country.

By the end of 1814, the United States and Great Britain were tired of fighting and eager for peace. Neither side had succeeded in winning the war. In December, the two countries signed a peace treaty. Also, Indians in the Midwest made peace with the Americans. As a result, the danger of Indian attacks was greatly reduced.

More settlers come to the Midwest. With much of the land safe from Indian attacks, settlers came to the Midwest in ever-increasing numbers. Some came from the parts of our country we call the South and the Northeast. Others came from European countries such as Germany and Great Britain.

Settlers traveled to the Midwest in different ways. Some came in covered wagons loaded with furniture, kitchen utensils, and food. Others, who were poorer, carried their few belongings in carts or on their backs. Many settlers traveled by land only as far as the Ohio River. There they built flatboats and floated downstream until they saw a place that seemed suitable for building a home.

As the years passed, improvements in transportation helped settlers to reach the Midwest more easily. The Erie Canal, opened in 1825, enabled settlers to travel by boat for a longer part of their westward journey. About this same time, steamboats came into

A flatboat on the Ohio River. In the late 1700's and early 1800's, thousands of settlers traveled down the Ohio River in flatboats to new homes in the Midwest. As the years passed, improvements in transportation made it easier for settlers to reach this part of our country.

Planting corn. Life was not easy for the first settlers in the Midwest. Before they could build homes and plant fields of crops, they had to clear trees from their land. Gradually, however, the Midwest was changed from a wilderness into a land of neat farms and busy towns.

common use on the Ohio and Mississippi rivers. They helped to make water travel faster and easier. Also, the National Road helped settlers travel more easily by land. In 1840, this road extended from Cumberland, Maryland, as far west as Vandalia, Illinois.

How did the settlers use and change the land? The wilderness lands of the Midwest were not easy to clear. To see how the settlers met the challenge of these lands, let us visit one of the first families to move into the land that is now Ohio. The family has been here less than a year. Most of their land is still covered with dense forest. Near the creek, however, is a small area where the trees have been cut down to make a clearing. At one side of the clearing

is the crude building in which the family lived until a few days ago. It has only three walls and a roof. A blazing fire was kept burning at the open side of this shelter to keep out prowling animals and to provide a little warmth. At the other side of the clearing is a newly completed log cabin. The men from neighboring farms helped the family build this cabin.

Close to the clearing we see several acres of blackened tree trunks. Last summer the father and his two sons chopped rings around the trunks of these trees to kill them. In the winter they set fire to the dead trees. When spring came, they planted corn among the tree trunks. Next year, they plan to clear out these tree trunks and make an open field here. This will be difficult, for they must do the work by hand, using simple tools.

To see whether the settlers were discouraged by the hard work and discomforts of frontier living, let us visit the same part of Ohio thirty years later. We can scarcely believe this is the same territory. Except for a few patches of woodland, the forest is gone. In its place are plowed fields, neat farmhouses, and busy towns.

Settlers Come to the Plains

As You Read,
Ask Yourself Questions

1. Texas was settled much sooner than the other Great Plains states. Why was this so?
2. What finally brought settlers to other parts of the plains?

Texas was the first of the Great Plains states to be settled. At the time the Midwest was becoming a land of farms and towns, the part of our country we call the Great Plains states was still largely a wilderness. Most of this wilderness was located in the vast territory of Louisiana, which the United States had bought from France. Texas, however, belonged to the country of Mexico, which had won its independence from Spain in 1821. Texas was a land of rich resources, but few Mexicans had settled here.

In the early 1800's, there were many Americans who wanted to make use of the rich resources of Texas. An American named Stephen Austin made arrangements with the Mexican government that permitted him to bring settlers from the United States to this vast, thinly settled land. The Mexican government asked, however, that the Americans agree to certain conditions, such as pledging their loyalty to Mexico. The settlers agreed, and by 1830 more than twenty thousand Americans were living in Texas.

Disagreements arose between the American settlers and the Mexican government as the years passed. This is not surprising, for the settlers still thought of themselves as Americans even though they had pledged their loyalty to Mexico. By 1835, the disagreements had grown so great that the Americans living in Texas revolted. Soon they declared their independence. The Americans suffered two terrible defeats in their fight for independence, but they were finally victorious. Texas became an independent nation in 1836.

Texas did not want to remain a separate nation, however. Its people felt as though they were Americans, and they wanted their new nation to become part of the United States. In 1845, the United States annexed Texas. This angered many Mexicans, who believed that the United States had encouraged the revolution in Texas in order to gain control of this area. In 1846, war broke out between Mexico and the United States. The Americans were victorious in this war, and Mexico was forced to recognize Texas as an American state.

A wagon train crossing the plains. Except in Texas, few settlers made their homes on the plains in the early 1800's. However, many people traveled through this area on their way to the far west.

Wagon trains crossed the plains on their way to the far west. Except in Texas, almost the only people living on the plains during the early 1800's were Indians. Many other people crossed this territory on their way westward, however. Fur trappers on their way to the Rocky Mountains were among the earliest travelers. The routes these men found were later used by pioneer families, missionaries, traders, and gold seekers going to the far west. As the years went by, the wagon trains of these travelers became a familiar sight to the Plains Indians.

To the travelers, the plains did not seem a very good place in which to live. This land of vast, open spaces was strange and frightening to people who were used to woods and hills. There were not enough trees here to provide wood for houses. Also, the climate was too dry for growing many of the crops they were used to planting. Besides, matted grass roots made it difficult for people to work the soil. Not until the middle of the 1800's did people begin to overcome their doubts about the plains and move here to make their homes. Only a few came at first, and they stayed on the eastern edge of the plains.

The Kansas-Nebraska Act brings settlers to the area that is now the Great Plains states. In the 1850's, a conflict that had started outside the plains helped to bring settlers to the part of our country that is now the Great Plains states. This conflict was the quarrel between the northern and southern states over slavery. Many people in the north believed that the federal government should prohibit slavery in the new territories that were being formed in the western part of our country. Southerners, on the other hand, generally felt that slavery should be permitted throughout the new territories.

In an attempt to resolve this question, Congress passed the Kansas-Nebraska Act in 1854. This act divided into two territories a vast area that included what are now the Dakotas, Nebraska, and Kansas. The settlers who came to these two territories were to vote on whether or not slavery should be permitted in the states that would later be formed there.

The Kansas-Nebraska Act helped bring the quarrel over slavery to a boiling point. The few settlers already living in the Kansas Territory generally felt that slavery should not be permitted there. Many people in the northern states also were determined to keep slavery out of Kansas. A special committee was formed in New England to send antislavery settlers to the territory. Southerners were just as determined to make Kansas a slave state. They encouraged proslavery settlers to move there.

As time went on, bitter fighting broke out in Kansas between people who were for slavery and those who were against it. The settlers in Kansas finally voted slavery down, but the bad feelings that had grown up over the Kansas question were not forgotten. They helped to divide the country and bring on a bitter war, called the Civil War, between the North and the South. (See map below.)

Railroads are built across the plains. By the time of the Civil War, a network of railroads spread throughout most of the eastern part of our country. In order to reach the west coast, however, people had to travel by wagon or stagecoach across the plains and mountains.

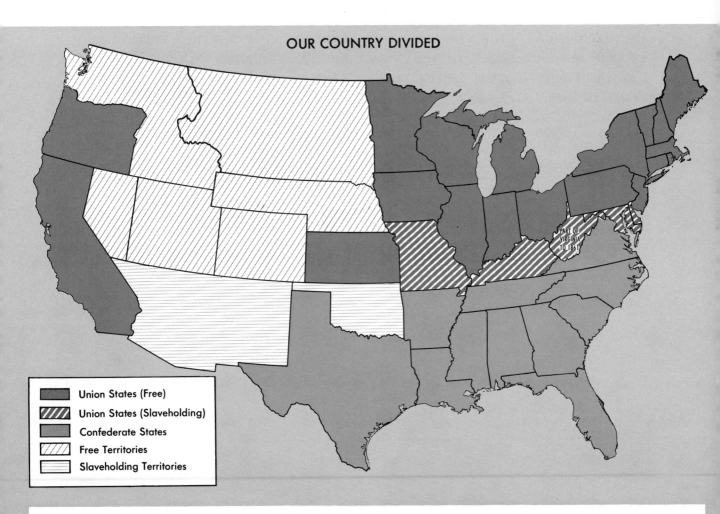

OUR COUNTRY DIVIDED

Union States (Free)
Union States (Slaveholding)
Confederate States
Free Territories
Slaveholding Territories

From 1860 to 1865, the United States was a divided country. In 1860, Abraham Lincoln was elected president. None of the southern states had wanted Lincoln as president, however, mainly because Lincoln was against slavery in the territories and new states of our country. Shortly after the election, South Carolina seceded from the Union.

During 1861, ten more states seceded. These states, together with South Carolina, became a separate nation called the Confederacy. The western part of Virginia remained in the Union, and later became the state of West Virginia. In 1865, the northern states finally won the war, and our country was no longer divided.

The United States government recognized the need for a railroad that would link our country's east and west coasts. Finally, Congress chartered two companies to build such a railroad. These were the Central Pacific and the Union Pacific railroad companies. Each company was to receive ten square miles of land along the railroad line for every mile of track it laid.

The building of the first transcontinental railroad was one of the most exciting events in our country's history. The two railroad companies raced to see which could lay the most track and get the most free land. In 1863, the Central Pacific started laying track eastward from Sacramento, California.

The Union Pacific began laying track at Omaha, Nebraska, and worked westward.

The crews of both companies faced great difficulties as they raced toward each other. Workers for the Central Pacific had to lay their track across rugged mountains, and many bridges and tunnels had to be built. The route followed by the Union Pacific lay across land inhabited by hostile Indians. Sometimes half the workmen had to fight Indians while the others laid the track.

On May 10, 1869, the tracks of the Union Pacific and the Central Pacific met at Promontory, in Utah. As hundreds of people watched, officials of the two companies drove a golden spike into

Building a railroad. By the time of the Civil War, a network of railroads spread throughout most of the eastern part of our country. However, no railroads linked the east and west coasts. Our country's first transcontinental railroad was completed in 1869.

the final railroad tie. The news was telegraphed across the nation. Bells chimed and cannons boomed in many cities to celebrate the completion of the railroad. The Union Pacific had laid 1,086 miles of the new track, and the Central Pacific had laid 689 miles.

As time passed, more railroads were built across the plains. (See map on page 94.) These railroads joined the eastern and western parts of our vast country. As the following pages will show, the railroads brought many people to the plains and helped to change the plains from an Indian hunting ground to a land of ranches and farms.

The buffalo herds are destroyed. One group of people the railroads brought to the plains were white men who hunted buffalo. Some of these men came to shoot buffalo for sport. Others were hired by the railroads to kill buffalo in order to prevent stampeding herds from overturning trains. The hired hunters also provided buffalo meat for the men working on the railroads. Between the 1860's and the 1880's, the buffalo hunters killed off almost all the great herds that had once roamed the plains.

The Indians are forced onto reservations. The large-scale killing of buffalo destroyed the way of life of the Indians who lived on the plains. As Chapter 4 explains, the Indians depended on the buffalo for food, clothing, and shelter. When the herds disappeared, the Indians faced starvation.

Starvation was not the only problem the Indians faced. Their land was being taken away, also. At one time the United States government had promised that the plains would be their hunting ground forever. Now that white men were moving into the plains, however, this promise was being broken.

The Indians tried desperately to hold onto their lands. From about 1860 to 1890, they fought many bloody battles with United States Army troops. In the end, however, the Indians were defeated, and were forced onto reservations.

The plains become the cattle kingdom. During the years when the Indians were being forced to move onto reservations, a new way of life came to the plains. This new way of life was based on cattle raising.

To understand how the plains became an important cattle-raising area, we need to go back to the time when Texas was still part of Mexico. (See page 89.) On the grasslands of southern Texas, Mexicans were raising livestock such as cattle and horses. Cattle, which had originally been brought to the New World by early Spanish settlers, were allowed to run wild over the open range.

Americans who settled in Texas in the early 1800's took over thousands of the wild cattle that were roaming the plains here. In order to control these animals, expert horsemen were needed who could ride the range for mile after mile, day after day. Eventually, these men came to be known as cowboys.

After the Civil War, Texas cattle could be sold for very high prices in the large cities in the north and east. However, there were no railroads leading from Texas to these cities. Cattlemen began driving their herds to railroads in Missouri and Kansas. Cowboys tended the cattle on these long drives. From Missouri and Kansas,

Major railroads of the United States in 1890. Many railroads were built across the western part of our country in the late 1800's. The railroads brought thousands of settlers to the plains, and helped to change the plains from an Indian hunting ground to a land of farms and ranches.

the cattle were shipped by rail to cities in the north and east.

Cattlemen soon realized that the plains north of Texas were also suitable for raising cattle. During the 1870's and the 1880's, the plains became the cattle kingdom of America. The cattle here grazed on the open range, just as the buffalo had in the past. At roundup time, cowboys herded the cattle together and drove them to the nearest railroad.

Abilene, Dodge City, and other towns where the cattle were brought for shipment became known as "cow towns." Here the cattle were sold, and the cowboys received their wages. They celebrated the end of a long drive by spending their money freely. Occasionally, some of the cowboys got into gunfights. This colorful time in the history of the plains is kept alive in the "Westerns" that people enjoy today in motion pictures or on television.

Farmers come to the plains. The railroads helped bring to the plains many people who wanted to farm. Before the railroads were built, it was not profitable to raise crops in the plains. In most areas, the only way a farmer could send his goods to market was by wagon. This was slow and expensive. After the railroads were built, however, farmers could ship their products from the plains to other parts of the country more quickly and cheaply. This helped make it profitable to raise crops in the plains.

The railroads were not the only reason why many farmers began to come to the plains, however. The development of new farming methods and tools also encouraged people to come to this part of our country. By the time the railroads were built, steel plows had been developed that could cut through the heavy sod of the plains. Labor-saving machines such as the McCormick reaper had also been developed. Windmills had been perfected that pumped water up from wells sunk deep into the ground. Barbed wire, which was first manufactured in the early 1870's, could be used in making fences. All of these developments made it easier for people to farm the land in the plains.

Another important reason why settlers came to the plains was that they could obtain land free or for a very low price. The railroads were anxious to sell the land they had obtained from the government. They knew that if more people settled in the plains, the railroads would have more business. Railroad land sold for as little as a dollar an acre. Government land was also available. In 1862, the government passed the Homestead Act,* which made it possible for settlers to obtain free land.

*See Glossary

A sod house in Nebraska. Thousands of farmers settled on the Great Plains in the late 1800's. Because trees were scarce, the first houses built by settlers here were usually made of blocks of sod. Life was difficult and lonely for these hardy pioneers.

The combination of good transportation, effective farm tools, and cheap land brought a great flood of people to the plains in the last part of the 1800's. These people came from other parts of the United States, and also from Europe. The barbed wire fences which they put up cut across the open range where the cattlemen had grazed their herds. This caused many quarrels between the cattlemen and farmers. The cattlemen, however, were soon forced to realize that the days of the open range were coming to an end.

How did the plains farmers work and live, and what changes did they bring to the land? To see what the life of an early plains farmer was like, let us visit a Nebraska farm in the late 1800's. It is summer, and the sun is beating down on us as we ride across the vast expanse of land. There is not a hill or a tree to break the view. Far ahead of us, looking small and lonely, is the farmer's house. It is built of blocks of sod.

When we reach the house, the mother and her two small children greet us warmly. It has been weeks since they have seen anyone but members of their own family. The mother is especially lonesome, because she grew up in a town and is used to having neighbors close by.

Loneliness is not the only hardship this family has faced since coming to Nebraska. Three years ago, the winter was so bitterly cold that their horses died. Last fall, grasshoppers ate all the crops. The farmer's wife wants to sell the farm so that the family can go back east where life is easier. However, her husband refuses to give up.

Many men like this pioneer farmer made their homes on the plains during the late 1800's and early 1900's. They refused to be discouraged by the hardships faced here. Thanks to the courage of these men, the plains were changed from a wilderness to a land of fertile farms.

Arrange Historical Events in Order

Below is a list of some of the events in the early history of our country that had important effects on what is today the Midwest and Great Plains. Arrange these events in the order in which they occurred.

The first transcontinental railroad is completed.

Britain recognizes the United States as an independent country.

The United States buys the territory of Louisiana from France.

The Kansas-Nebraska Act brings settlers to what is now the Great Plains states.

The Erie Canal is opened.

Indians living in the Great Plains are forced onto reservations.

Texas becomes part of the United States.

Share an Imaginary Experience

Imagine that it is the year 1815. You and your family have moved from Connecticut to Ohio. Write a letter to a friend back home, describing your journey and telling something about your everyday life. Explain what hardships you face as you and your family clear the land and start a farm. Refer to the suggestions on page 351 for writing good paragraphs and creating clear images.

Your letter will be more interesting if you include one of the following:

1. a map showing the route you followed from Connecticut to Ohio
2. a drawing of your farm in Ohio, showing the kind of home you live in

When you have finished your letter, share it with your class.

Detroit, Michigan, before the century of progress began. A century ago, at the time of the Civil War, the Midwest and Great Plains was a land of farms, forests, and grasslands. There were few large cities here. In the following hundred years, great changes took place. Industry developed rapidly, and large numbers of people moved from farms to cities to take jobs in factories. The Midwest and Great Plains became closely tied to the rest of our nation and world.

6 A Century of Progress

As You Read,
Ask Yourself Questions

1. What four great changes have taken place in the Midwest and Great Plains during the past century?

2. What are two great ideas that have helped to cause these four changes?

3. How have the four great changes helped the people of the Midwest and Great Plains?

The Midwest and Great Plains one hundred years ago. A century ago, at the time of the Civil War, the Midwest and Great Plains was a land of farms, forests, and grasslands. Most of the vast forest and mineral resources of this part of our country were still unused. Farming was the main way of earning a living. Few mills and factories had been built to provide other kinds of jobs. Most of the people lived on farms, and there were only a few large cities. In 1860, St. Louis and Cincinnati were the two largest cities in the Midwest and Great Plains. Each had a population of about 160,000.

The way people lived and worked one hundred years ago was very different from the way people live and work today. Some machines were used, such as horse-drawn reapers and sewing machines run by foot treadles. However, people still did much of their work by hand. Railroads had been built to transport passengers and freight between cities, but most people still used horse-drawn buggies and wagons. Many children went to grade school, but very few went on to high school and college.

Four Great Changes Come to the Midwest and Great Plains

In the century following the Civil War, great changes took place in the Midwest and Great Plains. People cut down forests and dug minerals from the earth. Many mills and factories were built, especially in the Midwest. Thousands of farmers left their farms and took jobs in industry. This helped great industrial cities to grow up in the Midwest and Great Plains.

In this chapter you are going to read more about these changes. As you read, watch for two great ideas at work. These ideas are individualism and the scientific attitude.

What is individualism? The belief that every individual is important and should be permitted to determine the course of his own life is called individualism. This way of thinking developed in Europe over a period of hundreds of years. Many of the people who came to America from Europe were strong individualists.

Most of the pioneers who settled in the Midwest and Great Plains also believed strongly in individualism. During the past century, this belief has given many people here the courage to try out new ideas. It has also helped to give people the faith and the freedom they need for individual growth.

What is the scientific attitude? The scientific attitude is a way of thinking about the world in which we live. A person with this attitude has many questions about his environment. To find reasonable answers to his questions, he follows a procedure called the scientific method. First, he studies the subject about which he has a question until he can make an educated guess about what the answer might be. Then he gathers facts to test whether this possible answer is true, partly true, or false. At all times he has an open mind. Instead of trying to prove something he wants to believe, he looks for the truth.

Build Your Vocabulary

scientific attitude	Industrial Revolution	crucible	satellite
century of progress	Bessemer process	computer	Civil War
individualism	depression	automation	interdependent

Like individualism, the scientific attitude developed in Europe over a long period of time. Gradually, the people who viewed the world with this attitude made many important discoveries. They also began to realize that scientific knowledge could be put to practical use. In the 1700's, the scientific attitude helped bring about the Industrial Revolution. (See pages 102 and 103.)

The Industrial Revolution spread to the northeastern part of the United States in the early 1800's. By the time of the Civil War, it had spread to the Midwest and Great Plains. Here it helped to bring about the great changes discussed in the rest of this chapter.

FOREST AND MINERAL RESOURCES WERE USED TO HELP MEET HUMAN NEEDS

One of the great changes that came to the Midwest and Great Plains was the increased use of the rich resources of this part of our country. Before the Industrial Revolution spread to the Midwest and Great Plains, people made little use of the towering forests and vast mineral deposits here. The Indians cut down a few small trees to make the framework of their wigwams. They also dug small amounts of copper, which they used mainly for making ornaments. When the white settlers came, they cut down some of the forests so they could use the land for farming. They also mined small amounts of iron ore. Even so, much of the forest land and most of the mineral deposits remained untouched.

The Industrial Revolution encouraged the development of mineral resources. As the Industrial Revolution spread to the Midwest and Great Plains, the demand for iron and steel began to grow. People

Oklahoma's first successful oil well. During the century of progress, the people of the Midwest and Great Plains made fuller use of the petroleum, iron ore, and other mineral resources here.

needed these metals to make machines, farm implements, railroad tracks, and many other kinds of equipment.

To meet the growing demand for iron and steel, new supplies of iron ore were needed. Rich deposits of ore were discovered in the remote wilderness lands of northern Michigan. At first, it was difficult to transport the ore to steel-making centers. Then, in 1855, the first Soo Canal was opened. (See page 244.) This canal made it possible for boats to carry iron ore from the shores of Lake Superior directly to cities such as Chicago and Cleveland.

The increasing demand for steel also encouraged the development of cheaper and faster methods of producing this metal. Until the middle of the 1800's, most steel was made in small pots called

Lumberjacks in Michigan. In the years following the Civil War, the need for wood increased in the Midwest and Great Plains. To meet this need, many logging companies were started. Lumberjacks cut down millions of trees in the great forests of Wisconsin, Minnesota, and Michigan. Logs were floated downstream to sawmills to be cut into lumber.

crucibles, a little at a time. This slow process made steel so expensive that people could not afford to use it in large quantities. In the 1850's, two men independently worked out a new way of making steel. These men were an English inventor named Henry Bessemer and an American ironmaker named William Kelly. In the new method, which came to be known as the Bessemer process, steel was made in huge containers called converters. It was now possible to produce large amounts of steel at a low cost.

After cheap steel became available, industry grew rapidly in the Midwest and Great Plains. The demand for addi-

tional supplies of minerals increased enormously. Huge quantities of iron ore were mined in northern Michigan and Minnesota. Abundant supplies of many other minerals, such as coal, limestone, and oil, were found in various parts of the Midwest and Great Plains. To learn more about the mineral resources of this area, refer to pages 162-170.

Forests were cut down. The need for wood also increased as the Industrial Revolution spread to the Midwest and Great Plains. People used large amounts of wood for constructing homes and other buildings. Wood was also used for making furniture, railroad ties, and many other kinds of goods. To help meet this need for wood, many logging companies were started. Noise filled the forests as lumberjacks cut down the tall trees with their axes. Rivers were jammed with logs being floated downstream to sawmills where they would be cut into lumber. To learn more about the forests of the Midwest and Great Plains, refer to pages 174-177.

MILLS AND FACTORIES WERE BUILT TO PRODUCE GOODS FOR MEETING HUMAN NEEDS

While minerals were being dug and forests were being cut, another change was taking place. Many men with ideas and courage were building mills and factories in the Midwest and Great Plains. In these mills and factories, workers used machines to change raw materials into goods that people could use to meet their needs.

The Midwest became one of our nation's leading manufacturing areas. More mills and factories were built in the Midwest than in the Great Plains states. This was partly because more natural resources were available in the Midwest. Also, there were more people to work in industry and to buy the goods that the mills and factories produced. The Great Lakes and other waterways of the Midwest also helped industry to grow here. Bulky raw materials such as coal and iron ore could be transported cheaply along these water highways.

The McCormick Reaper and Mower Works at Chicago, in 1871. Manufacturing grew rapidly in the Midwest during and after the Civil War. Men with ideas and courage built mills and factories to manufacture farm machines, furniture, and many other products that people needed.

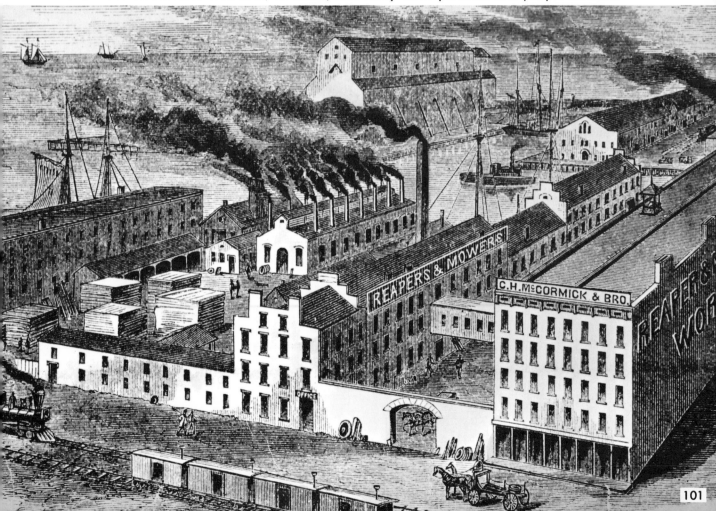

THE INDUSTRIAL REVOLUTION

New ways of producing goods are developed. People in many parts of the world still live much as their ancestors did hundreds or even thousands of years ago. We in America, however, as well as people in certain other parts of the world, are living in ways that are very different from those of our ancestors. One main respect in which our lives differ from theirs is the way we produce goods.

During the seventeenth century, most goods were produced by people in their own homes or on farms. Work was performed mainly by the muscle power of human beings or animals, although a few simple tools and machines were in general use. Wind and waterpower were used for certain work, such as grinding grain.

Beginning about the middle of the eighteenth century, three important developments occurred in the way goods were produced. First, many new machines were invented to help people make things more quickly and easily. Second, steam and other new sources of power came into use. Third, factories were built to house the new machines. Together these three main developments, which all began in England, are known as the Industrial Revolution.

One invention leads to another. Changes in England's textile industry during the eighteenth century illustrate the way the Industrial Revolution developed. In the early 1700's, workers

James Watt, a Scottish inventor, developed a steam engine that could be used to run machines.

Cotton-spinning machines in an early factory. In the 1700's machines were invented that made it possible to produce textiles and other goods more quickly and easily. The use of such machines was part of the Industrial Revolution.

used spinning wheels to make thread. Other workers wove the thread into cloth on hand looms. As the result of an improvement in the loom, made in 1733, weavers began to make cloth so fast that the spinners could not provide enough thread. During the 1770's, a spinning machine was developed that could be run by waterpower. This machine speeded up the making of thread. Toward the end of the century, a power loom was invented. By using the new loom, workers were soon able to speed up the weaving process.

Steam power. Spinning was the first manufacturing process to make use of steam power. Since the early 1700's, crude steam engines had been used for pumping water out of mines. In 1769, a Scottish inventor named James Watt patented* a much improved steam engine. Within a few years, the new engine was being used to run spinning machines. Soon, steam power was being used in making iron and pottery. In ironmaking, steam power was used to produce the steady blast of air needed for smelting iron ore with coke,* which had largely replaced charcoal for this purpose. The iron produced by using coke and steam power was cheaper and of better quality than the iron made by older methods. Better-quality iron, in turn, made it possible to build sturdier and more complicated machinery that could be run by steam engines.

The modern factory system begins. As machines became larger, heavier, and more complicated, they could no longer be placed in workers' homes. Instead, special buildings called factories were constructed, where workers could come to operate the machines. Machines run by waterpower had to be housed in factories located along streams. With the introduction of steam power, however, factories could be located wherever fuel was available.

The Industrial Revolution spreads. The new ways of producing goods soon spread from England to other parts of the world. The United States, Belgium, France, and Germany were among the first countries to adopt the new methods. Information about the development of modern industry in America is provided on pages 101, 104, and 105.

The Industrial Revolution has continued to spread. Today, it is in different stages in different countries. In much of the world, industry is just beginning to develop. Most parts of Europe and North America, however, are already highly industrialized. This is also true of Australia and New Zealand. The United States and several countries in western Europe are now beginning to move into a new stage of the Industrial Revolution. This new stage includes automation, which is the development and use of automatic machines. Through automation, it is now possible for an entire industrial plant to be run with few human operators.

Industrialization changes people's lives in several ways. For one thing, the standard of living is generally higher in nations that have experienced the Industrial Revolution. Also, more of the people in such nations live in cities. The people in industrialized nations are more interdependent than those who live in countries that have little industry. They depend on people in many parts of the world for raw materials. They also depend on other people to buy their products and services. We do not know just what the world of the future will be like as industrialization continues. We can be sure, however, that it will be different in many ways from the world of today.

*See Glossary

A control room in a chemical plant. By using computers, a few human operators can now control all the machinery of an entire industrial plant. The development and use of automatic machines that can be controlled in this way is called automation. The United States and several other countries are now beginning to move into a new stage of the Industrial Revolution that includes automation.

The Civil War spurred the growth of manufacturing in the Midwest. Until the Civil War, the number of mills and factories here was quite small. During the war, however, manufacturing grew rapidly. New factories were started to produce supplies for the northern armies, and older factories increased their production. After the war, industry continued to grow. Thousands of mills and factories were established here. Today, the Midwest is one of our country's leading manufacturing areas.

Different kinds of mills and factories were built in the Midwest. Many of the mills and factories built in the Midwest processed the rich resources of this part of our country. Some, such as sawmills and steel mills, processed forest and mineral resources. Others, such as flour mills and meat-packing plants, processed the farm products raised here.

Still other factories used the products from sawmills and steel mills to make goods for people to buy. Some of these factories manufactured farm machines to sell to the farmers of the Midwest and Great Plains. Others made furniture and carriages. In the early 1900's, automobile plants were established in the Midwest. Cars made here were soon being sold throughout our country.

Workers in a factory in the late 1800's. Some of the mills and factories built in the Midwest, such as flour mills and meat-packing plants, processed farm products. Others, including sawmills and steel mills, processed forest and mineral resources. Still other factories used products from sawmills and steel mills to make such goods as carriages and machinery.

Assembling Ford automobiles in 1914. Throughout the century of progress, inventors and factory owners in the Midwest and Great Plains developed new and better ways of producing goods. One of these people was Henry Ford, the first major manufacturer to make effective use of the assembly-line method. Today, this method is used in factories throughout our country.

Machines and manufacturing methods improved. Throughout the century of progress, inventors and factory owners worked to develop new and better ways of producing goods. They designed better machines and worked out more efficient manufacturing methods. One of the most important methods was developed in the factories of an automobile manufacturer named Henry Ford, in the early 1900's. This was the assembly-line method. Ford put the frame of an automobile on a conveyor belt that moved slowly past a line of workers. Each worker added a different part to the frame. When the last worker added his part, the automobile was completely assembled. The assembly-line method of manufacturing worked so well that it became widely used.

During the last half of the century of progress, manufacturers hired scientists and engineers to help them develop new products and better methods of production. The partnership of science and industry has led to great progress. Today, the mills and factories of the Midwest produce tremendous quantities of goods. These goods are sold in all parts of the world.

AS FARMING METHODS IMPROVED, FEWER FARMERS WERE NEEDED

During the years when factory methods and machines were being improved, people also learned better ways of farming. New and better farm machines were developed. The first machines were pulled by horses. In the early 1900's, however, farmers began to use gasoline-powered tractors. A farmer who used a tractor to pull his machines could farm more land than one who did not.

Farmers also began to use scientific farming methods. For example, they began to rotate their crops and to use chemical fertilizer. These new methods greatly increased the amount of food that could be produced on an acre of land.

Before the new farm machines and farming methods were used, a farmer could raise enough food for only a few people. Many farmers were needed to produce enough food for everyone. As the new machines and methods were developed, however, it became possible for a farmer to raise enough food for many people. This left large numbers of farmers available for other work.

GREAT CITIES GREW UP IN THE MIDWEST AND GREAT PLAINS

The growth of manufacturing and the changes in farming brought the fourth great change — the growth of great cities. Most mills and factories were built in towns and cities. Many people decided that they could make a better

A threshing machine, powered by a steam engine. New farm machines and farming methods were developed during the century of progress. As a result, one farmer could raise enough food for many people. This left large numbers of farmers available for other kinds of work.

living by working in these industries than by farming. As the years passed, thousands of people left their farms to live in cities. Many people in other countries, such as Germany and Italy, also left their homes and moved to the manufacturing cities of the Midwest and Great Plains. All of these developments helped great cities to grow up in this part of our country.

The cities grew because they met human needs. (See page 115.) Jobs available in cities gave people the opportunity to earn enough money to buy food, clothing, and other goods to meet their physical needs. Cities also offered people opportunities for meeting social needs. There were more libraries and schools in the cities than in rural areas. People had a greater chance to develop their abilities and achieve success. Throughout the century of progress, these opportunities continued to attract people to the cities of the Midwest and Great Plains.

Chicago in the early 1900's. During the century of progress, great cities grew up in the Midwest and Great Plains. There were generally more opportunities for people to meet their needs in the cities than there were in rural areas.

The Four Great Changes Have Helped the People of the Midwest and Great Plains

The standard of living in the Midwest and Great Plains today is much higher than it was one hundred years ago. The four great changes have made it possible for most people in the Midwest and Great Plains to enjoy a high standard of living. The new machines and methods that farmers and industrial workers use today make it possible for each worker to produce large quantities of goods. Since the average worker is highly productive, he can earn a good income. He can also obtain the food, clothing, and shelter he needs because the farms and factories produce so much that there is plenty for everyone.

More people have the opportunity to develop their abilities and to enjoy the arts. The four great changes have made it possible for more people to obtain the education they need to develop their abilities. Since people earn good incomes, they can pay the taxes needed to support schools and colleges. All students now have the opportunity to go to high school, and most students who

Explore Social Progress

During the past century, our country has made great progress toward solving a number of problems that formerly prevented large numbers of people from living full, happy lives. The measures taken to solve these important social problems have helped make life easier and happier for millions of Americans. Some of these measures are listed in the text below. To learn more about social progress in our country, you will need to do additional research, using many outside sources of information.

Better working conditions have been provided. During the century of progress, many steps have been taken to improve conditions in factories and other places of work. For example, laws have been passed forbidding child labor and limiting the length of the working day for women. Other laws require factory owners to protect the health and safety of their employees. All of the states have workmen's compensation programs, which provide insurance payments to workers injured on their jobs. Labor unions have been organized to bargain with employers on such issues as wages and working hours. You can find more information about these developments in encyclopedias and history books.

Progress has been made in helping the sick and the aged. In the past, people who could not work because of sickness or old age often had great difficulty meeting their needs. Today, considerable progress is being made toward solving this problem. Under the social security program set up by the federal government, employers and workers contribute to an insurance fund. Money from this fund is used in making regular payments to retired people and to workers' widows. Medical care for elderly people is also provided through social security. In addition, people can buy medical insurance from private companies to help meet the costs of serious illness. Many business firms offer pension plans for retired workers.

Equal rights for all people. During the past hundred years, many steps have been taken to help all our citizens gain the rights to which they are entitled. An amendment to the United States Constitution passed in 1920 guaranteed women the right to vote. In recent years, various laws and court decisions have helped Negroes and other minority groups gain equal rights in voting, employment, education, and other fields. You can read more about the civil rights movement in Chapter 8 of this book, as well as in other books and magazines.

have the ability and desire to go on to college can do so.

People also have a better opportunity to enjoy the arts. There are more libraries, art galleries, and museums in the Midwest and Great Plains today than there were one hundred years ago. Also, people have more leisure time for reading and other activities that make life interesting. One hundred years ago, factory workers were expected to work twelve to fourteen hours a day. Today, however, the average working day is only eight hours long.

THE MIDWEST AND GREAT PLAINS STILL HAS SOME SERIOUS PROBLEMS

Although the four great changes have helped most people in the Midwest and Great Plains to enjoy a high standard of living, there are still some serious problems in this part of the country. These problems are also found in other parts of the United States and the rest of the world.

Some people cannot meet their needs adequately. Some families in the Midwest and Great Plains do not share in the prosperity that the four great changes have brought to this part of the country. Parents in these families do not have jobs, or they work at jobs that pay very low wages. There are several reasons why they are not able to earn a better living. Many are ill or handicapped. Some lack the education they need, either because they attended poor schools or because they dropped out before graduation. Sometimes, members of minority groups are unable to obtain good jobs because of prejudice and discrimination. To learn more about these and other problems that affect people in the Midwest and Great Plains, refer to pages 124-144.

Many natural resources have been needlessly destroyed. The needless destruction of natural resources is another problem in the Midwest and Great Plains. Factories and cities have polluted air and water here. Lumbermen using careless methods have destroyed vast forests. Mining companies have left the surface of parts of the Midwest and Great Plains bare and ugly. Farmers have used methods that caused much valuable soil to be washed or blown away. To learn about the need for conserving the natural resources of the Midwest and Great Plains, refer to Chapters 9 and 10.

The Midwest and Great Plains Is Closely Tied to the Rest of Our Country and World

As You Read,
Ask Yourself Questions

1. Why is the Midwest and Great Plains more closely tied to the rest of our country and world today than it was a century ago?

2. In what ways do events in other parts of the world affect the lives of people in the Midwest and Great Plains?

THE WORLD SEEMS SMALLER

In the early 1800's, the Midwest and Great Plains seemed far away from other parts of our country and the rest of the world. Wagons, stagecoaches, and flatboats were the means of transportation used by most people to reach this part of our country. The journey from New York City to Indianapolis by stagecoach took about two weeks.

To reach the Midwest and Great Plains from other continents took much longer. Two months was the usual sailing time from Europe to North America. When travelers from Europe reached the coast of North America, they still had to make a long, hard journey inland to the Midwest and Great Plains.

News traveled as slowly as people did in the early 1800's. The telegraph and radio had not been invented. People in the Midwest and Great Plains often did not hear about important events in other parts of our country until six or seven weeks after they happened.

New ways of traveling and transporting goods were developed. Americans began to develop better ways of traveling even before the century of progress began. By 1860, many canals and roads had been built. Steamships were being used both on inland waterways and on the ocean. Railroads crisscrossed much of the eastern half of our country.

During the century of progress, transportation continued to improve. Railroads were extended across the plains to the west coast, making it possible to travel from New York to California in seven days. Steamships were improved, and the sailing time between Europe

Telstar II, a communications satellite, relays radio and television signals between continents. Modern methods of communication and transportation help to bring the Midwest and Great Plains much closer to the rest of our country and world.

and North America was cut to a few days. The automobile was developed, and paved highways were laid out across the land. The airplane was invented, providing man with a new and faster way of traveling. Today, jet airliners fly from the Midwest and Great Plains to Europe and other continents in just a few hours.

New ways of sending news were developed. Inventors also developed new and better methods of communication. By 1861, it was possible to send a message by telegraph from New York City to San Francisco. Before the 1800's were over, the telephone had been invented and was coming into common use. In the first half of the 1900's, radio and television were developed. Today, satellites orbit our earth, relaying radio and television signals from one continent to another.

The results of better transportation and communication. The methods of transportation and communication that were developed during the century of progress have made the world seem much smaller. Distant lands now seem as close as our nearest neighbors. Each year, many people from the Midwest and Great Plains travel to other parts of the world. Those who stay at home hear and see events that are taking place in other parts of our country and on other continents. Modern transportation and communication methods help to bring the Midwest and Great Plains much closer to the rest of our country and world.

WORLD EVENTS AFFECT THE MIDWEST AND GREAT PLAINS

Since the Midwest and Great Plains is closely tied to the rest of the world, it can be greatly affected by events that happen in other parts of our country and in distant lands. This circumstance has resulted mainly from the changes in the way people in the United States and many other lands live and work.

New ways of earning a living made people more dependent upon one another. The pioneers in the 1800's had fewer goods and comforts than we have today, but they were more independent. The pioneer farmer raised on his own land all the food his family needed. With the help of neighbors, he built his own house and farm buildings, often using trees from his own land. His wife made most of the clothing for the family. Although each family was independent in many ways, its members had to work hard from morning until night to provide the food and clothing that were needed.

The four great changes discussed earlier in this chapter brought new ways of earning a living to people in our country. Great numbers of people began to leave the farms and move to towns and cities where they did many different kinds of work. Usually, each person specialized in doing a particular job, such as running a machine in a factory or selling goods to customers in a store. These specialized workers earned money with which they bought the food and other goods they needed.

The new ways of earning a living in which a man specialized in doing one kind of work helped the people of the Midwest and Great Plains produce large amounts of goods. Because workers were highly productive, they could earn good incomes. At the same time, these new ways of earning a living made them very dependent upon people throughout the world. For example, most automobiles manufactured in Detroit, Michigan, are sold in other parts of the United States and in other countries. When car sales go down, many automobile workers in Detroit are laid off from work.

Several times during the past century, huge numbers of people in our country have been out of work. We call periods such as these depressions. The most serious of these was the Great Depression, which began in 1929 and lasted for several years. Millions of people in the United States and other parts of the world were without work during this difficult period. Many were unable to buy all the food they needed. In the late 1930's, conditions improved in our country and in the rest of the world. Many unemployed people were soon able to find jobs.

Wars in distant lands affect the Midwest and Great Plains. In the past one hundred years, our country has been involved in several wars in distant lands. (See feature below.) During these wars, hundreds of thousands of men from the Midwest and Great Plains were sent overseas to fight. Those who returned brought back a greater understanding of life in other parts of the world. During these wars, farms and factories increased production to furnish food and other supplies to our forces. In these and other ways, the wars affected the Midwest and Great Plains.

FIVE WARS

During the past one hundred years, American soldiers have fought in five wars in foreign lands. You may wish to do research to find out how the United States became involved in each of these wars.

The Spanish-American War took place in 1898. The only nations that fought in this conflict were Spain and the United States.

World War I, which began in 1914 and ended in 1918, was the first war in history to involve nearly every part of the world. The two groups of nations that opposed each other in World War I were the Allies and the Central Powers. The Central Powers were Germany, Austria, Turkey, and Bulgaria. The Allies included Great Britain, France, Russia, Japan, and the United States.

World War II, the second war that involved nearly every part of the world, began in 1939 and ended in 1945. The two groups of nations that opposed each other in this war were the Allies and the Axis. The Allies included China, the United States, Britain, and the Soviet Union. The Axis included Germany, Italy, and Japan.

The Korean War was a conflict between Communist and non-Communist forces in the country of Korea. This war began in 1950 and was halted by a cease-fire agreement in 1953.

Today in Vietnam, another bitter war is going on between Communist and non-Communist forces.

Events in other lands affect life in the Midwest and Great Plains. Events that happen in Europe and on other continents affect the people in the Midwest and Great Plains. For example, penicillin was discovered in England by Doctor Alexander Fleming, in 1928. After it was perfected, this drug gave doctors a powerful weapon for fighting diseases that were killing hundreds of thousands of people each year. Millions of Americans are alive today because of the discovery of penicillin.

In 1957, an event took place that greatly changed the thinking of many Americans. In October of that year, a powerful rocket launched from a base in the Soviet Union lifted a satellite far above the surface of the earth and placed it in orbit. News of this remarkable achievement by Soviet scientists took Americans by surprise. They were alarmed by the fact that the Soviet Union had put a satellite in orbit before the United States.

Following this achievement by the Russians, many schools in our nation began to spend more time in teaching science and mathematics. Many people thought we should train more young men and women to be scientists and mathematicians so that we could catch up with the Russians. Our government began spending larger amounts of money for scientific research. Better rockets were designed and built, making it possible for the United States to equal the achievement made by scientists in the Soviet Union.

These and thousands of other events prove how greatly the people of the Midwest and Great Plains are affected by what takes place in the rest of our country and world. The improvements that are being made each year in transportation and communication are tying countries throughout the world even more closely together. The need is now more urgent than ever for people to find better ways of cooperating.

Develop Important Understandings

1. What is individualism? Where did this way of thinking develop?
2. Describe the procedure followed by a person using the scientific method to find answers to his questions.
3. What three developments are included in the Industrial Revolution?
4. How have people in the Midwest and Great Plains made better use of their resources during the past one hundred years?
5. What changes in farming methods have taken place in the past one hundred years?
6. Why have many people moved to cities during the past century?
7. In what ways is life in the Midwest and Great Plains different today than it was one hundred years ago?
8. What are some of the serious problems that face the people of the Midwest and Great Plains today?
9. How have improved methods of transportation and communication affected the Midwest and Great Plains?

Examine Your Attitude Toward Change

1. Do you think the Midwest and Great Plains is now a better place to live than it was one hundred years ago? Give reasons for your answer.
2. Do you think the Midwest and Great Plains will change as much during the next one hundred years? Why, or why not?

Workers assembling television sets in Chicago

People enjoying a summer vacation in Missouri

Children in Detroit waiting for a school bus. About 67 million people live in the Midwest and Great Plains. This is more than one third of the total population of the United States. The population is not distributed evenly throughout the Midwest and Great Plains, however. About three times as many people live in the Midwest as in the Great Plains states.

7   People

A Study Guide

As you study about the people of the Midwest and Great Plains, look for answers to the following questions:

1. Why is the Midwest much more densely populated than the Great Plains states?
2. What three basic needs do all people have in common?
3. What are some of the reasons why people have come to live and work in the Midwest and Great Plains?
4. What are some contributions to the arts that have been made by people from the Midwest and Great Plains?

About 67 million people live in the Midwest and Great Plains today. They make up more than one third of our country's population. If you will study the map on page 117, you will see that the population is not distributed evenly throughout the Midwest and Great Plains. There are some places in which very few people live. Other areas are crowded with people. To learn more about the population of the Midwest and Great Plains, we will make two imaginary field trips.

First we drive along the shore of Lake Michigan from Chicago, Illinois, to Milwaukee, Wisconsin. (See map on page 140.) During our ninety-mile journey, we do not see any large stretches of open countryside. In fact, we are seldom outside a city or town. In some of the cities that we visit, we notice large apartment buildings where many families live. We also pass through sprawling suburbs that contain thousands of homes. Any crowded area such as the one through which we are driving is said to be densely populated.

On our next field trip, we travel across the Great Plains in western Nebraska. Our highway passes through broad grasslands where few people live. Sometimes we drive for miles without seeing a single farmhouse. At last we reach a crossroads with a gasoline station and two or three houses nearby. The gas station attendant tells us that the nearest town of any size is forty miles away. Any area like this one, which contains very few people, is said to be thinly or sparsely populated.

The Midwest is densely populated. About 49 million people make their homes in the Midwest. This part of our country is more densely populated than any other part except the Northeast.* If all the people in the Midwest were evenly distributed throughout these states, there would be about 109 persons for each square mile of land.

The main reason why the Midwest is so densely populated is that there are many opportunities here for people to satisfy their basic needs. (See feature below.) The Midwest is a great manufacturing, farming, and trading region. Because there are many job opportunities here, most people are able to earn

*See Glossary

ALL HUMAN BEINGS HAVE SIMILAR NEEDS

According to scientists who study human behavior, all persons share certain basic needs. These needs are the same whatever your skin color, your religion, or your national origin may be. There are three kinds of basic needs.

1. **Physical needs.** Some of your basic needs are so important that you will die or become seriously ill if they are not satisfied. These are called physical needs. They include:

. . . food to eat
. . . air to breathe
. . . sleep
. . . protection from heat and cold

2. **Social needs.** There are certain other needs that must also be satisfied if a person is to lead a happy, useful life. Some of these are called social needs. Every human being has certain social needs, such as:

. . . belonging to a group of people who respect him and whom he respects
. . . a chance to develop and use his abilities
. . . a chance to make decisions
. . . goals to work for
. . . a feeling of accomplishment

3. **The need for faith.** In addition to physical and social needs, every person also has a need for faith. A person may be sustained by different kinds of faith, such as:

. . . faith that his life will be happy and useful
. . . faith that he can solve his problems if he plans intelligently and works hard
. . . faith in the orderliness of the universe
. . . faith in God

enough money to satisfy their physical needs. The cities and towns of the Midwest also provide many opportunities for education and recreation, which help people to satisfy their social needs.

Some of the most sparsely populated areas in the Midwest are in northern Michigan, Wisconsin, and Minnesota. Here winters are severe, and the growing season is too short for many kinds of crops. Also, much of the soil is thin and sandy. Only a small part of the land is used for farming. The rest is mainly forested. There is little manufacturing in these remote areas. Therefore, fewer job opportunities are available here than in most other parts of the Midwest.

The Great Plains states are more thinly populated than the Midwest. Although the Great Plains states cover a larger area than the Midwest, they have only about one third as many people. About eighteen million people live in the Great Plains states. More than half of these people live in just one state, Texas. In the Great Plains states, the population density is only twenty-eight persons per square mile.

The main reason why the Great Plains states are more thinly populated than the Midwest is that there are fewer opportunities here for people to meet their needs. The Great Plains states have less industry than the Midwest. (See Chapter 12.) Huge cattle ranches and wheat farms cover much of the land.

Few people are needed to work on the wheat farms, because one man can farm many acres with modern machinery. Also, a small number of cowboys can take care of thousands of cattle on a large ranch. It is not surprising that job opportunities are scarce in many parts of the Great Plains states.

Since the 1930's, some parts of the Great Plains states have been losing population. These are generally areas in which farming is the main type of work. Each year, many people who are unable to make a good living by farming move to the cities in order to get jobs in industry. The great drought that helped create the Dust Bowl* in the 1930's caused many farmers in the Great Plains states to move to other parts of our country.

The only Great Plains state whose population has been growing rapidly is Texas. In this state are several large manufacturing cities. Factories, stores, and offices provide jobs for many people. Other Texans work on farms or in oil fields. The United States government has started a number of space and defense projects in Texas. These projects employ thousands of persons. Some people have moved to Texas because they enjoy the mild, sunny climate along the Gulf coast. These reasons help to explain why the population of Texas has nearly doubled since 1930.

Who lives in the Midwest and Great Plains? About nine tenths of the people

Build Your Vocabulary

descendant	basic needs	immigrant	Dust Bowl
reservation	urban	drought	suburb	homestead

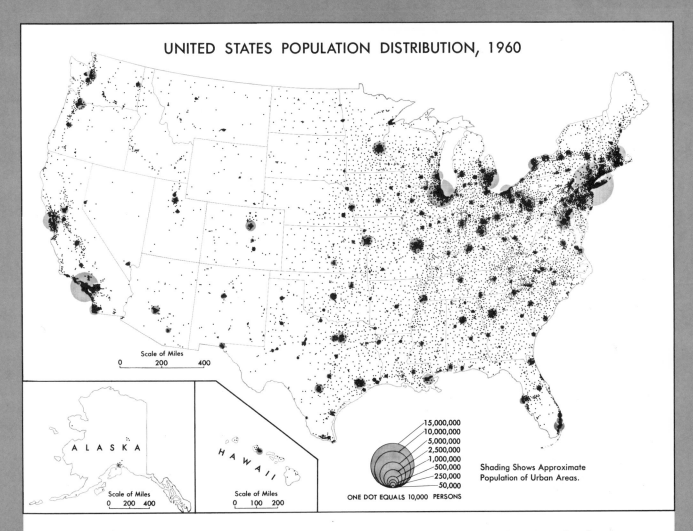

UNITED STATES POPULATION DISTRIBUTION, 1960

Scale of Miles
0 200 400

ALASKA

Scale of Miles
0 200 400

HAWAII

Scale of Miles
0 100 200

15,000,000
10,000,000
5,000,000
2,500,000
1,000,000
500,000
250,000
50,000

ONE DOT EQUALS 10,000 PERSONS

Shading Shows Approximate
Population of Urban Areas.

The map above shows the distribution of population in the United States. Each tiny black dot stands for ten thousand people. In some places on the map the dots are far apart. These are thinly populated areas. In other places, the dots are closer together. These areas are more densely populated.

In many places on the map, the dots are so close together that they form irregular black spots. These spots show densely populated communities such as cities or towns. The gray circles indicate the approximate number of people who live in each urban* area that has a population of fifty thousand or more.

*See Glossary

in the Midwest and Great Plains are white. Most of the others are Negroes, but there are also some American Indians and people of Asian descent.

Whites. Many of the white people in the Midwest and Great Plains are descended from people who came to our country from the British Isles. The pioneers who settled the Midwest in the late 1700's and early 1800's were largely

of English, Scotch, or Irish descent. Throughout the 1800's, people continued to come to America from Ireland and other parts of the British Isles. Some of these immigrants* settled in the Midwest and Great Plains. The people from the British Isles brought not only the English language but also many ideas and traditions that have had a great influence on our way of life.

117

Samuel Clemens, who wrote under the name of Mark Twain, was one of our country's greatest writers. He grew up in Hannibal, Missouri.

THE ARTS

The wooded hills and rolling prairies of the Midwest and Great Plains have inspired many writers, painters, and other artists. Some of these men and women are discussed in this special feature. You will probably want to do research in other books to learn more about the arts and the artists of the Midwest and Great Plains.

LITERATURE

The nineteenth century. In the nineteenth century, the Midwest and Great Plains produced one of America's greatest writers. This was Samuel Clemens, who wrote under the name of Mark Twain. Clemens grew up in Hannibal, Missouri, a town on the Mississippi River. His boyhood experiences helped him to create some of his best-loved books, such as *The Adventures of Tom Sawyer* and *Life on the Mississippi.*

Several other writers of the Midwest and Great Plains became famous during the late 1800's. One of these was Hamlin Garland, who was born in Wisconsin and grew up in Iowa and South Dakota. Garland wrote many novels and short stories. He is best known, however, for his autobiography *A Son of the Middle Border.* Indiana's James Whitcomb Riley was a popular poet of this period. You may have read some of his poems, such as "Little Orphant Annie." Eugene Field was another midwestern poet. He wrote "Wynken, Blynken, and Nod" and many other poems for young people.

Twentieth-century writers of the Midwest. During the present century, the Midwest has produced dozens of fine writers. Many of these men and women wrote novels and short stories about the people and history of this part of our country.

Booth Tarkington and Edna Ferber wrote many entertaining novels that are popular with young people as well as adults. Tarkington's books include *Penrod, Seventeen,* and *The Gentleman from Indiana.* Some of Ferber's novels, such as *So Big,* are about people in the Midwest. *Cimarron* tells about people who settled the Great Plains states.

Several of our country's greatest twentieth-century novelists were born in the Midwest and are strongly identified with this area. These include Sherwood Anderson, Theodore Dreiser, Sinclair Lewis, and James T. Farrell. In their books, these men portrayed people who were faced with some of the most serious problems of life in modern America. Anderson's best-known book is *Winesburg, Ohio.* Dreiser's novels include *An American Tragedy* and *Sister Carrie.* Many of Lewis' novels became best sellers. These include *Main Street,* which is about life in a small town in Minnesota. Farrell's most famous work is *Studs Lonigan,* a series of novels about a young man growing up in Chicago.

F. Scott Fitzgerald and Ernest Hemingway were also born in the Midwest but later moved to other areas. Fitzgerald was born in St. Paul, Minnesota. One of his most important novels is *The Great Gatsby.* Hemingway grew up in Oak Park, Illinois, and began his career in Kansas City. He wrote *A Farewell to Arms* and many other novels and short stories.

The Midwest has produced many important poets during the twentieth century. These include Vachel Lindsay and Carl Sandburg. Lindsay experimented with new and interesting verse rhythms in poems such as "The Congo." Some of his poems, such as "Abraham Lincoln Walks at Midnight" and "Bryan, Bryan, Bryan, Bryan" were about famous people of the Midwest. Sandburg's works include *Chicago Poems* and *The People, Yes*. He has also written a fine biography of Abraham Lincoln.

Some of the famous poets who were born in the Midwest are better known in connection with other parts of our country. These include Marianne Moore, Archibald MacLeish, Mark Van Doren, and Richard Eberhart. T. S. Eliot, who influenced many other writers, was born in St. Louis. He later became a British citizen.

Twentieth-century writers of the Great Plains states. Many fine writers of the present century have lived in the Great Plains states. Willa Cather, who grew up in Nebraska, wrote a number of novels and short stories about the settlement of the western prairies. Among these are *O Pioneers!* and *My Ántonia*. O. E. Rölvaag was a Norwegian immigrant who lived in South Dakota. His greatest work, *Giants in the Earth*, describes the lives of Norwegian settlers in South Dakota. Katherine Anne Porter, who was born in Texas, is known for her fine short stories and also for her novel *Ship of Fools*.

Poets of the Great Plains states include Edgar Lee Masters, who was born in Kansas. His most famous book is *Spoon River Anthology*. The poems in this book tell about the lives of the people buried in the cemetery of a midwestern village. Gwendolyn Brooks was also born in Kansas. She is noted for two collections of poems, *Annie Allen* and *A Street in Bronzeville*.

OTHER ARTS
Painters and sculptors of the Midwest and Great Plains. During the nineteenth century, George Caleb Bingham painted many scenes showing life in the Midwest. Among his paintings are "Fur Traders Descending the Missouri" and "The Jolly Flatboatmen."

Three twentieth-century artists of the Midwest and Great Plains also became famous for their paintings of everyday life in this part of our country. The paintings of Iowa's Grant Wood include "American Gothic," which is shown on this page. Thomas Hart Benton, who lived in Missouri, created many murals* and other paintings showing life in the Midwest. John Steuart Curry portrayed farm life on the plains of Kansas.

Other artists who lived and worked in the Midwest and Great Plains include the sculptors Lorado Taft and Carl Milles. In some of the cities of the Midwest are beautiful fountains and statues created by these men.

Architects. Some of our country's greatest architects worked in the Midwest and Great Plains. Louis H. Sullivan designed many of Chicago's early skyscrapers. Houses and other buildings designed by Frank Lloyd Wright are located in many different parts of the Midwest and Great Plains. Eliel Saarinen and his son Eero Saarinen came to America from Finland in 1923. Each of them designed many buildings. Eero Saarinen's design for a huge steel arch was used for the Jefferson National Expansion Memorial in St. Louis. (See picture on page 268.)

*See Glossary

Grant Wood's "American Gothic." Wood was one of a group of famous twentieth-century artists who painted scenes of everyday life in the Midwest and Great Plains.

A foreign quarter of Chicago in 1906. In the 1800's and early 1900's, millions of immigrants came to the Midwest and Great Plains. Large numbers of these people settled in Chicago and other cities. People of one nationality often lived in the same section of a city, speaking their native language and following their own customs.

During the last half of the 1800's, a steady stream of immigrants came to the Midwest and Great Plains from Germany. Some of the newcomers took up homesteads* and became farmers. Others settled in the cities, where they worked in factories, stores, or offices. Today, the German influence is still noticeable in cities such as Milwaukee, St. Louis, and Cincinnati.

People from other countries in northern Europe also came to the Midwest and Great Plains during the last half of the nineteenth century. Dutch immigrants settled in Michigan, Iowa, and other states. Large numbers of people came from the Scandinavian countries of Norway, Sweden, and Denmark. They settled mainly in Wisconsin, Minnesota, and the Dakotas. Many of them became farmers. Some worked as lumberjacks in the northern woods or as fishermen on the Great Lakes. Today, many people in the Midwest and Great Plains bear the Dutch or Scandinavian names of ancestors who came here long ago.

After 1890, millions of immigrants came to America from eastern and southern Europe. Among these people were Russians, Poles, Italians, Czechs, Hungarians, and Greeks. By the time they arrived, most of the good farmland in the Midwest had been taken. Some went farther west and established farms on the Great Plains. However, a much larger number of immigrants went to Chicago and other cities. Here, many of them worked in steel mills, machine shops, and other kinds of factories. They helped to supply the labor needed to make the Midwest a great industrial region. Other immigrants became businessmen, doctors, lawyers, or teachers. The descendants of many of these people still live in the cities of the Midwest today.

Since about 1920, immigration to the United States has decreased sharply. This is largely the result of laws passed by the United States Congress to limit the number of immigrants entering this country each year. Today about one sixth of the people in the Midwest and Great Plains are foreign born or have at least one foreign-born parent. These people are said to be of foreign stock. The three largest groups of people of foreign stock living in the Midwest and Great Plains today are the Germans, Poles, and Canadians.

In the Midwest and Great Plains, there are more than 800,000 people of Mexican descent. More than three fourths of these people live in Texas. Some are members of families that have been here since

Workers in a laboratory. The people who live in the Midwest and Great Plains represent a variety of races, nationalities, and religions. Together, these people have helped to make the United States the strong and prosperous nation it is today.

Texas was part of Mexico. (See page 89.) Others have come from Mexico in recent years to work on farms, in fruit orchards, or in factories. Spanish is spoken by many people in Texas today. Some cities, such as El Paso and San Antonio, have a colorful Spanish atmosphere.

Negroes. About one out of every thirteen persons in the Midwest and Great Plains is a Negro. Nearly all of the Negroes are descended from people who were brought from Africa as slaves during the 1600's and 1700's. Most of the slaves worked on large farms, called plantations, in the southern part of the United States. Slavery was abolished in 1865, after the end of the Civil War. (See page 91.) In the years that followed, most of the Negroes remained in the South. There they worked mainly as farmers or as household servants. Usually they earned very little money.

In an Indian reservation hospital. Many American Indians of the Midwest and Great Plains live on reservations. Some, however, have moved to the cities to get jobs.

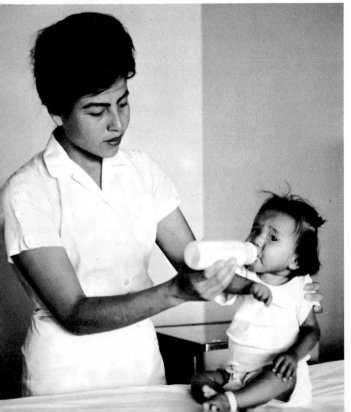

During World War I and World War II, factories in the Midwest needed large numbers of workers. Hundreds of thousands of Negroes from the South came to the Midwest in the hope of getting good jobs in industry. The movement of Negroes from the South to the Midwest has continued to the present time.

Today many Negroes live in all the large cities of the Midwest. In Chicago and Detroit, for example, about one out of every four persons is a Negro. More than one million Negroes live in Texas, the only Great Plains state with a large Negro population.

Indians. There are about 120,000 American Indians in the Great Plains states and another 50,000 in the Midwest. Some are descended from the Indians who roamed the prairies and the forests here long ago. (See Chapter 4.) Others are members of certain tribes, such as the Cherokee and Choctaw, who moved here from the eastern part of our country during the 1800's.

When our country was being settled, the United States government forced most Indian tribes to move onto reservations. These reservations were usually located in barren areas where few white persons cared to live. Today many Indians still live on their tribal reservations. Most of them earn their living by growing crops or raising livestock. Some Indians, however, have left the reservations and moved to the cities to get jobs in business and industry.

The people of the Midwest and Great Plains worship God in different ways. In the Midwest and Great Plains, as in other parts of our country, people of different religious beliefs live side by side in friendship. Some are members of

A Methodist church service in Iowa. In the Midwest and Great Plains, as in other parts of our country, people of different religious beliefs live side by side in friendship.

the Roman Catholic Church. Others belong to various Protestant groups, such as the Methodists, the Baptists, the Lutherans, and the Presbyterians. In a number of cities, there are Eastern Orthodox churches. Thousands of people in the Midwest and Great Plains are Jews.

Develop Important Understandings

1. Why have some parts of the Great Plains states been losing population since the 1930's?

2. What facts help to explain why the population of Texas has nearly doubled since 1930?

3. Why has immigration to our country decreased sharply since about 1920?

4. What facts help to explain why many people of Mexican descent live in Texas?

5. Why did large numbers of Negroes move to the Midwest during World War I and World War II?

6. How do most of the Indians on reservations in the Midwest and Great Plains earn their living?

Learn More About Immigrants

Immigrants from many nations have made important contributions to life in America. The following list includes the names of some famous people who came to the Midwest and Great Plains as immigrants.

O. E. Rölvaag   Joseph Pulitzer
Knute Rockne   William W. Mayo

Do research about one of these people. Then write an interesting report about his life and work. The suggestions on pages 346-351 will be helpful in finding information and in writing your report.

Replacing run-down tenements with modern apartment buildings helps to solve the problem of city slums. Although most of the people in the Midwest and Great Plains have the things they need for a comfortable way of life, people here also face a number of serious problems. With hard work and cooperation, people are making progress toward solving some of these problems.

8 Problems and Progress

Few parts of the world are as productive and prosperous as the Midwest and Great Plains. Farms, mines, and factories here produce great quantities of goods. Most of the people who live in the Midwest and Great Plains have the things they need for a comfortable way of life.

At the same time, people in the Midwest and Great Plains face a number of serious problems. Some of these problems are especially important to farmers, businessmen, or industrial workers. Others affect mainly Negroes, Indians, or other groups of people who differ in some way from the majority of the population. There are also serious problems shared by all the people who live in large cities. In this chapter, you will learn how the people of the Midwest and Great Plains are trying to solve some of their problems and plan for the future.

Farm Problems

A Study Guide

Farmers in the Midwest and Great Plains face several problems, but progress has been made toward solving them. As you study this section of the chapter, try to answer the following questions:

1. Why has there been an increase in farm production?
2. How has this increase in production affected farmers?
3. What is being done to help solve the problems of farmers?

Many farmers have had to seek new ways of earning a living. In the Midwest and Great Plains, as in other parts of our country, many people who would like to earn a living by farming are no longer able to do so. This problem is largely the result of changes that have occurred in farming methods during the last one hundred years. (See feature on page 148.) New methods and equipment have made it possible for a farmer today to produce much larger quantities of crops than a farmer could in the past. As more crops are produced by each farmer, fewer farmers are needed to supply our country with food.

Today, a farmer must produce a large amount of crops in order to earn enough money to support his family. To do this, he needs modern equipment. If he raises wheat and other field crops, he also needs many acres of farmland. Both land and equipment are expensive. Many farmers cannot afford to buy all the land and equipment they need. Each year, thousands of these people leave their farms and move to cities to find jobs in industry. Others continue to live in the country while holding part-time or full-time jobs in nearby towns. As a result, the number of farmers in the United States has been steadily decreasing.

The United States government is helping farmers adjust to the changes that have been taking place in agriculture. It has set up agencies that lend money to farmers who want to buy land or machinery. If a person decides to change from farming to another occupation, the government will give him information about jobs that are available. It will also lend him money to help him get the training he needs.

Build Your Vocabulary

minority group   surplus   urban   strike   slums   discrimination

migrant workers   automation   prejudice   segregation   air pollution

Prices of farm products are sometimes low. The people who remain in farming face the serious problem of getting enough money for their products. To understand why, let us use potatoes as an example. In some years, the supply of potatoes is smaller than usual. Farmers are able to sell all of their potatoes promptly at a high price. This is because there are enough people who want the potatoes and are willing to pay a price that is higher than usual. In other years, however, farmers produce a very large supply. When this happens, farmers may have to accept a lower-than-usual price in order to sell all of their potatoes in a reasonable period of time. It is expensive to store any crop, and if potatoes are stored for a long time, they may spoil. In the past, the price of some farm products remained low year after year.

A number of years ago, the federal government set up a special program to keep the price of some farm products from falling too low. It began buying large amounts of wheat, corn, and certain other products at prices that were usually higher than the farmers would get if they sold their products to other

Filling a government storage bin with corn. A number of years ago, the federal government set up a special program to keep the price of corn, wheat, and certain other farm products from falling too low. It began buying large amounts of these products at prices that were usually higher than farmers would get if they sold their products to other buyers.

buyers. However, farmers who wanted to sell products to the government had to follow certain rules. The government told each farmer how much land he could use to grow a particular crop. It also set a limit on the amount of the crop that the farmer could sell to other buyers.

The farm products purchased by the government were kept in large bins or warehouses. Part of the surplus was given to schools and hospitals. Some was sold to buyers in foreign countries.

Although the government's farm surplus program is still carried on today, it has never been completely successful. The cost of farming has risen so high that some farmers still do not earn as much money as they feel they should. At the same time, many people believe that the government should not use tax money to buy surplus farm products. Also, farmers who sell products to the government do not always like the rules they must follow.

Farm surpluses have been dwindling. In recent years, the amount of surplus farm products stored by the government has been decreasing. There are several reasons for this. First, the United States has been selling or giving away large amounts of farm products to countries that do not have enough food for all their people. For example, about one fourth of all the wheat produced in the United States in 1966 was shipped to India. In addition, our country's population has been growing steadily, so there are more American customers for farm products.

Another reason why surpluses have been decreasing is that new uses have been found for many farm products.

Unloading American wheat in India. Recently, farm surpluses have been dwindling. This is partly because the United States has been selling or giving away large amounts of farm products to countries that do not have enough food for their people.

Soybeans, for instance, were once used mainly as food for animals. Today, soybean oil is used in making paints, plastics, soap, and many other products. Soybean meal is used as fertilizer. New ways of using farm products are helping farmers to sell larger quantities of crops.

Some experts believe that the problem of farm surpluses will soon be solved. Before long, the government may no longer need to buy surplus farm products. Instead, it may have to encourage farmers to produce more crops in order to supply not only customers in the United States but hungry people throughout the world.

Problems of Industry

A Study Guide

There are certain problems that affect businessmen and industrial workers in the Midwest and Great Plains. As you read about these problems, try to answer the questions below. The feature on pages 132-133 contains additional information about these problems.

1. What are some of the causes of unemployment in the Midwest and Great Plains?
2. What is being done to help solve the unemployment problem?
3. How has automation been helpful to industry in the United States?
4. What are some of the job opportunities available for trained people in our country?

Many workers in the Midwest and Great Plains are unemployed. One of the serious problems facing industry in the Midwest and Great Plains, as well as in other parts of our country, is unemployment. At the present time, more than one-half million workers in the Midwest and Great Plains cannot find jobs.

Some areas that once employed many factory workers now lack industry. There are several reasons for this. In some cases, companies that no longer could sell their goods at a profit have been forced to shut down factories or to lay off some of their workers. Sometimes a business firm has moved from one location to another that offered more advantages for industry. In many towns and cities, a single company employs a large part of the factory workers. When such a company stops production or moves away, many people in the community are left without jobs.

Automation is taking jobs away from unskilled workers. There is another reason, too, why some workers are unemployed. Automatic machines are doing more and more of the work that used to be done by people. With modern machinery, for example, a glass factory that employs only fourteen workers can produce about nine tenths of all the electric light bulbs used in the United States. The use of machinery that requires few, if any, human operators is called automation.

Automation has been very helpful to industry in the United States. Factories using the new machines can produce larger quantities of goods at lower costs than ever before. Therefore, it seems likely that automation will become even more widespread in the future.

Although automation has brought great benefits to industry, it has also caused certain problems. Thousands of factory workers are now unemployed as a result of automation. Most of these people do not have much education or special training. In the past, many job opportunities were available for unskilled workers. Today, however, these people often have difficulty getting jobs because they lack the education or the special training needed to work in automated industries. They must be trained for jobs that are available at the present time and that will continue to be available in the future.

There are many job opportunities for trained people. Although automation is taking jobs away from unskilled workers, it is creating new job opportunities for engineers and other highly skilled people. Skilled workers are needed to build the new machines and to keep them running. In fact, manufacturing companies often have difficulty finding enough people with the education or the special training needed to hold certain kinds of jobs.

There are also thousands of jobs available in other fields besides manufacturing. In our country today, large numbers of people are needed to perform various kinds of services. For example, we need more doctors, dentists, nurses, teachers, policemen, and firemen. There is a shortage of people who know how to repair automobiles and household appliances. Bricklayers, plumbers, and other skilled craftsmen are in demand today, as are office workers such as clerks and typists. Our country also needs barbers, waiters, hospital attendants, and many other kinds of service workers.

Some service jobs require a considerable amount of education or special training, but others require very little. Many unemployed workers probably

Automatic machinery is used to run this oil refinery at Tyler, Texas. Only three men are needed to control the machinery. In our country today, automatic machinery does more and more of the work that used to be done by people. Although automation is taking jobs away from many unskilled workers, it is creating new job opportunities for engineers and other skilled people.

could obtain service jobs if they were given the right training and if they were informed about the jobs that are available.

What is being done to reduce unemployment? The people of the Midwest and Great Plains are making a serious effort to solve the problem of unemployment. To provide more jobs, the governments of some states are carrying on campaigns to attract new industries. Schools in many cities offer vocational courses in which young people can learn job skills. In some cities, there are also evening classes for adults who want to learn new trades. In addition, many private business firms have on-the-job training programs to teach workers the skills they need.

Our federal government, also, is trying in many ways to provide job training for those who need it. The Economic Opportunity Act, passed by Congress in 1964, set up the Job Corps. Young people who are unemployed can stay for a few months at special Job Corps centers located in different parts of our country. Here they are given a chance to earn money and to learn valuable job skills. The Economic Opportunity Act also set up programs that help young people to obtain jobs and vocational training in their own hometowns. In addition, the government has started programs to teach job skills to unemployed adults. All of these programs are helping to prepare jobless workers for successful careers in the modern world.

Young men learning how to weld at a Job Corps center. In 1964, our federal government set up the Job Corps. Young people who are unemployed can stay for a few months at a Job Corps center, where they are given a chance to earn money and to learn valuable job skills.

Strikes affect large numbers of people. In industry, disputes sometimes arise between workers and employers. For example, the workers in a particular factory may want higher wages or better working conditions. If their employer refuses to meet their demands, the workers may go on strike. In other words, they may join together and refuse to work.

Strikes can cause trouble and inconvenience for many people. Workers who are on strike are not able to spend much money because they are not receiving their regular wages. This hurts business at the stores where they usually shop.

A strike in one industry may also affect other industries. For instance, a strike of railroad engineers would be harmful to industries that depend on trains for bringing in raw materials and shipping manufactured products.

Today, most disagreements between employers and workers are settled before a strike occurs. Representatives of both sides meet together and try to settle their differences. If these two groups cannot agree, other persons may be called in to help end the dispute. The federal government has an agency that tries to settle disagreements between employers and workers.

Problems of Minority Groups

A Study Guide

In the United States today, members of certain minority groups face serious problems that are not shared by most other Americans. As you read this section, try to answer the following questions:

1. What is prejudice? What is discrimination? How do prejudice and discrimination affect members of minority groups?
2. What serious problems are being faced by (a) Negroes? (b) Indians? (c) Mexican-Americans?
3. What steps are now being taken to help solve the problems of minority groups?

In the Midwest and Great Plains, there are many groups of people who differ from the majority of the population in race, religion, or national origin. These are called minority groups. Some of these groups face serious problems that are not shared by most other Americans. Among the groups with especially serious problems are Negroes, Indians, and people of Mexican descent.

Negroes. Negro slavery was ended in the United States after the Civil War. (See page 91.) At that time, however, most Americans still were not willing to give Negroes all the rights and freedoms enjoyed by other citizens. Many states in the southern part of our country passed segregation* laws. These laws kept Negroes from sharing schools and other public facilities with white people.

*See Glossary

FIVE SOCIAL PROBLEMS

Sometimes, through no fault of their own, people cannot satisfy their basic needs. (See page 115.) Many of our citizens are unable to provide food, clothing, and shelter for themselves or their families. Some do not receive enough education to develop their abilities completely. Others lack the faith that might help them solve their problems.

Every country in the world has certain conditions that prevent large numbers of people from satisfying their needs. These conditions are called social problems. At the present time, the people of the United States are especially interested in finding solutions to five serious social problems.

1. Lack of jobs. Although the rate of unemployment has been decreasing in recent years, more than three million workers in our country are still unable to find jobs. Our unemployed workers lack jobs for various reasons. Some of them live in areas where the land is not well suited to farming and there is little

An adviser talks with unemployed workers. Both government and industry have set up programs to help our country's unemployed workers find jobs.

industry. Others, however, live in areas where there are plenty of jobs. They cannot find employment because they do not have the education or the special skills needed to hold the jobs that are available.

The number of jobs that can be held by unskilled workers is growing smaller every year, mainly because of automation. (See pages 128-129.) At the same time, automation is creating many new jobs for engineers and other people with special training. One way in which we can reduce unemployment is to provide more opportunities for workers to learn the skills needed by modern industry.

2. Lack of education. Many of our country's young people are not receiving the education they need. There are many reasons for this. Some communities do not have enough money to support good schools. Other communities do not provide equally good schools for all the children who live there. For example, in some cities less money is spent on schools in sections where the people are poor.

Often, young people leave school before they have fully developed their abilities or acquired the skills they need for life in our modern world. Some become discouraged and drop out. Others leave school to go to work. Many young people who would like to continue their education after high school cannot afford to go to college.

More and more opportunities for education are being made available to the young people in our country. Many students learn job skills in vocational schools or on-the-job training programs. Some schools make special arrangements for educating handicapped or especially talented children. In addition, scholarships make it possible for many students to continue their education.

3. Handicaps and illness. Although Americans are among the healthiest people in the world, sickness is a serious problem for many of our citizens. Government figures show that more than twenty-two million people in our country suffer from permanent or long-lasting illnesses and handicaps. Of these, more than three million have arthritis or similar diseases, and about the same number suffer from heart conditions. More than one million people have some form of mental illness.

Today important steps are being taken to improve the health of our citizens. First, medical care is being made available to larger numbers of people. For example, various government and private agencies help sick and handicapped people to obtain the medical care they need. Second, better methods of preventing and treating illness are being developed through research.

4. Prejudice. The dislike of certain persons because of their race, religion, or national origin is called prejudice. It is a serious problem throughout the world.

People who are prejudiced judge their fellow citizens as members of groups rather than as individuals. For example, an employer may be unwilling to promote a certain worker just because the man is of Mexican descent. A prejudiced person may refuse to sit next to a Negro on a bus. Some people will not vote for a candidate for public office if he is a Roman Catholic or a Jew.

When we become better acquainted with people, we are usually able to judge them as individuals. Therefore, prejudice nearly always lessens when people play together, work together, or go to school together. As we have more opportunities to know the members of different groups, prejudice in our country will gradually decrease.

5. Discrimination. The withholding of rights from people on account of their race, religion, or national origin is called discrimination. It is one of our country's serious problems, even though our courts have ruled many kinds of discrimination unconstitutional.

Examples of discrimination can be found in almost every part of the United States. In many of our cities, members of certain minority groups, such as Negroes, Jews, and Mexican-Americans are unable to purchase homes in

American students. Prejudice nearly always lessens when people of different groups go to school together, work together, or play together.

certain neighborhoods. Often, Negro children must attend all-Negro schools because they live in districts where there are no white children. Discrimination is also possible in our courts. If citizens who serve on juries are prejudiced against certain minority groups, they may make unjust decisions.

In our country, Negroes suffer more from discrimination than the members of any other minority group. Many of them are unable to exercise all of their constitutional rights and freedoms, which are generally referred to as civil rights. Even the right to vote has sometimes been denied to Negroes, especially in the South. (See page 134.)

In recent years, our federal government and some of the states have passed important laws concerning civil rights. Some of these laws have helped to end segregation in public places such as schools, parks, hotels, and restaurants. The Civil Rights Act passed by Congress in 1964 and the Voting Rights Act of 1965 are helping many Negroes to obtain equal voting rights and employment opportunities.

Some states also passed laws that required citizens to pass a literacy* test or pay a special tax before they could vote. Such laws helped to keep Negroes from voting or from being elected to government posts.

Most states in the northern part of our country did not have segregation laws. In these states, however, discrimination often resulted from the actions of private groups or individuals. For example, many hotels and restaurants throughout our nation refused to serve Negroes. Employers often denied jobs to qualified Negro workers. Sometimes labor unions refused to let Negroes become members.

Today, discrimination against Negroes is lessening. The United States Supreme Court ruled in 1954 that segregation in public schools is unconstitutional. Since that time, many schools that were formerly segregated have admitted Negro students. The federal government and a number of states have passed laws to end segregation in hotels, restaurants, and other public places. A federal law, the Voting Rights Act of 1965, forbids the use of literacy tests and other measures to keep Negroes from voting. As a result, more and more Negroes are gaining the opportunity to vote and to hold public office.

Progress is also being made toward ending job discrimination. Many business firms and labor unions have voluntarily taken steps to end unfair treatment of Negroes. The Civil Rights Act

A skilled toolmaker. In recent years, discrimination against Negroes has been lessening. New laws are helping many Negroes to obtain the voting rights and employment opportunities enjoyed by other American citizens.

passed by Congress in 1964 states that companies engaged in interstate* commerce must hire workers without regard to race. It also forbids discrimination by labor unions. Many states have passed similar laws and have set up commissions to make sure that the laws are enforced.

In spite of these gains, discrimination against Negroes is still a problem in the United States today. It is especially serious in the field of housing. Many white people do not want to have Negroes living near them. As a result, Negroes often find it difficult to buy homes or rent apartments in certain neighborhoods. In all the large cities of the Midwest and Great Plains, as in other parts of our country, there are neighborhoods that are made up entirely of white persons or of Negroes. Because children usually attend the school nearest their home, segregation in housing has often resulted in segregated schools as well.

Negro families who live in large cities face other problems in addition to discrimination. Many of these people came to the cities from rural areas in the South. They lack the education or the special skills needed to hold good jobs in industry. Because they earn little money, they are forced to live in poor neighborhoods called slums. Some of the problems faced by people who live in slums are discussed on pages 139-143.

Today our Negro citizens are becoming impatient to make progress toward a better way of life. In many cities, Negroes have held marches and other demonstrations to demand equal opportunities in housing and employment. Sometimes these demonstrations have led to conflict with people who are unwilling to grant the Negroes' demands. Serious riots have taken place in Chicago, Cleveland, and other cities.

Efforts are now being made to solve the problems that still face Negroes in the United States. For example, some states and cities have passed "fair housing" laws. The purpose of these laws is to permit members of minority groups to buy houses or rent apartments without being discriminated against. Many church groups and community agencies have started programs to help Negro families find suitable housing. The government training programs described earlier in this chapter are helping many Negroes learn the skills they need to obtain good jobs. Much remains to be done, however, before Negroes enjoy the same opportunities as white citizens.

Indians. More than half of the Indians in our country live on reservations. Many of these people have great difficulty earning a living. Often the land on the reservations is not well suited to growing crops. Also, many Indians are not familiar with modern farming methods, and they lack the money to buy expensive equipment. The reservations are usually located in areas that have little industry. Even if there were factories nearby, many Indians would have trouble getting good jobs because they do not have enough education. Today more than one third of the Indians on reservations are unemployed, and most of the others earn very little money.

On the reservations, the standard of living is much lower than it is in most other parts of our country. Many families live in one-room shacks or log cabins without running water. Often they lack

An Indian harvesting wild rice by hand. Many Indians in the Midwest and Great Plains lack the education or skills needed to earn a good living.

warm clothing and nourishing food. It is not surprising that large numbers of Indians suffer from tuberculosis and other serious diseases. On the average, Indians do not live as long as white Americans.

When Indians leave the reservations and move to the cities, they face many new problems. They have to give up their old customs and adjust to a way of life that often seems strange to them. Because most of the Indians do not have enough education, they cannot find steady, well-paying jobs. Sometimes they are the victims of discrimination. Eventually many of the Indians become dissatisfied and homesick, and return to the reservations.

Today the federal government is trying to help the Indians achieve a better way of life. It has built schools on the

reservations and has set up training programs to teach Indian workers the skills they need to hold good jobs. It is teaching the Indians modern farming methods and lending them money to buy necessary equipment. With government help, many tribes have started new industries on the reservations to provide jobs for their people. Indians who want to build new homes for themselves can get money from the government to buy building materials and to hire skilled help. To improve the Indians' health, the government is providing hospitals and other medical services. Indians who move to the cities are being helped to find jobs and to adjust to their new way of life.

Mexican-Americans. The people of Mexican descent in the Midwest and Great Plains face many of the same problems as the Negroes and Indians. They, too, often suffer from discrimination. A Mexican-American may have difficulty finding a job or buying a home in a certain neighborhood simply because of his national origin. Many Mexican-Americans speak Spanish instead of English. This has made it harder for them to get jobs and become accepted as American citizens.

Like the members of other minority groups, many people of Mexican descent lack the education they need to be successful in the modern world. They are forced to work at low-paying jobs that require hard physical labor. Some of these people live in the slums of San Antonio, Houston, and other large cities. Others live in rural areas and work as hired laborers on farms.

Many Mexican-Americans are migrant workers. Throughout the year they travel around the United States, helping farmers harvest their crops. Life is hard for the migrant workers. They usually work long hours in the hot sun for very low wages. Often they are housed in crowded shacks without adequate heating or plumbing. Because the migrant workers travel almost constantly, their children never stay in one place long enough to receive a good education.

With assistance from their fellow citizens, the people of Mexican descent are making a serious effort to solve their problems. Local organizations such as church groups are helping Mexican-American families to obtain better housing, education, and medical care. Also, the federal government is giving money to states and cities to help meet the needs of migrant workers. Several states have recently passed laws to protect the rights of the migrants. Training programs sponsored by business and government are preparing many Mexican-American workers for jobs in industry. With more opportunities for education and employment, our Mexican-American citizens should make rapid progress toward a better life.

An electrical-equipment repairman. People of Mexican descent often suffer from discrimination in housing and employment. With assistance from their fellow citizens, these people are making a serious effort to solve their problems. For example, programs sponsored by business and government are training many Mexican-Americans for jobs in industry.

Problems of the Cities

A Study Guide

The people who live in the large cities of the Midwest and Great Plains share a number of problems. As you study this section, look for the following:

1. ways in which transportation problems of urban areas are being solved

2. causes of air pollution, and ways in which it can be prevented

3. problems faced by people who live in slums, and ways in which these problems are being solved

4. why crime costs taxpayers so much money, and what steps might be taken to lower the crime rate

More than half of the people in the Midwest and Great Plains live in or near large cities. (See map on page 140.) When many people live close together, as they do in huge urban areas, certain problems are likely to arise. The rest of this chapter describes some of the problems that affect city dwellers in the Midwest and Great Plains.

Transportation problems. As an urban area grows in size and population, it becomes more difficult for people to travel from one part to another. Many people who live in the suburbs must travel twenty miles or more to reach their work. Most cities have buses, trains, or other forms of public transportation, but these are often inconvenient, crowded, and dirty. Some people do not care to use them. Instead, they travel by car. During the hours when most people are going to work or coming home, there is often so much traffic that cars have to move very slowly. It is sometimes difficult to find a parking place in downtown areas, and all-day parking is likely to be expensive.

The cities of the Midwest and Great Plains are trying to find ways to solve their transportation problems. Some cities have built broad expressways that have no traffic lights or crossroads. Cars can travel rapidly on these highways. As new expressways are completed, there is less traffic on the older, narrower streets. In many cities there are huge parking garages, where drivers can leave their cars while they work or shop. A few cities are planning to expand or improve their bus lines or railway systems to encourage more people to use public transportation.

Air pollution. Clean water and air must be provided for the people who live in large urban areas. If water or air contains impurities, it is said to be polluted. Chapter 10 tells about water pollution in the Midwest and Great Plains. Air pollution is also a serious problem, especially in large cities.

Air becomes polluted when smoke and fumes are allowed to enter the atmosphere. For example, people burn oil, gas, or coal to heat houses and other buildings. These fuels are also burned in plants that produce electric power. In backyards and city dumps, trash is often destroyed by burning it. The smoke from all these fires enters the air, together with exhaust fumes from motor vehicles and trains. Also, factories may give off harmful fumes in the manufacture of certain products. Sometimes the air in a city contains so many impurities that it is dark and smoky. Breathing polluted air may cause people to become seriously ill.

Various steps are being taken to prevent air pollution. For example, Cincinnati and other cities require industries to use special methods to prevent harmful fumes from entering the air. Laws have been passed in some cities to control the burning of trash. Engi-neers are studying ways to reduce exhaust fumes from motor vehicles.

Slums. In the large cities of the Midwest and Great Plains, there are many poor neighborhoods of run-down houses and apartment buildings. Areas like these are known as slums. In some cities, slums grow larger every year.

Problems of slum dwellers. Life is not very pleasant for most people in the slums. The homes in which they live are dirty, ugly, and overcrowded. Fires are a constant danger in these old, run-down buildings. The people who live in slum tenements* may not get enough heat during the winter. They may lack running water for drinking and bathing. Also, slum buildings and streets are usually filthy. There are many rats and insects, which may carry disease germs.

Air pollution is a serious problem in our country's cities. Air becomes polluted when smoke and fumes are allowed to enter the atmosphere. People may become very ill from breathing polluted air.

Main Cities

The map above shows the location of the main cities of the Midwest and Great Plains. It includes all cities that have a population of 100,000 or more. State capitals are also shown, including those with a population of less than 100,000. The names of capitals are underlined.

More than half of the people in the Midwest and Great Plains live in or near the cities shown on the map above. A densely populated area that includes at least one large city together with neighboring towns and settled sections is a metropolitan area. For example, the Detroit metropolitan area includes the central city of Detroit as well as dozens of smaller cities and towns. Less than half the people in the Detroit metropolitan area live in the central city.

In the Midwest and Great Plains, as in other parts of our country, cities have grown up because they help to meet human needs. (See page 115.) By comparing the map above with the map on pages 194 and 195, you can see that many of the cities are centers of large industrial areas. During the past one hundred years, well-paying jobs in factories have attracted millions of people to cities in the Midwest and Great Plains. Other people have come to the cities to take jobs in stores and offices.

As you study the map above, you will see that there are no large cities in some parts of the Midwest and Great Plains. In these thinly populated areas, most of the people earn a living by farming.

In the slums, the rate of sickness is always high. To have good health, people need sunlight, pure water, fresh air, and wholesome food. They also need protection from infectious diseases, such as tuberculosis and diphtheria. People in slum areas lack most of the things that are needed for good health.

Children who live in slums must often work harder than other children in order to succeed in school. This is not because they are less intelligent than other children, but because they have had less preparation for doing schoolwork. In many families, both the father and the mother must work long hours in order to earn a living. They have little time to help their children with their homework. Many of the homes lack toys, books, or writing materials. It is not surprising that children from slum areas must often work harder to keep up with their classmates.

The battle against slums. People in the Midwest and Great Plains have been trying in a number of ways to solve the

A nursery school. Some cities have started nursery schools to help prepare children from slum areas for kindergarten or first grade. In these nursery schools, the children are taught many of the things that most other children learn at home.

problem of slums. Many cities have been tearing down old tenements and replacing them with modern apartment buildings where people can live without paying high rents. Our federal government is helping to pay for slum clearance projects. In some cases, people living in slums have decided to improve their homes and clean up their neighborhoods by themselves. By working together, they have succeeded in changing slums into pleasant, attractive residential areas.

Cities are taking steps to improve the health of their citizens. In some communities, there are inspectors who check houses and apartment buildings to make sure they are safe and reasonably clean. Before children enter school, they usually receive "shots" to protect them from certain infectious diseases. These shots may be given free or at a very low cost. Many cities provide clinics

A health clinic. Sickness is a serious problem for people who live in slums. Many cities provide clinics and other services for people who have little or no money.

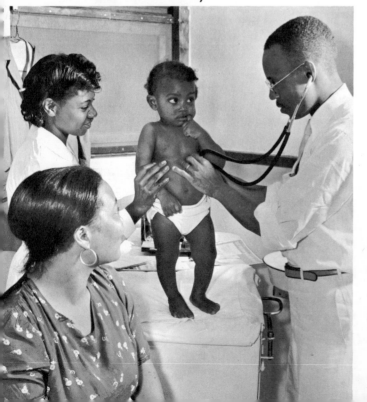

and other medical services for people with little or no money. Often, however, there is not enough medical help available for all the people who need it.

Some cities are now spending more money on schools in slum areas than they are on other schools. Part of this money is being used to buy new books and to hire well-qualified teachers. In addition, many old school buildings are being remodeled or replaced with well-equipped modern structures. The federal government and many of our state governments are providing funds to help improve schools in slum areas.

In many slum areas, nursery schools have been started for children who are three or four years old. In nursery school, these children are taught many of the things most other children learn at home. This helps to prepare them for kindergarten or first grade. Special classes are sometimes provided for older children who have difficulty in school.

Much has been done to help the people who live in slums, but even more must be accomplished in the future. Cities must provide slum dwellers with even more opportunities for obtaining a good education. They must break down the barriers of discrimination that have kept some members of minority groups from moving out of the slums. Better planning is needed to prevent the growth of new slums in the future. These are some of the important things that must be done before the slum problem can be solved.

Crime. In the Midwest and Great Plains, as in other parts of our country, the number of crimes committed each year has been increasing. The slums of

In a youth center. Many communities and private organizations sponsor recreational programs for young people. If young people can take part in worthwhile activities during their spare time, they are less likely to commit crimes. However, the battle against crime can succeed only if every citizen does his part in maintaining law and order.

large cities have an especially high crime rate. This is caused partly by the poor living conditions in slum areas, and by the fact that many slum dwellers do not have steady jobs. However, crime is not limited to the slums. In recent years, the crime rate has been rising in the suburbs as well as in the central* cities.

Crime not only is a threat to lives and property, but also costs American taxpayers billions of dollars each year. Part of the tax money paid by every citizen is used for police protection and for courts where lawbreakers are brought to trial. In addition, money is needed for prisons and reformatories.*

Today, city and state governments are trying to do more than merely arrest and punish criminals. They are trying to prevent crimes from taking place. Cities may be able to lower the crime rate if they can do away with some of their slums and find jobs for more people. This is not enough, however. All citizens must have respect for the law and for people in authority. Each person must obey the law, cooperate with police, and report any crime that he sees. The battle against crime can succeed only if every citizen does his part in maintaining law and order.

Looking toward the future. In this chapter, you have studied certain problems that affect different groups of people in the Midwest and Great Plains. You have seen that progress is being made toward solving some of these problems. With hard work and cooperation, the people of the Midwest and Great Plains can look forward to a future that is even better than the present.

Exploring Farm Problems

Imagine that you are a farmer in the Midwest and Great Plains who can no longer make a living by farming. You have been asked to write an article for a farm magazine, explaining why you have decided to sell your farm and move to a city. Include information such as the following in your article:

1. where your farm is located and how large it is
2. what main crop, or crops, you grow on your farm
3. reasons why you have found it difficult to earn a living from your farm

In addition to using the information in this chapter, you may wish to refer to Chapter 9 and to the Farming sections of Chapters 13-26. The suggestions on pages 346-351 will help you to locate other sources of information and to write your article.

Learn by Sharing Ideas

Some minority groups in our country face serious problems. As a class, discuss the following question:

Why do certain minority groups face serious problems?

To prepare for your discussion, read pages 131-137. The following questions will guide your reading:

1. What is a minority group? Name three of the minority groups in our country.
2. What serious problems do these minority groups face?
3. What is prejudice? Why do some people become prejudiced against members of certain minority groups?
4. What is discrimination? How can discrimination affect members of minority groups?

Make a Study of Automation

Automation is bringing great changes to our country. Do research to learn more about automation, and then prepare an oral report for your class. Your report should include answers to the following questions:

1. What does the word "automation" mean?
2. What is "feedback"?
3. What is "programming"?
4. What new jobs are being created by automation?
5. Why do companies often have difficulty in finding people to fill these jobs?

In addition to using the information in this chapter, you will need to do outside research. Refer to pages 346-352 for suggestions on finding information and preparing oral reports.

Learn From a Guest Speaker

One of the serious problems facing our big cities today is crime. What can you, as a citizen, do to prevent crime? Invite a member of your local police department or a social worker to speak to your class on this subject. Consider the following suggestions as you carry out this project:

1. Prepare for the speaker's visit by reading about crime prevention in newspapers and magazines.
2. Give the speaker your full attention.
3. Take brief notes on the parts of the speech that seem especially important.
4. When the speaker has finished, he may allow a question-and-answer period. Be prepared to ask him specific questions.

Keep Informed About City Problems

In addition to crime, other problems facing our cities today include air pollution, slums, and transportation problems. Newspapers and magazines frequently contain articles about these problems and about the progress that is being made in solving them. Keep a clipping file of articles on city problems and then make a bulletin board display of them. As a class, discuss the articles that are the most interesting.

Part 4
Earning a Living

Growing tomatoes in an Ohio greenhouse

Assembling tractors in an Illinois factory

Farmland in Iowa. Nature has provided the Midwest and Great Plains with large areas of level, fertile land and a climate that is generally well suited to farming. By using these resources wisely and by following modern, efficient farming methods, farmers here have made the Midwest and Great Plains our nation's most important farming area.

9   Farming

A Problem To Solve

The Midwest and Great Plains is one of the greatest farming areas in the world. **Why has farming become so important in this part of our country?** To solve this problem, you will need to make several hypotheses. In forming your hypotheses, you will want to consider facts about each of the following:

a. the soil and land features of the Midwest and Great Plains
b. the climate here
c. the farming methods used in this part of our country

See TO THE STUDENT, pages 8-10.

The Midwest and Great Plains is the most important farming area in the United States. Farmers here earn about half of our country's total farm income each year. Eight of our ten leading farming states are located in the Midwest and Great Plains. Farms in this part of our country provide us with many of the foods we eat. For example, more than half of our nation's beef cattle and four fifths of its hogs are raised here. Much of our clothing is made from cotton or wool produced in the Midwest and Great Plains. Hundreds of other products also come from the vast farmlands in this part of our country.

There are several reasons why farming is so important in the Midwest and Great Plains. Nowhere else in the world are there such large areas of fertile soil. Most of the land in the Midwest and Great Plains is level enough to be cultivated with modern farm machinery. The long, warm summers in most of this area are very good for growing crops. Rainfall is plentiful in the Midwest. Although many parts of the Great Plains states receive little rainfall, farmers here can earn a good living if they use the soil and water wisely.

Pioneer farming in the Midwest and Great Plains. Farms in the Midwest and Great Plains were not always as productive as they are today. To find out what farming was like a little over one hundred years ago, imagine that it is the year 1850. George Owen, his parents, and his brothers and sisters have recently arrived in Iowa from New York State. In a letter to a friend in New York, George describes his new home:

Dear William,

We've just finished building a log cabin on our new forty-acre farm. Pa says that we ought to be able to raise almost all the food we need on a farm of this size.

When we came here, the land was covered with tall prairie grass. This grass was so thick and the roots were so tough that ten oxen could hardly pull our plow through the fields. After we finally plowed the land, we planted corn, wheat, and a vegetable garden.

Our neighbors tell us that we can produce about twenty-five or thirty bushels of corn on one acre of land. We hope to harvest enough corn this year to fatten the hogs we brought with us from New York. Every day, my brothers and I spend six or seven hours in the fields with our hoes, helping Pa weed the corn. We also help feed the hogs and do a lot of other farm chores. If you want to work hard, come to Iowa!

Your friend,
George

A great revolution in farming. In the last one hundred years, great changes have taken place in our country's agriculture. As a result, most farms in Iowa today are very different from the one George described. To learn about some of the differences, we will visit a present-day farm in Iowa.

This farm covers more than four hundred acres, compared to the forty acres of the pioneer farm. The large frame house is much more comfortable than the crude log cabin George Owen's

Build Your Vocabulary

contour plowing   erosion   strip-cropping

dry farming   hybrid   irrigation   thresh   cash crop

cultivate   silage   crop rotation   fallow   combine

A REVOLUTION IN FARMING

Farming has changed greatly since the early days of our country. At that time, most farmers produced barely enough food for themselves and their families. Today, the average farmer in our country produces enough food for about thirty people.

There are many reasons why farm production has increased. Scientists have developed new varieties of plants that produce larger yields than older varieties. Better breeds of livestock have also been developed. It is now possible for farmers to enrich their soil with more effective chemical fertilizers. They can also kill harmful insects with newly developed chemicals. As a result of such advances, larger yields can now be produced on each acre of farmland. The invention of new farm machines has also helped increase production. For example, a harvesting machine called a combine not only cuts grain but also threshes* and cleans it. With modern equipment, one man can farm much more land than in the past.

Increased farm production in the United States has resulted in two important trends. First, the number of farmers needed to feed our people is decreasing. In the early years of our country, about nine out of every ten persons worked on farms. Today, only seven out of every one hundred workers are farmers. Second, the size of farms is increasing. This is partly because a farmer must produce a large amount of farm products in order to earn an adequate living. Also, most farm machines are too large and expensive to be used effectively on small farms. Today, the size of the average farm in the United States is about three hundred acres.

The use of modern farm machinery helps farmers to increase their production.

family lived in. Not far from the house are more than half a dozen other farm buildings. We see a large barn for cattle, a long, low building for hogs, three metal corncribs, and two large sheds for tractors and other farm machinery.

It is September, and the farmer has just finished plowing a field in preparation for planting oats next spring. We watch him drive his tractor into one of the sheds. This tractor can do the work of many horses or oxen. When the farmer uses it to pull his heavy plow, he can turn over more soil in a few hours than a pioneer farmer could in several days.

We go with the farmer to look at one of his cornfields. The corn here will soon be ready to harvest. It is so tall that we have to look up in order to see the tops of the stalks. The farmer says this field will produce about one hundred bushels of corn an acre.

We ask the farmer how he is able to produce such large yields of corn. He replies that several things make it possible. Nature has given him fertile soil, hot summer days, and plentiful rainfall. To get such large yields, however, the farmer also needs the help of modern science. For example, he plants hybrid* corn. This kind of corn was developed by plant scientists in the 1930's. It produces up to one-third more corn per acre than older varieties. The farmer also adds chemical fertilizers to the soil to keep it in good condition for growing crops. He uses newly developed chemicals to kill weeds and insects and to prevent diseases that might harm the growing corn.

As on many other farms in Iowa, much of the corn grown here is fed to

*See Glossary

148

Farm experts inspecting hybrid wheat in Kansas. To succeed in farming today, farmers must be able to do more than just raise crops and livestock. They must keep up with the latest scientific developments in agriculture. In addition, farmers need to know how and when to sell their products to earn the most profit, and how to manage money wisely.

hogs. The farmer that we are visiting raises several hundred hogs each year. Most of these are sold to a large meat-packing company, which will slaughter them and prepare the meat for market.

The farmer tells us that to succeed in farming, he must be able to do more than grow crops and raise livestock. He must know how and when to sell his farm products in order to earn the most profit. From time to time, the farmer must buy more supplies or a new piece of farm machinery. To meet these expenses, he must be able to manage his money wisely.

The farmer's oldest son is now attending college, where he is studying both agriculture and business. This will help prepare him for a career in farming. Even after his schooling is finished, however, he will still have to study books and magazines to keep up with the latest developments in agriculture.

Our visit to a modern Iowa farm has shown us some of the great changes that have taken place in American farming during the last one hundred years. These changes are part of a great "revolution" in farming, which is described in the feature on page 148.

Saving nature's riches. Nature gave farmers in the Midwest and Great Plains vast areas of fertile land. In the past, however, many farmers did not take good care of this valuable resource. Some farmers planted the same crop, such as corn, on the same land year after year. This removed large amounts of plant foods from the soil. As a result, the soil gradually became less fertile.

Sometimes poor farming methods caused soil erosion.* Before the Midwest and Great Plains was settled, most of the land was covered with grass or trees. The roots of these plants held the soil in place, keeping it from being washed away by rainwater or carried away by the wind. When the land was cleared and used for growing crops, the soil was no longer protected from erosion. In some places, rainwater washed away much fertile topsoil and cut deep gullies in the surface of the earth. In other places, strong winds picked up large amounts of topsoil and carried it away. This was the main cause of the Dust Bowl* in the 1930's. After the fertile topsoil had been removed, the land could no longer be used for growing crops.

Farmers have learned that if they wish to produce large crops, they must take good care of their land. In other words, they must practice conservation. Throughout the Midwest and Great Plains, just as in other parts of our country, farmers use various methods to keep the soil fertile and to prevent erosion.

An abandoned farm, covered with dust. In the past, many farmers in the Midwest and Great Plains did not take good care of their land. Wind and rainwater carried away large amounts of fertile topsoil. After the topsoil had been removed, the land could no longer be used for growing crops. Farmers have learned that if they wish to produce large crops, they must take care of their land.

Today many farmers no longer grow the same crop on the same land year after year. Instead, they grow different crops on the same land in different years. This procedure is called crop rotation. For example, one year a farmer may plant a crop such as corn, which removes large amounts of plant foods from the soil. The next year or two, he may raise a rotation crop such as soybeans, clover, or alfalfa. These crops require smaller amounts of certain plant foods than corn does. Sometimes the farmer may plow a rotation crop into the soil to help restore fertility. By the third or fourth year, the land is ready for growing corn again.

Many farmers today use chemical fertilizers to help keep their soil productive. These fertilizers replace some of the plant foods that corn and other crops take out of the soil.

Farmers use various methods to lessen soil erosion. To conserve soil on sloping land, they often plow rows that curve around the hillsides instead of up-and-down rows. (See picture on this page.) This is known as contour plowing. The furrows made by the plow catch the rainwater so that it cannot rush down the hillside and wash the fertile topsoil away.

In parts of the Great Plains states where rainfall is light, farmers must conserve moisture as well as soil. They have developed certain methods of growing crops without irrigation. This kind of farming is known as "dry farming."

Farmers who practice dry farming leave part of their land idle, or fallow, each year. Rain that falls on the fallow land is stored in the soil. When crops are grown on this land the following

Contour plowing in Michigan. To conserve soil on sloping land, farmers often plow rows that curve around hillsides instead of up-and-down rows. This helps prevent rainwater from rushing down hillsides and washing away fertile topsoil.

year, they can use the stored-up moisture. Therefore, they will not need so much rainfall.

When land is left fallow, the strong winds that sweep across the plains may blow much soil away. To prevent this, many wheat farmers practice "strip-cropping." They plant their wheat in long, narrow strips between strips of fallow land. The stalks of wheat slow down the wind so that it does not strike the bare soil with its full force. Many farmers also plant rows of trees along the edges of their fields. These are known as "windbreaks" or "shelterbelts." They, too, break the force of the wind and help to prevent soil erosion.

In order to make a good profit, farmers raise the crops and animals best suited to the land and climate where they live. Within the Midwest and Great Plains are several large areas where the land and climate favor a particular kind of farming. The map on the opposite page shows these main farming areas. It is important to remember, however, that other crops and animals are raised in addition to the main ones in each area.

The dairy belt. Most of Wisconsin, Minnesota, and Michigan lie in the dairy belt. Here, the raising of cows for milk is the main type of farming. Several facts help explain why dairying is so important in these areas. Summers

In the dairy belt, raising cows for milk is the main type of farming. This belt includes most parts of Wisconsin, Minnesota, and Michigan. Midwestern cities provide a huge market for dairy products.

here are generally cooler than they are elsewhere in the Midwest, and rainfall is plentiful. This kind of climate is very good for growing grass, which can be cut for hay or used for grazing. Also, cows give more milk if the weather is not too hot in the summertime. In many parts of the dairy belt, the land is too hilly or the soil is too poor for growing most crops. Even so, these areas can be used as pasture for dairy cattle.

By comparing the maps on pages 140 and 153, you can see that a number of large cities lie in or near the dairy belt. Because fresh milk is bulky and spoils quickly, it is seldom shipped long distances. Therefore, dairy farms are usually located as close as possible to their customers. The cities of the Midwest provide a huge market for dairy products.

Wisconsin produces more milk than any other state in our country. If you were to travel through this state in the summertime, you would see many herds of dairy cattle grazing in rolling green pastures. You would also see large, well-kept barns with tall, round silos.

Most farms in the dairy belt are not very large. Because the grass here is thick and nourishing, large areas of grazing land are not needed. Many dairy farmers raise alfalfa, clover, or timothy for hay. Corn is also grown on many farms. In places where the growing season is too short for corn to ripen fully, the corn is harvested before it is ripe and chopped into silage.*

Farmers who live near cities usually sell their milk to dairies. These plants

MAJOR TYPES OF FARMING IN THE UNITED STATES

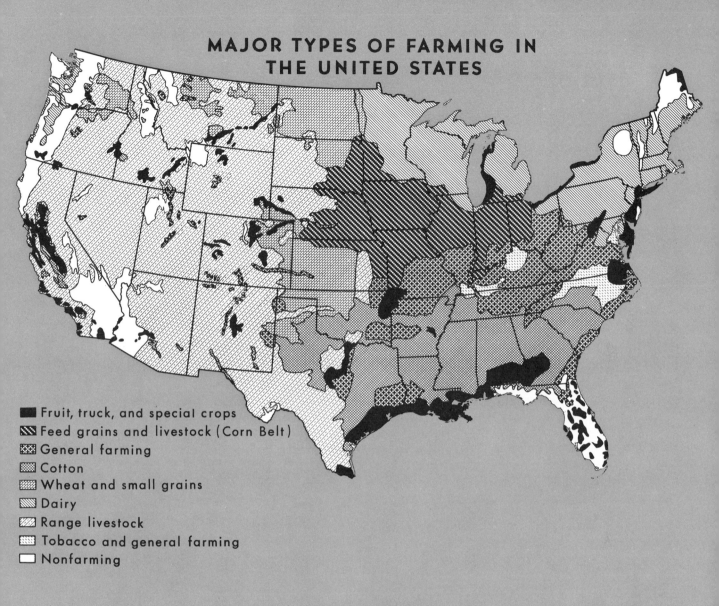

Fruit, truck, and special crops
Feed grains and livestock (Corn Belt)
General farming
Cotton
Wheat and small grains
Dairy
Range livestock
Tobacco and general farming
Nonfarming

Major types of farming. The map above shows the major types of farming in the conterminous United States. Within the Midwest and Great Plains are several large areas, such as the corn belt, where the land and climate favor a particular kind of farming.

pasteurize the milk and put it into bottles or cartons for sale to customers. Farmers who do not live close to cities sell milk to nearby plants that make such products as butter, cheese, and ice cream. If they are properly stored, these products keep for a long time without spoiling. Therefore, they can be shipped long distances. About 40 percent of the cheese made in the United States comes from Wisconsin. Minnesota produces

more butter than any other state. Plants in Michigan make large quantities of ice cream.

The corn belt. The corn belt covers part of every state in the Midwest and Great Plains except Texas and Oklahoma. It is the most fertile farming area of its size in the world. The rich, black soil and warm, humid summers here are especially well suited for growing corn.

153

Each year, farms in the corn belt produce about three fourths of our country's corn and about two fifths of all the corn grown in the world. Iowa and Illinois are our nation's leading corn-producing states.

The corn belt could also be called the "meat belt." Most of the corn grown here is used by farmers to fatten many millions of hogs and cattle. When these animals are fat enough, they are shipped to stockyards in Omaha, Chicago, and other cities. About three fourths of the money earned by farmers in the corn belt comes from the sale of livestock. Iowa and Illinois lead all the states in the amount of money earned from the sale of hogs, and Iowa and Nebraska lead in earnings from cattle.

Corn is not only used as feed for livestock, but it is also an important raw material for industry. Factories use it in making cornstarch, cooking oil, breakfast cereal, and other items that you can probably find on the kitchen shelves in your home. Various substances obtained from corn are used in manufacturing hundreds of different products, including soap, glue, and paper.

In recent years, soybeans have become an important cash* crop in the corn belt. The soybean plant has many

Harvesting corn in Illinois. The corn belt covers part of every state in the Midwest and Great Plains except Texas and Oklahoma. Each year, farms in the corn belt produce about two fifths of all the corn grown in the world. Most of the corn grown in this area is used to fatten hogs and beef cattle. Several other crops are also raised in the corn belt, including soybeans and oats.

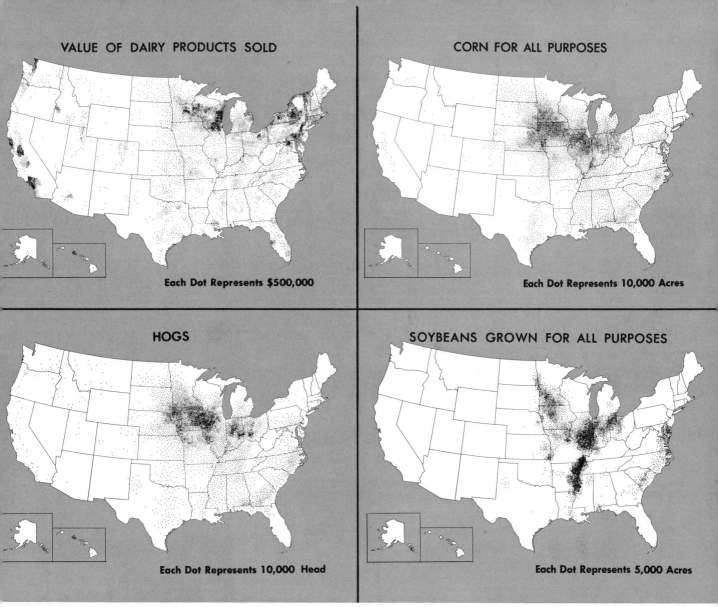

VALUE OF DAIRY PRODUCTS SOLD

Each Dot Represents $500,000

CORN FOR ALL PURPOSES

Each Dot Represents 10,000 Acres

HOGS

Each Dot Represents 10,000 Head

SOYBEANS GROWN FOR ALL PURPOSES

Each Dot Represents 5,000 Acres

Dairy products, corn, hogs, and soybeans come from farms in all the states of the Midwest and Great Plains. Wisconsin produces more milk than any other state in the nation. Illinois and Iowa are our country's leading producers of corn, hogs, and soybeans.

uses. Farmers feed the vines to animals or plow them back into the soil to replace plant foods taken from it by other crops. Manufacturers make both meal and oil from the beans. Soybean meal is a good feed for livestock, and soybean oil is used in making margarine, linoleum, and many other products. Our nation's leading producers of soybeans are Illinois and Iowa.

Other crops are also raised in the corn belt. After corn, the two most im-

portant feed crops are oats and hay. These are often planted as rotation crops on land where corn is grown. Soybeans or wheat sometimes take the place of oats or hay as rotation crops.

Two wheat belts. It is a warm, sunny morning in late June. We are visiting a wheat farm that covers nearly five hundred acres in western Kansas. The owner has invited us to see how his wheat is harvested. From the cab of his truck, we look out on golden fields of wheat separated by brown strips of fallow land.

To the right of the truck, a machine called a combine is moving slowly through the wheat. As the combine moves, it cuts and threshes* all the wheat in its path. Then the grain is blown through a long spout into the back of the truck. Before long, the farmer tells us that we have a full load of wheat. We take the wheat to a nearby railroad station, where it is put into a huge grain elevator. The wheat will be kept in this elevator until a train comes to carry it to Kansas City, where it will be made into flour.

More wheat is produced in the Great Plains states than in any other part of our country. In much of this area, the land and climate are better suited to growing wheat than any other crop. There are large areas of fertile soil. Rainfall in many parts of the Great

Combines harvesting wheat in Nebraska. More wheat is produced in the Great Plains states than in any other part of our country.

Plains states is too light for growing such crops as corn and soybeans, but there is usually enough rain for wheat. Because so much of the land here is level, farmers can use modern farm machines to plant and harvest their wheat.

There are two main wheat-producing areas in the Great Plains states. The most important is the winter wheat belt, which extends across central and western Kansas and Oklahoma and the Texas Panhandle. Here, farmers plant their wheat in late summer or early fall. The young plants grow about six inches before winter comes, and then do not grow again until spring. By early summer, the grain is ripe and ready to harvest. More than three fourths of all the wheat grown in our country is winter wheat. Kansas produces more wheat than any other state.

North of the winter wheat belt is another large wheat-producing area. Here, winters are too cold for young wheat plants to survive. Farmers in this area plant their wheat in the spring. For this reason, this area is called the spring wheat belt. Spring wheat is ready to harvest in late summer or early fall. North Dakota is our country's leading producer of spring wheat.

Sometimes, in the winter wheat belt, rainfall may be especially light for months or even years at a time. A severe drought can ruin the wheat crop and cost farmers large sums of money. To protect themselves against a loss of this kind, many farmers raise other things in addition to wheat. Beef cattle, for example, are often raised on wheat farms. They are allowed to graze on the young wheat stalks during the winter months. Farmers in the winter wheat

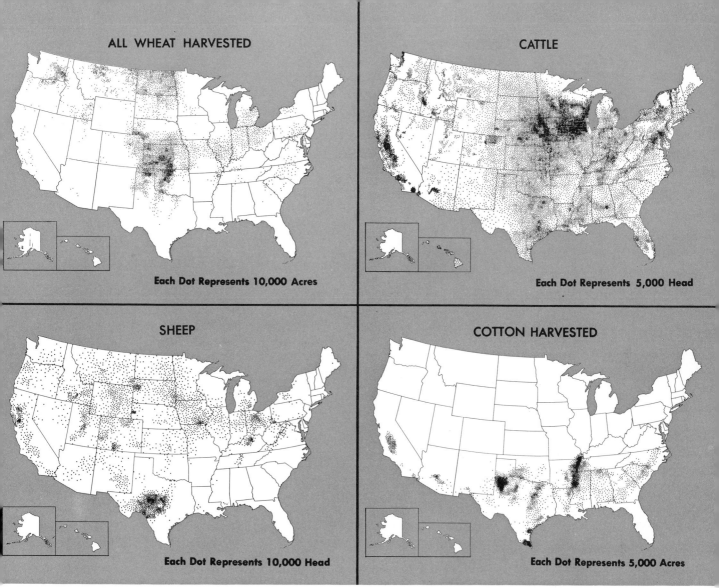

ALL WHEAT HARVESTED

Each Dot Represents 10,000 Acres

CATTLE

Each Dot Represents 5,000 Head

SHEEP

Each Dot Represents 10,000 Head

COTTON HARVESTED

Each Dot Represents 5,000 Acres

Wheat, cattle, sheep, and cotton. Kansas and North Dakota lead all our states in wheat production. Cotton, which needs a long growing season, is grown only in the southern part of the Midwest and Great Plains. Cattle and sheep are raised in every state in this part of our country. The cattle map above includes both beef and dairy cattle.

belt also raise sorghum. This crop grows well even in places where the weather is very dry. Large amounts of sorghum are used for fattening cattle in feedlots in the Great Plains states.

Rangelands. Some parts of the Great Plains states are too dry or too rugged for growing crops. Here much of the land is covered with short grass. At one time, great herds of buffalo fed on these grasslands, which are called ranges. Today the rangelands are used for grazing beef cattle and other livestock.

In the rangelands, livestock are usually raised on large farms called ranches. These vary in size from two or three thousand acres to more than one-half million acres. Ranches must be large because as many as fifty acres of grassland may be needed to feed each animal. In some places, cattle drink from streams or water holes. Where surface water is scarce, wells are an important source of drinking water for cattle. On many ranches, tall windmills pump this water from deep underground.

A cattle ranch. Some parts of the Great Plains states are too dry or too rugged for growing crops. Here, beef cattle and other livestock graze on the short grass that covers much of the land.

Three of the Great Plains states rank next to Iowa in the production of beef cattle. These are Nebraska, Texas, and Kansas. Some of the cattle raised on grasslands in these states are shipped directly to stockyards in cities such as Omaha, Chicago, and Kansas City. However, cattle fed only on grass may be too lean to slaughter for meat. Many grass-fed cattle are sold to farmers in the corn belt. These cattle are put into feedlots, where they are fattened on corn and other grains. After they have been fattened, trucks or trains carry them to the stockyards.

Ranchers in the drier parts of the Great Plains states also raise many thousands of sheep and Angora goats. These animals do not need as much grass and water as cattle do. Sometimes, cattle, sheep, and goats are raised on the same ranch. Cattle are given the best land, and the goats and sheep graze on the rest. Angora goats are valued for their long, silky hair, which is used to make mohair.* Most of the sheep that graze on the Great Plains are raised for their wool. Those raised for meat are sent to feedlots for fattening.

The cotton belt. Every fall, many fields in Texas turn almost snow-white. These are fields of cotton. During the long, warm summer, the seed pods, or bolls, on the cotton plants have been ripening. When they are fully ripe, they burst open, exposing the white, fluffy cotton fibers. Cotton-picking machines move slowly along the rows, stripping the ripe bolls from the plants. The cotton is taken to large buildings in nearby towns where gins* separate the fibers from the sticky cotton seeds. Then machines press the cotton into tightly packed bundles, called bales. The baled cotton is shipped to textile mills, where it is spun into yarn for making cloth.

Texas produces nearly one third of all the cotton grown in our nation. This crop is raised in many parts of the state. However, the state's most important cotton-growing area is in western Texas, near New Mexico. (Compare maps'on pages 157 and 333.) This is one of the most productive cotton-growing areas in the United States.

Western Texas has become a major cotton-producing area only within the last fifty years. Before 1900, nearly all of our country's cotton was grown in an area extending from South Carolina and Georgia westward into eastern Texas.

In the early 1900's, many cotton farmers faced a growing number of problems. In some areas, the land had been used so many years for growing cotton that it was no longer very fertile. Also, poor farming methods had caused serious soil erosion in some places. In addition, an insect known as the boll weevil had begun to cause great damage to cotton crops all the way from Texas to the Atlantic coast.

Gradually, many new cotton farms were started in areas west of the old cotton belt. One of these areas was western Texas. Here, there were large stretches of level, fertile land. The growing season was long enough for cotton. Although rainfall was fairly light in this area, there was usually enough for growing cotton. Also, farmers could irrigate their fields with water from nearby wells. Even more important,

the boll weevil was not a problem to farmers in western Texas. Here, the weather was too dry and the winters were too cold for this insect to survive.

The development of cotton-harvesting machines in the 1930's and 1940's gave farmers in western Texas another advantage over farmers in many other cotton-growing areas. With the new machines, farmers could harvest their cotton much more quickly and efficiently than was possible by hand. However, in states east of Texas, much of the land where cotton was grown was too hilly for using these machines successfully. Also, the machines were expensive to buy and operate. Many farms in the old cotton belt were small, and it was not profitable for farmers to buy such expensive machines. In western

Harvesting cotton. Texas produces almost one third of our country's total cotton crop each year. There are large areas of level, fertile land in Texas, and the growing season is long enough for cotton in nearly every part of the state.

Texas, on the other hand, many cotton farms covered hundreds of acres. Because most of the land was level, farmers could easily use machines to harvest their cotton crops.

Although Texas is by far the most important cotton-growing state in the Midwest and Great Plains, cotton is also produced in Missouri and Oklahoma. (See map on page 157.) Missouri's cotton-growing area is located in the southeastern tip of the state, in the Coastal Plain. Oklahoma's cotton is grown mainly in the southwestern part of the state.

Orchards and truck farms. In a few parts of the Midwest and Great Plains, farmers grow large amounts of fruits and vegetables. Along the eastern shore of Lake Michigan and the southern shore of Lake Erie, the climate is well suited to growing fruit. (See page 62.) For example, Michigan is one of the nation's leading fruit-growing states. Farmers here grow such fruits as apples, cherries, and peaches.

In the lower Rio Grande Valley of Texas, there are many groves of grapefruit and orange trees. Citrus fruits such as these cannot be grown where winters are cold. Winters in the lower Rio Grande Valley are usually mild and sunny. Occasionally, however, cold winds from the north sweep across the valley, killing thousands of fruit trees. Rainfall is light here, so the fruit trees must be irrigated with water from the Rio Grande.

Many different kinds of vegetables are grown on irrigated truck* farms in the lower Rio Grande Valley. During the winter months, large crops of carrots, cabbages, and other vegetables are shipped from here to colder parts of our country.

During the summer months, vegetables are raised in many parts of the Midwest and Great Plains. Farmers in each area grow the kinds of vegetables that are best suited to the soil and climate of that area. For example, potatoes can be raised where the growing season is too short and cool for many other kinds of crops. The chapters in Parts 5 and 6 of this book provide information about the main types of vegetables grown in the different states of the Midwest and Great Plains.

Questions To Help You Learn
1. Describe some of the methods used by farmers in the Midwest and Great Plains to take good care of their land.
2. What are some of the causes of soil erosion?
3. Why is dairying the most important kind of farming in the northern part of the Midwest?
4. Name some of the main uses for corn raised in the corn belt.

Discuss the Revolution in Farming
Great changes have taken place in farming in our country during the past hundred years. As a class, discuss these changes. In your discussion, consider:
1. scientific developments that have been helpful to farmers
2. changes in the way in which work is done on farms

Use Your Reasoning Ability
Choose a state in the Midwest and Great Plains that you, as a farmer, would find well suited to raising each of the following:

spring wheat   cotton
beef cattle   dairy cows
corn   winter wheat

State the reasons for each choice.

Oil derricks in Oklahoma City, Oklahoma. The Midwest and Great Plains has abundant natural resources, including minerals, forests, and fisheries. By using their resources wisely, the people of the Midwest and Great Plains can enjoy a high standard of living.

10 Natural Resources

A Study Guide

As you read about the natural resources of the Midwest and Great Plains, try to answer the following questions:

1. What are some of the important natural resources of the Midwest and Great Plains?
2. In what ways have the people here used their resources?
3. Why are some of these resources less plentiful today than they once were?
4. What is being done to conserve natural resources in the Midwest and Great Plains?

The Midwest and Great Plains has abundant natural resources. Rich soil, plentiful rainfall, and warm sunshine are among nature's most important gifts to the people of the Midwest and Great Plains. In addition to these resources, the Midwest and Great Plains has vast deposits of useful minerals. It also has valuable forests and fisheries.

Today, the people who live in this part of our country usually make good use of the gifts nature has given them. Chapter 9 tells how some resources have been used to make the Midwest and Great Plains a productive farming area. By using all of their resources wisely, the people here can enjoy a high standard of living.

Mineral Resources

The Midwest and Great Plains is rich in mineral resources. The Midwest and Great Plains has deposits of many different kinds of minerals. Each year, this part of our country produces minerals worth more than eight billion dollars. This is nearly half the value of our country's total mineral output. The minerals produced in the Midwest and Great Plains are used as sources of heat and power, and as raw materials from which thousands of different products are made.

PETROLEUM AND NATURAL GAS

The leading mineral resources of the Midwest and Great Plains. Petroleum and natural gas are the most valuable minerals produced in the Midwest and Great Plains. These two important resources account for more than half the value of the total mineral production of this part of our country.

Petroleum and natural gas affect the lives of everyone in the United States, either directly or indirectly. In the wintertime, millions of homes, factories, and other buildings are heated by furnaces that burn fuel oil or natural gas. Many power plants use oil or gas for generating electricity. Fuels for automobiles, airplanes, and diesel locomotives are made from petroleum. In addition, petroleum and natural gas provide raw materials for the manufacture of hundreds of different products. These include synthetic* fibers for textiles, synthetic rubber, and medicines.

Most deposits of petroleum are located far beneath the surface of the earth. The special feature on page 163 explains how these deposits were formed. Because petroleum usually lies buried under thousands of feet of rock, it is very hard to find. The only sure way to discover a deposit of petroleum is to drill for it. Oil companies spend many millions of dollars every year drilling wells in areas where oil has not previously been found. These are called wildcat wells. Only about one out of every nine wildcat wells succeeds in striking oil.

Deposits of petroleum are always accompanied by natural gas. Gas, however, sometimes occurs alone. Natural gas provides additional mineral products called natural-gas liquids. These are valuable liquids, such as natural gasoline, which are separated from the gas before it is forced into pipelines for distribution as a fuel.

Our country's greatest deposits of petroleum and natural gas are found in the Great Plains states. Maps on page 169 show where our country's main deposits of petroleum and natural gas are located.

*See Glossary

Build Your Vocabulary

wood pulp	fisheries	coke	bituminous coal
taconite	iron ore	groundwater	reservoir
petroleum	natural gas	crude oil	lignite	Mesabi Range

Where We Get Our Oil

Drilling an oil well. To obtain petroleum, oilmen must drill wells deep into the earth.

Petroleum, or crude* oil, is one of man's most useful mineral resources. Hundreds of important products are made from this valuable mineral.

How oil is formed. Most scientists believe that oil was formed millions of years ago, long before man appeared on earth. Much of the earth that is now dry land was then covered by shallow seas. Billions of tiny plants and animals lived in the water. As they died, they sank to the bottom. Over a period of millions of years, sand and soil were carried down to the sea by rivers. They covered the remains of the dead plants and animals. Gradually, the sand and soil turned into rock. The pressure of the layers of rock helped change the plant and animal matter into petroleum. In many places the land later rose, causing the seas to recede.

Where we find oil. As the diagram on this page shows, deposits of oil, gas, and water have accumulated in traps deep beneath the earth's surface. Through the centuries, the crust* of the earth has heaved and shifted many times, forming traps like these. Anticline traps, such as the one shown on the diagram, were formed when layers of rock bent upward to form an arch, or anticline. Fault traps were formed by the shifting of layers of rock. Oil, gas, and water moved upward through tiny openings in porous* rock, such as sandstone. Finally, they were stopped by a layer of nonporous rock, such as shale.

How we drill for oil. To obtain oil from underground traps, oilmen must drill wells deep into the earth. A tool called a rock bit is attached to the bottom of a long column of drill pipe. (See picture on this page.) The drill pipe is supported by a tall, steel derrick. Powerful machinery makes the drill pipe rotate, and the bit bores through the earth and hard rock.

Finally, the bit reaches the underground oil deposit. In some wells, the pressure of water or natural gas in the deposit causes the oil to flow to the surface by itself. At other times, pumps must be used to bring the oil up from the well. After the oil is brought to the surface, it is sent to refineries, where it is made into gasoline and other useful products.

*See Glossary

A natural-gas pumping station in Kansas. Petroleum and natural gas are the most valuable minerals produced in the Midwest and Great Plains. Our country's greatest deposits of petroleum and natural gas are found in the Great Plains states.

Deposits in the Great Plains states provide almost half of the nation's petroleum and more than half of its natural gas. No other part of our country has such abundant supplies of these important mineral resources.

Texas leads all of our states in the production of petroleum, natural gas, and natural-gas liquids. Oklahoma ranks fourth in the production of these minerals. Kansas, Nebraska, and North Dakota are also important producers. Large quantities of oil have been produced in Texas since 1901, when the state's first great oil field was discovered. Today, there are about 200,000 oil wells in various parts of the state. In recent years, wells have also been drilled off the coast of Texas. Here, oil is pumped from deposits that lie deep in the earth beneath the Gulf of Mexico.

Crude* oil is processed in industrial plants called refineries. These plants produce gasoline, kerosene, and other petroleum products. Some of the oil pumped from wells in the Great Plains states is sent by pipeline, boat, truck, or train to refineries in other parts of our country. Much of it, however, is refined within the area, especially along the Gulf coast of Texas. Here are also many plants that use petroleum and natural-gas products to make petrochemicals.* Texas leads the nation in the refining of petroleum and in the manufacture of petrochemicals.

Petroleum and natural gas are also found in the Midwest. In some parts of the Midwest there are valuable deposits of petroleum and natural gas. Illinois ranks eighth in the nation in the production of petroleum. Other states of the Midwest that produce important amounts of oil are Ohio, Michigan, and Indiana. Altogether, however, the states of the Midwest produce only about one twelfth as much petroleum as the Great Plains states. Ohio and Michigan are the Midwest's leading producers of natural gas.

COAL

A visit to a coal mine. We are visiting an open-pit coal mine in southern Illinois. (See picture on page 165.) This kind of mine is also called a strip mine. It looks like a narrow valley, or trench, several blocks long. In the picture, the land that has not yet been stripped of coal is shown at the left. The area that has already been stripped of coal is at the right.

Several different operations are going on in the mine. The largest machine in the trench is a giant excavator. This machine is removing soil from the surface of the land at the left and piling it far to the right on top of ridges of waste material. On the ledge made by the excavator, rock is being drilled in preparation for blasting with explosives. The blasting will loosen the rock. A huge power shovel is picking up rock that has already been loosened and is dumping it along the opposite side of the trench. Gradually, this huge shovel is uncovering the long seam of coal that lies under the rock.

A smaller power shovel, shown in the foreground of the picture, is digging coal from the bottom of the trench and loading it onto a truck. The truck will carry the coal to a nearby preparation plant where it will be cleaned and sorted. Then the coal will be loaded onto railroad cars and carried to power plants, factories, and retail dealers.

Coal that lies fairly near the surface of the earth is easily obtained by strip mining. About one third of all the coal produced in the United States is mined by this method. The rest comes from underground mines. As you can see from the picture below, strip mining leaves the land unfit for farming. Many coal mining companies, however, try to restore strip-mined areas to usefulness. Sometimes the land is smoothed, replanted with grass, and used for grazing. Much of the strip-mined land in Illinois and Indiana has been made into lakes and recreational areas.

There are huge deposits of coal in the Midwest and Great Plains. The Midwest and Great Plains has enormous coal

An open-pit coal mine in southern Illinois. There are huge deposits of coal in the Midwest and Great Plains. Illinois, Ohio, and Indiana are among our nation's ten leading coal-producing states. Most of the coal mined in the Midwest and Great Plains is used as fuel for generating electricity and for heating buildings.

resources. (See map below.) Several states in the Midwest are among our nation's leading producers of coal. Illinois ranks fourth, Ohio fifth, and Indiana eighth. The coal mined in the Midwest is high-grade soft coal, also called bituminous coal. Very little bituminous coal is mined in the Great Plains states. North Dakota has our country's largest deposits of a kind of coal called lignite.

Bituminous coal. The most useful kind of coal found in our country is bituminous coal. (See below.) There are two main types of bituminous coal, coking and noncoking. When coking coal is roasted in airtight ovens, it forms a mass of grayish-black material called coke. This is the fuel used in blast furnaces for smelting* iron ore. Almost all of the good coking coal mined in

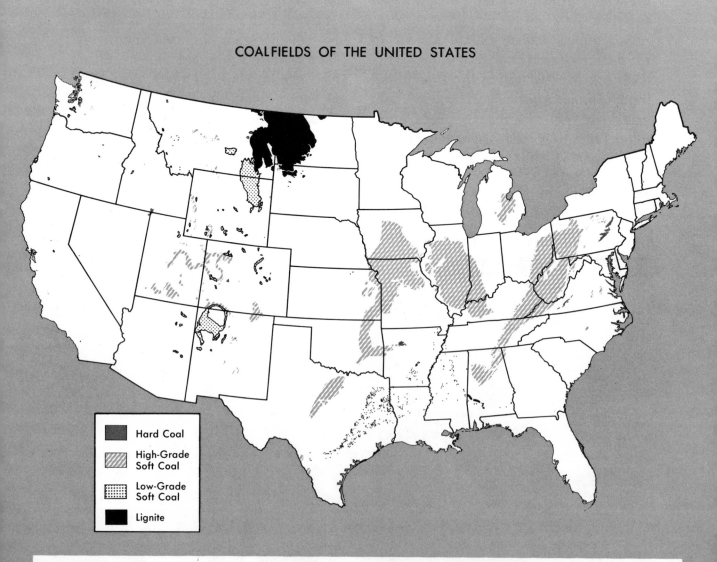

COALFIELDS OF THE UNITED STATES

Hard Coal

High-Grade Soft Coal

Low-Grade Soft Coal

Lignite

Coal is a rocklike substance composed mainly of carbon* and water. There are four main kinds of coal. Hard coal, or anthracite, has a very high carbon content, and burns with little smoke. High-grade soft coal, or bituminous coal, also has a high carbon content, but it generally gives off more smoke than anthracite does. Low-grade soft coal, or subbituminous coal, is about three-fourths carbon and one-fourth water. Lignite, a still poorer quality coal, is about half water.

The main coal deposits in the conterminous* United States are shown on the map above. Notice that there are large deposits of high-grade soft coal in several states of the Midwest and Great Plains. Our country's largest deposits of lignite are found in North Dakota.

our country comes from the Northeast and the South. (Compare map on page 21 with map on page 166.) Although the bituminous coal found in the Midwest gives off just as much heat, very little of it can be used for making coke.

The noncoking coal mined in the Midwest has several important uses. It is used in heating homes, factories, and other buildings. It is also used as a fuel in the production of cement. About two thirds of all the Midwest's coal is used for generating electricity. At power plants, the coal is used to heat water, producing the steam needed to turn powerful engines called turbines. The turbines run machines called generators, which produce electricity. Most of the electricity used in the Midwest comes from steam power plants that burn coal.

Lignite. Most of the coal found in the Great Plains states is lignite. When lignite is burned, it does not give off as much heat as bituminous coal. About 90 percent of all the lignite mined in the United States is produced in North Dakota. It is used mainly as a fuel for generating electricity and for heating homes and other buildings.

IRON ORE

Iron mining in Minnesota. Thousands of people in Minnesota earn their living by working in iron mines. Most of the mines are located along a line of low hills called the Mesabi Range. This range extends for more than one hundred miles through northeastern Minnesota. The width of the range varies from about one to three miles.

Most of the iron ore that comes from the Mesabi Range is dug from open-pit mines. (See picture on page 168.) An open-pit iron mine may be as much as a mile across and five hundred feet deep. At the bottom, workers operate huge power shovels that scoop up tons of iron ore from the earth. Trucks or conveyor* belts carry the ore up out of the mine.

Each year, millions of tons of iron ore dug from mines in the Mesabi Range are carried by train to Duluth and other ports on Lake Superior. Here, the ore is dumped into huge ore boats. These boats carry the ore to Chicago, Detroit, and other Great Lakes port cities.

The history of the Mesabi Range. Iron ore was first discovered in Minnesota in the 1850's. By the end of the century, several companies were mining iron ore from the Mesabi Range. This ore contained over 50 percent iron. Until the 1950's, Minnesota's Mesabi Range continued to produce enormous quantities of high-grade iron ore. Gradually, however, much of the richest ore was used up, and some mines were forced to close.

Vast deposits of a low-grade iron ore called taconite remained in the Mesabi Range. Taconite is a hard rock that contains only about 20 to 30 percent iron. Because there is so little iron in taconite, it is not profitable to use it in blast furnaces for making iron and steel.

One hope remained for Minnesota's iron-mining industry. If a way could be found to turn taconite into a richer ore, the Mesabi Range could still provide huge amounts of iron. After many years of experimenting, scientists worked out a method for producing high-grade ore from taconite at a reasonable cost. The taconite is crushed and ground into a fine powder. Magnets are used

An open-pit iron mine in Minnesota. About three fifths of the iron ore mined in our country comes from Minnesota. Michigan is also a major producer of this important mineral.

to separate particles that contain iron from the waste materials in the powder. Then these iron-rich particles are formed into grape-sized pellets and baked. The pellets are over 60 percent iron. This is a higher iron content than is found in most natural ores.

During the 1950's, several new taconite mines were opened in the Mesabi Range. A number of plants for processing taconite were also built, and additional plants are now under construction. Each year, millions of tons of taconite pellets are shipped from northern Minnesota to steelmaking cities on or near the Great Lakes.

Minnesota leads the nation in the production of iron ore. About three fifths of all the iron ore produced in our country comes from Minnesota. The Mesabi Range is the state's main producing dis-

trict, but iron ore is also mined from two smaller ranges in northern Minnesota.

Today, much of Minnesota's iron ore production is in the form of taconite pellets. In the Mesabi Range are many new taconite mines, as well as mills for crushing the ore. Whole new towns have been built up around some of the huge taconite-processing plants. By the time Minnesota's vast supplies of taconite are used up, there will probably be ways of using even poorer quality ore from the Mesabi Range.

Iron ore in other states of the Midwest. Minnesota's iron ranges are part of a large iron-bearing district near Lake Superior. This district extends into Michigan's Upper Peninsula. At one time, more iron ore was mined in Michigan than in Minnesota. As the richer ores were used up, production declined. Today, Michigan ranks second among our states in iron ore production.

Michigan, like Minnesota, is beginning to produce pellets from low-grade iron ore. In fact, the largest pelletizing plant in the world is located near Marquette, in Michigan's Upper Peninsula. A kind of rock called jaspilite,* which is similar to taconite, is used for making the pellets. It is concentrated by a somewhat different process than the one used for taconite. The pellets produced in northern Michigan are shipped to steel mills on or near the Great Lakes.

Iron ore has been mined in Missouri for many years. Today this state ranks fourth in the nation in the mining of iron ore. Most of the deposits are in the southeastern part of the state, in the Ozarks. Recent discoveries of iron ore in Missouri have helped to increase the state's production of this mineral.

OTHER MINERALS

Copper, lead, and gold. In addition to iron, the Midwest and Great Plains has deposits of several other valuable metals. Michigan ranks fifth in the United States in the production of copper. (See pages 242 and 243.) Missouri ranks first among all the states of our country in the production of lead ore. Lead is a soft, heavy metal. It is used in making storage batteries, ammunition, and many other products. In addition, chemicals that contain lead are used in paint and gasoline. South Dakota is famous as our country's chief producer of gold. A huge mine here, called the Homestake Gold Mine, produces more of this precious metal than any other mine in our country.

Limestone. The Midwest and Great Plains has enormous deposits of limestone. (See map on this page.) This is a kind of rock that varies in color from white to dark gray or brown. It is taken from huge open pits called quarries.

Large amounts of limestone are used in construction. Good-quality limestone that can be cut into blocks is used as a building stone. Indiana leads the nation in the production of this variety of limestone. Crushed limestone is widely used in road building and other kinds of rough construction work. Limestone for such uses is quarried in many parts of the Midwest and Great Plains.

Limestone is one of the three main raw materials used in making iron and steel. For this purpose, it must be free

Iron ore, limestone, natural gas, and oil are important resources of the Midwest and Great Plains.

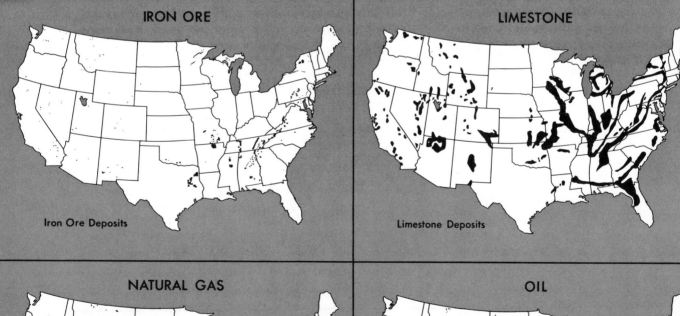

IRON ORE

Iron Ore Deposits

LIMESTONE

Limestone Deposits

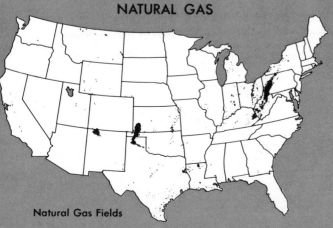

NATURAL GAS

Natural Gas Fields

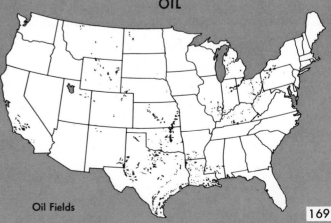

OIL

Oil Fields

of most impurities. Michigan leads the nation in the production of limestone for the iron and steel industry.

Limestone is the main raw material from which cement is made. To make this valuable mineral product, limestone is ground up with a smaller amount of shale* or clay. The mixture is heated in a huge oven, or kiln, until it forms lumps called clinkers. The clinkers are cooled and ground into a fine powder. This material is cement. Texas, Michigan, and Indiana are leading cement-producing states.

In addition, limestone is used as a raw material for the manufacture of various other industrial products. Lime, a white substance made by heating limestone in a kiln, is used as a fertilizer. It is also used in the manufacture of glass and paper. An important industrial chemical called soda ash is made from limestone and salt.

Salt. About half of all the salt produced in our country comes from Michigan, Ohio, and Texas. Each year, mines and wells in these states produce more than fifteen million tons of salt. To learn more about salt production in Michigan, see page 243. Most of the salt produced in our country is used to make chemicals and chemical products. Large quantities are also used in food processing.

Sulfur. Another important mineral found in the Midwest and Great Plains is sulfur. The state of Texas produces more than half of our country's supply of this useful, yellow mineral. Large deposits of sulfur are found along the Gulf coast. Sulfur is usually obtained by drilling a well and forcing hot water down into the deposit. The hot water melts the sulfur, which is forced to the surface as a liquid. Large amounts of sulfur are used to make sulfuric acid, a vitally important basic chemical. Sulfuric acid is used as a raw material for the manufacture of hundreds of other chemicals and chemical products. These include fertilizers, explosives, and synthetic fibers.

Water Resources

THE MIDWEST

The Midwest has a plentiful supply of water. Water is one of the most important natural resources of the Midwest. Most parts of the Midwest receive more than thirty inches of rainfall each year. Throughout this part of our country, there is enough rainfall for growing crops. As a result, farmers do not need to irrigate their fields.

Much of the rain that falls in the Midwest drains into the rivers and streams that flow through this part of the United States. The Mississippi River and its tributaries, including the Ohio and Missouri rivers, make up the largest river system in our country. (See feature on page 31.) The rivers of the Midwest provide large amounts of water for cities and industries along their banks.

Some of the Midwest's rainwater is stored in lakes. Four of the five Great Lakes border or lie in this part of our country. Cities and industries near

Lake Erie, at Cleveland. Four of the five Great Lakes border or lie in the Midwest. These lakes provide an abundant supply of water for cities and industries located nearby.

these lakes have an abundant supply of fresh water. There are also many smaller lakes that supply water to the people of the Midwest.

Part of the rain that falls in the Midwest seeps into the ground. It soaks down into layers of rock and soil beneath the surface. Because these layers are full of tiny holes and cracks, they can hold large amounts of water. The water stored in rock and soil beneath the ground is called groundwater. It can be obtained by digging or drilling wells. Many towns and farms in the Midwest depend on wells to supply the water they need.

The people of the Midwest must use their water resources carefully. Unfortunately, people in the Midwest have sometimes misused their plentiful water resources. Many of the lakes and rivers in this part of our country have been polluted by waste materials from homes and factories. Water that is polluted may contain disease germs or harmful chemicals and may have a very unpleasant odor. It must be treated before it can be used for drinking, bathing, and other purposes.

A striking example of water pollution in the Midwest is Lake Erie. It has become so polluted with waste materials dumped into it by industries and cities that it has been called a "dying lake." Our federal government has become alarmed by the misuse of this valuable water resource. Now it is cooperating with state governments and private agencies to cleanse the water in Lake Erie.

In the future, the people of the Midwest must take better care of their water resources. Industries must avoid dumping harmful waste materials into rivers and lakes. Cities must dispose of sewage in such a way that it does not pollute the water supply. Each citizen must realize that water is a precious resource. Only by conserving their water supplies can the people of the Midwest provide pure, fresh water to meet the needs of a growing population.

THE GREAT PLAINS STATES

In the eastern part of the Great Plains states, water supplies are adequate. People who live in the eastern part of the Great Plains states generally have enough water. There is sufficient rainfall here for growing most crops without irrigation. (See map on page 49.) Rivers and lakes provide water for many cities and industries in this area. Just as in the Midwest, however, people here must be careful not to waste their water or let it become polluted.

Water Resources

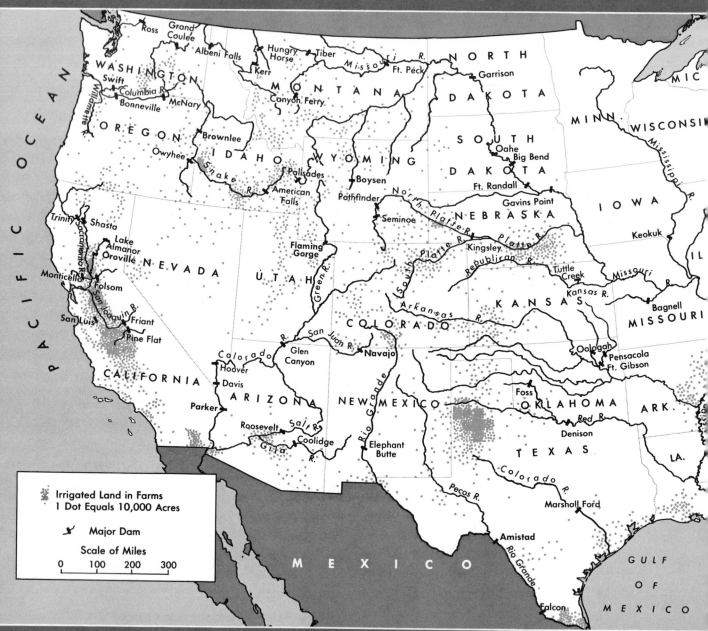

The map above shows some of the most important rivers and dams in the western part of the conterminous* United States. It also shows areas of irrigated farmland.

There are a number of large dams in the Great Plains states. Some of them are made of concrete. Others consist of many layers of earth packed tightly together. The chief purpose of some of these dams is to control floods. Other dams were built mainly to store water for irrigation. The water stored in reservoirs* behind the dams may also be used for recreation and for the production of hydroelectric* power.

The largest dam in the Great Plains states is Oahe Dam, on the Missouri River in South Dakota. It is made of earth. Other large dams on the Missouri include Garrison, Fort Randall, and Gavins Point.

The map shows that there are many thousands of acres of irrigated farmland in the northwestern part of Texas. Cotton is the main crop here. Water for irrigating the cotton fields is brought from nearby wells. Other large areas of irrigated farmland lie near the Platte River in Nebraska and along the Rio Grande, near the southern tip of Texas.

*See Glossary

Water is scarce in the western part of the Great Plains states. The people who live in the western part of the Great Plains states sometimes have difficulty obtaining water for all their needs. The average rainfall here is less than twenty inches a year. In addition, there are very few lakes in the western part of the Great Plains states. Only a few large rivers flow across this area. Most of these rivers, such as the Missouri, the Platte, and the Arkansas, flow down from the Rocky Mountains, where rainfall is heavier.

The lack of water in the western part of the Great Plains states affects people here in several ways. To grow crops in this area, farmers must irrigate their fields or use dry-farming* methods. Because many industries require vast quantities of water every day, the lack of water has kept some companies from building factories in this area. At times when rainfall is especially light, people must be careful not to use any more water than they absolutely need. Sometimes they are not allowed to wash their cars or sprinkle their lawns.

<u>Dams.</u> People in dry areas of the Great Plains states have worked hard to obtain the water they need. Dams have been built on the Missouri, the Platte, and other rivers that flow across the plains. These dams hold back the water of the rivers to form large reservoirs. The feature on the opposite page tells more about dams and reservoirs in the Great Plains states.

Some of the water stored in reservoirs is used for irrigation. It flows from the reservoirs through pipelines, canals, and ditches to farms where it is needed. There are about nine million acres of irrigated farmland in the Great Plains states. (See map on page 172.)

Dams and reservoirs are also valuable for other reasons. They help control the amount of water in the Missouri and other rivers. In the past, these rivers often rose so high they flooded the land along their banks. Today the dams and reservoirs help to prevent floods. When the rivers are high, some of the water is stored behind the dams so it will not flood the land. When the rivers are low, some of the water stored in the reservoirs is released. Reservoirs in the Great Plains states are also used for recreation, such as swimming, boating, and other water sports.

Hydroelectric* power plants have been built near some of the dams in the Great Plains states. Water from the reservoirs is allowed to flow through

Garrison Dam in North Dakota. Many dams have been built across rivers in dry areas of the Great Plains states. The reservoirs behind the dams store water for irrigation and other purposes.

huge pipes inside the dams. The rushing water turns large engines called turbines. Shafts leading from the turbines run machines called generators, which produce electricity. Most of the electricity used in the Midwest and Great Plains is produced in steam power plants that use coal, oil, or natural gas as fuel. (See page 167.) However, hydroelectric power is important in some areas. For example, most of the electricity used in North Dakota and South Dakota comes from hydroelectric power plants.

Wells. People in parts of the Great Plains states also obtain some of the water they need from wells. Each winter large amounts of snow fall on the Rocky Mountains, to the west. As the snow melts, some of the water seeps into underground layers of rock that extend all the way from the mountains to the Great Plains. This water can be obtained by digging or drilling wells and pumping it to the surface. There are thousands of wells in the Great Plains states. They supply pure water to many towns and farms here.

Forests and Fisheries

FORESTS

Dense forests once covered most of the Midwest. When settlers first came to the Midwest, they found most of the land covered with dense forests. The map on page 175 shows some of the main types of trees that grew here. In the northern part of the Midwest were forests of pine, hemlock, and other evergreen trees. Some of these trees were as tall as a fifteen-story building. Farther to the south were great forests of hardwoods, such as oak, maple, and hickory trees. Even on bright summer days, these forests were cool and dark, because the thick canopy of leaves overhead shut out most of the sunlight.

The climate of the Midwest helps explain why there were such large forests in this part of our country. Trees need about twenty inches of rainfall a year. They cannot survive long periods of dry weather. Trees also need about fourteen consecutive weeks without severe frosts each year. In the Midwest, rainfall is plentiful throughout the year, and the growing season is long enough for trees to thrive.

In some parts of the Midwest, the early settlers found grasslands instead of forests. These treeless areas, called prairies, covered large parts of Illinois, Iowa, and western Minnesota. (See map on page 175.) No one knows for sure why these areas were not forested, since they also receive plentiful rainfall and have a long enough growing season.

Today about one fourth of the Midwest is forested. Most of the great forests in the Midwest were cut down during the 1800's. The early settlers removed thousands of trees to clear the land so they could grow crops. Later, logging companies began cutting down the great pine forests in the northern parts of Michigan, Wisconsin, and Minnesota. At that time, the cities of the Midwest were growing rapidly. Large amounts of lumber were needed for building houses and for making such articles as furniture, wagons, and railroad ties. Logs from the northern forests were floated down rivers and streams to sawmills, where they were cut into lumber. The lumber was shipped by boat to Chicago, Detroit, and other cities.

Today, forests cover about one fourth of the land in the Midwest. Most of the trees in these forests are second growth. They have grown up in place of the ones that were cut down many years ago. These trees are generally smaller than the trees that grew in the original forests.

Most of the forests in the Midwest today are located in areas that are not well suited to farming. For example, there are large forests of evergreen trees in the northern parts of Michigan, Wisconsin, and Minnesota. Here the soil is poor, and the growing season is too short for most kinds of crops. Forests of oak and other hardwoods cover much of the hilly land in the Ozarks of southern Missouri and in the Appalachian Plateau of eastern Ohio. Small patches of

Natural forest regions of the conterminous* United States. At one time, dense forests of evergreen trees and hardwoods covered most of the land in the Midwest. However, during the 1800's settlers and logging companies cut down most of the Midwest's great forests. Today, forests cover only about one fourth of the land in this part of our country. Except for eastern Texas and Oklahoma, most areas of the Great Plains states are treeless.

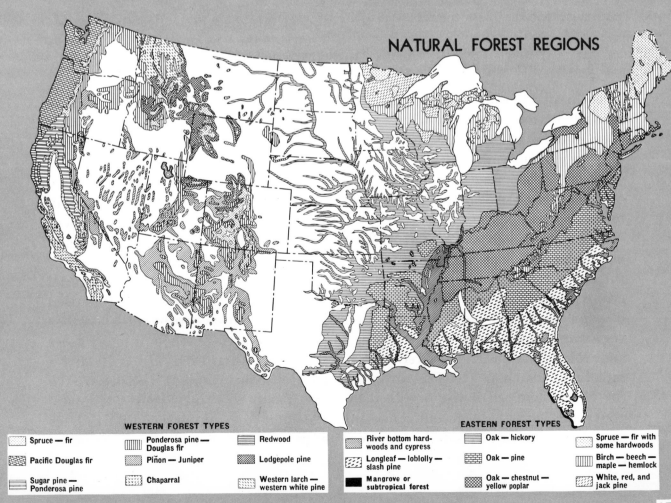

NATURAL FOREST REGIONS

WESTERN FOREST TYPES

Spruce — fir	
Pacific Douglas fir	
Sugar pine — Ponderosa pine	
Ponderosa pine — Douglas fir	
Piñon — Juniper	
Chaparral	
Redwood	
Lodgepole pine	
Western larch — western white pine	

EASTERN FOREST TYPES

River bottom hardwoods and cypress	
Longleaf — loblolly — slash pine	
Mangrove or subtropical forest	
Oak — hickory	
Oak — pine	
Oak — chestnut — yellow poplar	
Spruce — fir with some hardwoods	
Birch — beech — maple — hemlock	
White, red, and jack pine	

175

In a Wisconsin state forest. There are more than 170 state and national forests in the Midwest and Great Plains. In these forests, men called rangers protect the trees from fires, insects, and disease.

forest known as woodlots are scattered throughout the farmlands of the Midwest. These woodlots supply the farmers who own them with fence posts, fuel wood, and other useful items. Farmers often sell timber from their woodlots to nearby sawmills.

Forests cover much land in eastern Texas and Oklahoma. The largest forests in the Great Plains states are in the eastern parts of Texas and Oklahoma. (See map on page 175.) Here summers are very warm, the growing season is long, and rainfall is plentiful. Trees grow rapidly under these conditions. As in the Midwest, most of the forests that grew here long ago were cut down to provide lumber or to clear the land for

farming. However, new forests have grown up to take their place. In some areas, there are large forests of oak and other hardwoods. In other places, huge pine forests stretch for miles across the plains.

Most parts of the Great Plains states are treeless. Settlers who came to the Great Plains states in the 1800's found much of the land covered with grass instead of trees. This was mainly because of the lack of rainfall here. As you learned in Chapter 3, most of the western part of the Great Plains states receives less than twenty inches of rainfall a year. Sometimes weeks may pass without a drop of rain. In pioneer days, trees grew mainly along riverbanks. There were also forests in the Black Hills of South Dakota, where rainfall was heavier than on the plains nearby.

The farmers who settled on the grasslands of the Great Plains states often planted trees near their houses for protection against the fierce winds that swept across the plains. In recent years, many farmers have planted rows of trees around their fields to prevent wind erosion. (See page 151.)

How the forests are used. The forests of the Midwest and Great Plains supply wood for making a number of different products. The most important of these are wood pulp and lumber.

Wood pulp is a soft, damp material made up of tiny wood fibers. It is used in making paper, cardboard, and other useful products. Although many trees in the second-growth forests of Michigan, Wisconsin, and Minnesota are too small to be cut into lumber, they are excellent for making wood pulp. Logs of pine, hemlock, and other evergreens are floated down streams or carried by truck to nearby pulp mills. At the mills, the logs are cut into small chips, which are cooked with chemicals to produce pulp. There are many pulp and paper mills in Wisconsin and neighboring states. The manufacture of pulp and paper is also an important industry in eastern Texas. Mills here use large amounts of pulpwood from nearby pine forests.

Lumber is another forest product of the Midwest and Great Plains. Each year, forests in Missouri, Ohio, and other midwestern states supply thousands of hardwood logs to nearby sawmills. There the logs are cut into lumber. Because the wood of oak, maple, and other hardwood trees is sturdy and beautiful, much of it is used in making furniture. Some is used in the construction of houses and other buildings. Sawmills in eastern Texas and Oklahoma produce large amounts of lumber from pine logs cut in nearby forests.

Several other products also come from the forests of the Midwest and Great Plains. Logs of certain sizes are used as telephone poles or fence posts. A building material known as fiberboard is made from wood chips. Sap obtained from pine trees in Texas is used in making turpentine* and rosin.* Many farmers in the Midwest earn money by raising Christmas trees.

The forests of the Midwest and Great Plains not only supply many products, but they are valuable in other ways. For example, the roots of trees help hold the soil in place, preventing erosion by wind and rainwater. Forests are also used for recreation. People come to the woods for camping, hiking, hunting, and other outdoor activities.

In addition, forests provide food and shelter for many kinds of wildlife.

Protecting our forests. In the past, people in our country did not always take good care of their forest resources. Sometimes logging companies cut down all the trees in a certain area and moved on without planting new trees. Branches and wood scraps left behind by the loggers were often burned as waste. These fires sometimes got out of control and spread over wide areas, destroying thousands of acres of valuable trees.

Today most people realize that the forests must be protected if they are to supply our needs in the future. When logging companies cut down forests, new trees are usually planted. Ways have been found to use branches and wood scraps that were formerly wasted. Some companies hire men to protect their forests from fire. Often the forests are sprayed with chemicals to kill insects and diseases that might harm the growing trees.

Some of the forests in the Midwest and Great Plains are protected by our federal and state governments. There are 21 national forests and more than 150 state forests in this part of our country. The men who take care of these forests are called rangers. It is their job to protect the trees from fire, insects, and disease. Sometimes a private company is allowed to cut down a certain number of trees in a national or state forest. However, the rangers make sure that enough new trees will grow up to replace the ones that have been cut down. Through careful use, forests will continue to be a valuable natural resource of the Midwest and Great Plains.

FISHERIES

Most parts of the Midwest and Great Plains do not border on any ocean, so fishing is not a major industry in this part of our country. Texas, which lies along the Gulf of Mexico, leads the states of the Midwest and Great Plains in the value of fish caught. Smaller quantities of fish are caught in the Great Lakes and in the Mississippi River and its tributaries.

Fishing in the Gulf of Mexico. Each year, Texas fishermen bring millions of pounds of fish to ports along the Gulf coast. Most of these fish are shrimp or menhaden. Large quantities of shrimp are packaged and frozen in processing plants in or near the fishing ports. Then they are sent by train or truck to grocery stores throughout our country. Menhaden are seldom used as food for people. However, they are made into livestock feed, fertilizer, and oil. Menhaden oil is used in making soap, paint, and other products.

Fishing in lakes and rivers. In Michigan and other states that border on the Great Lakes, there are several thousand people who earn their living by fishing. From the lakes they bring in large catches of yellow perch, lake herring, chubs, alewives, and other kinds of fish. Alewives, like menhaden, are used mainly for making oil. The other kinds of fish are used as food. They are smoked, frozen, or sold fresh in grocery stores and fish markets.

In recent years, the number of fish caught in the Great Lakes has been decreasing. This is partly because cities and industries have been dumping harmful waste materials into the lakes. (See page 171.) Some kinds of fish cannot live in water that is badly polluted.

Large rivers such as the Mississippi and the Illinois also yield considerable amounts of food fish. Among these are catfish, carp, and buffalo fish. They are usually sold fresh in nearby towns and cities.

Explore Conservation

The Midwest and Great Plains has abundant natural resources. However, if these resources are to continue to be plentiful, they must be used wisely. The wise use and protection of natural resources is called conservation. Select one of the natural resources listed below and then prepare an oral report for your class. In your report, tell about some practices that should be followed to conserve this resource.

soil water
petroleum forests

This chapter and Chapter 9 contain useful information about conservation. For help in locating more information and in presenting your report, refer to the suggestions on pages 346-352.

Learn by Sharing Ideas

Do research to find out what the most important natural resources are in the area where you live. Then, as a class, discuss ways in which you can help to conserve these resources. If possible, invite a conservation official to take part in the discussion.

Make a Chart of Resources and Their Uses

Make a chart showing the important resources of the Midwest and Great Plains. Divide your chart into three columns. In the first column, name the resource. In the second column, name the state or states of the Midwest and Great Plains where it is important. In the third column, tell some of the ways in which the resource is used or name some of the products made from it.

A railroad yard near Chicago. An excellent system of roads, railroads, airways, and waterways serves the Midwest and Great Plains. This system makes it possible to transport goods quickly and cheaply from place to place. Good transportation routes also connect the Midwest and Great Plains with other parts of the United States and with foreign countries.

11 Transportation

A Problem To Solve

Good transportation is important to the development of any area. **How has transportation affected the development of the Midwest and Great Plains?** To solve this problem, you will have to learn about the history of transportation in this part of our country and about the transportation facilities available there today. Then you will need to make hypotheses about the ways in which transportation has affected:

a. the settlement of the Midwest and Great Plains
b. industry in these states
c. the growth of cities in these states

See TO THE STUDENT, pages 8-10.

Entering Chicago by train. We are riding in a glass-domed observation car on a modern passenger train. The train is moving slowly through the vast railroad yards on the southwest side of Chicago. Our hostess tells us that more railroads serve this city than any other city in the world.

From the observation car, we can see long freight trains carrying goods to and from Chicago. These trains are made up of many kinds of railroad cars. Some are boxcars full of corn grown on farms in Iowa or wheat grown in Kansas. Others are refrigerator cars bringing fresh fruits and vegetables from Texas. Stockcars loaded with beef cattle are bound for the Chicago stockyards. We also see gondola cars loaded with coal, which will be used by industries in the Chicago area. In addition, there are flatcars loaded with steel beams, tractors, and generators. These products were manufactured in the Chicago area and are being carried to distant cities.

Some of the railroad cars are being disconnected from one train so they can be connected to another. Chicago is a great transfer point for rail cargo from all parts of our country. For example, oranges grown in California may be transported by one train to Chicago. Here, the railroad car carrying the oranges may be connected to another train that is going to New York City.

Not all of the trains we see are freight trains. Some are passenger trains, like the one on which we are riding. Each day, thousands of people enter and leave Chicago by train. Many of these people are businessmen or vacationers traveling long distances. Others are commuters, who travel by train between their homes in the suburbs and their places of work in downtown Chicago.

Transportation helps people meet their needs. Our train ride into Chicago reminds us of the importance of transportation in our lives. Farmers must have a way of getting their products to market. Factories depend on trains, trucks, and other means of transportation to bring them the raw materials they need and to carry the goods they manufacture to customers. In our country, transportation is comparatively cheap. If this were not so, we would have to pay higher prices for many of the things we use every day. This is because transportation costs are included in the prices that people pay for goods.

People need good transportation for many other purposes besides the shipment of goods. Workers usually need some kind of transportation to get to work. When people decide to visit friends or relatives in a distant city, they must have a way of traveling there. Doctors, policemen, and firemen depend on transportation to get them quickly where they are needed in times of emergency. In these and many other ways, transportation is vitally important to all of us.

The development of transportation in the Midwest and Great Plains. When pioneers began coming to the Midwest, in the late 1700's, travel was more difficult and much slower than it is today. Locomotives, automobiles, and airplanes had not been invented. Trees had to be cleared from the land before roads could be built for wagons and other horse-drawn vehicles.

Build Your Vocabulary

cloverleaf   Great Lakes — St. Lawrence Waterway   piggyback

barge   commuter   interstate highways   locks   gondola car

The waterways of the Midwest provided excellent transportation routes, however. The Ohio and Mississippi rivers became major water highways. Thousands of pioneers from the eastern part of our country traveled in boats down the Ohio River to new homes on the frontier. At first, people who settled near the Ohio and Mississippi rivers used flatboats to transport farm products and other goods to markets. In the early 1800's, steamboats were developed. Soon they were carrying large amounts of freight and many passengers up and down the Ohio and the Mississippi. Gradually, steamboats also came into use on the Great Lakes, another major water highway of the Midwest.

In what are now the Great Plains states, there were few inland waterways that could be used for transportation. Although the Missouri River was an important transportation route, most people traveled by land in this part of our country. In the 1840's and 1850's, large numbers of pioneers moved westward across the plains in covered wagons and stagecoaches.

In the last half of the 1800's, railroads were built across the Midwest and Great Plains. The generally level land here made railroad building easy. Many railroads were built in the Midwest in the 1850's, connecting cities here with cities along our country's Atlantic coast. After the Civil War, railroads were built to link the Midwest with the Great Plains states. Chapter 5 discusses the importance of railroads in the settlement and development of the Midwest and Great Plains.

In the 1900's, the automobile and the airplane changed transportation in the

Pioneers crossing the plains. In the mid-1800's, thousands of pioneers journeyed westward across the plains in covered wagons and stagecoaches.

Midwest and Great Plains even more. Many new highways, paved with concrete or asphalt, were built to handle the growing amount of automobile traffic. By 1930, airlines connected most of the major cities in this part of our country.

Transportation in the Midwest and Great Plains today. An excellent system of roads, railroads, airways, and waterways serves the Midwest and Great Plains. People and goods can be transported from place to place much faster and more easily now than in pioneer days. In 1850, for example, it took about thirty-five hours for pioneers to travel by covered wagon from Columbus, Ohio, to Indianapolis, Indiana. Today, this trip takes about four hours by car and about one hour by airplane.

Roads. The Midwest and Great Plains is served by more than one and one-half million miles of roads. Some of these are broad superhighways that are used by hundreds of thousands of cars, trucks, and buses each day. Others are narrow, dirt or gravel roads. Most of these are located in thinly populated rural areas, and are used mainly by farmers. Roads reach many areas in the Midwest and Great Plains that are not served by railroads or airways.

Many highways in the Midwest and Great Plains are four or more lanes wide and are designed for high-speed traffic. These superhighways avoid crossroads and railroad tracks by means of overpasses, underpasses, and curving intersections called cloverleafs. By using superhighways, people can travel more quickly and safely from place to place.

Among the superhighways of the Midwest and Great Plains are the interstate highways. These are part of a nationwide system of superhighways being paid for mainly by our federal government. More than 7,500 miles of interstate highways have been built in the Midwest and Great Plains, and about 7,000 more miles are scheduled to be built.

A few of the interstate highways are toll roads. To use these interstate highways, motorists must pay a fee, called a toll. This money is used to pay the cost of building and repairing the roads. The toll roads that extend across northern Ohio and Indiana are among the nation's busiest highways.

The Indiana Toll Road. There are more than one and one-half million miles of roads in the Midwest and Great Plains, ranging from broad superhighways to narrow, dirt roads. Superhighways such as the Indiana Toll Road avoid crossroads and railroad tracks, enabling people to travel more quickly and safely from place to place.

Chicago's O'Hare International Airport is the busiest airport in the world. Cities of the Midwest and Great Plains are served by many airlines. Planes fly not only between cities in this part of our country but also to other parts of the United States and to foreign countries.

Railroads. Most of our country's major railroad lines serve the Midwest and Great Plains. Although millions of people travel by train each year, the main work of the railroads is hauling freight. As you have learned, trains carry a wide variety of manufactured goods and raw materials. Many trains also carry loaded truck trailers "piggyback." For example, a trailer may be loaded with furniture at a factory in Grand Rapids, Michigan. The trailer is then put aboard a flatcar and carried to Boston, Massachusetts. There the trailer is taken off the train and hauled to the place where the furniture is needed.

Piggybacking is cheaper than hauling goods long distances entirely by truck.

Airways. The routes of many airlines crisscross the Midwest and Great Plains. The planes of some of these airlines fly mainly between cities in this part of our country. Others serve cities not only in the Midwest and Great Plains but also in other parts of the United States. Many planes fly directly from Chicago, Detroit, Houston, and other cities to cities in foreign countries.

Chicago's O'Hare International Airport is the busiest airport in the world. Each month, it handles nearly two million passengers. Many people who are

183

Great Lakes–St.

The Great Lakes–St. Lawrence Waterway is made up of the five Great Lakes, the St. Lawrence River, and several smaller connecting waterways. Oceangoing ships can sail on this great water highway all the way from the Atlantic Ocean to the western end of Lake Superior. In making this journey, ships travel a distance of about 2,300 miles. They also rise from sea level to an elevation of 600 feet.

Although the Great Lakes–St. Lawrence Waterway follows natural water routes, it

MINNESOTA

Port Arthur / Fort William

Taconite Harbor
Silver Bay

(600 Ft.)

Lake Superior

Duluth / Superior

Presque Isle Harbor
Marquette

M

CAN

Soo Canals and Locks
St. Marys R.
Drummond Island

Port Inland
Port Dolomite

WISCONSIN

Escanaba

GREEN BAY

Calcite
Stoneport
Alpena

Lake Huron

GEORGIAN BAY

Green Bay
Kewaunee

Lake Michigan

Frankfort

(579 Ft.)

Manitowoc

M
I
C
H
I
G
A
N

Ludington

SAGINAW BAY

Toronto

Milwaukee
Oak Creek

(579 Ft.)

Muskegon
Grand Haven

Hamilton
Welland Ship Canal
Port Colborne

Lake

Niagara R.

Buffalo

St. Clair
St. Clair R.

Chicago

Detroit
Detroit R.
L. St. Clair

(570 Ft.)

Lake Erie

Erie

Indiana Harbor
Buffington Harbor   Gary

Conneaut
Ashtabula

Toledo

Fairport
Cleveland

ILLINOIS

Sandusky   Lorain
Huron

PENN

⚓ Major Ports

= Locks

▪▪▪▪ Canals

—·— International Boundary

Numbers in Lakes Indicate
Height Above Sea Level

INDIANA

OHIO

Scale of Miles

0   50   100

WEST

VIRGINIA

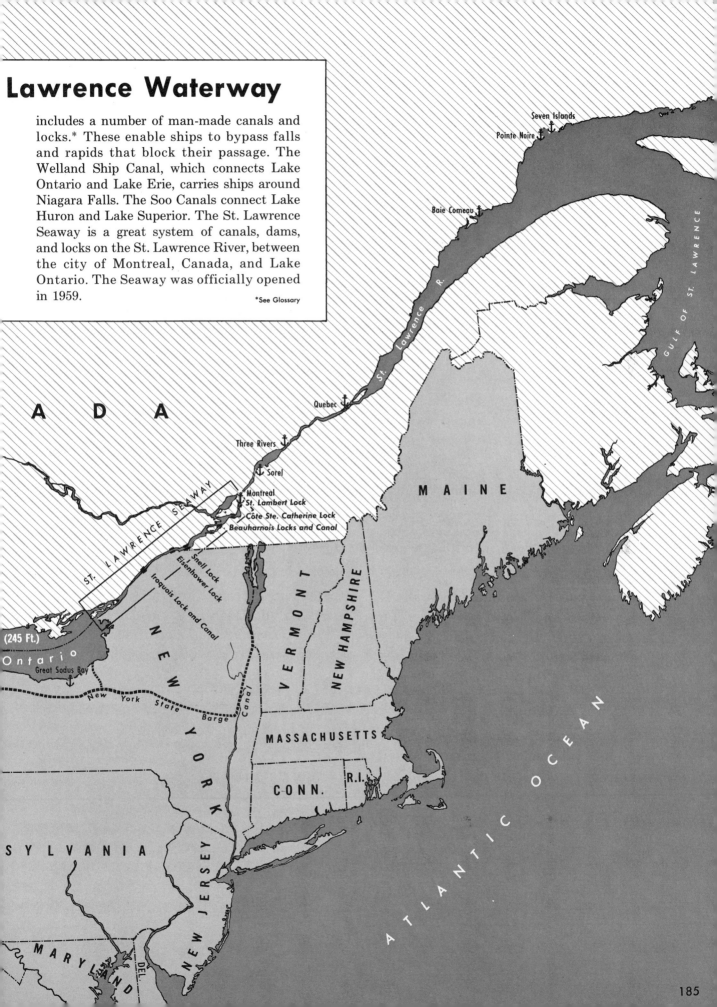

Lawrence Waterway

includes a number of man-made canals and locks.* These enable ships to bypass falls and rapids that block their passage. The Welland Ship Canal, which connects Lake Ontario and Lake Erie, carries ships around Niagara Falls. The Soo Canals connect Lake Huron and Lake Superior. The St. Lawrence Seaway is a great system of canals, dams, and locks on the St. Lawrence River, between the city of Montreal, Canada, and Lake Ontario. The Seaway was officially opened in 1959.

*See Glossary

Seven Islands

Pointe Noire

Baie Comeau

St. Lawrence R.

GULF OF ST. LAWRENCE

Quebec

A D A

Three Rivers

Sorel

MAINE

Montreal

St. Lambert Lock

Côte Ste. Catherine Lock

Beauharnois Locks and Canal

ST. LAWRENCE SEAWAY

Snell Lock

Eisenhower Lock

Iroquois Lock and Canal

VERMONT

NEW HAMPSHIRE

(245 Ft.)

Ontario

NEW YORK

Great Sodus Bay

New York State Barge Canal

MASSACHUSETTS

CONN.

R.I.

SYLVANIA

NEW JERSEY

ATLANTIC OCEAN

MARYLAND

DEL.

flying from one part of our country to another must change planes at O'Hare.

Airplanes are faster than any other means of transportation available to people today. Therefore, large numbers of businessmen and other people travel by plane when they want to get from one place to another quickly. Airplanes are also used to carry goods that must be moved in a hurry. Much of our country's mail is transported by plane, as are certain perishable goods such as flowers. An increasing number of companies are also sending manufactured products to customers by air, especially when the goods are needed urgently.

Inland waterways. The Midwest is served by the greatest inland waterway in the world. This is the Great Lakes –

St. Lawrence Waterway. It is made up of the five Great Lakes, the St. Lawrence River, and several smaller connecting waterways. (See map on pages 184 and 185.)

Ships traveling on the Great Lakes carry many kinds of raw materials and manufactured products. Although water transportation is slower than other means of transportation, it is generally cheaper. Therefore, ships are often used to transport heavy cargoes that do not need to be moved in a hurry. Many long, low boats like the one shown in the picture below carry wheat, iron ore, and other raw materials to the mills and factories where they will be processed. Other ships carry manufactured products, such as automobiles and steel, between lake

The Soo Canals make it possible for ships to travel between Lake Huron and Lake Superior. These canals form an important link in the Great Lakes–St. Lawrence Waterway, which is the greatest inland waterway in the world. Ships can travel on this great water highway all the way from the Atlantic Ocean to Great Lakes ports in the Midwest.

ports. Most shipping on the Great Lakes must stop during the winter, however. Ice blocks many harbors from about December to April.

If you were to visit the ports at Chicago, Cleveland, Toledo, and several other cities along the Great Lakes, you would see ships from many different countries. The St. Lawrence Seaway makes it possible for large oceangoing ships to sail from the Atlantic Ocean to the Great Lakes. (See feature on pages 184 and 185.)

The Ohio and Mississippi rivers are also important transportation routes in the Midwest. Long strings of barges like those in the picture on page 32 move slowly up and down these rivers carrying cargoes of coal, grain, sand, petroleum, or other raw materials. A series of waterways connects the Mississippi River with the Great Lakes. At Chicago, goods can be transferred directly from riverboats to lake freighters.

Gulf coast shipping. Texas is the only Great Plains state that is served by important waterways. This state borders on the Gulf of Mexico, an arm of the Atlantic Ocean. Ships carry large amounts of goods to and from ports at Houston, Corpus Christi, Port Arthur, and other Texas cities. Among the goods exported from ports in Texas are petroleum products, chemicals, cotton, and sulfur. Imports include bauxite, iron ore, and other raw materials for Texas industries. Houston's port is one of the busiest in the United States. (See pages 342 and 343.)

Texas is also served by the Gulf Intracoastal Waterway, which extends along the Gulf coast from Texas to Florida. This waterway makes it possible for riverboats and barges to transport goods between Gulf coast ports without traveling on the open sea. In some places, the waterway is protected by offshore islands. In other places, the waterway lies inland. (See map on page 333.) Many barges carry freight on the Gulf Intracoastal Waterway from ports in Texas to New Orleans. From there, the barges travel northward on the Mississippi River and connecting waterways to Chicago, St. Paul, and other ports in the Midwest.

Questions To Guide Your Reading
1. What waterways became important transportation routes for pioneers moving to the Midwest in the late 1700's?
2. What important changes in transportation took place between 1850 and 1930 in the Midwest and Great Plains?

An Adventure on the Great Lakes – St. Lawrence Waterway

The Midwest is served by the greatest inland water highway in the world. Learn about this waterway by studying the feature on pages 184 and 185 and by doing outside research. Then plan a boat trip from Quebec, Canada, to Duluth, Minnesota. Write an account of your imaginary trip to share with your class. Include the following information in your account:

1. the names of the lakes on which you traveled
2. the goods you saw being loaded and unloaded at the port cities along the way
3. the kinds of ships that you saw
4. interesting or unusual sights you noticed along the way

In writing your account, use your imagination, but be sure the statements you make are based on facts.

Assembling automobiles in Michigan. Industry is much more important in the Midwest than in the Great Plains states. Midwestern factories turn out more than 65 billion dollars' worth of goods each year. Factories in the Great Plains states produce less than one sixth this amount.

12   Industry

A Problem To Solve

Why has industry grown more rapidly in the Midwest than in the Great Plains states? In order to solve this problem, you will need to make hypotheses about how each of the following has affected the growth of industry in these two parts of our country:

a. transportation
b. availability of raw materials
c. location of markets
d. supply of skilled workers
e. water supplies

See TO THE STUDENT, pages 8-10.

We are traveling by automobile from Chicago, Illinois, to Detroit, Michigan. Although we are moving at a speed of sixty miles an hour, we are as comfort- able as if we were sitting in our own living room. Soft music comes from the radio speaker. The carpet underfoot is thick and luxurious. Tinted glass helps shield us from the hot sunlight. At the touch of a button, the window beside us slides down as if by magic. Our driver presses the accelerator, and our new station wagon surges ahead. In less than five hours, we are able to complete a journey of 275 miles.

Now, let's go back in time about sixty years. We are traveling by automobile from Lansing, Michigan, to Detroit, a distance of less than one hundred miles. As we move along at a speed of twenty miles an hour, we are tossed and jolted nearly out of our seats. There is no protection from the burning rays of the sun. Dust seeps in under our goggles and leather coats. We can hear nothing over the chugging of the engine. Our car has stalled three times, and the driver tells us that his arm is very sore from cranking up the engine. Including the time we have lost during breakdowns, it will take us nearly twenty-four hours to complete our trip to Detroit.

Many people today take for granted the ease and speed with which automobiles carry them from place to place. However, little more than seventy years ago, there were only four automobiles in the entire United States. By 1905, the number had increased to more than 75,000, but automobiles were still costly, slow, and uncomfortable. Worst

A Model T Ford. Henry Ford was the first man to make cars that large numbers of people could afford to buy. In his factory, low-cost cars were produced by using the assembly-line method. Today, automobiles are our country's most important manufactured product.

of all, they were undependable. No one could trust an automobile to get him anywhere on time.

Today, automobiles are our country's most important manufactured product. About ten cents of every dollar spent by consumers in this country goes for the purchase of new automobiles. In addition, about one fifth of all workers in the United States have jobs related in some way to the automobile industry. Some of these workers produce steel for auto bodies. Others make glass for windshields or rubber for tires. Thousands of people repair automobiles or build and maintain highways. Two of our nation's ten leading manufacturing companies make automobiles. Four others make petroleum products, including gasoline and oil for automobiles.

Automobiles have created a new way of life in the United States. People in our country travel more now than they ever did before. Today, there are few places in the nation that cannot be reached by automobile. Sixty years ago, a journey of twenty or thirty miles was considered long and difficult. Now, many workers travel even farther than that to work every day. Friends and relatives easily drive long distances to visit each other. On holidays and vacations, families are able to travel to interesting places far from home. In these and many other ways, automobiles have brought people and places in our country closer together than ever before.

A visit to one of our country's greatest manufacturing plants. In southeastern Michigan is one of the greatest manufacturing plants in the United States. It is made up of dozens of buildings spread out over more than one thousand acres. If you were to fly over this plant in a helicopter, you could look down at large factories with tall smokestacks and blast* furnaces ten stories high. You would see raw materials being unloaded from large boats at the company's docks. Also, you would notice the many miles of roads and railroad tracks connecting the various parts of this plant.

All of these facilities are part of the vast River Rouge plant of the Ford Motor Company at Dearborn, Michigan. (See picture on page 191.) To learn about this plant, we will go on a guided tour. Our tour begins at the company's main office building, about two miles from the plant. Here we board a bus and are welcomed by our guide.

The Ford Motor Company, our guide tells us, is a very large manufacturing company with plants and offices in various parts of the world. It was founded at the beginning of this century by Henry Ford, a pioneer of the automobile industry. Ford made his first automobiles in a small workshop. Then, in the hope of making a profit, a group of businessmen lent Ford the money he needed to build a factory.

Henry Ford was the first man to produce an automobile that large numbers

*See Glossary

Build Your Vocabulary

raw materials   market   interchangeable parts   coking coal

profit   mass production   chemicals   assembly line   consumer

The Ford Motor Company's River Rouge plant at Dearborn, Michigan, is one of the greatest manufacturing plants in our country. This picture shows some of the plant's main features. (1) coal, iron ore, and limestone storage bins, (2) blast furnaces, (3) coke ovens, (4) power house, (5) basic oxygen furnace building, (6) warehouse, (7) ore boats, (8) boat slip, (9) steel mill plant, and (10) stamping plant.

of people could afford. In order to do this, Ford used a method of manufacturing called mass production. Thousands of each automobile part were made in his factory. The automobile frames were placed on a moving belt called a conveyor belt. The belt carried the frames along, past a row of workers. As each frame came along, a man on the "assembly line" added a different part, such as a wheel or a nut and bolt. By using this method, Ford lowered the cost of making each car. As a result, the price charged to customers was also lowered. At the Rouge plant, we will learn

more about the mass production of automobiles.

During our bus ride, our guide tells us that the ideas, talents, and skills of many thousands of workers are needed to mass-produce automobiles. In buildings in another part of Dearborn, more than twelve thousand scientists, engineers, designers, and technicians plan the kind of car that they think people will buy and that will bring the company a profit. They spend many months designing the body and other parts of the car. At the same time, the methods by which the car will be produced are also being developed. When the design has been completed, test models of the car are manufactured. These models are given a series of rugged tests. As a result of these tests, some parts may have to be redesigned so that the car will meet the company's standards. Finally, the car is ready to be mass-produced.

The Rouge plant itself needs thousands of workers to perform hundreds of different jobs. Some workers are employed in the company's steel mill. Others work in the foundry, in the glass factory, or at the company's docks. There are also factories where engines, radiators, frames, and other automobile parts are made. Workers at the Rouge plant also perform such jobs as running diesel locomotives and operating cranes.

The Rouge plant also needs managers to supervise the many operations that take place here. Without good management, it would be impossible to operate a plant as large as this one. The managers are responsible for running each division of the plant as efficiently as possible so that the company can make a profit. People who have invested money in the company expect a good profit on their investment.

Our bus has now entered the plant grounds. The first stop on our tour is the company's docks. From early spring to late fall, boats arrive here carrying huge cargoes of iron ore, coal, and limestone. These raw materials are piled high in storage bins near the three blast furnaces of the company's steel mill. Iron ore, coal, and limestone are the three main raw materials needed for making iron and steel. About half of the iron and steel needed by the Rouge plant is made here.

Our next stop is the assembly plant, where workers put together more than thirteen thousand parts to make one shiny new automobile. Our guide explains that there are several assembly lines in this plant. The frame of the automobile is carried by conveyor belt along the main assembly line. Certain parts of the car, such as the body, move along other assembly lines to the main line, where they are added to the frame.

We stop to watch a powerful engine being lowered onto the frame of a car. Our guide tells us that this engine is identical to thousands of other engines made at the Rouge plant. It will fit another car of the same model as perfectly as it fits this one. In other words, it is an interchangeable part. The same is true of all other parts in this car. Without interchangeable parts, the mass production of automobiles would not be possible. Instead, each part would have to be made laboriously by hand to fit a particular car. Furthermore, when a part wore out, it could not easily be replaced by another just like it. A new one would have to be specially made, and it would be very expensive.

At many places along the assembly line, we notice inspectors checking the car. They must make sure that it will meet the quality standards set up by the company. After the car has been completely assembled, other inspectors give it a final test. When the car is finally approved, it is driven from the assembly plant. Less than a minute later, another new car follows this one off the assembly line. These cars will be carried by truck or train to an automobile showroom somewhere in our country.

Newly assembled automobiles are loaded on railroad cars and trucks for shipment to showrooms in all parts of our country. Industries depend on trains, trucks, and other means of transportation to bring them raw materials and to carry finished products to customers.

Our guide tells us that not all Ford cars are assembled here at the Rouge plant. The Ford Motor Company, like other major automobile manufacturers, operates assembly plants in various parts of the United States and in some foreign countries as well. Automobile parts are shipped to these plants to be assembled. It is much cheaper to ship automobile parts than to ship fully assembled automobiles.

As we leave the plant, our guide tells us that the efficient methods of production we have seen at the Rouge plant are not limited to the automobile industry. We could see many examples of mass production in manufacturing plants throughout our country.

The Midwest is a great industrial region. Factories in the Midwest employ more than one third of our country's industrial workers. Automobiles are only one of many thousands of products made here. Each year, factories in the Midwest turn out more than 65 billion dollars' worth of steel, machinery, food products, and other goods. This is more than one third the value of all goods manufactured in the United States.

The Midwest has many advantages for industry. The Midwest is a great manufacturing region because it has nearly

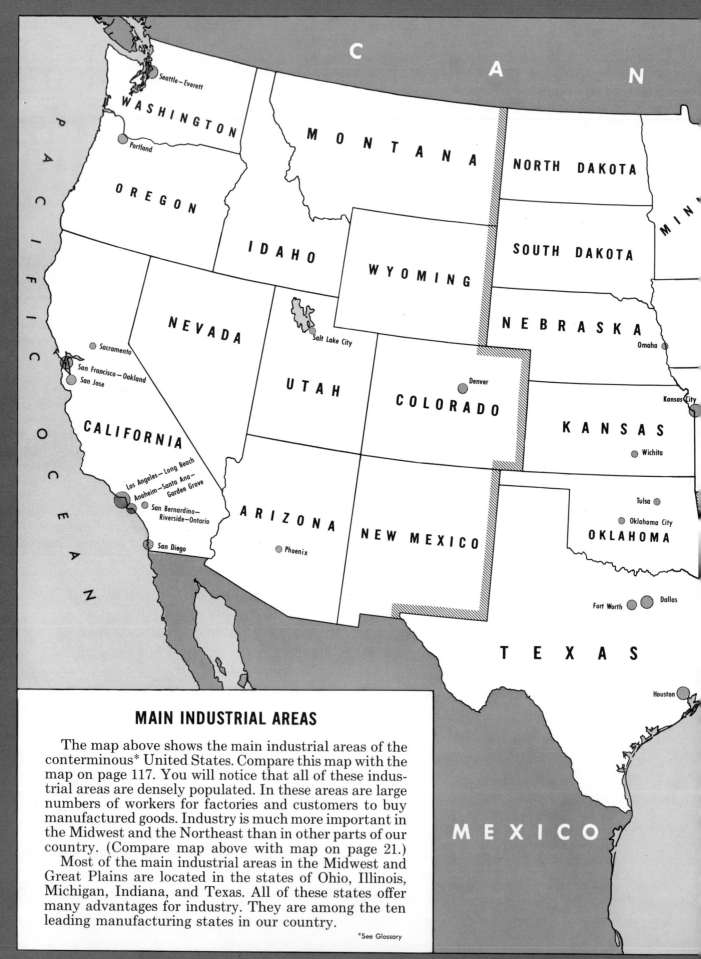

MAIN INDUSTRIAL AREAS

The map above shows the main industrial areas of the conterminous* United States. Compare this map with the map on page 117. You will notice that all of these industrial areas are densely populated. In these areas are large numbers of workers for factories and customers to buy manufactured goods. Industry is much more important in the Midwest and the Northeast than in other parts of our country. (Compare map above with map on page 21.)

Most of the main industrial areas in the Midwest and Great Plains are located in the states of Ohio, Illinois, Michigan, Indiana, and Texas. All of these states offer many advantages for industry. They are among the ten leading manufacturing states in our country.

*See Glossary

CANADA

WISCONSIN

Minneapolis—St. Paul

MICHIGAN

Muskegon—Muskegon Heights
Grand Rapids
Saginaw
Flint
Lansing
Ann Arbor
Milwaukee
Kalamazoo

IOWA

Rockford
Chicago
South Bend
Gary—Hammond—East Chicago
Fort Wayne
Peoria

ILLINOIS

INDIANA

Anderson
Indianapolis
Cincinnati

Davenport—Rock Island—Moline

St. Louis

MISSOURI

Detroit
Toledo
Cleveland
Lorain—Elyria
Akron
Dayton
Columbus

OHIO

Youngstown
Steubenville—Weirton
Canton
Pittsburgh
York
Harrisburg

PENNSYLVANIA

Buffalo
Rochester
Syracuse
Utica—Rome
Binghamton

NEW YORK

Erie
Lancaster
Philadelphia

MAINE

VT.
N.H.

MASS.
CONN.
R.I.

Boston

New York City

N.J.

DEL.
MD.

Evansville
Louisville

KENTUCKY

WEST VIRGINIA

Washington, D.C.

Baltimore

Richmond

VIRGINIA

Nashville

TENNESSEE

Knoxville

Chattanooga

Memphis

ARKANSAS

Winston-Salem
Greensboro—High Point

Charlotte

NORTH CAROLINA

Greenville

SOUTH CAROLINA

Birmingham

Atlanta

Augusta

ALABAMA

GEORGIA

MISSISSIPPI

LOUISIANA

Texarkana

Beaumont—Port Arthur

New Orleans

FLORIDA

Tampa—St. Petersburg

Miami

ATLANTIC OCEAN

Scale of Miles
0   100   200   300

Thousands of Industrial Workers

- 25 to 50
- 50 to 100
- 100 to 500
- 500 and Over

A

VT.
N.H.

Albany—Troy—Schenectady

Lawrence—Haverhill

N.Y.

MASSACHUSETTS

Boston

Springfield—Holyoke

Worcester

CONNECTICUT

Providence

New Britain
Hartford

New Bedford

Waterbury

New London—Groton—Norwich

R.I.

Bridgeport
New Haven

Scale of Miles
0   40   80

B

NEW YORK

Scranton

Wilkes-Barre—Hazleton

Paterson—Clifton—Passaic
Newark
Jersey City

New York City

Allentown—Bethlehem—Easton

Reading

Trenton

PENNSYLVANIA

NEW

JERSEY

Philadelphia

Wilmington

MD.

DEL.

Scale of Miles
0   40   80

all the things that industry needs. One of the Midwest's most important advantages for manufacturing is its excellent system of land, water, and air transportation. By comparing the map on pages 18 and 19 with the map on pages 194 and 195, you can see that most of the Midwest's main industrial areas are located on or near major waterways. Low-cost water transportation is used to take raw materials to factories and to carry manufactured goods to customers. Also, vast networks of roads, railroads, and airways crisscross the Midwest.

To carry on manufacturing, industries need raw materials, water, and power. The Midwest has an abundant supply of iron ore, coal, and other important mineral resources for factories. The farms and forests here also provide valuable raw materials. Many industries require huge amounts of water. For example, the Rouge plant uses more than 250 million gallons of water every day. Rivers, lakes, and underground water supplies in the Midwest provide plentiful sources of water for factories. Industries also need electric power to run machinery. Coal mined in the Midwest provides fuel for plants that produce electricity.

The 49 million people who live in the Midwest provide another major advantage for industry here. Hundreds of

Managers and skilled workers in an Ohio factory. The 49 million people who live in the Midwest provide a major advantage for industry here. Hundreds of thousands of these people have the skills, talents, and ideas that are needed by modern industry.

thousands of these people have the skills, talents, and ideas needed by modern industry. The people of the Midwest also provide a huge market for manufactured goods. Every day, they buy food, clothing, and hundreds of other items made here. Not all of the goods made in the Midwest are sold to individual consumers, however. Midwestern factories also sell large quantities of goods such as machinery to other factories in this part of our country.

The Great Plains states have much less industry. Manufacturing is much less important in the Great Plains states than in the Midwest. Factories here make only about ten billion dollars' worth of goods every year. As the map on pages 194 and 195 shows, there are about three times as many main industrial areas in the Midwest as there are in the Great Plains states.

A combination of disadvantages has held back the growth of industry in the Great Plains states as a whole. First, most parts are not served by major waterways. Therefore, bulky goods such as coal and steel have to be shipped by train or truck. It is more expensive to ship goods by these means of transportation than by boat. Second, the Great Plains states lack some of the mineral resources essential for modern industry, especially iron ore and high-grade coal. Iron ore, for example, is needed to make steel, which is the main raw material used by factories that make machinery and hundreds of other products. Many parts of the Great Plains states also lack adequate water supplies for industry. Finally, the Great Plains states as a whole are sparsely populated. As a result, markets here are

At a petroleum refinery in Texas. Although the growth of industry has been slow in most parts of the Great Plains states, Texas is one of the ten leading manufacturing states in our nation.

small and there is not a large supply of factory workers.

Although industry is lacking in most parts of the Great Plains states, Texas is one of our nation's ten leading manufacturing states. Texas has rich deposits of minerals that can be used by industry. The state's location on the Gulf of Mexico makes it easy to bring in raw materials and to ship manufactured goods to customers. In eastern Texas, where most of the state's industries are located, there are adequate supplies of water for manufacturing. In addition, Texas has a large population. More than half the people in the Great Plains states live here. Thus there are plenty of workers for factories and large markets for manufactured goods.

Products of Industry

Iron and steel. One of the leading industries in the Midwest and Great Plains is the manufacture of iron and steel. Factories here use millions of tons of steel each year to make automobiles, machinery, and countless other products. Ohio, Indiana, Illinois, and Michigan rank just after Pennsylvania as our nation's chief iron- and steel-producing states.

About one third of the steel made in the United States each year comes from five industrial areas of the Midwest—Youngstown, Cleveland, Detroit, Gary–Hammond–East Chicago, and Chicago. (See the map on pages 194 and 195.) The main raw materials needed in making iron and steel can be easily shipped to these industrial areas. Lake freighters carry iron ore from iron-mining areas near Lake Superior to ports along the southern shores of Lake Michigan and Lake Erie. Trains carry the ore to steel plants that lie inland. Limestone from midwestern quarries and coking*coal from mines in the Appalachian Plateau are also transported to steel plants by water and by rail.

Pouring white-hot steel into molds. About one third of the steel made in the United States each year comes from mills in Ohio, Indiana, Illinois, and Michigan. Factories in the Midwest and Great Plains need steel to make automobiles, machinery, and countless other metal products.

Assembling tractors. Factories in Illinois, Iowa, Wisconsin, and Michigan make almost two thirds of our nation's farm machinery. Each year, factories in the Midwest and Great Plains produce more than sixteen billion dollars' worth of machinery.

There are large markets nearby for steel produced in these five industrial areas. Hundreds of factories that make machinery, automobiles, or other products requiring large amounts of steel are located near the steel plants. These factories can obtain the steel they need without having to pay high transportation costs.

Machinery. Another leading industry in the Midwest and Great Plains is the manufacture of machinery. This industry is especially important in the midwestern states. Each year factories here produce more than two fifths of the total value of machinery made in our country.

Hundreds of factories in the Midwest and Great Plains make industrial or construction machinery. Plants in Michigan, Ohio, and the other midwestern states make nearly two thirds of the nation's machine tools. These machines cut, grind, and shape metal to make parts needed in the manufacture of other machines. Factories here also make such industrial machinery as refrigeration equipment and printing presses. The Chicago industrial area is a leading producer of construction equipment, such as bulldozers and concrete mixers. In Texas and Oklahoma, which are important petroleum-producing states, there are factories that make oil-field equipment.

Factories in Illinois, Iowa, Wisconsin, and Michigan make almost two thirds of our nation's farm machinery. Farmers in the Midwest and Great Plains need machines for planting, cultivating, and harvesting crops. Many farm machines, such as tractors and combines, require large amounts of steel. Because they are bulky, these machines are difficult and costly to transport. Therefore, farm machines are usually made in factories that are close to both steel mills and major farming areas.

Plants in the Midwest and Great Plains also produce several other kinds of machinery. Many people here work in factories that manufacture household appliances, such as refrigerators and air conditioners. Electronic equipment, such as computers and television sets, is made in Chicago, Dallas, and other cities.

Transportation equipment. The manufacture of transportation equipment is another major industry in the Midwest and Great Plains. More transportation equipment is made here than in any other part of our country. This industry

Manufacturing helicopters at Fort Worth, Texas. Plants in the Midwest and Great Plains make airplanes, locomotives, and other kinds of transportation equipment besides automobiles.

includes the production of aircraft and railroad equipment, as well as cars, trucks, and buses.

Michigan ranks first in the nation in the production of motor vehicles. The world's three leading automobile manufacturers—General Motors, Ford, and Chrysler—have their home offices in the Detroit area and operate large plants in Michigan. Another major automobile producer—American Motors—also has its headquarters in Detroit, although it makes most of its cars in Wisconsin.

Several other industries supply automobile manufacturers with products they need. Plants in Toledo, Ohio, for example, supply auto makers in nearby Michigan with glass for car windows. Most of the tires used by the automobile industry come from factories in Akron, Ohio.

Plants in the Midwest and Great Plains also make railroad equipment and aircraft. Powerful diesel-electric locomotives are manufactured in La Grange, Illinois. More than half of the small, private airplanes made in this country come from Wichita, Kansas. In Texas, there are plants that make helicopters, large airliners, and spacecraft.

Food products. Farms in the Midwest and Great Plains provide huge quantities of raw materials for industry here. In food-processing plants, meat, grain, and other farm products are prepared for sale to customers throughout our country.

One of the most important types of food processing in this part of our country is meat-packing. Omaha, Nebraska, processes more meat than any other city in the United States. There are

Preparing wheat for milling. Farms in the Midwest and Great Plains provide huge amounts of grain and other products for food-processing plants here.

also large meat-packing plants in Chicago, Sioux City, Fort Worth, and many other cities. Farmers prefer to sell their cattle, hogs, and other livestock to meat-packing firms in cities located fairly close to their farms. Livestock may lose too much valuable weight if they are shipped to markets located far away.

In many cities of the Midwest and Great Plains, there are mills and factories that make food products from grain. Trains and trucks bring vast amounts of grain from our country's wheatlands to flour mills in Kansas City, Missouri. In our nation, this city ranks second only to Buffalo, New York, in flour milling. Large plants at Battle Creek, Michigan, make much of our nation's breakfast cereal from wheat, corn, and other grains. In Milwaukee, St. Louis, and other cities, brewers use a grain called barley to make beer.

In the dairy belt of the Midwest, there are many plants that process milk to make such products as cheese and butter. More cheese is produced in Wisconsin than in any other state, and Minnesota, Wisconsin, and Iowa are the nation's leading butter producers. These dairy products are sold in stores in many parts of the United States.

Petroleum products. There are many petroleum refineries in the Midwest and Great Plains. These refineries make gasoline, fuel oil, and other valuable products from crude* oil. Texas, Illinois, Indiana, Oklahoma, and Kansas all rank among our nation's ten leading petroleum-refining states.

Texas leads the nation in petroleum production and also ranks first in petroleum refining. Although there are refineries in many parts of Texas, the petroleum-refining industry is especially important along the state's Gulf coast. (See page 341.) Texas refineries produce hundreds of thousands of barrels of petroleum products each day. Ocean tankers and pipelines carry large amounts of these products to other parts of our country.

Chemicals and chemical products. Texas, Illinois, Ohio, and Michigan are among our nation's ten leading producers of chemicals and chemical products. Many plants in these states make basic* chemicals, such as hydrochloric acid and ammonia. Basic chemicals are used in the manufacture of hundreds of different products, ranging from household detergents to drugs.

Texas is outranked only by New Jersey in the manufacture of chemicals and chemical products. The chemical industry of Texas, like the state's petroleum-refining industry, is located mainly along the Gulf coast. Chemical plants here use large quantities of raw materials from nearby refineries to make petrochemicals.* You can learn more about the chemical industry of Texas by reading pages 340 and 341.

Questions To Help You Learn
1. In what ways is the automobile industry important to our country?
2. Explain what the term "mass production" means.
3. Where do iron and steel mills in the Midwest obtain the main raw materials they need?

Exploring Industry in Your Community
Invite a businessman from a manufacturing plant in your community to come to your classroom for an interview. Take notes during the interview for use later in a class discussion. Ask your visitor questions such as the following:

1. What products do you make?

2. What raw materials are used in making these products?
3. Where do these raw materials come from and how are they shipped to your plant?
4. What is done to these raw materials to change them into finished products?
5. Does your company have difficulty in finding skilled workers? If so, explain why.
6. How are your finished products shipped to customers?

Hold a class discussion on the ways in which this industry depends on people in other places as well as on people in your own community. The suggestions on pages 352 and 353 will help you.

Part 5

States of the Midwest

States of the Midwest. Part 5 of this book provides information about the eight states in the Midwest. Here you will find the facts you need for solving many problems about this part of our country. The text, the maps, and the vivid pictures will give you the most important information about the land, climate, people, and resources of each state in the Midwest.

Reading the fact tables. The following explanation will help you understand the information in the fact table at the beginning of each state chapter. The figures in these tables are the latest that were available from the United States government at the time this book was published. Some of these fig-

ures are amounts of money. These tell how many dollars the people of the state received in a year from such activities as farming, mining, and fishing. The figures for manufactures show the actual value added to goods or raw materials by factories in the state. The value added in manufacturing was figured out in an interesting way. From the amount of money received from the sale of goods, the cost of the materials needed to make them was subtracted. The amount of money left is the value added by the factories.

The fact tables also show the rank of each state in comparison with all the other states of our country. In cases where figures were not available, the rank is not given.

13 Illinois

Facts About Illinois		
	Number or Value	Rank
Area (square miles)	56,400	24
Population	10,722,000	5
Capital — Springfield		
Admission Date:		
December 3, 1818		21
Colleges and Universities	112	4
Farm Products	$2,214,158,000	4
Corn	521,920,000	1
Cattle and calves	448,240,000	6
Hogs	444,677,000	2
Fish	$ 745,000	27
Forest Products	$ 12,400,000	35
Minerals	$ 591,136,000	8
Coal	208,448,000	4
Petroleum	205,592,000	8
Stone	56,553,000	4
Manufactures	$14,557,060,000	4
Nonelectrical machinery	2,181,630,000	1
Food and kindred products	2,043,377,000	2
Electrical machinery	1,781,288,000	3

LAND

Illinois is one of our country's greatest farming and manufacturing states. If you were to fly over this state in the summertime, you would see that most of the countryside resembles a vast, flat checkerboard of green and gold. The squares of the checkerboard are fields of corn, wheat, and other crops. In only a few places would you see forests or steep hills. In some parts of the state you would see busy industrial cities. In other places, villages and towns dot the countryside.

As the map on pages 28 and 29 shows, nearly all of Illinois lies in the Central Lowland. The Interior Highlands and the Coastal Plain extend into the southern tip of the state.

Farmlands in the Central Lowland of Illinois. Nearly all of Illinois lies in the Central Lowland section of our country. Most of the land here is flat or gently rolling. The Interior Highlands and the Coastal Plain extend into the southern tip of Illinois.

The Central Lowland. Most of the Central Lowland of Illinois is flat or gently rolling. During the Great Ice Age,* huge glaciers moved over most of this area. They leveled off hills, filling in valleys with soil and rock.

As the map on this page shows, small areas in the Central Lowland of Illinois were not covered by glaciers. The land in these unglaciated areas is quite different from the rest of the Central Lowland. Here are steep hills and narrow valleys. It is difficult to raise crops in these hilly areas. Much of the land is in forest or pasture.

The Interior Highlands. A small area in southern Illinois lies in the Interior Highlands region of our country. Narrow valleys and forested hills make up most of the land here. Orchards of apple and peach trees cover many of the hillsides.

The Coastal Plain. A tiny part of the Coastal Plain extends into southern Illinois. (See map on this page.) The land here is mostly low and flat. This area borders on both the Mississippi and the Ohio rivers. Some farmers grow cotton in the fertile soil of the Coastal Plain in Illinois.

Important waterways serve Illinois. Some of our country's most important water highways serve the state of Illinois. One of these is the Great Lakes–St. Lawrence Waterway. (See pages 184 and 185.) The great city of Chicago, which is located on Lake Michigan, handles more freight than any other port on the Great Lakes–St. Lawrence Waterway. Since the opening of the St. Lawrence Seaway section of this waterway, oceangoing ships from many parts of the world have been able to come to Chicago.

Illinois is served by important waterways. Lake Michigan borders the state on the northeast. The Mississippi River flows along Illinois's western boundary.

Illinois is served by several other important water highways. The Mississippi River forms the state's entire western boundary. The Ohio River flows along the southern border and empties into the Mississippi. The Illinois Waterway* connects Lake Michigan and the Mississippi River. This waterway includes the Chicago River, the Des Plaines River, and the Illinois River.

*See Glossary

205

A summer day on a farm in northern Illinois. The warm, humid summers in Illinois are excellent for growing crops such as corn and soybeans. The growing season here ranges from five to seven months. Winter in most of Illinois is a cold, snowy season, with changeable weather.

CLIMATE

The climate of Illinois differs from one part of the state to another. The southern tip of Illinois lies almost four hundred miles closer to the equator than the northernmost part of the state. Temperatures in the south are usually several degrees warmer than those in the north. The feature on pages 50 and 51 will help you to understand how distance from the equator affects temperatures.

The length of Illinois's growing season ranges from five to seven months. (See map on page 60.) In the southern tip of the state, the growing season is long enough for growing cotton. In the rest of Illinois, farmers grow corn, oats, hay, and other crops that do not need as much time to ripen.

In Illinois, the weather changes greatly from season to season. These changes are typical of the kind of climate found in most of the Midwest and Great Plains. This is called a continental climate. (See pages 46-48.)

Winters in most of Illinois are generally cold and snowy. However, the weather is very changeable. Sometimes icy winds from the northwest sweep across the land, piling the snow into deep drifts that make travel difficult. At other times, warm winds from the south melt away ice and snow. Temperatures may rise or fall twenty degrees in one hour.

Summers in Illinois are very warm and humid. This type of weather is excellent for growing such crops as corn and soybeans. However, the combination of heat and humidity makes people uncomfortable. Near Chicago, cool breezes from Lake Michigan help to make summer weather more pleasant.

Throughout Illinois, there is enough rain for growing crops. Moist winds from the Gulf of Mexico bring most of the state's rainfall. As the map on page 49 shows, the yearly rainfall is generally heavier in southern Illinois than it is in the northern part of the state.

NATURAL RESOURCES

Illinois's mineral resources have helped it to become a great manufacturing state. It ranks fourth in the nation in the value of coal produced and eighth in the value of petroleum.

Some of the largest bituminous coalfields in the United States underlie much of Illinois. (See map on page 166.) More than half of the coal produced in Illinois is found near the surface of the earth. This coal is dug from the ground by giant power shovels. (See pages 164 and 165.) In other places in Illinois, coal deposits are located far beneath the surface. To obtain this coal, miners must work deep within the earth.

A huge power shovel in an open-pit coal mine in Illinois. Illinois ranks fourth in the nation in coal production. Nearly two thirds of Illinois's coal is used in steam power plants to produce electricity. Some coal is also used to heat factories and homes.

Almost two thirds of the coal in Illinois is used by steam power plants to produce electricity. These plants supply nearly all of the electric power needed by the large number of people and the many industries in the state. Some coal is used to heat homes and factories. A small amount of Illinois's coal is used to make coke* for the iron and steel industry. Most of Illinois's coal, however, is not suitable for making coke. Steel mills here must import coking coal from West Virginia and other states.

Illinois is the Midwest's leading oil-producing state. Most of the oil comes from oil fields located in southeastern Illinois. (See map on page 169.) Crude* oil is piped from these fields to refineries, where it is made into gasoline, fuel oil, and other useful products. Illinois does not produce all the oil needed by its large population and its many industries, however. Crude oil and petroleum products must also be brought by pipeline from Oklahoma and other oil-producing states.

Illinois is also a leading producer of stone, sand, and gravel. These mineral resources are used mainly by the construction industry. Sand is also used by some factories in the state as a raw material for making glass. Most of the stone quarried in Illinois is limestone. Besides being used in the construction of roads and buildings, limestone is the main raw material used in making cement.

An oil refinery at Joliet. Illinois produces more oil than any other state east of the Mississippi River. Most of its oil wells are in the southeastern part of the state. Crude oil from wells is piped to oil refineries, where it is made into gasoline and many other useful products.

FARMING

When pioneers came to Illinois in the early 1800's, much of the land was treeless prairie, covered with tall grass. They found the prairie sod very difficult to plow. Many of them believed that since trees did not grow on the prairie, crops could not be grown either. As a result, most of the pioneers settled in wooded areas. Then, in the 1840's, an Illinois blacksmith named John Deere began to manufacture steel plows. With these new plows, farmers were able to turn over the tough prairie sod much more easily. They soon found that the black soil of the prairies was excellent for growing crops.

Illinois ranks fourth in the nation in agriculture. Today, Illinois ranks fourth among our states in the value of its farm products. The level land, rich soil, and plentiful rainfall in Illinois are favorable for agriculture. Also, the growing season here is long enough for raising corn and other grain crops. An excellent system of highways and railroads makes it easy for farmers to ship their products to markets in Chicago and other cities.

Corn is the leading farm crop. Farmers in Illinois earn more money from corn than from any other farm product. This state ranks first in the country in the production of this important crop. As the map on page 153 shows, much of Illinois lies in our country's great corn belt. By late summer, the corn stands taller than a man. In autumn, large corn-picking machines rumble through the fields, harvesting the ripened ears of corn.

More than half of the corn raised in Illinois is fed to beef cattle and

Harvesting corn on an Illinois farm. Illinois ranks fourth among our states in the value of farm products sold. Corn is the leading crop.

hogs. Much of the corn raised in the state, however, is sold to food-processing plants. These plants use corn in making such products as breakfast cereals, cornstarch, and corn syrup.

Livestock. The sale of livestock accounts for about four tenths of Illinois's total farm income each year. Farmers in Illinois raise more hogs than are raised in any other state except Iowa. Illinois is also an important cattle-raising state. Many beef cattle are brought from ranches in states farther west to feedlots in Illinois. Here, cattle are fattened on corn and other grain before they are shipped to market.

Other important farm products. Illinois leads the nation in the production of soybeans. Meal and oil are obtained from this crop. Soybean meal is fed to livestock. Margarine, paints, soap, and

Beef cattle in an Illinois feedlot. Ranchers in states farther west often ship their cattle to feedlots in Illinois. Here, farmers fatten the animals for market by feeding them corn and other grain. Many farmers in Illinois also raise hogs.

other useful products are made from soybean oil. Many farmers in Illinois grow soybeans as a rotation* crop to help keep the soil fertile. You can read more about crop rotation on page 151.

Milk and eggs are other important farm products in Illinois. Most dairy and poultry farms are located in the northern part of the state. They supply large quantities of fresh milk and eggs to people in the Chicago metropolitan area. Dairy farms in southwestern Illinois supply milk to customers in the St. Louis, Missouri, area.

INDUSTRY

A great manufacturing state. Illinois ranks fourth in our nation in manufacturing. Factories here turn out almost fifteen billion dollars' worth of goods each year. More than two thirds of this amount is produced in the Chicago industrial area.

A combination of advantages has helped industry to grow in Illinois. One of the major advantages is the state's location. Illinois is situated in a very densely populated and heavily industrialized part of the United States. (See maps on pages 117,

194, and 195.) The millions of people who live in and near Illinois create a huge market for products from the state's factories. This state's large population also provides an excellent supply of skilled industrial workers. Thousands of factories in the Midwest buy machinery and other goods produced in Illinois. Automobile plants, for example, use large metalworking machines and enormous quantities of steel made in Illinois's mills and factories.

Another advantage for industry in Illinois is its outstanding network of land and water transportation routes. These routes enable manufacturers here to ship their products to customers in all parts of the United States as well as in foreign countries. Major water highways, such as the Great Lakes–St. Lawrence Waterway, serve Illinois. (See page 205.) In addition, roads and railroads link Illinois with all parts of our country.

Although farms and mines in Illinois provide many raw materials for industry, certain raw materials must be brought in from other states. For example, large shipments of coal and iron ore are brought to steel mills in Illinois by train and boat.

Products of Illinois's industry. The manufacture of iron and steel is one of the leading industries in Illinois. Steel is the main raw material used by many factories in the state. Most of Illinois's iron and steel plants are located in the Chicago industrial area, which is part

Assembling combines at a factory in Moline. Illinois is one of our nation's leading producers of farm machinery. In the farming areas of the Midwest and Great Plains, there is a large market for combines, tractors, and other farm machines.

of a great steelmaking district along the southern shore of Lake Michigan. Iron ore, coal, and limestone can be brought here easily by water and rail.

Much of the steel made in Illinois is used in the manufacture of machinery. Illinois leads the nation in the production of nonelectrical machinery. Road graders, bulldozers, and other kinds of heavy construction equipment are made in several cities in the state. Factories in Illinois also manufacture equipment such as machine* tools and other types of metalworking machines. In addition, this state is one of our nation's leading producers of farm machinery. There is a large market for tractors, combines, and other farm machines in the farming areas of the Midwest and Great Plains.

Illinois ranks third among the states of our country in the production of electrical machinery. More than three fourths of all the electrical machinery made in the state is manufactured in the Chicago area. Factories here make household appliances, radios, television sets, and many other kinds of electrical equipment.

Another major industry in Illinois is the manufacture of food products. (See fact table on page 204.) This state is outranked only by California in food processing. Illinois farms provide huge quantities of corn, soybeans, and other

Manufacturing road graders and other earth-moving equipment in Decatur. Factories in Peoria, Decatur, and other Illinois cities make heavy construction equipment. Illinois leads the country in the production of nonelectrical machinery.

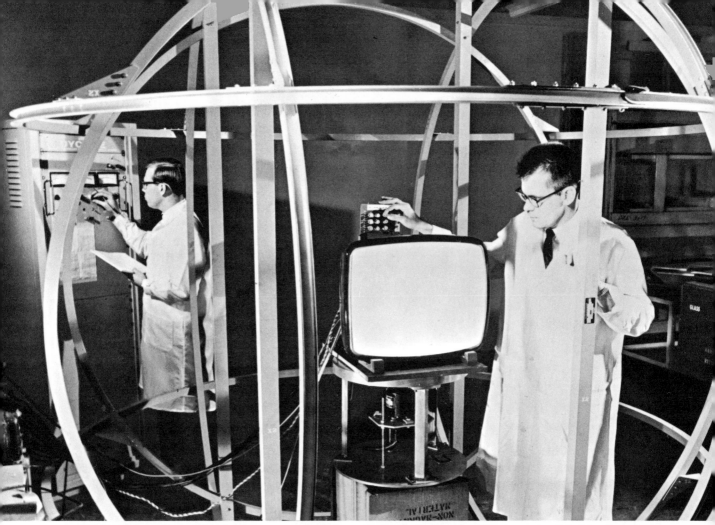

Technicians in a television research laboratory in Chicago. Illinois ranks third in the nation in the manufacture of electrical machinery. Factories in the Chicago area make household appliances, radios, television sets, and other electrical equipment.

raw materials for processing plants here. In addition, trucks and trains bring farm products from other states.

Many kinds of food products are made in Illinois. Large plants in Decatur, Chicago, and other cities process corn to make such products as corn syrup and cornstarch. Other plants process soybeans to make soybean oil and meal. Many mills in the state grind wheat into flour. Fruits and vegetables are processed in canneries and freezing plants.

Meat-packing is also an important type of food processing in Illinois. There are slaughterhouses in cities throughout the state. Each year, work-ers in these plants butcher hundreds of thousands of hogs, beef cattle, sheep, and lambs from farms in Illinois. The meat is then prepared for sale to stores and restaurants.

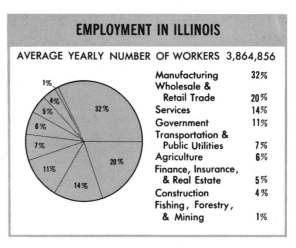

EMPLOYMENT IN ILLINOIS

AVERAGE YEARLY NUMBER OF WORKERS 3,864,856

Manufacturing	32%
Wholesale & Retail Trade	20%
Services	14%
Government	11%
Transportation & Public Utilities	7%
Agriculture	6%
Finance, Insurance, & Real Estate	5%
Construction	4%
Fishing, Forestry, & Mining	1%

PEOPLE AND CITIES

More people live in Illinois than in any other state in the Midwest and Great Plains except Texas. Illinois ranks fifth in population among all the states in the nation. However, most of Illinois is not densely populated. More than half of the people in the state make their homes in or near the great city of Chicago. Only two other cities in Illinois (Rockford and Peoria) have populations of more than 100,000.

Chicago (population 3,520,000; altitude 595 feet) is located in the northeastern part of Illinois. (See map on page 205.) It is our country's second largest city. Only New York is larger.

A visit to Chicago. The great city of Chicago spreads along the southwestern shore of Lake Michigan for about twenty-five miles. If you were to visit this city, you would see beautiful parks, broad expressways, and sandy beaches along the lakefront. Near the point where the Chicago River joins Lake Michigan, many tall buildings rise high into the sky. This is Chicago's central business district. Here are most of the city's largest office buildings, stores, banks, and hotels. Each day, hundreds of thousands of people come to the central business district to work or shop.

From the central business district, Chicago spreads out to the north, west, and south. To the north, along Lake

A view of Chicago, looking westward from Lake Michigan. Near the lakeshore is Chicago's central business district. From here, this great city spreads out to the north, west, and south. More than half of Illinois's people make their homes in or near Chicago.

Michigan, modern apartment buildings line Lake Shore Drive. To the west, we see factories, apartment buildings, and thousands of small homes. O'Hare International Airport, which covers about ten square miles, is located northwest of the city.

South of the central business district, we see the buildings and campus of the University of Chicago. This is one of many colleges and universities located in or near Chicago. As we travel southward along the shore of Lake Michigan, we see giant steel mills and oil refineries. Several long ore boats and oil tankers are docked along the waterfront.

Chicago is the central city of a huge metropolitan* area. North of Chicago, a series of smaller cities and towns extends to the Wisconsin border. West of the city the land is dotted with small towns and factories. To the southeast, a vast industrial area extends into northwestern Indiana. The manufacturing cities of Gary, Hammond, and East Chicago, Indiana, are located here. Altogether, more than seven million people live in the Chicago metropolitan area.

How Chicago grew. In 1803 a detachment of American soldiers built a small fort at the mouth of the Chicago River. It was named Fort Dearborn. This fort stood on the main route between the Great Lakes and the Mississippi River. Explorers and fur traders had used this route for many years. They traveled between Lake Michigan and the Mississippi River almost entirely by water, paddling their canoes along the Chicago, Des Plaines, and Illinois rivers.

A small settlement grew up around Fort Dearborn. For many years the settlement grew slowly. Then, in the 1850's, railroads were built connecting the eastern part of our country with settlements in the Midwest. From then on, Chicago grew rapidly. Settlers poured into the Midwest. They shipped their grain, livestock, and other farm products to Chicago to be processed. Many factories were started in this city to supply the growing population of the Midwest with manufactured products. Thousands of people came from eastern cities to work in Chicago. Many immigrants from Europe also came here to live and work. By 1870, the population of Chicago had increased to more than 300,000.

In 1871, a terrible fire swept through Chicago. It destroyed the entire business district and left about one third of the population homeless. Chicago quickly recovered from this disaster, however. Within three years the city was almost entirely rebuilt. It continued to grow rapidly. By 1890, the tiny settlement that had started around Fort Dearborn had become one of the great cities of the world. At that time, it had a population of more than one million.

Chicago today. Except for New York, Chicago is our country's leading trading and manufacturing city. It is the most important transportation center in the nation.

A great web of highways and railroads leads into Chicago. This city is the busiest rail center in the world. Each weekday, about 35,000 carloads of freight are handled in railroad yards in and near Chicago. More travelers pass through O'Hare International Airport than any other airport in the world.

Chicago also benefits from water transportation. Millions of tons of oil, coal, and other products are carried by barge on the Illinois Waterway, which connects Lake Michigan with the Mississippi River. Ships from all parts of the world come to the port of Chicago by way of the Great Lakes–St. Lawrence Waterway.

The value of goods manufactured in Chicago is greater than that of goods made in any other city in our country except New York. Factories in the Chicago area produce about ten billion dollars' worth of goods each year. Many manufacturing plants in the Chicago area use steel that is produced here. This steel is used to make machinery and many other kinds of metal products. Other important industries in the Chicago area include printing and publishing, the manufacture of chemicals, and petroleum refining. Pages 210-213 tell more about industry in the Chicago area.

More trade is carried on in Chicago than in any other city in our country except New York. Raw materials and manufactured goods are shipped to Chicago from many parts of the United States as well as from foreign countries. The products of Chicago's factories are sold in many parts of the world. Chicago is noted for its huge trade shows where thousands of products are exhibited. Owners of stores and factories from all over our nation send buyers to Chicago to see these products.

Chicago is the cultural center of the Midwest. If you were to visit this great city, you would find many interesting things to do. You could attend several different plays. You could also hear a concert by the Chicago Symphony Orchestra. Each day, thousands of peo-

ple from Chicago and other parts of the Midwest visit the city's great museums. In the Art Institute, you would see paintings and sculptures by some of the world's greatest artists. A large art school is also part of this institute. In the huge Museum of Science and Industry, there are hundreds of exhibits showing achievements in science and manufacturing. Here, you can also see a model farm and coal mine. More than a million visitors go through the Field Museum of Natural History each year. Among the popular exhibits in this museum is a series of bronze and stone sculptures called the "Races of Man."

Other cities of Illinois. Compared to the great city of Chicago, other cities in Illinois are small. The largest urban area outside of Chicago is made up of a group of cities clustered around East

Peoria is located on the Illinois River. It is a river port and an important manufacturing city.

St. Louis. (See map on page 205.) Almost half a million people live in this urban area. East St. Louis has a population of about 82,000. None of the other cities in this urban area is as large.

Rockford (population 133,000; altitude 715 feet) is the second largest city in Illinois. It is located along the banks of the Rock River, about eighty-five miles northwest of Chicago. Rockford is noted for producing manufactured goods requiring highly skilled workers. Factories here make precision machine tools, bolts and nuts, hardware, and other metal products. Rockford also serves as a trading center for a large area of prosperous farms and small towns.

Peoria (population 130,500; altitude 470 feet) is Illinois's third largest city. It is located on the Illinois River. (See map on page 205.) Peoria is the main trading city for a prosperous farming area in the north central part of the state. It is also a river port and an important manufacturing city. Peoria's largest industry is the manufacture of earth-moving machines and other construction equipment. Caterpillar tractors, bulldozers, and other large machines are shipped from Peoria to many parts of the world.

Springfield (population 87,000; altitude 610 feet) is the capital of Illinois. It is located in the central part of the state. (See map on page 205.) Although there are a number of small factories in Springfield, manufacturing is not as important here as it is in many other Illinois cities. Many people in Springfield are employed by government agencies. Abraham Lincoln lived in Springfield from 1837 to 1861, and he is buried here. Many tourists come to Springfield to see the house Lincoln lived in and to visit his tomb.

Questions To Guide Your Reading
1. In what section of our country is most of Illinois located?
2. How does the Interior Highlands region in Illinois differ from the part of the state that lies in the Coastal Plain?
3. Name four important waterways that serve Illinois.
4. What are some of the uses of coal mined in Illinois?
5. Why is Illinois well suited for agriculture?
6. What facts help to explain why Illinois is a great manufacturing state?
7. Name several products of Illinois's factories.
8. What is the capital of Illinois?

Learn About Chicago
Read about the great city of Chicago and then prepare an oral report about it to share with your class. The questions below will guide your research.
1. Where is Chicago located?
2. How did Chicago begin?
3. What helped the city to grow?
4. What disaster once destroyed much of Chicago?
5. What are some of the ways in which Chicago is important to the rest of our country?
6. What are some of the interesting things to see and do in Chicago?

This chapter contains much useful information for your report. If you wish to do outside research, refer to the suggestions on pages 346-352 for locating information and making your report. You may also want to conclude your report with several sentences explaining why you would, or would not, like to live in Chicago.

14 Indiana

Facts About Indiana		
	Number or Value	Rank
Area (square miles)	36,291	38
Population	4,918,000	12
Capital — Indianapolis		
Admission Date:		
December 11, 1816		19
Colleges and Universities	40	21
Farm Products	$1,202,577,000	8
Hogs	283,234,000	3
Corn	217,957,000	3
Soybeans	168,075,000	3
Fish	$ 132,000	35
Forest Products	$ 14,850,000	29
Minerals	$ 211,783,000	23
Coal	57,246,000	8
Cement	48,695,000	6
Stone	39,978,000	10
Manufactures	$7,687,872,000	8
Primary metal industries	1,417,541,000	3
Electrical machinery	1,137,752,000	7
Transportation equipment	1,092,402,000	6

Land. Indiana is the smallest state in the Midwest and Great Plains. It lies entirely in the Central Lowland. (Compare map on the opposite page with map on pages 28 and 29.) Indiana has forty-five miles of shoreline on Lake Michigan, which borders the northwestern corner of the state. The Ohio River flows along Indiana's entire southern border. Part of the state's western boundary is formed by the Wabash River, which empties into the Ohio.

Most of Indiana was smoothed by glaciers during the Great Ice Age. (See page 36.) The glaciers leveled off hilltops and filled in valleys, leaving broad lowlands and low, rounded hills. Almost all of this glaciated area is in our country's fertile corn belt. The only

Harvesttime in Indiana. Indiana lies entirely in the Central Lowland section of our country. Most of the land in this state is level or gently rolling and is well suited to farming.

part of Indiana that was never covered by glaciers is the Southern Hills and Valleys. (See map at right.) This area is generally more hilly than the rest of the state.

The northern third of Indiana is mainly flat or gently rolling. Pastures and cornfields cover much of the countryside. In the northeastern part of the state is an area of valleys and low hills. The land here is dotted with hundreds of lakes formed by glaciers during the Great Ice Age. Parts of northern Indiana that were once marshy have been drained, leaving rich, black soil called muck.* Among the crops grown in this fertile soil are onions and mint.

The northwestern corner of Indiana is part of the Midwest's greatest industrial district. A belt of steel mills, oil refineries, and cement plants stretches for miles along the Indiana shore of Lake Michigan. Three cities located here—Gary, Hammond, and East Chicago—form an industrial area that adjoins the Chicago industrial area. (See map on pages 194 and 195.) East of Gary, beautiful white sand dunes rise along the lakeshore. Indiana Dunes State Park is located here. This park provides summer recreation for thousands of visitors.

Indiana's most fertile farmlands are in the central part of the state. Fields of corn, soybeans, wheat, and oats stretch for miles across the level land of central Indiana. Farmers here also raise many hogs and beef cattle. Indiana's capital, Indianapolis, is located in this part of the state.

The Southern Hills and Valleys area of Indiana is not so well suited to farming as the rest of the state. In the valleys and on some of the slopes, however,

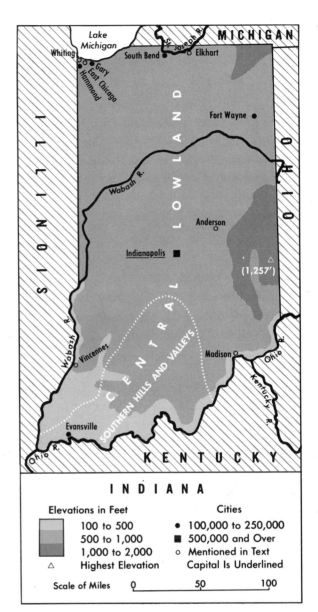

Indiana is the smallest state in the Midwest. It is bordered by Lake Michigan on the northwest and by the Ohio River on the south.

farmers raise crops such as corn, wheat, and soybeans. Cattle graze on hillsides where the soil is too thin and poor for growing crops. In this area are many rounded, tree-covered hills called knobs, which make a picturesque landscape. Underground streams have hollowed out huge caves in the beds of limestone that lie beneath the surface of the land. In the southwestern corner of Indiana,

*See Glossary

where the Wabash River joins the Ohio, the land is low and level.

Climate. Indiana has a continental climate, with long, warm summers and generally cold winters. This kind of climate is found in the parts of our country that lie far inland from the oceans. (See pages 46-48.) Since there are no ocean breezes to moderate the climate, such areas are marked by extremes of temperature.

Indiana's climate is well suited to farming. The growing season lasts from five to six months in most of the state. In parts of southern Indiana, the frost-free period is from six to seven months long. (See map on page 60.) All parts of the state receive an average annual rainfall of thirty inches or more. The southern part receives from forty to fifty inches of rainfall each year. (See map on page 49.) Most of the rain is brought by winds blowing northward from the Gulf of Mexico.

Each season brings a change of weather to Indiana. Winter brings cloudy skies, cold winds, and drifting snow. Spring is a time of soaking rains and warm sunshine. Fields of corn flourish during the warm, humid summer, and by August, the corn stands much taller than a man. Autumn brings cool days and clear, starry nights. This is the season when, as James Whitcomb Riley* wrote, "the frost is on the punkin and the fodder's in the shock."

Farming. Indiana ranks eighth in the nation in the value of farm products sold. In the early 1800's, Indiana's broad areas of level, fertile land attracted thousands of pioneers. The settlers cleared the land and started farms. They found that corn would grow es-

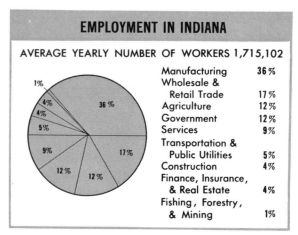

EMPLOYMENT IN INDIANA

AVERAGE YEARLY NUMBER OF WORKERS 1,715,102

Manufacturing	36%
Wholesale & Retail Trade	17%
Agriculture	12%
Government	12%
Services	9%
Transportation & Public Utilities	5%
Construction	4%
Finance, Insurance, & Real Estate	4%
Fishing, Forestry, & Mining	1%

pecially well in Indiana. Most of the state lies in the corn belt, a large area of our country where the soil and climate are favorable for growing this crop. (See map on page 153.) The corn belt is also well suited for growing many other crops and for raising livestock.

Today, Iowa and Illinois are the only states in our country that grow more corn than Indiana. In every part of Indiana, some corn is grown. (See map on page 155.) Many farmers grow corn as feed to fatten hogs and cattle

Cultivating soybeans. Indiana ranks third in the nation in the production of both soybeans and corn. Most of the state lies in the corn belt.

An Indiana farm in the wintertime. Much of the corn grown in Indiana is used to fatten hogs, which are the state's most valuable farm product. Farmers in Indiana also raise several other kinds of livestock, including beef cattle and sheep.

for market. Others sell their corn to processing plants, where it is made into such products as corn oil, cornstarch, and cereal.

Soybeans are Indiana's second most valuable crop. They are grown in the same areas where corn is grown. Soybeans are used chiefly as livestock feed and in making food products such as cooking oil. The oil from soybeans is also used in the manufacture of a variety of other products, including soap and paint.

Indiana farmers raise many other crops. Wheat, oats, and rye are grown throughout the state. Large quantities of tomatoes are grown in the east central part of Indiana. Canneries in this area process tomatoes to make such

foods as tomato juice, tomato sauce, and canned tomatoes. These products are shipped to all parts of our country. Spearmint and peppermint grow well in the rich, black muck of northern Indiana. They are used to provide flavoring for candy, gum, and other products. Onions and other vegetables are also grown in northern Indiana. Some farmers in southern Indiana grow tobacco.

Raising livestock is also important in Indiana. The sale of hogs brings more money to the state than the sale of corn or soybeans. In feedlots* throughout Indiana's corn belt, hogs are fattened on corn. The animals are then sold to meat-packing plants, which prepare ham, bacon, sausage, and other pork products. Indiana farmers also earn

Quarrying limestone in Indiana. Limestone is one of Indiana's most important mineral resources. Some of the limestone is used to make cement. Quarries here also supply fine-quality limestone for use as a building stone. The leading mineral resource of Indiana is bituminous coal. Nearly two thirds of Indiana's coal is burned in steam power plants to generate electricity.

large sums of money from cattle. Beef cattle are raised throughout the state. Dairy farming is also important, especially in the northwestern corner of Indiana. The many people who live in this part of the state provide a large market for dairy products. Indiana farmers also raise sheep and poultry.

Natural resources. Indiana has many other important natural resources besides fertile soil and a climate favorable to agriculture. The state has deposits of coal, petroleum, and other nonmetallic minerals. In addition, valuable hardwood forests cover parts of Indiana.

Bituminous coal is Indiana's leading mineral resource. Large quantities

of coal are taken from the coalfields located in the southwestern part of the state. (See map on page 166.) Some of the mines are deep underground, while others are surface, or strip, mines. In strip mines, the coal is so near the surface that it can be dug with giant power shovels. Nearly two thirds of Indiana's coal is burned in steam power plants to generate electricity.

Limestone is also one of Indiana's most important mineral resources. Some of the limestone is used to make cement. Indiana ranks sixth in the nation in the production of this useful mineral product. (See fact table on page 218.) Quarries in the state also supply fine-quality limestone for use as a building stone. Indiana limestone has been used in the construction of some of the most famous buildings in our country. These include the Rockefeller Center buildings in New York City and the Pentagon in Washington, D.C. Indiana also produces large amounts of crushed limestone for use in road building and other kinds of construction work.

Other useful natural resources are found in Indiana. Oil wells in the southwestern part of the state produce some petroleum, but not enough to meet all of Indiana's needs. Indiana clay is used in making bricks, tile, and pottery. Forests, which cover about one sixth of the state, provide hardwoods such as oak, hickory, maple, and walnut. These woods are used for making furniture and other wood products.

Industry. Indiana ranks eighth in the nation in manufacturing. Several facts help to explain why so much industry has developed here. Indiana is located near many of the Midwest's largest cities. These cities provide a huge market for Indiana's manufactured goods. Indiana is served by convenient water, air, and land transportation. The state also has abundant supplies of minerals, farm products, and other raw materials for manufacturing. In addition, Indiana has a large labor force available to work in its mills and factories.

A steel plant in Gary, along Lake Michigan. The manufacture of primary metals is Indiana's leading industry. Steel is the main product of this industry. Much of the steel produced in Indiana is used by factories here to make such products as refrigerators and automobile parts.

The manufacture of primary metals is Indiana's leading industry. Steel is the main product of this industry. Iron and steel plants are located in an industrial belt that stretches for more than fifteen miles along the shore of Lake Michigan. Here, lake freighters unload their cargoes of iron ore and limestone. Long trains bring coking* coal from the Appalachian Plateau. In the daytime, clouds of gray and orange smoke billow from tall smokestacks. At night, the entire area glows with light from blast-furnace fires. Sometimes, showers of sparks fly into the night sky.

The steel produced in Indiana is used in the manufacture of many different products. Some of it is shipped to other states for use in making automobiles, airplanes, and other goods. Much of Indiana's steel, however, is used within the state. Many factories here use steel in the manufacture of electrical machinery, which is Indiana's second most important industry. Products of this industry include refrigerators, washing machines, and radio and television sets. Large amounts of steel are also used by factories that make transportation equipment, such as automobile and aircraft parts. The manufacture of transportation equipment ranks third among the state's industries.

Although northwestern Indiana is the state's busiest manufacturing area, many products are made in other parts

In an aluminum plant near Evansville. Barges on the Mississippi and Ohio rivers bring alumina* from states in the southern part of our country. Aluminum made in this plant is used by factories in Indiana to manufacture wire and many other products.

Indianapolis is located near the center of Indiana. It is the state's capital and largest city. Indianapolis is the leading manufacturing city in central Indiana. Among the goods manufactured here are jet engines, drugs, and parts for motor vehicles.

of Indiana. A large plant near Evansville produces aluminum from alumina.* Barges on the Mississippi and Ohio rivers bring alumina from plants in the southern part of our country. Elkhart, in northern Indiana, is known for the manufacture of drugs, musical instruments, and house trailers. Food-processing plants in various parts of Indiana make cheese, flour, and other foods.

People and cities. About two thirds of Indiana's population lives in large towns and cities. Many people live in urban areas that spread into Indiana from cities in other states. These cities include Chicago, Illinois; Louisville, Kentucky; and Cincinnati, Ohio.

Indianapolis (population 530,000; altitude 710 feet) is Indiana's capital and largest city. Located near the center of the state, Indianapolis is served by a network of fine highways, railways, and airways.

Indianapolis is the leading manufacturing city in central Indiana. It is also a center of business and culture. Factories in the Indianapolis area make jet engines, electrical machinery, drugs, and parts for motor vehicles. The stockyards here are among the largest in the nation. More than fifty insurance companies have their home offices in Indianapolis. Several colleges and universities are also located in this city.

225

Each year on Memorial Day, Indianapolis attracts huge crowds. People come here from all over the world to watch the famous "Indianapolis 500." This is a 500-mile automobile race held at the Indianapolis Motor Speedway.

Gary–Hammond–East Chicago metropolitan* area (population 610,500; altitude 590 feet). The three industrial cities of Gary, Hammond, and East Chicago are located in the northwestern corner of Indiana. They are the chief cities of a large metropolitan area that also includes Whiting and several other towns.

Gary, with a population of about 179,000, is Indiana's second largest city. It was founded in 1906 as the home of an enormous iron and steel plant. Today, in addition to its large steel industry, Gary has industrial plants that make products such as machine parts and cement. Hammond (population 115,000), East Chicago (population 58,000), and Whiting (population 8,000) are located west of Gary. Whiting has one of the largest oil refineries in the world.

Fort Wayne (population 172,000; altitude 790 feet), Indiana's third largest city, is located in the northeastern part of the state. The city grew up around a fort built by General Anthony Wayne* in the late 1700's. Today, Fort Wayne is an important trading city for the rich farming country that surrounds it.

Fort Wayne is also a manufacturing city. Products made here include washing machines and railroad-car wheels.

The "Indianapolis 500" is an automobile race held at the Indianapolis Motor Speedway each year on Memorial Day. People come here from all over the world to watch this famous 500-mile race.

In addition, the city is a leading producer of gasoline tanks and pumps for service stations.

Evansville (population 138,500; altitude 385 feet) is the largest city in southern Indiana. It is a port city on the Ohio River. Evansville was founded early in the nineteenth century. The little settlement along the river soon grew into a busy river port and trading town. Today, factories in the Evansville area make many different kinds of products, from aluminum to refrigerators. Food processing and furniture manufacturing are also important industries in Evansville.

South Bend (population 135,000; altitude 710 feet) is the central city of a metropolitan area in northern Indiana. South Bend was founded by a French fur trader in 1823, at the site of an old Indian village on the St. Joseph River.

Today, South Bend is an important manufacturing city. For many years, South Bend was known as the home of the Studebaker automobile. Although automobiles are no longer made here, the manufacture of automobile parts is

The South Bend metropolitan area is located in northern Indiana, along the St. Joseph River. South Bend was founded by a French fur trader in 1823. Today it is an important manufacturing city.

one of the city's chief industries. Factories here make brakes for both automobiles and airplanes. Farm machinery and machine tools are also made in South Bend.

Learn About Indiana With Maps

Study the map on page 219, and then answer the following questions:

1. What river forms the southern boundary of Indiana?
2. What large body of water borders Indiana's northwestern corner?
3. What is the capital of Indiana? In what part of the state is this city located?

Discover Important Facts About Indiana

1. Name Indiana's two leading crops. What are some uses of each crop?
2. What are three ways in which Indiana's limestone is used?
3. How is much of Indiana's coal used?
4. What is the leading industry in Indiana? How do other industries in the state depend on this industry?

Reading for Pleasure

Listed below are three books that tell about life in Indiana in the past. For outside reading, choose one of these books or some other book about Indiana. Share the parts you find most amusing or interesting with your family and classmates.

Seventeen, by Booth Tarkington

Penrod and Sam, by Booth Tarkington

Friendly Persuasion, by Jessamyn West

Facts About Iowa		
	Number or Value	Rank
Area (square miles)	56,290	25
Population	2,747,000	25
Capital — Des Moines		
Admission Date:		
December 28, 1846		29
Colleges and Universities	51	13
Farm Products	$2,685,758,000	2
Cattle and calves	943,415,000	1
Hogs	701,636,000	1
Corn	377,038,000	2
Fish	$ 300,000	31
Forest Products	$ 7,350,000	37
Minerals	$ 106,630,000	29
Cement	48,245,000	7
Stone	33,038,000	14
Sand and gravel	13,546,000	26
Manufactures	$2,275,928,000	24
Food and kindred products	653,063,000	10
Nonelectrical machinery	476,344,000	14
Electrical machinery	256,121,000	16

Land. Have you ever flown over Iowa in spring or summer? If so, you will never forget this beautiful state. Looking down from your plane, you discover a checkerboard of fields and pastures stretching to the horizon. (See picture below.) Flying mile after mile over farmlands that seem endless, you begin to realize that Iowa is truly a great farming state. No other area of this size in the world has so much rich farmland.

Iowa lies entirely in the Central Lowland section of our country. (Compare map on opposite page with map on pages 28 and 29.) Although Iowa is generally level, the land slopes slightly upward from southeast to northwest.

Farmland in western Iowa. All of this state lies in the Central Lowland section of our country. The land here is generally level, and the soil is very fertile. Almost all of the land in the state is used for farming.

The Mississippi River winds southward along Iowa's entire eastern border. The state's western boundary is formed by the Big Sioux and Missouri rivers.

Almost all of Iowa was smoothed by massive glaciers during the Great Ice Age. (See page 36.) These huge ice sheets leveled off hilltops and filled in valleys, leaving vast, gently rolling plains. Today, these plains are covered with rich, dark soil, which has helped make Iowa one of our most productive farming states.

The Driftless Area in the northeastern corner of Iowa is the only part of the state that was not smoothed by glaciers. (See map at right.) This area is generally too rugged for cultivation. However, much of the land is used for grazing cattle. Along the eastern border of the Driftless Area, steep, pine-topped bluffs rise high above the Mississippi River.

Climate. Iowa's climate is much like that of the other states in the interior of our country. The weather varies greatly from one season to another. Winters here are bitterly cold, and summers are warm. This kind of climate is found in areas that lie far from any large body of water. The weather in Iowa also may vary greatly from one day to the next. Since the state has no sheltering mountains, winds blow freely over the land, bringing sudden storms and changes of temperature.

Iowa's climate is especially well suited to farming. Although the winters are long and cold, the danger of frost is generally over by early May. In most parts of the state, the growing season lasts from five to six months. (See map on page 60.) This is long enough for

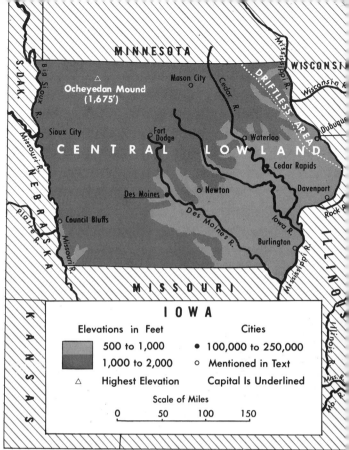

Iowa. The Mississippi River flows along the entire eastern border of Iowa. The western boundary of the state is formed by two other rivers, the Missouri and the Big Sioux.

farmers to grow corn and many other crops. Iowa also receives plenty of rain. Most of the rain comes during the summer months, when it is most needed by growing crops. To learn more about Iowa's climate, you may wish to read pages 46 and 47.

Farming. Iowa is the leading farming state in the Midwest and Great Plains. Among all the states of our country, it ranks second only to California in the total value of farm products. Favorable climate and fertile soils have encouraged the development of agriculture in Iowa. Today, almost 97 percent of the land here is used for farming. Out of every hundred workers in Iowa, about thirty earn their living by farming.

Farmers in Iowa receive more money from the sale of livestock than from

Harvesting corn in Iowa. Almost all of Iowa lies in the corn belt. Farmers here have increased their production of corn through the use of hybrid seed and chemical fertilizers. Most of the corn grown in Iowa is used to fatten hogs and cattle.

Judging cattle. Iowa is our nation's leading producer of beef cattle and hogs. Farmers here earn more money from livestock than from crops.

crops. Iowa leads the entire nation in the production of both hogs and beef cattle. (See fact table on page 228.) These animals are produced throughout the state. Most farmers in Iowa buy cattle raised on the grazing lands of states farther west and fatten them for market. A few raise their own beef cattle. Iowa ranks second in the raising of sheep, and many farmers in the state keep dairy cattle or poultry.

Corn is Iowa's leading crop. Almost all of the state lies in the corn belt, which is the richest farming area of its size in the world. (See pages 153-155.) In recent years, Iowa's corn production has greatly increased. This increase has resulted partly from the use of hybrid* seed and chemical fertilizers. Also, modern farm machines such as

*See Glossary

the mechanical corn picker have made it easier for farmers to harvest their huge crops of corn. Most of the corn grown in Iowa is fed to hogs and cattle. Some corn is cut green and stored as silage* for winter feeding.

Iowa farmers produce many crops in addition to corn. The state ranks second in the nation in the production of oats and soybeans. These important feed crops are grown throughout the state, often as rotation* crops. In various parts of Iowa, fruits such as apples, peaches, and grapes are grown. Near the cities, truck farmers grow cabbages, onions, tomatoes, and other vegetables.

Natural resources. The people of Iowa benefit from many valuable gifts of nature. These include fertile soil, abundant rainfall, and warm sunshine. Although Iowa does not have any important supplies of metal ores or petroleum, it does have large deposits of certain useful minerals such as stone, gypsum, and coal.

One of Iowa's most important mineral resources is limestone. Large amounts of this mineral are used in road building and other kinds of rough construction. Limestone is also used to make cement, Iowa's leading mineral product. (See fact table on page 228.)

To make cement, limestone is combined with smaller amounts of clay or shale. These minerals are found close together in various parts of the state. Large quantities of cement are made near Mason City, in north central Iowa.

The pictures on this page show three main steps in producing cement. First, the limestone is loosened by blasting. After the limestone is dug from the quarry, it is taken to the cement plant.

Blasting limestone in a quarry

Crushing limestone

Heating "raw mix" in a kiln

There it is dumped into huge crushing machines. The crushed limestone is mixed with small quantities of crushed shale or clay, and the mixture is ground into a fine powder called "raw mix." The raw mix is heated to a high temperature in an enormous round oven, or kiln. As it is heated, the material forms small lumps called clinkers. These are ground into the light-colored, powdery material we call cement.

Besides limestone, Iowa has deposits of other minerals used by the construction industry. These include sand and gravel, which are used mainly in road building. Iowa leads the nation in the production of a white, chalky mineral called gypsum. Large deposits of this useful mineral are located near Fort Dodge. The gypsum mined here is made into building materials such as plaster and wallboard.

Soft coal is mined in central and southern Iowa. Most of the coal is close enough to the surface to be scooped out by giant power shovels. This method of obtaining coal is called strip-mining. All of the coal mined in Iowa is used within the state, mainly in power plants to generate electricity.

Quarrying gypsum near Fort Dodge. Iowa is the nation's leading producer of gypsum. This useful mineral is made into plaster and other building materials. Coal is mined in central and southern Iowa. Most of it is used in power plants in Iowa to generate electricity.

Cooking canned hams in a meat-packing plant in Waterloo. Food processing is the leading industry in Iowa. Ham, bacon, and other products from meat-packing plants here are sold in many parts of our country. Other food products of Iowa include oatmeal and corn oil.

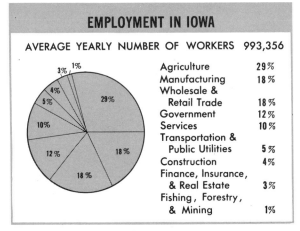

EMPLOYMENT IN IOWA

AVERAGE YEARLY NUMBER OF WORKERS 993,356

Agriculture	29%
Manufacturing	18%
Wholesale & Retail Trade	18%
Government	12%
Services	10%
Transportation & Public Utilities	5%
Construction	4%
Finance, Insurance, & Real Estate	3%
Fishing, Forestry, & Mining	1%

Industry. The people of Iowa earn almost as much money from manufacturing as they do from agriculture. (See fact table on page 228.) Nearly one fifth of all the workers in the state have jobs in industry. Most of the factories are in the eastern half of the state.

Iowa's leading industry is food processing. This industry depends on the state's huge production of crops and livestock for its raw materials. The chief branch of the food-processing industry in Iowa is meat-packing. Trucks and trains carry thousands of animals from Iowa farms to livestock markets such as Sioux City and Waterloo. Meat-packing plants in these cities process enormous quantities of pork and beef. Meat products are shipped from Iowa to many different parts of our country.

233

Other kinds of food processing are also important in Iowa. Factories in Cedar Rapids and other cities use corn as a raw material for making food products such as corn oil and cornstarch. Cedar Rapids has one of the largest cereal mills in the world. If your mother served you oatmeal for breakfast this morning, the chances are that the oats were grown in Iowa and processed at this huge cereal mill. This plant also makes livestock feed from oats and other grains. Milk from Iowa dairy farms is processed in various cities in the state to make dairy products such as butter and ice cream.

The second most important industry in Iowa is the manufacture of nonelectrical machinery. Many factories in the state produce farm implements or construction equipment. Farm tractors, for example, are made in Waterloo and Dubuque. Electrical machinery is also made in Iowa. Refrigerators, refrigeration equipment, and washing machines manufactured in Iowa are sold throughout the United States.

People and cities. Iowa's population is distributed fairly evenly throughout the state. (See map on page 117.) Only two cities in Iowa have more than 100,000 people. These are Des Moines and Cedar

Assembling washing machines at Newton. Many factories in Iowa manufacture machinery. Some make washing machines, refrigerators, and other kinds of electrical machinery. Factories here also manufacture nonelectrical machinery, such as farm implements and construction equipment.

Des Moines is the capital and largest city of Iowa. It is located on the Des Moines River, in the central part of the state. Des Moines is noted for being an insurance and printing center. It is also the main trading city for the surrounding farming area.

Rapids. Out of every hundred people in the state, only fifty-three live in cities and towns.

Des Moines (population 216,000; altitude 805 feet) is Iowa's capital and largest city. It is the main trading city for a prosperous farming area in the central part of the state. The city grew up around a military fort built by the United States government on the Des Moines River in the 1840's.

Although Des Moines has many factories, it is better known as an insurance and printing center. More than

fifty insurance companies have their home offices in Des Moines, and many others have branch offices here. Printing plants in the city supply vast amounts of printed materials needed by the insurance business. Several farm and home magazines published in Des Moines are sold throughout the United States. Factories in the city make a variety of manufactured goods, such as meat products, clothing, farm implements, and aircraft engines.

Each year, at the end of summer, the Iowa State Fair is held in Des Moines.

Thousands of people come to the fair to see the exhibits, which feature products of Iowa agriculture and industry. Prizes are awarded for the best cattle, hogs, sheep, and other livestock. Prizes are also given for the best grains, vegetables, and fruits exhibited at the fair. Farm equipment and other manufactured products are displayed in the exhibition buildings at the fairgrounds.

Cedar Rapids (population 103,500; altitude 730 feet) is the second largest city in Iowa. It is located near rapids in the Cedar River, in the eastern part of the state. (See map on page 229.) Cedar Rapids serves as the main trading city for the surrounding agricultural area.

Although Des Moines is larger, Cedar Rapids is Iowa's leading manufacturing city. Food processing is the chief industry. At grain mills, corn and oats are made into food products such as cereal, cornstarch, and corn oil. Several large meat-packing plants are also located here. An electronic-products plant in Cedar Rapids provides electronic communication systems for some of our country's most important space projects. Farm implements and radios are among the other products manufactured in Cedar Rapids.

The Iowa State Fair is held each year, at the end of summer, in Des Moines. Thousands of people come to the fair to see the exhibits, which display products of farms and factories in Iowa. Prizes are awarded for the best hogs, cattle, sheep, and other livestock.

Cedar Rapids is Iowa's second largest city. It is also the state's leading manufacturing city. Food processing is the most important industry here.

Other cities. Five cities in Iowa have populations between 50,000 and 100,000. One of these is Waterloo (population 74,000; altitude 850 feet). This city is located on the Cedar River about fifty miles northwest of Cedar Rapids. It is an important trading city for livestock and other farm products. Several meat-packing plants are located here. Trac-tors and other kinds of farm machinery are made in Waterloo.

Two of the oldest cities in Iowa are located on the Mississippi River. They are Davenport (population 95,500; altitude 590 feet) and Dubuque (population 56,500; altitude 645 feet). Davenport and Dubuque both grew up as river ports in the mid-1800's. Today, these cities are still important ports. Here, goods such as grain and cement are loaded onto river barges, which are pushed along the Mississippi by diesel* tow-boats. Davenport and Dubuque are also important manufacturing cities. Davenport has an enormous aluminum rolling mill, and Dubuque produces lumber products and farm machinery.

The chief cities of western Iowa are Sioux City (population 91,000; altitude 1,110 feet) and Council Bluffs (popu-lation 58,500; altitude 990 feet). Both of these cities are on the Missouri River. Sioux City has extensive stock-yards and large meat-packing plants. Council Bluffs is an important trading and transportation city, served by sev-eral major railroads. Many of the peo-ple who live in Council Bluffs work in the city of Omaha, Nebraska, just across the Missouri River.

Build Your Vocabulary
Listed below are some of the words and terms you will need to know as you read about Iowa. Refer to the suggestions on page 353 for finding the meanings of words or terms that are new to you. Then, test your understanding by using each of these words or terms in a sentence.

silage	gypsum
hybrid seed	strip mining
rotation crop	fertilizer

Solve an Interesting Problem About Iowa
Iowa is one of our country's most important farming states, ranking second to California. **Why has Iowa become such an important farm-ing state?** To solve this problem, you will need to make hypotheses. (See To the Stu-dent, pages 8-10.) In forming hypotheses, consider each of the following:
a. the land and soil of Iowa
b. the climate of Iowa
You will find useful information in Chapter 9, as well as in this chapter.

Facts About Michigan		
	Number or Value	Rank
Area (square miles)	58,216	23
Population	8,374,000	7
Capital — Lansing		
Admission Date:		
January 26, 1837		26
Colleges and Universities	70	8
Farm Products	$ 790,948,000	17
Dairy products	224,160,000	6
Vegetables	117,447,000	4
Cattle and calves	89,928,000	22
Fish	$ 2,522,000	21
Forest Products	$ 48,750,000	17
Minerals	$ 555,495,000	9
Iron ore	143,979,000	2
Cement	89,270,000	4
Copper	45,014,000	5
Manufactures	$13,003,804,000	6
Transportation equipment	5,068,299,000	1
Nonelectrical machinery	1,758,378,000	3
Primary metal industries	1,143,823,000	5

Land. The state of Michigan is made up of two large peninsulas separated by a narrow water passage called the Straits of Mackinac. (See map on opposite page.) The Lower Peninsula, which is shaped like a mitten, lies mainly between Lake Michigan and Lake Huron. The Upper Peninsula, which extends eastward from Wisconsin, has a long, jagged shoreline along Lake Superior.

Michigan's peninsulas were formed as the Great Ice Age came to an end. (See page 36.) During this period, huge glaciers crept southward, covering much of what is now the Midwest. These glaciers scooped out thousands of depressions in the earth's surface. With the retreat of the last glacier, water from the melting ice began to fill some of these

The Mackinac Bridge links the two large peninsulas that make up Michigan. Most of Michigan's farms and large cities are located in the southern half of the Lower Peninsula. Few people live in the Upper Peninsula. Forests of pine, spruce, and birch cover much of this area.

depressions. As water rose in the enormous hollows that became the Great Lakes, many peninsulas and islands were formed.

Michigan's Lower Peninsula lies entirely in the Central Lowland. (See map on this page.) Most of the land here is level or gently rolling. On the western side, however, high bluffs and sand dunes line the Lake Michigan shore. The most fertile soil in Michigan is in the southern half of the Lower Peninsula. Most of the state's farms and large cities are located here. In the northern half of the Lower Peninsula, the soil is thin and sandy. Much of this area is forested.

Michigan's Upper Peninsula is a wild and beautiful land of woods and waters. Forests of pine, spruce, and birch cover much of the land. The eastern half of the Upper Peninsula lies in the Central Lowland. (See map on this page.) Parts of this area are low and swampy. The western half of Michigan's Upper Peninsula is in the Superior Upland. In this region, two low mountain ranges rise along the shore of Lake Superior. These are the Hurons and the Porcupines.

The state of Michigan includes a number of islands. The largest of these is Isle Royale in Lake Superior. This rugged island is a forested wilderness, preserved as a national park. Mackinac Island, in the Straits of Mackinac, has a romantic history as an Indian meeting place and the site of an early fur-trading post.

More than eleven thousand lakes dot the state of Michigan. Some are very small, but others are quite large. Most of these lakes were formed by glaciers. There are a number of small

Michigan. Most of Michigan lies in the Central Lowland section of our country. The western half of the Upper Peninsula is in the Superior Upland region.

rivers in the state that flow into the Great Lakes. Many of the northern rivers are noted for their rapids and waterfalls. Because of its thousands of lakes and streams, Michigan has been called the "Water Wonderland."

Climate. The climate varies from one part of Michigan to another. This is partly because the state extends about four hundred miles from north to south. Also, the Great Lakes have a moderating effect on climate, just as all large bodies

239

A ski race at a winter resort in Michigan.
Winters in the state are cold and snowy.
Summers are warm in most of the Lower Peninsula but mild in the rest of Michigan.

of water do. (See pages 61 and 62.) The effect of the Great Lakes on Michigan's climate is especially noticeable along Lake Michigan. Winds blowing across the lake cool the lakeshore in spring and delay the coming of frost in fall. These conditions help to make this area well suited for growing fruit.

In southern Michigan and along most of the Lake Michigan shore, the growing season is between five and six months. (See map on page 60.) The growing season in the rest of the state is less than five months.

Winters are long and cold throughout Michigan, but the Upper Peninsula is generally colder than the Lower Peninsula. Some places in the Upper Peninsula receive as much as 160 inches of snow during the winter. Lake Superior harbors freeze solid, and in some years people can even cross the Straits of Mackinac on the ice.

Summers are warm and humid in much of the Lower Peninsula. As you go north, however, the summer weather becomes cooler. In the Upper Peninsula, summers are mild and pleasant.

Farming. Agriculture is not as important in Michigan as it is in the other states of the Midwest. There are several reasons for this. In the northern parts of the state, much of the soil is poor for farming. Also, the growing season in some areas is not long enough for raising many crops successfully. In addition, manufacturing industries in Michigan's industrial areas have attracted many workers away from farms.

In spite of these disadvantages for agriculture, Michigan still produces many farm products. Dairying is the most important kind of farming. Even in areas where summers are short and cool, pasturelands provide enough grass for cattle. Hay and other kinds of fodder can also be grown in these areas. Throughout much of the state, the soil and climate are suitable for growing corn for silage.* Much of the milk produced by Michigan's dairy herds is sold fresh in Detroit and other large cities. Some is used in making dairy products such as butter, cheese, and ice cream.

Michigan is a leading producer of vegetables. Many different kinds of vegetable crops are raised, mainly in the southern part of the Lower Peninsula. In southwestern Michigan, swamps and small lakes have been drained, leaving patches of black, fertile soil called muck. This kind of soil is especially good for growing vegetables such as celery and onions. In addition to these vegetables, Michigan produces

240

*See Glossary

large amounts of cabbages, potatoes, and carrots. The state leads our country in the production of cucumbers for pickles. It also ranks first in the production of dry beans, such as navy beans and red kidney beans.

The western part of the Lower Peninsula is an important fruit-growing area. The climate along the shore of Lake Michigan is well suited for growing fruits such as cherries, apples, peaches, strawberries, grapes, and melons. Michigan leads the nation in the production of sour cherries, which are grown chiefly in an area around Traverse City. In the spring, the cherry trees suddenly burst into bloom. A fluffy white blanket of cherry blossoms stretches for mile after mile, covering much of the countryside.

Michigan farmers also earn money from a variety of other products. Many of them raise beef cattle or hogs. In the southwestern part of the state there are many chicken hatcheries and large turkey farms. Large quantities of sugar beets grown in Michigan are sent to sugar refineries in Bay City and other cities in the state.

Natural resources. Michigan is rich in minerals and other natural resources. Iron ore is the leading mineral produced in the state. The ore is found in the western part of the Upper Peninsula, in the Superior Upland region. For more than one hundred years, mines in the

Orchards near Traverse City. Farming is not as important in Michigan as it is in the rest of the Midwest. However, the part of the Lower Peninsula that borders Lake Michigan is one of the most productive fruit-growing areas of North America.

Upper Peninsula of Michigan have supplied ore for our country's iron and steel industry.

Although Michigan once led the nation in the production of iron ore, the state now ranks second to Minnesota. Much of the iron ore now shipped from Michigan's Upper Peninsula is in the form of grape-sized pellets. These pellets are produced by a special process from iron-bearing rock called jaspilite.* (See page 168.) The Upper Peninsula has vast deposits of this kind of rock. Nearly all of Michigan's iron ore is shipped by boat to Great Lakes port cities. Steel plants in the Detroit area use large amounts of Michigan ore to make iron and steel for the automobile industry. (See page 192.)

Copper is another of Michigan's important mineral resources. This familiar metal is made into hundreds of different products, such as coins, tubing, and pots and pans. However, about half of the copper used in this country is made into wire and other electrical supplies. Michigan's copper deposits are found in the Upper Peninsula, on a long, narrow strip of land that juts into Lake Superior. Here, in the 1840's, prospectors uncovered some of the richest copper deposits in the world. In the nineteenth century, Michigan led the nation in the production of copper. Now the state

A copper mine in the Upper Peninsula. Michigan is rich in mineral resources. There are large deposits of copper and iron ore in the Superior Upland region. This state ranks second in the nation in the production of iron ore and fifth in the production of copper.

ranks fifth in copper mining. Recently, however, new reserves of copper have been discovered near some of the old mines. Plans are being made to start mining these deposits.

Michigan is one of our nation's leading salt producers. Immense beds of salt underlie much of Michigan's Lower Peninsula. Rock* salt is mined from deposits more than one thousand feet beneath the city of Detroit. In several parts of the state, salt is obtained by forcing water down into a salt deposit. The salt dissolves in the water, forming an artificial brine.* The brine is pumped up and evaporated to produce salt. Natural brines also occur in Michigan. In addition to salt, these brines yield valuable chemicals that contain bromine* and magnesium.* Michigan's chemical industry uses these substances, as well as salt, as raw materials for the manufacture of drugs and other chemical products.

Other important minerals in Michigan include limestone, gypsum, and petroleum. Limestone is found in various parts of the state. Quarries along the shore of Lake Huron provide large amounts of this mineral for steelmaking and other industrial uses. Lake freighters carry the limestone to Detroit and other ports. Limestone is also used to make cement, which is Michigan's second most important mineral product. The world's largest cement plant is located at Alpena. Michigan has large gypsum deposits along Lake Huron and near Grand Rapids. Gypsum is used in making plaster and wallboard. Michigan's oil wells are mainly in the central and southern parts of the Lower Peninsula.

About half of Michigan is covered with forests. One hundred years ago, Michigan was a famous lumbering state. Lumberjacks cleared vast tracts of pine and hardwood trees. Now many of Michigan's cutover areas are being reforested. Millions of acres are included in state and national forests. In the Upper Peninsula, lumbering is still an important industry. Wood from Michigan's forests is used to make lumber, pulp, charcoal, and many other products.

Michigan is the leading fishing state in the Midwest. In the Great Lakes, fishermen catch whitefish, perch, trout, and herring. Several years ago, the trout in the Great Lakes were nearly destroyed by eel-like animals called lampreys, which came here from the ocean through the Great Lakes–St. Lawrence Waterway.* Now the lampreys are under control, and the lake trout are increasing. Michigan's rivers also provide fish. Each spring, commercial fishermen take large catches of smelt from rivers that empty into the Great Lakes.

Transportation. Michigan has an excellent transportation system. Highways, railroads, and airways connect the state's major cities. They also link these cities with other parts of our country. At the Straits of Mackinac, the Mackinac Bridge spans four miles of deep, blue water. This great highway bridge, completed in 1957, links the two peninsulas of Michigan. Railroad freight cars are ferried across the straits.

Water transportation on the Great Lakes has helped Michigan become a great industrial state. For example, huge lake freighters carry iron ore from the shores of Lake Superior to the busy docks at Detroit and other major Great

Freighters loading limestone at Rogers City, on Lake Huron. Water transportation on the Great Lakes has helped Michigan to become a leading manufacturing state. Lake freighters and oceangoing ships load and unload goods at many ports in Michigan.

Lakes ports. The freighters pass from Lake Superior into Lake Huron by way of the Soo Canals. These canals bypass falls and rapids in the St. Marys River, which connects the two lakes. Locks* in the canals lower southbound boats to the level of Lake Huron. On the return journey, the locks raise the boats to the level of Lake Superior. Each year, more freight is carried through the Soo Canals than through the Panama Canal.

The Great Lakes are part of an important water highway called the Great Lakes–St. Lawrence Waterway. (See map on pages 184 and 185.) The canals and locks of the St. Lawrence Seaway* make it possible for oceangoing ships to travel from the Atlantic Ocean all the way up the St. Lawrence River to the Great Lakes. Several Michigan cities are ports of entry for foreign goods.

Industry. Michigan is one of our country's leading manufacturing states. Industrial development began here in the nineteenth century, with the construction of sawmills and furniture factories. The state's plentiful supply of useful raw materials, including iron ore and salt as well as timber, encouraged manufacturing. Michigan's excellent transportation facilities have also helped industry to grow.

Besides raw materials and convenient transportation routes, Michigan has other advantages for industry. Because of the state's large population, many workers are available for employment in manufacturing plants. The millions of people who live in Michigan's industrial areas buy many of the products manufactured in the state. Other industrial areas of the Midwest, such as Chicago and Cleveland, are close to Michigan. (See map on pages 194 and 195.) These areas also provide huge markets for Michigan products.

When you think of industry in Michigan, you probably think of automobiles. This is only natural, since Michigan is our country's leading producer of cars.

In fact, so many motor vehicles are manufactured in Michigan that the state has become the nation's leading producer of transportation equipment. Each year, hundreds of thousands of automobiles roll off assembly lines in Detroit, Flint, and other Michigan cities. Perhaps your family car came from Michigan. Even if your car came off an assembly line in some other state, most of its parts were probably made in Michigan factories. For example, parts of its body might have been made in Grand Rapids. Its engine may have come from Lansing, and its steering mechanism from Saginaw. Hundreds of factories in Michigan's Lower Peninsula turn out parts and accessories for cars, trucks,

Assembling automobile engines at Dearborn. Michigan is our country's leading producer of automobiles. Many plants in the state make iron and steel or special machinery needed for making automobiles. Still other plants make auto parts and accessories.

and buses. To learn more about the manufacture of automobiles in Michigan, read pages 190-193.

Michigan ranks third in the nation in the manufacture of nonelectrical machinery. Factories in the state make many of the special machines and machine tools used in making automobiles. Other kinds of machinery made in Michigan include farm implements, construction equipment, and pumps.

The production of primary metals, such as iron and steel, is one of Michigan's leading industries. Only four other states in our country rank higher. Steel plants in the Detroit area provide much of the metal needed by the automobile industry. These plants use Michigan's iron ore and limestone, but coal is brought here from other states.

Many factories in Michigan make chemicals and chemical products. An enormous plant in Midland manufactures plastics, medicines, weed killers, and hundreds of other chemical products. This plant got its start in the 1890's by using natural brine as a raw material. Several large chemical plants are located along the Detroit River. Two of the leading drug-manufacturing plants in our country are located in

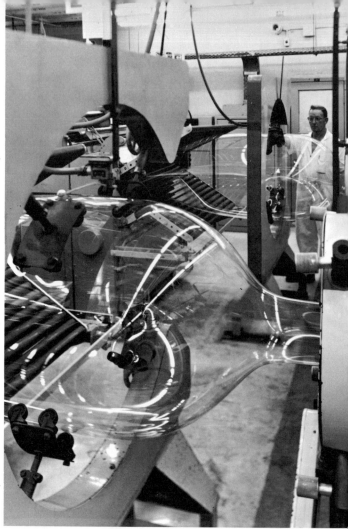

Manufacturing plastic wrap in a chemical plant at Midland. Among the hundreds of chemical products made in Michigan are plastics and medicines.

Michigan. One of these is in Kalamazoo, and the other is in Detroit.

Michigan's abundant resources supply raw materials for many other industries. Food-processing plants are scattered throughout the state. Paper mills in Kalamazoo and other cities use wood from Michigan's forests to make pulp and paper. Factories in Michigan also manufacture wood products such as fine furniture and sporting goods. Large amounts of Michigan limestone are used to make cement in the world's largest cement plant, which is located at Alpena, on Lake Huron.

Recreation. Each year, more than ten million people come to Michigan to

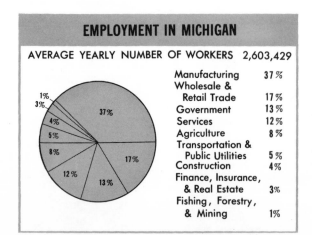

EMPLOYMENT IN MICHIGAN

AVERAGE YEARLY NUMBER OF WORKERS 2,603,429

Manufacturing	37%
Wholesale & Retail Trade	17%
Government	13%
Services	12%
Agriculture	8%
Transportation & Public Utilities	5%
Construction	4%
Finance, Insurance, & Real Estate	3%
Fishing, Forestry, & Mining	1%

enjoy many kinds of recreation. Fishing, boating, and other water sports are popular throughout the state. Summer campers enjoy fine beaches and wilderness areas. In the fall, deer hunters stream into the Upper Peninsula from all parts of the Midwest. Michigan usually issues more hunting licenses than any other state in our country. Skiing, tobogganing, and other winter sports are also popular in Michigan.

People and cities. About nine tenths of the people of Michigan live in the southern half of the Lower Peninsula. Almost all of the large cities are in this part of the state. (See map on page 117.)

There are many small cities and towns scattered throughout Michigan.

Detroit (population 1,600,000; altitude 585 feet) is the largest city in Michigan and the fifth largest in the nation. More than four million people live in the Detroit metropolitan area, which includes such adjoining cities as Dearborn, Royal Oak, Wyandotte, and Warren.

Detroit is located on the busy Detroit River, which is part of a waterway that connects Lake Erie with Lake Huron. (See map on page 184.) In 1701, a Frenchman named Cadillac* established a fort on the Detroit River. Here the French traded with the Indians for furs. Later

Detroit is located on the busy Detroit River in the southeastern part of Michigan. It is the largest city in the state and the fifth largest in the nation. Detroit is a major port city on the Great Lakes–St. Lawrence Waterway. It is also the world's leading producer of automobiles and trucks.

the fort and the settlement that grew up around it were taken over by the British. Finally, the United States gained possession of Detroit. From 1837 to 1847 Detroit served as the first capital of the state of Michigan.

After the Civil War, manufacturing developed rapidly in Detroit, and the city's population grew. Among Detroit's products were bicycles and carriages. In the early 1900's, inventive men such as Henry Ford and Ransom E. Olds began manufacturing automobiles. As the first small factories grew into huge automobile plants, thousands of people came from rural areas and even from abroad to work in Detroit.

Today, America's four largest automobile manufacturers all have their headquarters in the Detroit area. Detroit leads the world in the production of automobiles and trucks. In addition to its assembly plants, Detroit has many factories that make automobile parts and accessories. Here, too, are technical centers for automobile research, testing, and design. One of the fine cars manufactured in Detroit is the Cadillac, which was named for the man who founded the city over two and one-half centuries ago.

Factories in the Detroit area make a large variety of goods in addition to automobiles and automobile parts. Much of the metal needed by the automobile industry is produced in steel plants here. Metal products made in the Detroit area include machine tools and other industrial machinery. A large number of factories in Detroit make miscellaneous metal products such as hardware, valves, and pipe fittings. Among the many other kinds of goods made in Detroit are chemicals and rubber products.

Detroit has excellent transportation facilities. The city is served by most major airlines and a network of fine roads and railroads. It is also a major port city on the Great Lakes–St. Lawrence Waterway. Ships from other Great Lakes ports bring raw materials to Detroit's busy docks. By using the St. Lawrence Seaway, large ships from foreign countries are also able to reach Detroit. Automobiles and hundreds of other manufactured products are exported from this city.

Detroit is prosperous and up-to-date. About one third of the workers in the Detroit area are employed in the automobile industry, which pays high wages. In recent years, many of Detroit's slums have been replaced with new housing developments. A large, modern civic center has been built on Detroit's waterfront. Several broad expressways now connect Detroit with different parts of the fast-growing urban area that has spread out from the city.

Detroit has many cultural and educational institutions. Among these are Wayne State University, the University of Detroit, and several other colleges and technical institutes. Located near Detroit is a well-known group of schools called Cranbrook Institutions. One of these is the Cranbrook Academy of Art, which provides advanced education for students of architecture, sculpture, and other arts. The Detroit area also has many fine museums. These include Greenfield Village in Dearborn. In the village are dozens of historic buildings that have been moved here from other parts of our country and restored. One

People in Grand Rapids, Michigan's second largest city. Although Grand Rapids has long been known for the manufacture of fine furniture, factories here also make many other products. These range from auto parts to refrigerators. Printing and publishing are also important industries in the city.

of these is the workshop where Thomas Edison invented the first practical electric light bulb.

Grand Rapids (population 209,000; altitude 610 feet) is Michigan's second largest city. It is located in western Michigan, on the Grand River. Grand Rapids has long been famous for the manufacture of fine furniture. Factories here originally used pine, oak, beech, and maple from nearby forests. Today, furniture companies in Grand Rapids

import wood from other states as well as from other countries. The manufacture of metal furniture has now become one of the city's chief industries. Other metal products made in Grand Rapids include automobile parts, refrigerators, industrial machinery, and hardware. The city also has several printing and publishing companies.

Flint (population 202,000; altitude 715 feet) is Michigan's third largest city. It is located about sixty miles

northwest of Detroit. (See map on page 239.) Flint was originally a lumbering town. Its factories used Michigan lumber to make wagons and carriages. Flint's large automobile industry developed from the carriage business. Flint ranks second only to Detroit in the production of automobiles in our country. Factories in Flint also produce machinery and chemical products.

Lansing (population 120,500; altitude 830 feet), Michigan's capital city, is located in the south central part of the state. Here, several thousand workers are employed by the state government. Lansing is also a manufacturing city. Among its leading industrial products are automobiles and trucks. Factories in Lansing also make automobile parts, farm implements, and machine tools. Michigan State University is located in the adjoining city of East Lansing. About 38,000 students attend this well-known university.

Flint is the third largest city in Michigan. This city ranks second only to Detroit in the production of automobiles in our country.

Discover Important Facts About Michigan

1. Explain how Michigan's peninsulas were formed.
2. How do the Great Lakes affect Michigan's climate?
3. Why is farming not as important in Michigan as it is in the other states of the Midwest?
4. Why is dairying Michigan's most important type of farming?
5. What advantages does Michigan have for industry?
6. What is Michigan's leading industry?
7. What facts help to explain why few people live in the northern areas of Michigan?

Learn by Sharing Ideas

As a class, discuss the following question:
In what ways is Michigan important to the rest of our country?

Prepare for your discussion by reading about Michigan and taking notes. Look for information about natural resources, industry, and recreation facilities. In addition to studying this chapter, you may wish to use other sources of information. Refer to the suggestions on pages 346-348 and 352-353 for help in finding information and in carrying on a successful discussion.

Explore an Interesting Topic

To learn more about Michigan, choose one of the topics below and prepare a report about it to share with your class. You will find the suggestions on pages 346-352 helpful in locating and organizing your information.

A Visit to Detroit
The Life and Work of Henry Ford
Cherry Growing Near Lake Michigan

Facts About Minnesota		
	Number or Value	Rank
Area (square miles)	84,068	12
Population	3,576,000	20
Capital — St. Paul		
Admission Date:		
May 11, 1858		32
Colleges and Universities	46	16
Farm Products	$1,492,722,000	5
Dairy products	339,437,000	4
Cattle and calves	329,872,000	8
Hogs	204,089,000	5
Fish	$ 965,000	26
Forest Products	$ 42,900,000	20
Minerals	$ 497,495,000	13
Iron ore	449,289,000	1
Sand and gravel	25,907,000	10
Stone	12,297,000	29
Manufactures	$2,827,660,000	20
Food and kindred products	585,189,000	13
Nonelectrical machinery	486,977,000	13
Electrical machinery	224,139,000	19

Land. Minnesota is the largest state in the Midwest. This is a land of prosperous farms, rushing rivers, and green forests dotted with sparkling lakes. Our country's greatest river, the Mississippi, begins in the beautiful lake country of northern Minnesota.

During the Great Ice Age, glaciers moved across nearly all of Minnesota. (See page 36.) These huge ice sheets leveled off hills, filled in valleys, and gouged many hollows in the surface of the land. When the glaciers melted, water filled these hollows, creating thousands of lakes. The retreating glaciers left behind huge amounts of material called drift. This material is a mixture of clay, sand, gravel, and finely ground rock. In some places, the drift

A fertile valley in southeastern Minnesota. Most of Minnesota lies in the Central Lowland. In this part of the state are fertile plains and valleys, low hills, and thousands of beautiful lakes. Our country's greatest river, the Mississippi, begins in the Central Lowland of Minnesota.

was deposited evenly over the land. In other places, it was piled in mounds and ridges.

Most of Minnesota lies in the Central Lowland section of our country. (See map on pages 28 and 29.) The rugged Superior Upland extends across the northeastern part of the state.

The Central Lowland. The northwestern part of the Central Lowland of Minnesota lies in the valley of the Red River of the North. This river, which flows northward into Canada, forms much of Minnesota's western border. (See map on this page.) During the last part of the Great Ice Age, the Red River Valley was covered by a huge lake, called Lake Agassiz. (See pages 310 and 311.) Gradually the lake waters drained away, leaving behind a flat, fertile plain. Today, prosperous farms cover the land in the Red River Valley. Farmers grow wheat, sugar beets, and other crops in the deep, black soil here.

East of the Red River Valley is an area known as the hill and lake country of Minnesota. Here, glaciers piled drift material into knobby hills. Cold, clear lakes lie in some of the shallow depressions between the hills. This land is generally not well suited to growing crops, but dairy cattle graze on hillside pastures. Woods cover much of the land that is not used for farming.

In the southern third of Minnesota, most of the Central Lowland is level or gently rolling. This is a fertile farming area. Herds of dairy cattle graze in lush, green pastures near fields of corn, oats, and other crops. This is also the most densely populated part of Minnesota. The state's two largest cities — Minneapolis and St. Paul — are located here.

The southeastern tip of Minnesota's Central Lowland was never covered by glaciers. This part of the state is known as the Driftless Area. (See map below.) Here, the Mississippi and other rivers have carved deep valleys in the surface of the land. High bluffs rise above the Mississippi. Because most of the land is too hilly for growing crops, many farmers here raise dairy cattle. There is a good market for dairy products in the nearby cities of Minneapolis and St. Paul.

The Superior Upland. The northeastern part of Minnesota lies in the Superior Upland. (See map below.) This

Minnesota. Northeastern Minnesota lies in the rugged Superior Upland. Lake Superior borders this part of the state.

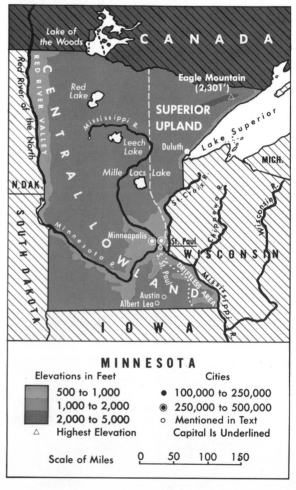

MINNESOTA

Elevations in Feet

500 to 1,000
1,000 to 2,000
2,000 to 5,000
△ Highest Elevation

Cities

● 100,000 to 250,000
◎ 250,000 to 500,000
○ Mentioned in Text
Capital Is Underlined

Scale of Miles   0   50   100   150

is an area of rocky, wooded hills. The Superior Upland includes both the highest and lowest elevations in Minnesota. The highest is Eagle Mountain, which rises 2,301 feet above sea level. The lowest land in the state lies along Lake Superior.

Much of Minnesota's Superior Upland is wilderness. Because the land is rugged and the growing season is short, this area is not well suited to farming. However, the riches that lie beneath the soil here make the Superior Upland a very important part of Minnesota. Each year, huge quantities of iron ore are taken from mines in this area. The ore is shipped from Duluth and other ports on Lake Superior. Buildings and bridges in many parts of the world are constructed with steel made from Minnesota iron ore.

In the Superior Upland of Minnesota is Superior National Forest. This is a paradise for campers. People can travel for hundreds of miles in canoes, making short portages* between the many lakes and rivers. Small islands and wooded shores provide excellent campsites.

Climate. Winters are long and cold in Minnesota. At this time of year, cold winds from Canada sweep across the state. In some places, the temperature drops to ten or more degrees below zero. Lakes and rivers freeze, and a blanket of snow covers the land. Many people in Minnesota enjoy skiing, skating, and other winter sports. In late January or early February, thousands of people visit St. Paul to take part in the city's Winter Carnival.

Spring is a season of dramatic change in Minnesota. Water from melting snow and ice fills rivers and streams. Colorful

Fishing in northern Minnesota. During the summer, many city dwellers go to the forests and lakes of northern Minnesota to escape the heat.

wild flowers bloom in the woods and fields. In the southeastern part of the state along the Mississippi River, farmers begin planting their crops in early May, when the danger of severe frost is past. In parts of northern Minnesota, however, there is danger of frost until June. The growing season here is only three to four months long. (See map on page 60.)

Summer days in most of Minnesota are long and warm. Sometimes, winds from the south or southwest bring short hot spells, when daytime temperatures may reach one hundred degrees or more. Thunderstorms frequently break the summer heat, however. The air feels cool and fresh after one of these storms. Summer weather is coolest in northern Minnesota. Many city dwellers go to the forests and lakes there to escape the heat.

*See Glossary

Beef cattle in a Minnesota feedlot. Beef and dairy cattle, hogs, and poultry are among the different kinds of livestock raised on Minnesota farms. The sale of livestock and livestock products provides about two thirds of the state's farm income.

Autumn is a beautiful season in Minnesota. Leaves change from green to brilliant shades of gold and scarlet. The first freezing weather is usually followed by a period known as "Indian summer." This is a time of mild and sunny days. The cold nights, however, are a reminder that winter is near.

Farming. Minnesota ranks fifth in the nation in income received from the sale of farm products. Although some farming is carried on in nearly every part of the state, Minnesota's best farmland is located in the Red River Valley and in the southern part of the state.

The sale of livestock and livestock products provides about two thirds of Minnesota's yearly farm income. As the map on page 153 shows, most of the state lies in the great dairy belt of the Midwest. There are dairy farms in many parts of Minnesota. Much of the milk from these farms is made into butter and cheese. Farmers in Minnesota also raise large numbers of beef cattle and hogs. These two kinds of livestock are especially important in the southern part of the state, where large crops of corn are grown for feed.

Wheat was once Minnesota's leading crop. In the late 1800's, golden fields of wheat covered about half of the state's cropland. At that time, more flour was produced in Minneapolis than in any other city in our country. Gradually, however, Minnesota's wheat production declined. One reason was that large amounts of wheat were being grown in states west of Minnesota. Therefore, Minnesota farmers could not always get good prices for their crops. In addition, farmers found that they needed to rotate their crops in order to keep the soil fertile. (See page 151.) For these reasons, farmers in Minnesota began to raise other crops in addition to wheat.

Today, Minnesota's most important crops are corn and soybeans. Both of these crops are raised mainly in the southwestern part of the state, which lies in our country's great corn belt. (See map on page 153.) Most of the corn raised in Minnesota is used as feed for livestock. Large plants in Minneapolis and other cities process soybeans for their oil, which is used in making paint, varnish, and many other products.

Farmers in Minnesota also grow a number of other crops. Wheat, sugar beets, and flax are important crops in the fertile Red River Valley. Minnesota is our nation's leading producer of oats. This grain is raised in most parts of the state. Among the other crops grown in Minnesota are barley and hay.

Natural resources. Minnesota's most valuable mineral resource is iron ore. This resource accounts for about nine tenths of the state's total yearly income from mineral production. Almost

Unloading iron ore at a processing plant near Lake Superior. Minnesota leads the nation in the production of iron ore. There are vast deposits of this important mineral in Minnesota's Superior Upland. Most of Minnesota's iron ore is shipped by lake freighter to port cities in the Midwest.

two thirds of the iron ore produced in the United States each year comes from mines in northeastern Minnesota. You can learn more about the iron-mining industry in this state on pages 167 and 168.

At one time, forests of tall evergreen trees covered millions of acres in northern Minnesota. Then, in the middle of the 1800's, lumberjacks began cutting down these great forests. People settling on the treeless prairies that lay to the west and south needed huge amounts of lumber to construct homes and other buildings. Timber from Minnesota helped to meet this need. However, the lumbermen did not plant new trees to replace the ones they had removed. By 1920, most of the state's great forests were gone.

Today, forests of pine, spruce, oak, and other trees cover two fifths of Minnesota. These second-growth trees are much smaller than those that grew in Minnesota before the lumbering days. They are best suited for making wood pulp.* There are pulp and paper mills in several Minnesota cities.

Transportation. Minnesota is served by a fine network of land, water, and air transportation routes. Long before the first white men came to this area, Indians traveled in canoes on the lakes and rivers here. Today, waterways are still important to Minnesota. Goods are shipped from ports along Lake Superior to ports in other parts of the United States and to foreign countries. Duluth is the westernmost port city on the Great Lakes–St. Lawrence Waterway. (See map on pages 184 and 185.)

The Mississippi River is another important transportation route for Minnesota. Barges carry coal, scrap steel, grain, and other products between river ports in Minnesota and ports in states farther south. In addition, railroads, highways, and airways crisscross the state. These connect Minnesota cities with cities in other parts of our country.

Industry. About one fifth of Minnesota's workers are employed in manufacturing. Factories in this state make a wide variety of products, ranging from paper bags to elevators. Although there are manufacturing plants in nearly every part of Minnesota, about half of them are located in the Minneapolis-St.Paul metropolitan* area.

Food processing is Minnesota's chief industry. In Minnesota, the most important type of food processing is meat-packing. There are large slaughterhouses and packing plants in Austin, South St. Paul, Albert Lea, and other cities. Here, beef cattle and hogs from Minnesota farms are butchered, and their meat is prepared for sale.

Plants in Minnesota also process other products from farms here. Dairies process milk to make butter and cheese. In the southern part of the state are many factories where vegetables are canned or frozen. Minnesota also has sugar-beet

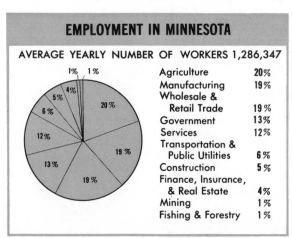

EMPLOYMENT IN MINNESOTA

AVERAGE YEARLY NUMBER OF WORKERS 1,286,347

Agriculture	20%
Manufacturing	19%
Wholesale & Retail Trade	19%
Government	13%
Services	12%
Transportation & Public Utilities	6%
Construction	5%
Finance, Insurance, & Real Estate	4%
Mining	1%
Fishing & Forestry	1%

An engineer checking a new computer made in Minneapolis. The leading industries in Minnesota are the processing of food and the manufacture of machinery. Among the many kinds of machinery made here are computers, mining machines, and farm machines.

refineries, breweries, and soybean-processing plants.

Machinery accounts for about one fourth of the value of Minnesota's manufactures. Thousands of tractors and other farm machines are produced here each year. There are also factories that make machines for the paper, mining, printing, and construction industries. Temperature-control devices and other types of electrical machinery are manufactured in Minneapolis and St. Paul.

People and cities. More than nine tenths of the people who live in Minnesota are native-born Americans. Many of these people are descended from European immigrants who came to Minnesota in the last half of the 1800's to work as farmers, miners, or lumberjacks.

Others are descended from Canadians who settled here. About 15,500 American Indians also live in Minnesota. Most of them live on reservations in the northern part of the state.

About two thirds of Minnesota's people make their homes in urban areas. The state's two largest cities are Minneapolis and St. Paul. Because these two cities are located so close together, they are called the "Twin Cities." About one third of the state's population lives in the Minneapolis-St. Paul metropolitan area. Minnesota's third largest city is Duluth.

The Twin Cities. Minneapolis (population 465,000; altitude 828 feet) and St. Paul (population 308,000; altitude 780 feet) are located in southeastern

257

Minnesota. The Mississippi River flows through both cities. St. Paul is the capital of Minnesota.

The Mississippi River played an important part in the development of both Minneapolis and St. Paul. Minneapolis grew up near the Falls of St. Anthony, a waterfall on the Mississippi River. Trees chopped down in the forests of northern Minnesota were floated down the Mississippi to Minneapolis. Mills at the falls used the waterpower to run machines that sawed logs into lumber. By the late 1800's, many flour mills had been built at the Falls of St. Anthony to process wheat grown in Minnesota. Minneapolis gained fame as the leading flour-milling city in our country. As the years passed, many other industries also grew up in Minneapolis.

For the city of St. Paul, the Mississippi River was important mainly as a transportation route. During the middle 1800's, St. Paul was a terminus* for river steamboat traffic. In the late 1800's, railroads became more important than steamboats. At St. Paul, railroads from the eastern part of our country connected with lines that extended to the northwestern part.

Today, Minneapolis and St. Paul are the central cities of one of our country's main industrial areas. (See map on pages 194 and 195.) Farm machines, construction and refrigeration equipment, and

Minneapolis is the largest city in Minnesota. Minneapolis and its twin city, St. Paul, are important manufacturing cities, making products ranging from chemicals to automobiles. They also serve as wholesale trading cities for a large area.

St. Paul is the capital of Minnesota and the second largest city in the state. Both St. Paul and Minneapolis owe their early settlement and growth to their location on the Mississippi River. St. Paul began as a fur-trading post, but later became an important river port.

computers are among the many kinds of machinery made here. Automobiles are assembled in St. Paul. Plants in the Twin Cities also make chemicals and chemical products.

Trade is also important to the Twin Cities. They serve as wholesale trading cities for an area that extends westward to the Rocky Mountains. One of our country's largest grain markets is located in Minneapolis. Although much less wheat is processed in this city today than in the past, five of our country's leading flour-milling companies still have their headquarters here.

The Twin Cities offer many recreational and cultural attractions. Twenty-two lakes and more than 150 parks lie within the city of Minneapolis. Several fine colleges and universities are located in the area. Minneapolis is the home of the University of Minnesota, the largest university in the Midwest and Great Plains. In the Twin Cities, people can attend a wide variety of plays, operas, concerts, and art exhibits.

Duluth (population 104,000; altitude 600 to 800 feet) lies at the extreme western end of Lake Superior, near the Wisconsin border. (See map on page 252.) The city's business district is located on a long, narrow plain along the lake. The rest of Duluth is built on a steep bluff that rises above the plain.

Duluth is a port city on the Great Lakes–St. Lawrence Waterway.* A long sandbar shelters the fine, deep harbor here. Duluth shares this harbor with the neighboring city of Superior, Wisconsin. (See map on pages 184 and 185.) From April to December each year, more than forty million tons of goods are handled by these twin ports. Iron ore is by far the chief export. During the long, cold winter, however, shipping must stop because the harbor freezes over.

Many of the people in Duluth have jobs in trade or industry. Among the goods manufactured here are iron and steel products, lumber, and cement. Duluth serves as a wholesale and retail trading city for a large area. Many hunters and fishermen stop here on their way to wilderness areas to the north.

Learn About Minnesota With Maps

Study the map on page 252, and then answer the following questions:

1. What country borders Minnesota on the north?
2. What river forms part of Minnesota's western boundary?
3. What large body of water borders part of Minnesota's Superior Upland?
4. What important river has its source in Minnesota?
5. Name the two largest cities in Minnesota. In what part of the state are they located?
6. Which states of the Midwest border Minnesota?

Discover Important Facts About Minnesota

1. How were thousands of lakes created in Minnesota?
2. Why do many farmers in the Driftless Area of Minnesota raise dairy cattle?
3. Minnesota's Superior Upland is not well suited for farming. Why is this so?
4. What event attracts many people to St. Paul in late January or early February each year?
5. Give two reasons why farmers in Minnesota raise less wheat today than they did in the late 1800's.
6. Why were most of the great forests in Minnesota cut down during the middle 1800's?
7. How is Minnesota's iron ore transported out of the state?
8. Why are St. Paul and Minneapolis called the Twin Cities?
9. For what reason is shipping discontinued from Duluth during the wintertime?

Share an Imaginary Adventure

Plan a vacation trip to Minnesota. You may wish to visit the hill and lake country or the Superior Upland region. Decide whether you would prefer to take your trip in the summertime or during the winter. Next, make a general plan for your trip in the form of an outline. Now imagine that you have taken your trip. Using your outline as a guide, write a story about your trip to share with your class. Make your story so interesting that your classmates would like to make the same trip. The suggestions on page 351 will help you create clear word pictures and write good paragraphs. Include in your story information such as the following:

1. the route you followed from your home to Minnesota and the means of transportation you used
2. a description of the countryside as you traveled through Minnesota
3. a description of the weather during your stay in Minnesota
4. what sports or other activities you enjoyed

In addition to the information in this chapter, you may wish to do outside research. The suggestions on pages 346-348 will help you locate other useful sources of information. A map of your trip will make your story more interesting.

18 Missouri

Facts About Missouri		
	Number or Value	Rank
Area (square miles)	69,686	19
Population	4,508,000	13
Capital — Jefferson City		
Admission Date:		
August 10, 1821		24
Colleges and Universities	64	9
Farm Products	$1,144,761,000	11
Cattle and calves	308,977,000	9
Hogs	222,295,000	4
Soybeans	140,477,000	5
Fish	$ 46,000	39
Forest Products	$ 22,250,000	24
Minerals	$ 189,305,000	25
Stone	47,984,000	7
Cement	43,664,000	9
Lead	31,479,000	1
Manufactures	$4,424,148,000	14
Transportation equipment	1,131,650,000	5
Food and kindred products	631,991,000	11
Chemicals and allied products	393,365,000	14

Land. Missouri is the second largest state in the Midwest. Only Minnesota is larger. On the east, Missouri is bordered by our country's greatest river, the Mississippi. The muddy Missouri River forms part of Missouri's western boundary and then winds eastward across the state. The Missouri empties into the Mississippi River a few miles north of St. Louis.

Missouri may be divided into three main parts. (See map on page 262.) Most of southern Missouri lies in the Ozark Plateau. An area in the southeastern part of the state, along the Mississippi, is in the Coastal Plain. The rest of Missouri lies in the Central Lowland section of our country.

The Ozark Plateau section of Missouri. Most of southern Missouri lies in the Ozark Plateau. Here are wooded hills and deep river valleys. The southeastern corner of Missouri lies in the Coastal Plain. The rest of the state is in the Central Lowland.

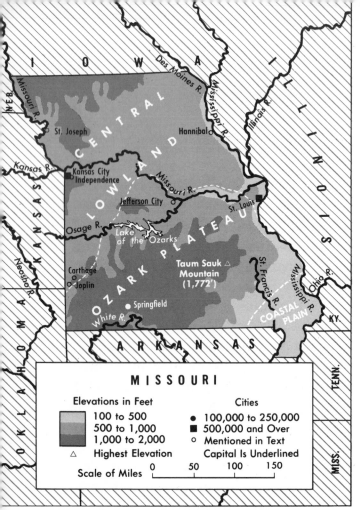

Missouri. The Mississippi River flows along the entire eastern border of Missouri. The Missouri River forms part of the state's western boundary.

The Central Lowland. The Central Lowland includes about half of Missouri. Pastures and fields of crops cover much of the land in this area, which lies almost entirely in the corn belt. (Compare map above with map on page 153.) Missouri's two largest cities, St. Louis and Kansas City, are located in the Central Lowland.

North of the Missouri River, Missouri's Central Lowland consists of a rolling plain. Almost all of this area was smoothed by glaciers during the Great Ice Age. (See page 36.) Much of the land here is now covered with deep, rich soil.

Parts of Missouri's Central Lowland were never covered by glaciers. The larg-

est unglaciated area lies south of the Missouri River, in the western part of the state. Although the soil in this area is not as deep or as rich as the soil in northern Missouri, the grass that grows here provides excellent pasture for dairy and beef cattle.

The Ozark Plateau. Most of southern Missouri is in the Ozark Plateau section of the Interior Highlands. (Compare map at left with map on page 29.) This section, which is often referred to as the Ozarks, is made up mainly of wooded hills and deep river valleys. In the southeastern part of Missouri's Ozarks, the land is mountainous, with many rugged ridges. The highest point in Missouri is located here. This is Taum Sauk Mountain, which rises 1,772 feet above sea level.

Each year, thousands of tourists and sportsmen come to the Ozarks of Missouri to camp in the woods or fish in the clear waters of the lakes and streams. Huge, sprawling Lake of the Ozarks is a popular recreation area. This beautiful lake, which was created by damming the Osage River, is the largest lake in Missouri. Tourists also visit the many caves in the Ozarks. Mysterious underground streams wind for miles through the huge limestone caverns in these hills.

The Coastal Plain. The southeastern corner of Missouri is part of our country's vast Coastal Plain. A severe earthquake occurred here in 1811. The earthquake changed the course of the Mississippi River and also caused large areas of land to sink below their former level. Water from the river poured over these sunken areas, creating swamps. Many of these swamps have now been drained, exposing dark, rich soil that is good for growing crops. Cotton is the leading farm product here, but farmers also grow other crops, such as soybeans and corn.

Climate. Missouri is located in the heart of our country, far from any oceans or other large bodies of water. It therefore has a continental climate. (See pages 46-48.) Throughout the state, summers are long and warm. Winters are generally colder in northern Missouri than they are in the southern part of the state. (See map on page 56.) In the Coastal Plain of Missouri, winters are especially mild. The growing season here lasts about two hundred days, which is long enough for farmers to grow cotton. (See map on page 60.)

Rainfall is plentiful in all parts of Missouri. The average yearly rainfall varies from about thirty inches in the northern part of the state to about fifty inches in the Coastal Plain. Missouri's rain is brought by warm, moist winds that blow northward from the Gulf of Mexico. (See page 52.)

The most pleasant time of year in Missouri is autumn. During this season, the fields are brown with the stubble of wheat and corn. On the wooded hills, the leaves of trees turn scarlet and gold.

Water-skiing on a reservoir in northern Missouri. Summers are long and warm in Missouri. In winter, the weather is generally colder in the northern part of the state than in the southern part. All of Missouri receives plentiful rainfall.

As autumn comes to an end, cold winds swirl into Missouri from the western plains.

Spring brings warm weather to Missouri. By late April, the danger of frost is usually over. In the Coastal Plain, the spring sunshine warms the young cotton plants. In the Ozarks, jack-in-the-pulpits and other wild flowers are in bloom. Farmers in northern Missouri are plowing their fields, preparing them for the planting of corn and other crops.

Farming. Missouri is one of our country's leading farming states. It ranks eleventh in the value of its agricultural products. Because the climate and soil are different in different parts of the state, farmers in Missouri grow a great variety of crops. Many kinds of livestock are also raised by Missouri farmers.

In Missouri, the raising of livestock is more important than the growing of crops. This state ranks fourth in the nation in the production of hogs, and ninth in cattle and calves. These animals are raised throughout the state. However, they are especially important in the corn belt.

Other kinds of livestock also bring money to Missouri farmers. Many dairy cows graze on the pasturelands of southwestern Missouri. Much of the milk produced in this area is processed in

Beef cattle on a Missouri farm. The sale of cattle and calves brings more money to Missouri's farmers than any other farm product. Many farmers here also raise hogs. Soybeans and corn are the two leading crops grown in Missouri. They are used mainly as feed for livestock.

Springfield. (Compare dairy products map on page 155 with map on page 262.) Sheep, horses, and mules are raised throughout the corn belt of Missouri. Chickens and eggs are produced in almost every part of the state. Farmers also raise large numbers of ducks, geese, and turkeys.

Soybeans and corn are Missouri's leading crops. They are grown throughout the Central Lowland and the Coastal Plain of Missouri. Corn is also grown in some parts of the Ozarks. (Compare map on page 262 with maps on page 155.) Missouri farmers grow both corn and soybeans mainly for livestock feed. However, these two crops are also used as raw materials in food-processing plants.

Missouri farmers raise many other crops. Cotton, Missouri's third most valuable crop, is grown in the southeastern part of the state, in the Coastal Plain. Here, the growing season is long enough for cotton to ripen. Farmers in the corn belt grow wheat and oats. Hilly land that is not suitable for most crops is often used for growing hay or for grazing.

Fruits and truck crops are also produced in Missouri. (See map on page 153.) In southwestern Missouri, the climate and soil are especially well suited for growing berries and tomatoes. Missouri usually leads the nation in the production of blackberries. Apple orchards flourish in most parts of the state. Other fruits and vegetables grown in Missouri include peaches, grapes, melons, and cabbages.

Natural resources. Early settlers in Missouri found that nature had given the state many advantages. Waterways

A limestone quarry near Carthage. The limestone found here is a very hard variety that is used as building stone. It is known as Carthage marble. Stone is Missouri's most valuable mineral resource.

such as the Mississippi and Missouri rivers provided convenient transportation routes. The climate and soils, especially in northern Missouri, were suitable for growing corn and other crops. In addition, settlers in Missouri found timber and useful minerals such as lead ore.

Stone is Missouri's most valuable mineral resource. Limestone is quarried mainly in the Ozarks, but it is also found in other parts of the state. Much of the limestone is used in construction and road building. A very hard variety of limestone found near Joplin and Carthage, in southwestern Missouri, is known as Carthage marble. It is used as a building stone. Other kinds of stone found in Missouri include granite and sandstone.

265

Mining lead ore in the Ozarks. Missouri is the nation's leading producer of this mineral. The largest deposits are in the southeastern part of the state, in the Ozarks. Here also are deposits of iron ore. Missouri ranks fourth in the country in iron ore production.

Cement is one of Missouri's most valuable mineral products. (See fact table on page 261.) Several large cement plants are located along the Mississippi River. Nearby quarries provide limestone and shale, which are used as raw materials in these plants. Barges on the Mississippi provide an inexpensive means of transporting the cement to distant markets.

Missouri produces several metal ores. The state ranks first in the nation in the production of lead ore. Missouri's largest deposits of this mineral are found in the southeastern part of the state, in the Ozarks. For many years, iron ore has also been mined in the Ozarks. Recently, new discoveries of rich iron ore deposits have been made here. The state now ranks fourth in the nation in the production of this mineral. Steel plants near St. Louis are expanding their facilities to take advantage of Missouri's increasing production of iron ore. Small amounts of copper and zinc are also produced in Missouri.

Other minerals found in Missouri include barite, coal, and various kinds of clay. There are large deposits of barite south of St. Louis. This mineral is used mainly in making paints and other chemical products. Deposits of high-grade soft coal extend through northwestern Missouri. (See map on page

166.) Most of the coal mined here is used by steam power plants to generate electricity. Clays from central Missouri are used in making products such as brick and tile.

About one third of Missouri is wooded. During the 1800's, most of the trees in Missouri's original forests were cut down for use in construction and manufacturing. Now there are large tracts of second-growth trees. Forests of oak, hickory, and other hardwoods cover much of the land in the Ozarks. These forests provide wood for the manufacture of products such as furniture and flooring. Some of Missouri's forests have been placed under the supervision of the National Forest Service. In years to come, these forests are expected to provide valuable timber for use in construction and manufacturing.

Industry. Factories in Missouri make a wide variety of goods, from airplanes to shoes. Manufacturing is carried on chiefly in the state's two largest industrial areas, St. Louis and Kansas City. However, several smaller cities, such as Springfield and St. Joseph, are also busy manufacturing communities.

Missouri ranks fifth in the nation in the manufacture of transportation equipment. This is the state's leading industry. Airplanes, automobiles, and railroad cars are made in large plants in the St. Louis and Kansas City areas. In addition, there are many factories in the state that manufacture parts for motor vehicles or aircraft.

Food processing is the second most important industry in Missouri. Huge flour mills are located at Kansas City, St. Joseph, and St. Louis. These cities also have large meat-packing plants.

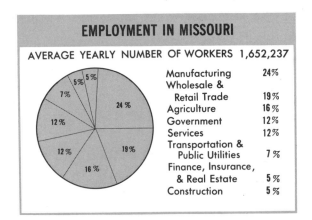

EMPLOYMENT IN MISSOURI

AVERAGE YEARLY NUMBER OF WORKERS 1,652,237

Industry	Percent
Manufacturing	24%
Wholesale & Retail Trade	19%
Agriculture	16%
Government	12%
Services	12%
Transportation & Public Utilities	7%
Finance, Insurance, & Real Estate	5%
Construction	5%

A huge dairy plant in Springfield processes about 125,000 gallons of milk each day.

Missouri's manufacturing plants make many other products. Among these are chemicals and chemical products such as detergents, drugs, paints, and fertilizers. Both electrical and nonelectrical machinery are made in Missouri. One

Making passenger cars for trains in a St. Louis factory. Missouri's chief industry is the manufacture of transportation equipment, such as automobiles, airplanes, and railroad cars.

of the state's newest industries is the manufacture of equipment for space exploration. Many of the capsules that have carried our astronauts into space were made in St. Louis. Rocket engines for unmanned spacecraft are also manufactured in Missouri.

People and cities. More than four million people live in Missouri. In recent years, the percentage of the population living in urban areas has steadily increased. Today, about two thirds of the people live in cities or towns.

Missouri's two largest cities are St. Louis, on the Mississippi River, and Kansas City, on the Missouri River. Springfield is the only other city in the state with a population of more than 100,000. Jefferson City, the capital, has a population of about 30,000. It is located on the Missouri River, in the central part of the state.

St. Louis (population 710,000; altitude 455 feet) is located along the west bank of the Mississippi River, a few miles south of the point where the river receives the muddy waters of the Missouri. It is the central city of a huge metropolitan area that sprawls across the Mississippi into Illinois. About two million people live in this area. St. Louis is an important manufacturing city, as well as one of our country's leading ports.

St. Louis was founded in 1764 as a French fur-trading post. The pelts of

Gateway Arch, in St. Louis, was built as a reminder of the time when this city was the main gateway to the western part of our country. St. Louis, located on the Mississippi River, is Missouri's largest city. It is both an important manufacturing city and a leading port.

beaver, buffalo, and other animals were brought to St. Louis from the western wilderness. Today, St. Louis is still a leading fur market.

During the early 1800's, St. Louis became a leading center of trade and transportation. In 1804, Lewis and Clark set out from St. Louis on their famous expedition into the Louisiana Territory. (See pages 84 and 86.) Other explorers and settlers followed, carrying food and other supplies purchased from St. Louis merchants. During the years of our country's rapid westward expansion, St. Louis served as the main gateway to the west.

Today, St. Louis produces a large variety of manufactured goods. The city's leading industry is the manufacture of transportation equipment. Plants in the St. Louis area produce airplanes, trucks, and automobiles. The next most important industry in this area is food processing. Several large breweries and meat-packing plants are located here. Tanneries in the St. Louis area process animal hides to make leather for shoes and other products.

St. Louis is a lively, up-to-date city, but it still has many reminders of the past. In the heart of the city is the handsome Memorial Plaza. Around the plaza are the Soldiers Memorial and other public buildings. A section of the city along the riverfront has been cleared and set aside as a national historic site. This is the Jefferson National Expansion Memorial, which covers forty city blocks. Here, the lofty, steel Gateway Arch, 630 feet high, recalls the time when St. Louis was the gateway to the western part of our country. From the top of the arch, visitors can see the

Kansas City, on the Missouri River, is the second largest city in Missouri. Its chief industry is the manufacture of transportation equipment.

entire city, stretching along the curving Mississippi River.

Kansas City (population 530,000; altitude 745 to 1,005 feet) is Missouri's second largest city. It is located at the western border of the state, along the Missouri River. Kansas City is part of a large metropolitan area that also includes Kansas City, Kansas, across the state line. Missouri's fourth largest city, Independence, is also part of the Kansas City metropolitan area. More than eighty thousand people live in Independence.

Kansas City grew up around a frontier trading post and settlement. During the 1840's, many pioneers moving westward stopped here for supplies.

269

After the Civil War, Kansas City became a busy cattle and grain market.

Today, Kansas City is one of the Midwest's chief trading and manufacturing cities. The leading industry in the Kansas City area is the manufacture of transportation equipment, such as airplanes and automobiles. Food processing is the second most important industry in the area. Kansas City is famous for its meat-packing plants and flour mills. Other products made in the city include chemicals and machinery. Kansas City also serves as a major distribution center for manufactured goods such as automobiles and farm implements.

Kansas City is the leading educational and cultural city of western Missouri. Several colleges and special schools have been established here. A branch of the University of Missouri is also located in Kansas City. The community has many excellent libraries and museums, such as the William Rockhill Nelson Gallery of Art. During the winter season, many people in the Kansas City area attend concerts given by the Kansas City Philharmonic Orchestra.

Springfield (population 103,500; altitude 1,292 feet) is Missouri's third largest city. It is the main trading and manufacturing city for the southwestern part of the state. Milk from nearby farms is brought to processing plants in Springfield to be made into butter, cheese, and other foods. Other industries here include meat-packing, flour milling, and the manufacture of trucks and trailers. Cement is also produced in Springfield. In addition, the city is an important poultry market.

Practice Using Your Map Skills

Study the maps on pages 11 and 262. Then answer the following questions:

1. What river flows along the entire eastern border of Missouri?
2. Into what three main parts may Missouri be divided?
3. Which Great Plains states border Missouri? What states of the Midwest border Missouri?
4. What important river flows across Missouri and empties into the Mississippi?

Questions To Guide Your Reading

1. What are some of the ways in which the Ozark Plateau section of Missouri differs from the Central Lowland section?
2. Why is the Coastal Plain region in Missouri well suited for growing cotton?
3. In which section of Missouri is winter weather mildest?
4. Why can farmers in Missouri grow a great variety of crops?

5. What are some of the uses made of Missouri's natural resources?
6. What are the two largest industrial areas in Missouri? Where is each located?
7. What are the two leading industries in Missouri?

Learn About One of Missouri's Cities

Missouri's two largest cities are St. Louis and Kansas City. Choose one of these cities and write a report about it to share with your class. Do outside research in addition to using the information in this chapter. The suggestions on pages 346-351 will help you locate good sources of information and organize your material into a good report. You may wish to use the following main headings:

  I. Location
 II. Early history
III. Main industries
IV. Places of interest

Your report will be more interesting if you illustrate it with a map or pictures.

19 Ohio

Facts About Ohio		
	Number or Value	Rank
Area (square miles)	41,222	35
Population	10,305,000	6
Capital — Columbus		
Admission Date:		
March 1, 1803		17
Colleges and Universities	72	7
Farm Products	$ 1,058,768,000	12
Dairy products	216,675,000	7
Cattle and calves	162,955,000	12
Hogs	139,494,000	7
Fish	$ 1,008,000	25
Forest Products	$ 18,600,000	27
Minerals	$ 454,937,000	14
Coal	137,776,000	5
Stone	61,814,000	3
Cement	53,774,000	5
Manufactures	$15,443,018,000	3
Transportation equipment	2,458,182,000	3
Primary metal industries	2,254,048,000	2
Nonelectrical machinery	1,919,086,000	2

LAND

Ohio may be divided into two main parts. (See map on page 272.) Almost all of the eastern half of Ohio is in the Appalachian Plateau section of our country. The rest of the state is in the Central Lowland. The beautiful Ohio River forms the state's entire southern boundary. Lake Erie borders part of the state on the north.

Most of the land in Ohio is level or gently rolling. During the Great Ice Age, glaciers scooped out the enormous hollows that later became the Great Lakes. (See pages 35, 36, and 37.) Then, creeping southward, these huge ice sheets rounded off hills and filled in valleys. The glaciers smoothed all of Ohio's

*See Glossary

Cutting corn for silage* in Ohio's corn belt. Ohio lies partly in the Central Lowland and partly in the Appalachian Plateau. Most of the Central Lowland in Ohio is in the corn belt. This part of the state is generally level and the soil is fertile. Fields of corn and other crops cover much of the land. This is Ohio's most important farming area.

OHIO

Elevations in Feet
- 100 to 500
- 500 to 1,000
- 1,000 to 2,000
- △ Highest Elevation

Cities
- • 100,000 to 250,000
- ◉ 250,000 to 500,000
- ■ 500,000 and Over
- ○ Mentioned in Text

Capital Is Underlined

Scale of Miles 0   50   100

Ohio. The beautiful Ohio River forms all of Ohio's southern boundary. Lake Erie borders much of the state on the north.

land except the southern two thirds of the Appalachian Plateau. This is the state's most rugged area.

The Central Lowland. The Central Lowland section of Ohio is an important farming area. By comparing the map above with the map on page 153, you will see that most of Ohio's Central Lowland is in the corn belt. The land here is generally level, and the soil is fertile. Fields of corn, wheat, soybeans, and other crops cover much of the land. In addition to growing crops, farmers in Ohio's corn belt raise livestock. Dairy cattle and sheep graze in rich pasturelands, and hogs thrive on

the corn and other feeds produced in this area.

Ohio's Central Lowland includes a narrow plain that borders Lake Erie. (See map at left.) Located on this plain is one of the leading trading and manufacturing districts of our country. Here are the sprawling industrial cities of Cleveland and Toledo. These and other port cities have grown up around natural harbors along Lake Erie. Nearby farms supply the people in the cities with dairy products and fresh fruits and vegetables. In some places, vineyards stretch for miles along the lakeshore.

The Appalachian Plateau. The Appalachian Plateau section of Ohio is an area of hills and valleys. The northern one third of this section is made up of low, rounded hills separated by broad valleys. This is part of the dairy belt. (See map on page 153.) In addition to raising cattle, farmers here grow crops such as corn, oats, wheat, and potatoes. Several important industrial cities are located in this part of Ohio. These include Akron, Youngstown, and Canton.

The southern two thirds of Ohio's Appalachian Plateau is a land of rugged beauty. Scattered among the steep hills here are many caves, waterfalls, and unusual rock formations. Forests cover many hillsides. Although the land in this part of the state is generally not well suited to growing crops, herds of cattle and sheep graze on hillside pastures. Farms and villages dot the valleys of several rivers that cut across the plateau.

CLIMATE

Ohio, like the rest of the Midwest, lies far inland from the great oceans that

272

border our country's coasts. There are no ocean breezes to moderate the climate here. (See page 48.) As a result, temperatures in Ohio differ greatly between summer and winter. Summers here are very warm, and winters are cold.

Ohio's climate is well suited to farming. No part of the state has a growing season less than four months long. (See map on page 60.) In some places, the frost-free period may last as long as seven months. Ohio also gets plenty of rain. In almost every part of the state, the annual rainfall is between thirty and forty inches. This is sufficient for growing most crops. The rain is brought mainly by warm, moist air masses that move northward from the Gulf of Mexico. Since the prevailing

winds in our country move from west to east, these moist air masses drift eastward rather than westward. As a result, Ohio and the other states of the Midwest generally receive more rain than the Great Plains states. (See map on page 49.)

In winter, cold winds from the northwest blow over Ohio. Sometimes these winds collide with warm winds from the south, causing snowstorms. Snowfall is heaviest near Lake Erie. This is partly because the cold winds from the northwest become warmer and pick up moisture as they blow over the Great Lakes. (See page 55.) When these winds reach the cold land along the southern shore of Lake Erie, they drop large amounts of moisture as snow. Average yearly

A farm in the Appalachian Plateau section of Ohio. Ohio's Appalachian Plateau is made up of hills and valleys. Much of the land is wooded or in pasture. Several of Ohio's large industrial cities are located in the northern third of this section.

snowfall in Ohio ranges from as much as sixty inches in the northeastern corner of the state to about fifteen inches along the Ohio River.

FARMING

Favorable climate and large areas of fertile soil have helped make Ohio an important agricultural state. It ranks twelfth in the nation in the value of farm products. Ohio's large population and its many food-processing plants provide a ready market for milk, meat, and other products supplied by its farms. Industry has now become so important in Ohio, however, that the state earns about fifteen times as much money from manufacturing as it does from farming. (See fact table on page 271.) Few other states rank so high in both agriculture and manufacturing.

Ohio has a long history as an important farming area. In the late 1700's and early 1800's, thousands of pioneers came here from the states along the Atlantic coast. Some settlers chose land along the Ohio River, which provided a convenient transportation route for shipping farm products. Soon, Ohio farmers were raising hogs and other livestock, as well as bountiful crops of corn and wheat.

In Ohio, raising livestock is more important than growing crops. The leading products of Ohio's farms are milk, cattle and calves, and hogs. Dairy and beef cattle are raised throughout the state. However, dairy farming is especially important in the northern part of Ohio's Appalachian Plateau, which is in the dairy belt. Milk produced here is shipped to Cleveland and other nearby cities. Hogs are raised mainly in the corn belt. Farmers in Ohio also earn money from the sale of turkeys, chickens, and eggs. Ohio leads all the states east of the Mississippi River in the production of sheep and wool.

Many different crops are raised in Ohio. The two most important are soybeans and corn. Farmers in the corn belt raise enormous quantities of these crops, mainly as feed for livestock. Hay is grown throughout the state. Farmers in various parts of Ohio grow wheat, potatoes, and other food crops.

Northern Ohio is noted for its fine fruits and vegetables. Many of these are processed at canneries in the area. Truck farms on the Lake Erie Plain provide fresh vegetables for people in the cities nearby. Some farmers here raise vegetables in greenhouses. In this way, they can supply fresh produce even in winter. Ohio ranks first in the nation in the production of greenhouse vegetables. The climate along Lake Erie is especially well suited to raising fruit. (See page 62.) Apples, peaches, pears, and grapes are grown here. Most of the grapes are used to make wine.

NATURAL RESOURCES

Nature has supplied Ohio with abundant resources. Among the most important of these are large areas of fertile soil and a climate well suited to farming. Rich mineral deposits have helped Ohio become one of our leading industrial states. Ohio also has forests and fisheries. Lake Erie and the Ohio River provide water for many of Ohio's large cities and manufacturing plants. They also provide convenient water transportation routes.

A huge power shovel at work in an open-pit mine in Ohio. There are large deposits of high-quality soft coal in the Appalachian Plateau section of Ohio. Other mineral fuels produced in Ohio include oil and natural gas.

Mineral fuels are among Ohio's leading natural resources. The state ranks fifth in the nation in coal mining. Large deposits of high-quality soft coal are located in the Appalachian Plateau section of Ohio. The state also has deposits of oil and natural gas. New oil wells drilled recently have boosted Ohio's production of petroleum. Additional oil must be brought in from other states, however, to meet Ohio's needs. Most of the power plants in Ohio generate electricity by burning either coal or natural gas.

Stone is another of Ohio's important natural resources. Almost all of the stone quarried in the state is limestone.

This useful mineral is found in several different parts of Ohio. (See map on page 169.) Large amounts of limestone are made into a mineral product called lime.* Ohio leads the nation in the production of this material. Limestone is also one of the three main raw materials needed by the iron and steel industry. In addition, some of the limestone quarried in Ohio is made into cement. The state ranks fifth in the nation in cement production.

Several other minerals that are useful to industry are found in Ohio. For example, large quantities of salt are mined in the state. Chemical companies in northeastern Ohio use salt as a raw material for the manufacture of soda* ash and other chemicals. Large amounts of soda ash are used in Ohio's glass-making industry. Ohio ranks second in the nation in the production of sand and gravel. These materials are used mainly in the construction industry. Clays are also abundant in Ohio, especially in the Appalachian Plateau. Some clays are used, along with limestone, to make cement. Clays are also used in the manufacture of products such as brick, tile, and pottery. Clays that resist high temperatures are made into firebrick. This material is needed for lining furnaces such as those used in making iron and steel.

Forests are a source of income for some of the people in Ohio. However, forests are not as important to the state as they once were. During the nineteenth century, vast amounts of hardwood timber were cut for use in construction and manufacturing. Today, through conservation and replanting, forests are gradually beginning to cover much of Ohio's cutover land. In the Appalachian Plateau, some hardwoods are now being cut for use in making wood products such as furniture.

Lake Erie has always provided the main fishing grounds for Ohio's commercial fishermen. The value of the fish catch is very low at present, however. There are two main reasons for this. First, lampreys have killed many of the food fish in the Great Lakes. (See page 243.) Also, Lake Erie is seriously polluted, and the most valuable fish do not thrive in polluted waters.

The pollution of Lake Erie has become a serious problem for the people of Ohio. This condition has resulted from the great quantities of waste materials dumped into the lake, or into streams that empty into the lake. Besides harming the fishing industry, pollution has ruined Lake Erie as a source of clean water for cities and industries. (See page 171.) It has also spoiled the lake as a recreation area, for many beaches are now smelly and dirty. State and national government officials are studying ways to control pollution. However, it will take billions of dollars and many years to make Lake Erie waters clean again. Fortunately, Ohio has other supplies of fresh water, such as rivers, groundwater,* and underground streams.

INDUSTRY

Advantages for industry. Ohio is the leading industrial state in the Midwest and Great Plains. It ranks third in the nation in manufacturing. (See fact table on page 271.) Only New York and California outrank Ohio as manufacturing states.

Ohio has become a great industrial state because it possesses many of the advantages needed for the growth of industry. Ohio's advantages include plentiful raw materials, excellent transportation facilities, skilled workers, and a vast market for manufactured products.

Raw materials. When industry first began to develop in Ohio, the state's farms, forests, and mines provided many different raw materials for manufacturing. Today, many of Ohio's industries, such as food processing and brickmaking, still depend on raw materials that are available within the state. However, it is no longer so important to have supplies of raw materials near at hand.

Excellent transportation systems bring raw materials to Ohio's industries from distant parts of our country.

Transportation. Convenient transportation routes favor the growth of industry. (See pages 193 and 196.) Ohio's position as a leading manufacturing state is closely related to its excellent transportation system.

Water transportation has been important throughout Ohio's history. In the early 1800's, the Ohio River provided a convenient means of shipping farm products and manufactured goods. Canals built during the 1820's and 1830's in New York and Ohio encouraged trade and travel between these states. The opening of Michigan's first Soo Canal, in 1855, also affected Ohio. By using the canal, large lake freighters could easily carry iron ore from the shores of Lake Superior to Ohio ports on Lake Erie. By the time of the Civil War,* Cleveland had become an important ironmaking city.

Today, water transportation is still important to Ohio. River barges provide an economical means of transporting bulky goods. For example, barges on the Mississippi and Ohio rivers carry alumina* from Louisiana to an aluminum plant at Hannibal. Freighters on the Great Lakes bring iron ore to Cleveland and other port cities on Lake Erie. Also, the St. Lawrence Seaway makes it possible for oceangoing ships to reach these ports. (See map on pages 184 and 185.)

In addition to waterways, Ohio has excellent land and air transportation facilities. Most of our country's main east-west transportation routes pass through Ohio. Networks of highways and railways crisscross the state. Planes of many major airlines serve Ohio's large cities.

Ohio's excellent transportation system makes it easy for factories to obtain raw materials from other states and from foreign countries. Manufacturers in Ohio are also able to ship finished products to markets throughout the United States and in many parts of the world.

Skilled workers. Ohio's large population provides many workers who are well qualified for jobs in industry. More than half of all the jobholders in the state are classified as skilled or semiskilled workers. Most of these people received their education and training in Ohio's schools and colleges.

Markets. Ohio is located in the heart of our country's greatest trading area. More than two thirds of all the people in the United States live within six

Assembling electronic equipment at Dayton. Ohio ranks third in the nation in manufacturing. One of the many advantages offered for industry in Ohio is a large supply of skilled workers.

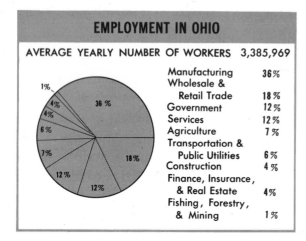

EMPLOYMENT IN OHIO

AVERAGE YEARLY NUMBER OF WORKERS   3,385,969

Manufacturing	36%
Wholesale & Retail Trade	18%
Government	12%
Services	12%
Agriculture	7%
Transportation & Public Utilities	6%
Construction	4%
Finance, Insurance, & Real Estate	4%
Fishing, Forestry, & Mining	1%

hundred miles of Ohio's borders. If you will compare the map on pages 194 and 195 with the map on page 117, you will see that many of our large population centers and industrial areas are within this distance of Ohio. Of the forty-two cities in the United States with populations of more than 300,000, only fifteen are farther than six hundred miles from Ohio.

The nearness of so many large cities and industrial areas gives industry in Ohio a tremendous advantage. Manufacturers can obtain partially processed goods more quickly and cheaply from suppliers that are located nearby. For example, lumber for use in the manufacture of furniture is brought into Ohio from neighboring states. Also, manufacturers in Ohio are able to ship their products to nearby markets quickly and inexpensively. The people who live in the vast trading area that surrounds the state buy many kinds of products made in Ohio. These include industrial materials such as steel, glass, and cement. Consumer goods such as food, clothing, appliances, and furniture are also sold by Ohio manufacturers and merchants to people in Ohio or in neighboring states.

Manufactured products. Ohio's leading manufacturing industries are closely related to one another. One of the most important of these industries is the making of iron and steel. Among all our states, only Pennsylvania produces more of these useful metals. Much of the steel produced in Ohio is used within the state as a raw material for making products such as truck bodies, automobile parts, machine tools, and boilers.

Most of Ohio's large iron and steel plants are in the northeastern part of the state, mainly in the Cleveland and Youngstown industrial areas. (See map on pages 194 and 195.) The main raw materials needed by these plants are iron ore, coking* coal, and limestone. Ohio has large deposits of limestone, but iron ore and coking coal must be brought in from other states. Iron ore from Minnesota and Michigan is carried by Great Lakes freighters to Cleveland and other ports on Lake Erie.

More of Ohio's workers are employed in the manufacture of transportation equipment than in any other manufacturing industry. Many of these people make automobile parts. Others work in huge plants that assemble automobiles or trucks. Most of these plants are located in large industrial areas such as Cleveland, Toledo, and Cincinnati. Aircraft manufacturing is also important in Ohio. Airplane engines are made near Cincinnati. Other kinds of aircraft parts are made in the Cleveland and Akron industrial areas. Airplanes are assembled at a large plant in Columbus.

Ohio ranks second in the nation in the manufacture of nonelectrical machinery. Factories in the Cleveland area make machine* tools and other kinds of metalworking machinery. Canton is well known for roller bearings. Other kinds of nonelectrical machinery produced in Ohio include construction and mining equipment.

The manufacture of electrical machinery is also important in Ohio. Much of this kind of machinery is designed for industrial use. For example, factories in Ohio produce electric motors and welding machines. Household appliances such as refrigerators and vacuum cleaners are also made in Ohio. Some factories in the state make television parts or other communication equipment.

Food processing is another major industry in Ohio. Hundreds of dairies supply milk and products such as butter and ice cream to the people who live in Ohio's many large cities. Plants in the city of Van Wert make all of our country's supply of a popular cheese called Liederkranz. Meat-packing plants and canneries process many other Ohio farm products.

Ohio ranks sixth in the nation in the production of chemicals and chemical products. One of the leading chemical industries is the making of soap. Cincinnati has the world's largest soap and detergent plant. Chemical plants in northeastern Ohio, near Lake Erie, use salt and limestone from nearby deposits to make soda ash. (See the natural resources section of this chapter.)

Other important products manufactured in Ohio include rubber goods, glass, and aluminum. More rubber products are made in Ohio than in any other state. Ohio's rubber industry is centered in Akron. Toledo is famous as a glassmaking city. Most of Ohio's rubber and glass products are used in the manufac-

ture of automobiles. Plants in Ohio also make aluminum or aluminum products such as pipes and tubes.

PEOPLE AND CITIES

Ohio ranks sixth in the nation in population. (See fact table on page 271.) It is the most densely populated state in the Midwest and Great Plains. About three fourths of the people in Ohio live in cities and large towns. Most of the main industrial areas are in the northeastern and southwestern parts of the state. (See map on pages 194 and 195.)

Cleveland (population 811,000; altitude 660 feet) is Ohio's largest city and a major Great Lakes port. It is located on the shore of Lake Erie, at the mouth of a small river. More than two million people live in the Cleveland metropolitan area.

Manufacturing rubber tires at Akron. Ohio is the nation's leading producer of rubber products.

Cleveland, Ohio's largest city, is located on the shore of Lake Erie. Cleveland is noted for being a center of education, culture, and scientific research. Factories in the Cleveland area manufacture iron and steel, auto parts, and hundreds of other products.

Cleveland was founded in 1796. This settlement was one of the first in northern Ohio. For many years, its population remained small. In the 1830's, however, Cleveland began to grow rapidly. The Erie Canal,* completed in 1825, made it possible for boats to travel all the way from New York City to settlements along Lake Erie. Then, Ohio began to build a canal connecting Lake Erie, at Cleveland, with the Ohio River. With the completion of this canal in 1832, trade between the Northeast and the Midwest developed rapidly. Cleveland soon became one of the leading ports on the Great Lakes and an important trading city.

Railroads first reached Cleveland during the 1850's. By that time, canals were becoming less important than rail-

roads as a means of transportation in our country. Cleveland soon became a busy transfer point for products shipped partly by lake freighter and partly by train. Among the goods that passed through the city were lumber, iron ore, coal, and farm products.

During the last half of the nineteenth century, Cleveland became a great manufacturing city. The iron industry here grew rapidly during the Civil War, when large amounts of iron were needed for making cannons and other military equipment. After the war, the steel industry began to develop. Much of the iron and steel produced in the Cleveland area was used by the city's factories to make products such as farm implements and industrial machinery. About the same time, plants were built in Cleveland to refine crude* oil from Pennsylvania's oil wells.

As more and more factories were built in Cleveland, more workers were needed. Large numbers of European immigrants came to the city to seek work. Today, Cleveland has a large supply of skilled workers for its many factories.

Cleveland's leading industries still include the manufacture of metals and metal products. Several of our country's largest iron and steel plants are located in the Cleveland area. Some of the factories here make transportation equipment such as automobile and aircraft parts. Other plants make machine tools, paints and varnishes, chemicals, clothing, and hundreds of other products.

Cleveland is noted for its educational, cultural, and scientific institutions. Several colleges and universities are located here. These include Western Reserve University and Case Institute of Technology. The city is the home of the Cleveland Orchestra, which is one of our country's leading symphony orchestras. The Cleveland Museum of Art is also well known. In addition, Cleveland has many scientific-research centers. One of these is the Lewis Research Center of the National Aeronautics and Space Administration.

Columbus (population 540,000; altitude 780 feet) is Ohio's capital and second largest city. (See map on page 272.) The city was founded in 1812, on the east side of the Scioto River. Later, an older community on the west side of the river also became part of Columbus.

Columbus grew rapidly. By 1832, canals connected the city with Lake Erie and the Ohio River. The National Road* reached Columbus in 1833. These transportation routes helped Columbus become an important trading city for the people of central Ohio. Today, Columbus is still an important trading city, served by excellent transportation facilities.

Ohio's capital is also one of the state's leading industrial cities. Factories in the Columbus area make many different kinds of machinery. These include mining and construction machinery, radio and television parts, and telephone equipment. The manufacture of transportation equipment is also important in Columbus. A large plant makes airplanes, and other factories make automobile and aircraft parts. Many new industrial plants, started in recent years, are helping Columbus to grow.

Columbus is an important center of education and research. It is the home of Ohio State University, as well as several other colleges and universities. At the Battelle Memorial Institute, several thousand workers solve industrial problems through scientific research.

Cincinnati (population 495,000; altitude 550 feet) is located in the southwestern corner of Ohio, along the Ohio River. (See map on page 272.) It is the central city of a huge metropolitan area that includes counties in the neighboring states of Kentucky and Indiana.

Cincinnati was founded in 1788 by settlers who came down the Ohio River on flatboats. The little settlement soon became an important supply point for pioneers moving farther west. During the 1820's, steamboats became common on the Ohio River. They brought farm products and other raw materials to Cincinnati to be processed. They also carried food products and manufactured

Cincinnati, on the Ohio River, is the third largest city in Ohio. It is the central city of a huge metropolitan area that includes counties in the neighboring states of Kentucky and Indiana.

goods from Cincinnati to farms and cities along the Ohio and Mississippi rivers.

Today, Cincinnati is one of Ohio's leading industrial and trading cities. The most important manufacturing industry in the Cincinnati area is the making of transportation equipment. Automobile bodies are manufactured here, and Cincinnati also has automobile-assembly plants. The manufacture of chemical products is also important in Cincinnati, which is the home of one of our nation's leading producers of soaps and detergents. Other major industries in Cincinnati are food processing and the manufacture of machine tools.

Toledo (population 354,000; altitude 585 feet) is the fourth largest city in Ohio. Located on a fine harbor at the western end of Lake Erie, Toledo is the state's leading port city. More coal is shipped from Toledo than from any other port in the world. Millions of tons of coal from mines in the Appalachian Plateau are brought to Toledo by rail. At Toledo, the coal is transferred to lake freighters for shipment to other Great Lakes ports, such as Chicago and Detroit. (See map on pages 184 and 185.) Incoming freighters bring products such as grain and iron ore to the wharves along Toledo's harbor.

One of the leading manufacturing industries in the Toledo area is the making of automobiles and automobile parts. Automobiles have been manufactured in Toledo since the early 1900's. Another of Toledo's leading industries is closely related to the automobile industry. This is glassmaking. Factories in Toledo supply most of the glass used by automobile manufacturers in Michigan and Ohio. Other glass products such as bottles, plate glass, fiber glass, and fine, hand-blown crystal are also made in Toledo.

Plants in the Toledo industrial area produce many other kinds of manufactured goods. Among these are foods, machinery, and petroleum products such as gasoline. Some of the oil refineries in Toledo were built when there were many oil wells in western Ohio. Today, most of the oil comes through pipelines from as far away as the Gulf coast.

Akron (population 298,000; altitude 950 feet) is located about thirty-five miles southeast of Cleveland. It is the home of the famous Soap Box Derby.

Akron is the world's leading manufacturer of natural and synthetic* rubber products. The city's rubber industry was established in 1870. In that year, Benjamin F. Goodrich opened a plant to manufacture rubber fire hose from imported natural rubber. Later, Goodrich began to make rubber tires for buggies and bicycles. By 1915, the growing automobile industry had created a huge demand for automobile tires. As a result, Akron's rubber industry grew rapidly. During World War II, when the United States was no longer able to import enough natural rubber to meet its needs, plants in Akron began to manufacture synthetic rubber.

Today, about one third of all the industrial workers in the Akron metropolitan area are employed in plants that make automobile tires or other rubber products. Many other manufactured items are made in Akron. Among these are machinery and chemicals.

Dayton (population 260,000; altitude 745 feet) is an important industrial city in southwestern Ohio. People from Cincinnati first settled here in the 1790's. Today, a great manufacturing belt stretches along the Miami River between Cincinnati and Dayton. Many of the factories along the river produce paper and paper products.

Dayton produces a wide variety of manufactured goods. These include machinery and transportation equipment. Many factories in the city make products that were invented or developed here. Among these are cash registers, automobile starters, and refrigerators. The aviation industry has also been important in Dayton's history. This was the home of the Wright brothers, and it was in Dayton that they built the first successful airplane. Today, Dayton has a research center for the aircraft industry. Near the city is the huge Wright-Patterson Air Force Base, which employs many of the city's workers.

Learn About Ohio With Maps

Study the map on page 272, and then answer the following questions:

1. What river forms Ohio's southern boundary?
2. What large body of water borders much of Ohio on the north?
3. In what two land sections of our country does Ohio lie?
4. What states of the Midwest border on Ohio? What states of the Northeast? (You may wish to refer to the maps on pages 18, 19, and 21.)
5. What is the capital of Ohio? What are the state's two largest cities?

Discover Important Facts About Ohio

1. Why is Ohio's climate well suited for farming?
2. What are Ohio's two leading crops? Give the main use of these crops.
3. Name some of the natural resources of Ohio that are useful to industry here.
4. What are some of the advantages that Ohio offers for industry?

Explore Ohio's History

Preparing a report about events or people in Ohio's history will help you learn more about this state. Choose one of the topics given below and prepare an interesting report to share with your class. For help in locating and organizing information, refer to the suggestions on pages 346-352. You may either write your report or give it orally.

The Story of Johnny Appleseed
The Battle of Fallen Timbers
The Work of the Wright Brothers
The Founding of Marietta
Ohio, the Birthplace of Presidents

20 Wisconsin

Facts About Wisconsin		
	Number or Value	Rank
Area (square miles)	56,154	26
Population	4,161,000	16
Capital — Madison		
Admission Date:		
May 29, 1848		30
Colleges and Universities	63	10
Farm Products	$1,151,285,000	10
Dairy products	629,253,000	1
Cattle and calves	151,226,000	15
Hogs	102,674,000	9
Fish	$ 2,195,000	22
Forest Products	$ 44,900,000	19
Minerals	$ 70,007,000	37
Sand and gravel	24,695,000	12
Stone	20,232,000	22
Cement	Not available	
Manufactures	$5,344,282,000	11
Nonelectrical machinery	981,227,000	7
Food and kindred products	769,381,000	8
Transportation equipment	733,739,000	9

Land. If you were to travel through the beautiful state of Wisconsin, you would see rolling plains, rounded ridges, and low hills. Forests cover large areas of northern Wisconsin. In the southern part of the state are many farms, towns, and cities. Dotting the Wisconsin countryside are thousands of clear, blue lakes.

Much of the scenic beauty of Wisconsin is due to the action of glaciers. During the Great Ice Age, glaciers spread across much of this state. (See map on page 36.) These huge masses of moving ice leveled off the tops of mountains, scooped out hollows, and filled in valleys. As the glaciers melted, they deposited a thick layer of sand, clay, and gravel over the land. In some

Fertile farmland in Wisconsin's Central Lowland. About two thirds of Wisconsin lies in the Central Lowland section of our country. The eastern half of this section is the state's richest farming area. In the western half, much of the land is too rugged for growing crops.

places this material, called drift, was piled into small hills, ridges, and mounds. Water from the melting glaciers remained in many hollows, forming lakes.

Glaciers did not spread across a large area in western Wisconsin. This part of the state is called the Driftless Area. (Compare map on this page with map on page 36.) Since the land here was not smoothed by glaciers, this area is more rugged than the rest of Wisconsin.

The Central Lowland. About two thirds of Wisconsin lies in the Central Lowland section of our country. To the east, Wisconsin's Central Lowland borders on Lake Michigan. The Mississippi River flows along most of its western edge.

The eastern half of Wisconsin's Central Lowland is called the Great Lakes Plain. This is Wisconsin's richest farming area. The soil in this part of the state is very fertile. The most important type of farming in the Great Lakes Plain is dairying. Thousands of dairy farms cover the countryside between cities and towns here. Herds of dairy cows graze in green pastures on these farms. Next to the pastures are fields of hay, corn, and other crops grown as feed for cattle.

The Great Lakes Plain is the most densely populated part of Wisconsin. (Compare map on this page with map on page 117.) The state's most important industries are located in the cities and towns here. Lake Michigan provides low-cost water transportation for some of these industries. Along the shore of Lake Michigan lies Milwaukee, Wisconsin's largest city.

The western half of the Central Lowland in Wisconsin is made up of the

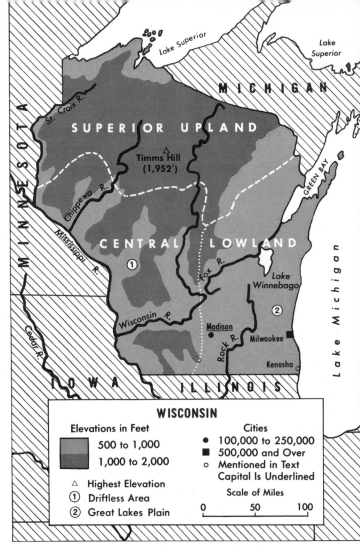

Wisconsin is bordered by two of the Great Lakes and the Mississippi River. Northern Wisconsin lies in the Superior Upland.

Driftless Area. Although a small part of this area lies in the corn belt, much of it is too rugged for growing crops. Farmers graze beef and dairy cattle on the ridges and hillsides here. Along the western edge of Wisconsin's Driftless Area, high wooded bluffs overlook the Mississippi River.

The Superior Upland. Northern Wisconsin lies in the Superior Upland region of our country. Lake Superior borders part of this region .(See map above.) Dotting Wisconsin's Superior Upland are thousands of beautiful lakes, surrounded by forests of pine, spruce, and other trees.

Few people make their homes in the Superior Upland of Wisconsin. The soil here is not fertile, and the growing season is short. Swamps cover large areas. However, the woods and lakes make this part of the state a popular vacationland. Thousands of people from other states come here each year to hunt, fish, and enjoy many other outdoor activities.

Climate. Winters are long and cold in Wisconsin. Even though this state borders on two of the Great Lakes, these bodies of water have little warming effect on winter temperatures. This is because winds in winter come mainly from the west or northwest, so they are not warmed by any large body of water before reaching Wisconsin. (See page 48.) Sometimes, masses of arctic air from Canada sweep across the state, causing severe cold waves. Winter days are short and often cloudy. Snowfall ranges from an average of thirty inches near the southern border of Wisconsin to more than sixty inches near Lake Superior. Skiing on Wisconsin's snow-covered hills is a popular winter sport.

Spring in Wisconsin is a short season, with changeable weather. Snow often falls in April, and the weather sometimes stays cool until the middle of May. This is about the time of the last killing frost. Then, suddenly, days become warm and sunny. Farmers begin plowing their fields to plant crops. Spring rains turn pastures green.

Summers are warm and pleasant in Wisconsin. Since this state lies in the northern part of our country, the weather seldom becomes uncomfortably hot. Many people from midwestern cities come to spend their vacations at lakes here. Thousands of children attend summer camps in Wisconsin.

Fall is a brisk and invigorating time of year in Wisconsin. Sometimes, there is an early snowfall in October. This may be followed by a short period of warm weather and clear days, which is called "Indian summer." Then the weather grows colder. By December, ice begins to thicken on lakes and streams. Cold, blustery winds are a sign that winter is near.

Wisconsin receives plentiful rainfall. Most of this rain is brought by moist winds from the Gulf of Mexico. (See page 52.) Wisconsin's rain comes mainly in the spring and summer, when it is most helpful to farmers.

The growing season varies from place to place in Wisconsin. (See map on page 60.) Most of the Great Lakes Plain, Wisconsin's main farming area, has five to six months of frost-free weather. This is more than enough for growing oats and fodder crops, or corn for silage.* Farmers in northern Wisconsin have less than five months in which to plant and harvest crops.

Farming. Wisconsin is one of our country's important farming states. It ranks

*See Glossary

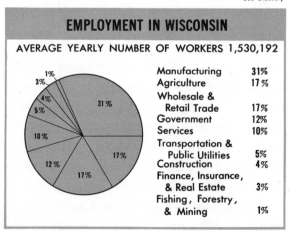

EMPLOYMENT IN WISCONSIN

AVERAGE YEARLY NUMBER OF WORKERS 1,530,192

Manufacturing	31%
Agriculture	17%
Wholesale & Retail Trade	17%
Government	12%
Services	10%
Transportation & Public Utilities	5%
Construction	4%
Finance, Insurance, & Real Estate	3%
Fishing, Forestry, & Mining	1%

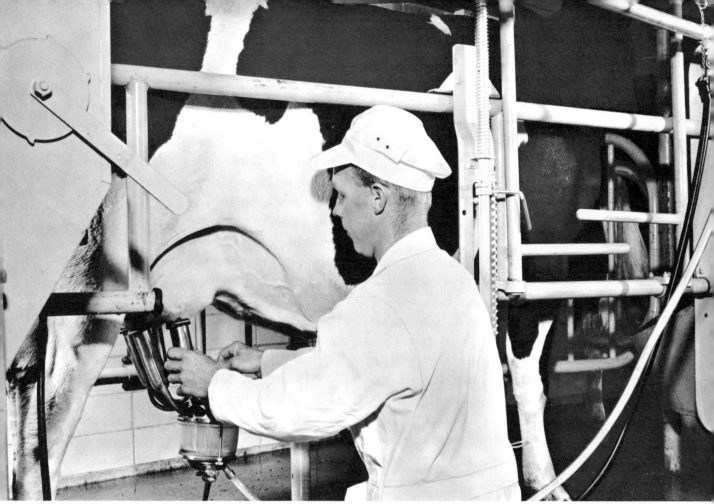

Milking a cow by machine. Wisconsin, our nation's leading producer of milk, is often called "America's Dairyland." The sale of milk provides more than half of the money received for farm products in Wisconsin. Much of the milk from farms here is made into cheese and other products.

tenth in the nation in the amount of money received for its farm products. This state is our country's leading producer of milk. Because Wisconsin supplies such large quantities of milk and milk products, it is often called "America's Dairyland."

More than half of all the money received for farm products in Wisconsin comes from the sale of milk. Although there are dairy farms in most parts of Wisconsin, the richest dairying area is in the Great Lakes Plain. Far more milk is produced in Wisconsin than can be used by its people. Therefore, much of the milk is made into cheese and other dairy products and sold to people in many parts of our country. Pages 152

and 153 tell more about dairy farming in the Midwest.

Several facts help to explain why dairying has become so important in Wisconsin. In the late 1800's, large numbers of Dutch, Swiss, and Scandinavian immigrants came to Wisconsin. Since many of these people had been dairy farmers in their homelands, they established dairy farms in Wisconsin. They found the climate here very favorable for dairying. The state's abundant rainfall keeps pastures green all summer long. Also, the short summers in Wisconsin are better suited for growing hay or silage crops than for growing crops that need long, hot summers in order to ripen.

Cattle and calves are Wisconsin's second leading source of farm income. Farmers who live in the more rugged parts of the state, such as the Driftless Area, graze beef cattle on slopes that are too steep for cultivating crops. Also, dairy cows that are no longer producing much milk are often sold by farmers for beef.

Some farmers in Wisconsin also raise other kinds of livestock. Hogs are raised on many farms in the Central Lowland, especially in the part that lies in the corn belt. (See map on page 153.) Farmers here grow crops such as corn and oats to feed their hogs. Hogs raised on dairy farms in Wisconsin are often fed skim* milk. In the Great Lakes Plain are many poultry farms that supply chickens and fresh eggs to people in nearby cities.

Wisconsin ranks tenth in our country in the production of vegetables. Green peas and sweet corn are the two leading vegetables grown here. These are grown mainly on large farms in the Great Lakes Plain. Wisconsin's summer weather is well suited to raising these two crops. After being harvested, most of the peas and sweet corn are sold to large canning or freezing plants. Pea vines and pods are made into silage to feed dairy cattle.

Natural resources. Forests are one of Wisconsin's most important natural resources. Wisconsin ranks nineteenth in the nation in the amount of money received for forest products. Forests cover about half of the state.

Wisconsin's forests are not as valuable as they once were. When the first settlers came here, thick forests of pine, birch, oak, and other trees covered most of the land. In the late 1800's, lumbermen seeking quick profits began to cut down the trees. Their ruthless cutting exhausted nearly all of the original forests.

Most of the trees that grow in Wisconsin today are second growth. They are used mainly for making wood pulp. Thousands of new trees are planted every year in Wisconsin to replace those cut down. If this practice is continued, there will be valuable forest resources here in the future for people to use.

Wisconsin has few important mineral resources. However, it does have a plentiful supply of sand, gravel, and limestone. Although much of the sand and gravel is shipped to neighboring states, some of it is used in the construction and paving of roads in Wisconsin. Large quantities of Wisconsin's limestone are also used in road building, but some is used in making iron and steel or cement.

Logging in northern Wisconsin. Forests cover about half of Wisconsin. They are one of the state's most important natural resources.

Making coal-mining machinery. The manufacture of power shovels, tractors, and other kinds of nonelectrical machinery is Wisconsin's leading industry. The state's location near the steelmaking centers of Indiana and Illinois has encouraged the growth of metal-products industries here.

Among the states of the Midwest, Wisconsin ranks second to Michigan in the value of fish caught each year. Wisconsin's fishermen take large catches of chubs, perch, and other valuable fish from the waters of Lake Michigan and Lake Superior. Many fish are also caught in the Mississippi and other rivers.

Industry. Although Wisconsin is an important farming state, manufacturing brings far more money to people here than the sale of farm products. About eight tenths of the value of all goods produced in the state comes from manufacturing. Most of Wisconsin's industries are in the towns and cities of the Great Lakes Plain. The main industrial area of the state is in and around the city of Milwaukee.

Wisconsin offers many advantages for industry. Its location near the great steelmaking centers of Indiana and Illinois has encouraged the development of industries that make metal products. The Great Lakes and the Mississippi River provide low-cost water transportation for bringing in steel and other raw materials and for shipping out manufactured goods. Chicago and other big cities of the Midwest provide large markets for goods produced in Wisconsin. Since the opening of the St. Lawrence Seaway, Wisconsin can also carry on trade with foreign countries. In addition, the state has a plentiful supply of skilled laborers to work in factories.

Wisconsin ranks seventh in the nation in the production of nonelectrical machinery. This is the state's leading industry. Iron and steel from mills in Indiana and Illinois are used in factories in Wisconsin to make machinery such as power shovels, turbines, and diesel engines. The location of Wisconsin's cities, near fertile farming areas, has encouraged the growth of factories that make tractors, cultivators, and other kinds of farm machinery.

Food processing is the second most important industry in Wisconsin. This state ranks eighth in our country as a supplier of food products. Although some of the milk from dairy farms here is sold fresh, much of Wisconsin's milk is made into cheese. This state is our country's leading producer of cheese. Large meat-packing plants in Wisconsin process the meat of beef cattle raised in the state. Canning and freezing plants here process peas, sweet corn, and other vegetables grown in Wisconsin. In the 1840's, German immigrants established breweries here and began making beer. Today, Wisconsin is one of our country's leading producers of beer.

Wisconsin's third leading industry is the manufacture of transportation equipment. (See fact table on page 284.) This industry also uses large quantities of steel. Automobiles are the main kind of transportation equipment made in Wisconsin. They are made at Kenosha. Auto parts and trucks are manufactured in several cities.

Wisconsin is our country's second most important producer of paper and paper products. Wood from Wisconsin's second-growth forests is shipped to pulp and paper mills. Many of these are located along the Fox River, which supplies the large amounts of water needed in making paper. Mills in Wisconsin make tissue paper, wrapping paper, and paper boxes.

People and cities. About two thirds of Wisconsin's people live in cities and towns. Most of the state's cities and large towns with populations of ten thousand or more are located on the Great Lakes Plain. (See map on page 285.)

Milwaukee (population 765,000; altitude 581 feet) is by far the largest city in Wisconsin. It is located along the western shore of Lake Michigan, at a point where three rivers join and empty into the lake. About 1,330,000 people live in the Milwaukee metropolitan area.

Milwaukee began as a French fur-trading post in the late 1700's. Gradually, a small settlement grew up around the post, and a town was established here. After the Territory of Wisconsin was opened for settlement, around 1836, many people from the eastern part of our country came and settled in the town of Milwaukee. By the late 1800's, railroads had been built across Wisconsin, linking it with states west of the Mississippi. Milwaukee then became an important port for shipping wheat and other grains from these states to flour-milling cities on the Great Lakes, such as Buffalo, New York.

After 1850, large numbers of German immigrants came to Wisconsin. (See page 120.) Many of them settled in Milwaukee. These hardworking, skillful people helped industry to grow in Milwaukee. By the late 1800's, the city had become a leading producer of lumber, machinery, and beer.

During the present century, Milwaukee has continued to grow. The opening

Milwaukee is by far the largest city in Wisconsin. This port city is located along the western shore of Lake Michigan. Oceangoing ships and lake freighters load and unload many kinds of cargo at docks along Milwaukee's fine harbor. Milwaukee is also an important manufacturing city. Among the products made here are turbines, farm machines, and beer.

of the St. Lawrence Seaway has encouraged the growth of trade with other countries. Milwaukee's fine harbor is open most of the year. Oceangoing ships from many different countries dock regularly at Milwaukee. They unload cargoes such as crude rubber and tin. They take away machinery, grain, and other goods. Lake freighters carry large amounts of goods between Milwaukee and other ports on the Great Lakes. Also, freight trains are loaded onto ferries and transported to ports in Michigan.

Factories in Milwaukee produce a great variety of manufactured goods.

Many of the city's skilled workers are employed in plants that make machinery, such as turbines and farm machines. Other workers here have jobs in meat-packing plants and breweries.

City leaders in Milwaukee have worked hard to make this city a pleasant place in which to live. As a result, they have succeeded in solving some of the problems that face all large cities. Milwaukee has one of the lowest crime rates in our country for a city of its size. There are fewer slum areas than in most large cities. Most homes here are tidy and well kept. Parks and other recreational facilities are scattered throughout Milwaukee. Wide, tree lined parkways wind through the city.

Madison (population 154,000; altitude 859 feet) is the capital and second largest city in Wisconsin. It is located in the south central part of the state, on a narrow strip of land between two beautiful lakes. Madison was chosen as the site for the capital of the Territory of Wisconsin in 1836. After Wisconsin became a state, Madison remained the capital.

Madison is a center of trade, government, and education. A rich farming area surrounds the city. Farmers from this area come into Madison to sell their farm products and buy the things they need. Many of the city's workers have jobs in food-processing industries, such as meat-packing plants and dairies. Still others work for federal, state, or local government agencies. The University of Wisconsin, located here, also employs large numbers of people.

Use Maps To Learn About Wisconsin

Study the map on page 285, and then answer the following questions:

1. In what two main land sections or regions does Wisconsin lie?
2. What large body of water borders Wisconsin on the east?
3. What large body of water borders Wisconsin on the northwest?
4. What river flows along much of the western boundary of Wisconsin?
5. What states of the Midwest border Wisconsin?

Develop Important Understandings

1. How did glaciers affect the land in Wisconsin?
2. What is the main difference between the Great Lakes Plain and the Driftless Area?
3. Why do the Great Lakes have little warming effect on winter temperatures in Wisconsin?
4. Why is Wisconsin often called "America's Dairyland"?
5. In what ways is Wisconsin's climate favorable for dairying?
6. Why are many trees planted each year in Wisconsin?
7. How has Wisconsin's location in the Midwest influenced industry in the state?

Learn About Wisconsin's History

Do research about the history of Wisconsin, and then write a report about it to share with your class. The following questions will guide your reading and help you decide what to include in your report.

1. What groups of Indians lived in the area that is now Wisconsin? Describe their way of life.
2. Who were the first explorers to travel through this part of North America?
3. Why did war break out between the Indians and the French here?
4. How did France lose its territory in Wisconsin?
5. What attracted settlers to Wisconsin? Where did most of these settlers come from?

For help in locating information and in writing your report, refer to the suggestions on pages 346-351.

Explore an Interesting Topic

Listed below are some interesting topics that will help you learn more about Wisconsin. Choose one of these topics and do some outside reading about it. Then present your findings to the class in the form of an oral report, a chart, or a classroom mural. Refer to pages 346-348 for help in locating information.

The Wisconsin Dells
How Cheese Is Made
The Work of a Dairy Farmer
A Vacation Trip Through Wisconsin's Superior Upland
A Visit to Milwaukee
How Paper Is Made From Wood

States of the Great Plains. Part 6 of this book provides information about the six Great Plains states. Here you will find the facts you need for solving many problems about this part of our country. The text, the maps, and the vivid pictures will give you the most important information about the land, climate, people, and resources of each Great Plains state.

Reading the fact tables. The following explanation will help you understand the information in the fact table at the beginning of each state chapter. The figures in these tables are the latest that were available from the United States government at the time this book was published. Some of these fig-

ures are amounts of money. These tell how many dollars the people of the state received in a year from such activities as farming, mining, and fishing. The figures for manufactures show the actual value added to goods or raw materials by factories in the state. The value added in manufacturing was figured out in an interesting way. From the amount of money received from the sale of goods, the cost of the materials needed to make them was subtracted. The amount of money left is the value added by the factories.

The fact tables also show the rank of each state in comparison with all the other states of our country. In cases where figures were not available, the rank is not given.

21 Kansas

Facts About Kansas

	Number or Value	Rank
Area (square miles)	82,264	14
Population	2,250,000	29
Capital — Topeka		
Admission Date:		
January 29, 1861		34
Colleges and Universities	45	17
Farm Products	$1,194,103,000	9
Cattle and calves	559,786,000	4
Wheat	279,924,000	1
Hogs	78,236,000	10
Fish	$ 11,000	46
Forest Products	$ 1,800,000	44
Minerals	$ 513,269,000	11
Petroleum	310,256,000	7
Natural gas	96,031,000	6
Cement	27,132,000	12
Manufactures	$1,436,874,000	29
Transportation equipment	433,130,000	15
Food and kindred products	238,511,000	26
Chemicals and allied products	192,217,000	25

Land. If you were to take an automobile trip from east to west across Kansas, you would discover that much of the land here is as flat as a tabletop. In some places, however, there are rounded hills separated by deep valleys. Many steep-sided buttes rise above the level plains in western Kansas.

The land in Kansas slopes upward from east to west. It rises from less than one thousand feet in the east to about four thousand feet along the state's western border. Eastern Kansas lies in the Central Lowland section of our country. (See map on pages 28 and 29.) The rest of the state is in the Great Plains.

<u>The Central Lowland</u>. In the northeastern part of the Central Lowland of

Level wheatlands in Kansas. Much of the land in Kansas is as flat as a tabletop. In some places, however, the Kansas plains are broken by rounded hills and steep-sided buttes.

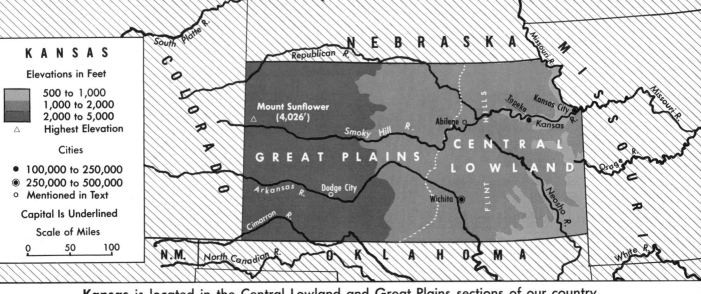

Kansas is located in the Central Lowland and Great Plains sections of our country. The land in Kansas rises from less than one thousand feet in the east to about four thousand feet along the state's western border.

Kansas, most of the land is level or gently rolling. This part of the state was smoothed by glaciers during the Great Ice Age. (See page 36.) When these ice sheets retreated, they left behind deposits of finely ground rock and other drift* materials. Later, winds spread a thick layer of silt over the land here. The soils that have developed from these deposits are very fertile. Today, this is a rich farming area. Corn and wheat are the leading crops grown here. Many farmers raise vegetables to sell in the nearby cities of Topeka and Kansas City.

The rest of the Central Lowland of Kansas was never covered by glaciers. Here, most of the land is hilly, and the soil is thin and stony. Livestock raising is the most important type of farming in this part of Kansas.

In the western part of the Central Lowland of Kansas is a band of rugged, stony ridges called the Flint Hills. (See map above.) These hills extend from the state's northern border to its southern border. Most of the land in the Flint Hills is not suited to growing crops. However, much of it is covered with tall grass that makes excellent pasture for livestock. Many fine herds of beef cattle graze on the slopes of the Flint Hills.

The Great Plains. All of Kansas west of the Central Lowland lies in the Great Plains section of our country. (See map above.) Much of the land here is level and is covered with very fertile soil. In some places, however, the countryside is very hilly.

The Great Plains section of Kansas is one of the greatest wheat-growing areas of the world. If you were to travel through western Kansas in early summer, you would drive for miles through a golden sea of ripening grain. Now and then you would pass a lone farmhouse or a tall grain elevator rising above the level plain. In parts of the Great Plains section where the soil is too sandy or the land is too hilly for growing wheat, there are large cattle ranches.

Several rivers have carved deep valleys in the Great Plains of Kansas. During periods when rainfall is light, some of these rivers may dry up completely. At other times, heavy rains or melting snow may cause rivers to overflow their banks and flood the land

*See Glossary

295

nearby. Sometimes floods have severely damaged towns, destroyed crops, and carried away much valuable topsoil. To prevent floods, dams have been built across some of these rivers. The reservoirs behind the dams store water for irrigation, for the production of hydro-electricity, and for recreation.

Climate. In Kansas, there are extreme changes in the weather from season to season and often from day to day. This is partly because Kansas is located hundreds of miles from any large body of water, which would help moderate temperatures. (See page 48.) Also, since the state is not protected by mountains, cold winds from the north and warm winds from the south can move swiftly across the land.

Winters in most of Kansas are cold. On frosty winter nights, when the air is clear and still, the temperature may drop far below zero. Strong winds sometimes whip up powdery snow, causing blizzards. The drifting snow blocks highways and railroads, making travel difficult. Then, after several days of very cold weather, warm winds from the Gulf of Mexico may sweep northward across the state. These winds send the temperature above the freezing point and quickly melt the snow.

Summers in Kansas are long and very warm. The growing season here lasts from five to seven months. (See map on page 60.) In summer, daytime temperatures in Kansas often rise above ninety degrees. Hot, dry winds sweep across the plains, raising clouds of brown dust. Thunderstorms are frequent during the summer months. Sometimes they are accompanied by hailstorms that flatten entire fields of wheat.

Many tornadoes strike Kansas each year. (See page 59.) These violent wind-storms usually occur in spring or early summer. They can cause great property damage and loss of life. Many farm homes have underground shelters called "storm cellars," where people can go if they see a funnel cloud approaching.

In Kansas, rainfall decreases from east to west. (See map on page 49.) The average annual rainfall is more than thirty inches in the eastern third of the state, and between twenty and thirty inches in the central part. This is enough rainfall for growing most crops. In the westernmost part of Kansas, the average yearly rainfall is less than twenty inches. Wheat farmers here use dry-farming* methods. Sometimes, for several years in a row, rainfall in western Kansas may be lighter than usual. Droughts have often destroyed crops and caused much hardship to farmers here.

Farming. Kansas is one of our nation's ten leading farming states. It ranks first in wheat production and fourth in the production of cattle and calves. Together, these products bring in about seven tenths of the state's yearly farm income.

Cattle and wheat have been important farm products in Kansas for many years. About one hundred years ago, Texas cowboys began driving huge herds of cattle to Abilene and other "cow towns" in Kansas for shipment by train to eastern markets. (See pages 93 and 94.) When they discovered that grasslands in Kansas provided excellent pasture for livestock, many cattlemen began grazing their herds here before shipping them eastward. This was the beginning of the cattle industry in Kansas.

During the 1870's and 1880's, thousands of settlers came to Kansas and started farms. They strung barbed wire fences around their land to keep out wandering cattle and plowed up the prairie grass in order to plant crops. These pioneers found that Kansas was very well suited to growing wheat. The cool, moist springs and sunny, dry summers were just right for this crop. Although winters were cold, they were not as severe here as in states farther north. As a result, wheat could be planted in the fall and harvested in the early summer. In addition, the soil was fertile, and the land was level enough for farmers to use farm machinery. These machines saved farmers much labor and enabled them to raise wheat on large areas of land.

Although Kansas was generally a good land for farming, settlers here faced many difficulties. Sometimes huge swarms of grasshoppers ate up their crops. Droughts and floods also caused much damage. However, most farmers were hardworking people who did not give up easily. By the early 1900's, Kansas was producing so much wheat that it was nicknamed the "wheat state."

For several years during the 1930's, little rain fell in western Kansas. Crops shriveled in the sun, and strong winds carried away huge amounts of fertile topsoil. Southwestern Kansas formed part of the area known as the Dust Bowl.* Since that time, farmers in Kansas have planted thousands of trees as windbreaks* and have taken other measures to conserve soil and water. Many

Harvesting wheat in Kansas. Kansas is the leading wheat-growing state of our country. The land and climate of Kansas are well suited for growing this crop. However, farmers in the state earn more money from cattle and calves than from any other farm product. Where winters are mild, beef cattle are grazed on the fields of young wheat.

farmers in the western part of the state now irrigate their crops with water from deep wells or from reservoirs. Another drought struck Kansas in the 1950's, but it caused much less damage because farmers had learned how to take better care of their land.

Today, wheat is by far the leading crop grown in Kansas. Although this crop is raised throughout Kansas, it is especially important in the central and western parts of the state. (See map on page 157.) You can read about a typical wheat farm in western Kansas on pages 155 and 156.

Although wheat is Kansas' main crop, farmers here earn more money from beef cattle than from any other product. The sale of cattle and calves provides nearly half of the state's total yearly income from farm products. Beef cattle are raised throughout Kansas. Wheat farmers often raise cattle on part of their land so they will have something to sell in case their wheat crop is poor. Where winters are mild, the cattle graze on the fields of young wheat. In the spring, they are moved to other pastures so that the wheat can grow.

Farmers in Kansas also raise several other kinds of crops and livestock. The state is a leading producer of sorghum, which is used mainly as feed for livestock. There are many fields of corn and soybeans in the eastern part of the state, where rainfall is plentiful. Much of the corn is fed to cattle and hogs. Dairy farms in eastern Kansas supply large amounts of milk to processing plants in nearby cities.

A natural-gas pipeline station in southwestern Kansas. Natural gas is forced through pipelines to homes, factories, and power plants for use as fuel. Petroleum and natural gas are the two leading mineral resources of Kansas. Most of the oil is sent by pipeline to refineries in Kansas and other states to be made into gasoline and other products.

Natural resources. Oil and natural gas are the most important mineral resources of Kansas. The state ranks seventh in the nation in petroleum production and sixth in the production of natural gas. Most of Kansas' electric power is produced in plants that burn natural gas or fuel* oil.

Petroleum brings in about three fifths of Kansas' total income from mineral production. There are more than 45,000 oil wells in this state. Pipelines carry oil from the wells to refineries in Kansas and in other states. At the refineries, such products as fuel oil and gasoline are made from the petroleum.

Kansas' largest deposits of natural gas are found in the southwestern part of the state. (See map on page 169.) Certain substances, such as helium* and natural gasoline, are removed from the natural gas at processing plants. Then the gas is piped to homes, factories, and power plants for use as a fuel.

Limestone is another important mineral resource of Kansas. Large quantities of limestone quarried here are used in the construction of roads and buildings. Limestone is also used in making cement, which is the state's third most valuable mineral product.

Assembling jet planes at Wichita. The manufacture of airplanes is one of the leading industries in Kansas. Factories here make small business planes and large jet bombers.

Industry. About sixteen out of every one hundred workers in Kansas earn their living from manufacturing. Twenty-five years ago, Kansas was mainly a farming state. Since then, however, industry has grown rapidly here, and today it is more important than farming.

One of the main industries in Kansas is the manufacture of aircraft. The state's airplane industry started here before World War I, partly because there was so much clear weather for flying and testing airplanes. During World War II, the city of Wichita produced more military airplanes than any other city in the United States. Because Wichita is located far inland, airplane plants here were considered safer from enemy attack than cities along the coast. Today, factories in the Wichita area make large numbers of small airplanes used by business firms and individuals. Large jet bombers and other

EMPLOYMENT IN KANSAS

AVERAGE YEARLY NUMBER OF WORKERS 726,196

Agriculture	21%
Wholesale & Retail Trade	18%
Government	16%
Manufacturing	16%
Services	11%
Transportation & Public Utilities	7%
Construction	6%
Finance, Insurance, & Real Estate	3%
Fishing, Forestry, & Mining	2%

military aircraft for the United States Air Force are also made here.

Other kinds of transportation equipment besides aircraft are made in Kansas. Factories here manufacture railroad equipment, such as freight and passenger cars and locomotive parts. Automobiles are assembled in the Kansas City area.

Since Kansas produces large quantities of farm products, it is not surprising that food processing is a major industry here. In several cities and towns, there are flour mills that process wheat grown on Kansas farms. Kansas produces more flour than any other state. Kansas also has many slaughterhouses and packing plants where cattle and other animals are butchered and the meat is prepared for sale. Factories in Kansas City use animal fats and oils in the manufacture of shortening and other products.

The manufacture of chemicals and chemical products is another important industry in Kansas. Oil refineries and gas-processing plants in the state provide raw materials that are used in producing a variety of petrochemicals.* There are also plants in Kansas that make such chemical products as explosives, drugs, and fertilizer.

People and cities. About five out of every six people in Kansas live in the eastern half of the state. All of the state's largest cities are located here. The western half of Kansas is a land of giant wheat farms and cattle ranches. In this area, there are no cities with more than twenty thousand people.

Wichita is the largest city in Kansas. It is located on the Arkansas River, in the south central part of the state. Wichita was an important cattle-shipping town in the late 1800's. Today, Wichita is still an important trading city for livestock and other farm products.

Wichita (population 275,000; altitude 1,290 feet) is the largest city in Kansas. It lies along the Arkansas River, in the south central part of the state. (See map on page 295.) The city is named for the Wichita Indians, who once lived in this area.

Settlers from the eastern part of our country founded Wichita in 1868. Soon the town became an important stopping point for cowboys who were driving cattle northward on the Chisholm Trail from Texas to Abilene. After the Santa Fe Railway was extended to Wichita, in 1872, cowboys from western Kansas and from Texas brought cattle here for shipment to eastern markets. Later, farmers settled near Wichita and began to grow wheat.

Today, Wichita is the main trading city for a large area. Grain, livestock, and other farm products are brought here to be sold. Retail stores in southern Kansas buy a variety of manufactured goods from wholesale firms in Wichita.

The leading industry in Wichita is the manufacture of aircraft, including bombers and private planes. Flour milling and meat-packing are also important industries here. Refineries in Wichita process large amounts of petroleum piped from nearby oil fields.

Kansas City (population 182,000; altitude 750 feet) is located on the eastern border of Kansas, near the point where the Kansas River empties into the Missouri River. Just across the state line is Kansas City, Missouri. These two cities are part of a metropolitan area with a population of more than one million.

Kansas City, Kansas, is an important transportation center and manufacturing city. Barges on the Missouri River carry bulky goods to and from the city. Kansas City is served by twelve railroad lines. Grain and livestock from Kansas farms are brought here to be processed in flour mills and meat-packing plants. There are also oil refineries and chemical plants here.

Topeka (population 127,500; altitude 930 feet) is the capital of Kansas. It is located along the Kansas River, in the heart of a rich farming area. The main offices of the Atchison, Topeka and Santa Fe Railway are in this city. Here, too, are shops that repair railroad equipment. Plants in Topeka also make many other goods, including tires, steel, flour, and meat products. Many people who live here work for the state government.

Learn About Kansas With Maps

Study the maps on pages 11 and 295, and then answer the following questions:

1. In what two sections of our country does Kansas lie?
2. What Great Plains states border on Kansas? What state of the Midwest borders on Kansas?
3. Name some of the rivers that flow across Kansas.
4. What is the capital of Kansas?

Discover Important Facts About Kansas

1. What facts help to explain why Kansas is the nation's leading wheat-growing state?
2. Why have many people in Kansas built underground shelters?
3. What are the two leading mineral resources of Kansas? What are some of the uses made of these resources?
4. In which half of Kansas do most of the people live?

Facts About Nebraska		
	Number or Value	Rank
Area (square miles)	77,227	15
Population	1,456,000	35
Capital — Lincoln		
Admission Date:		
March 1, 1867		37
Colleges and Universities	23	30
Farm Products	$1,299,414,000	6
Cattle and Calves	617,644,000	2
Hogs	159,329,000	6
Corn	159,103,000	4
Fish	$ 33,000	40
Forest Products	$ 950,000	47
Minerals	$ 91,959,000	31
Petroleum	51,605,000	16
Sand and gravel	15,748,000	20
Cement	Not available	
Manufactures	$ 743,087,000	36
Food and kindred products	314,679,000	24
Electrical machinery	65,055,000	27
Printing and publishing	50,238,000	30

Land. One hundred years ago, Indians and buffalo roamed the treeless plains of Nebraska. Today, prosperous farms and large cattle ranches cover the land.

Nebraska may be divided into two main parts. The eastern one fifth of the state is in the Central Lowland section of our country. (See map on pages 28 and 29.) The rest of Nebraska lies in the Great Plains.

The Central Lowland. As the map on the opposite page shows, the Central Lowland of Nebraska extends along the Missouri River. The richest farmland in the state is found here. Most of Nebraska's Central Lowland is level or gently rolling and the soil is very fertile. Corn is the main crop grown in the

Cultivating corn in Nebraska's Central Lowland. About one fifth of Nebraska lies in the Central Lowland section of our country. The state's most fertile farmland is located here. Nebraska's two largest cities and most of its industries are also located in the Central Lowland.

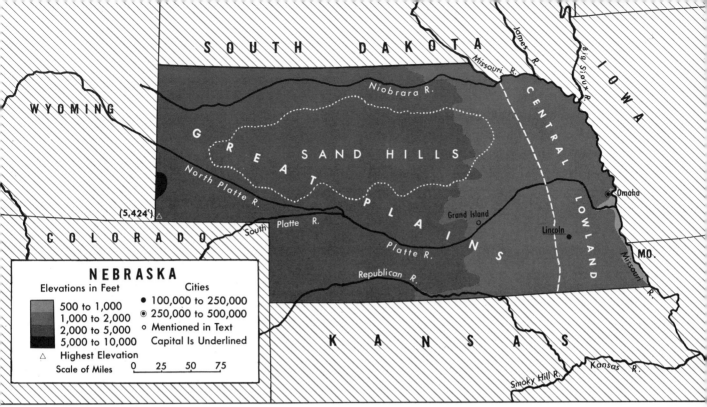

Nebraska. The Great Plains extend across the western four fifths of Nebraska. The land here slopes gently upward from east to west. Much of Nebraska's Great Plains section is better suited for grazing livestock than for growing crops.

rich, brown soil of Nebraska's Central Lowland.

About half the people of Nebraska live in the Central Lowland. The state's two largest cities, Omaha and Lincoln, are located here. Here also are most of the state's industries.

The Great Plains. All of Nebraska west of the Central Lowland lies in the Great Plains section of our country. The plains slope gently upward from about 1,500 feet above sea level in the east to more than 4,000 feet in the west. In some places in western Nebraska, the land rises to more than 5,000 feet above sea level. (See map above.)

To learn more about the Great Plains of Nebraska, let us take an imaginary trip. We board a plane at Lincoln and fly westward. In a few minutes, we reach the Great Plains section of the state. As we fly over the eastern part of this section, the land below us appears very flat. We see many fields of corn. This crop grows well in the rich soil here, which is similar to the soil in the Central Lowland.

Soon, we notice the wide, shallow Platte River winding across the plains. This river is formed by the North Platte and the South Platte rivers, which rise in the Rocky Mountains. They meet in western Nebraska to form the Platte. In the middle of the 1800's, pioneers journeyed westward in covered wagons along the banks of the Platte and the North Platte on their way to Oregon and California. Today, roads and railroads follow the route that was traveled long ago by the pioneers.

Our plane now follows the Platte River westward over south central Nebraska. Fields of corn, wheat, oats, and other crops stretch out as far as we can see. Since rainfall in this part of Nebraska is not very plentiful or dependable, many farmers here irrigate their fields. (See map on page 172.) Irrigation ditches carry water from the Platte, the Republican, and other rivers to some of the farms. Water for irrigation is also pumped from wells.

North of the Platte River is a vast area of sand dunes that are covered with grass. These are called the Sand Hills. (See map on page 303.) They make up more than one fourth of the state. The Sand Hills were formed many centuries ago when strong winds carried fine, yellow sand across the open plains and piled it up in hills and ridges. Today the grass covering the hills holds the sand in place.

Large herds of beef cattle graze on the tall, green grass of the Sand Hills. Ranchers here have found that it is not wise to plow the land for growing crops. Whenever grass is removed from the Sand Hills, winds quickly blow sandy

An irrigated bean field in Nebraska. Rainfall decreases from east to west in Nebraska. In areas where rainfall is not very plentiful or dependable, many farmers irrigate their fields.

soil away. Sometimes, so much soil is blown away that huge holes appear on the green hillsides. In Nebraska, these are called "blowouts."

Now we are flying over the western third of Nebraska. Most of this part of the state is a high, flat tableland. In places, however, rivers and streams have cut deep canyons in the land. In other places, rugged buttes rise sharply above the surrounding plain. We see herds of beef cattle grazing on large ranches in this part of Nebraska. Rainfall here is too light for growing most crops.

Climate. Winters in Nebraska are cold. Winds from the northwest blow across the treeless plains in winter, bringing bitterly cold weather. Temperatures sometimes drop far below zero. One reason for the cold winters here is that Nebraska lies far inland, away from any large bodies of water. Northwest winds travel over many miles of cold land surface before they reach Nebraska. They do not pass over any oceans or large lakes, which might have a warming effect. (See page 48.)

Snowfall is not extremely heavy in Nebraska. However, strong, cold winds sometimes accompany snow, creating severe blizzards. Deep snowdrifts may cover the roads for days at a time, making travel very difficult.

Summer days in Nebraska are often hot. Frequently, temperatures rise above one hundred degrees. Strong, hot summer winds sometimes dry up the land and carry away soil.

As in most of the Great Plains states, rainfall in Nebraska decreases steadily from east to west. Masses of warm, moist air from the Gulf of Mexico drift northward in summer and bring rain to Nebraska. However, this moist air seldom reaches the western part of the state. Here, the average annual rainfall is only ten to twenty inches. (See map on page 49.) In central Nebraska and much of eastern Nebraska, the average annual rainfall is between twenty and thirty inches. The southeastern part of the state receives the most rain. This area receives between thirty and forty inches of rain each year.

Nebraska does not receive the same amount of rainfall every year. In some years there is little rain, and crops and grass may wither and die for lack of moisture. In other years rain is abundant, and farmers harvest huge crops. Sometimes heavy rains cause rivers and streams to overflow their banks and wash away valuable topsoil.

During the summer months, storms are frequent in Nebraska. Violent thunderstorms sometimes crash across the plains. These storms may be accompanied by hail that destroys crops. Occasionally, tornadoes sweep across Nebraska. These fierce windstorms sometimes cause severe damage and loss of life.

Farming. Nebraska is an important farming state. Among all the states of

Cattle grazing in the Sand Hills. Farmers in Nebraska receive more money from cattle and calves than from any other farm product. Hogs and corn are the next most important sources of income.

our country, it ranks sixth in the value of farm products sold. Each year, farmers in Nebraska supply the nation with more than one billion dollars' worth of cattle, hogs, grain, and other farm products.

Nebraska is one of the great cattle-raising states of our country. Iowa is the only state that receives more money from the sale of beef cattle and calves. The Sand Hills and the grass-covered plains of western Nebraska make excellent grazing land for beef cattle. Many ranchers in these areas ship their calves to feedlots in eastern Nebraska. As the map on page 153 shows, most of the eastern half of the state lies in the corn belt. Corn and other grain crops grown here are fed to the calves to fatten them for market.

Nebraska farmers also raise hogs, sheep, dairy cattle, and poultry. Hogs

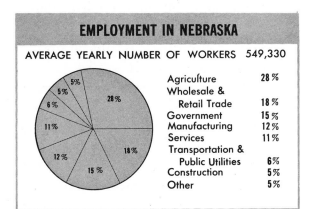

EMPLOYMENT IN NEBRASKA

AVERAGE YEARLY NUMBER OF WORKERS 549,330

Agriculture	28%
Wholesale & Retail Trade	18%
Government	15%
Manufacturing	12%
Services	11%
Transportation & Public Utilities	6%
Construction	5%
Other	5%

are raised mainly in the corn belt, where they can be fattened on corn and other grains. Flocks of sheep and lambs graze on the grasslands of western Nebraska. Most dairy and poultry farms are located in the eastern part of the state. These farms supply fresh milk, eggs, and poultry to people in nearby towns and cities.

Nebraska ranks fourth in the nation in the production of corn. This is the state's leading crop. In eastern Nebraska, cornfields stretch for mile after mile under the blue summer sky. Fertile soil, hot sunshine, and adequate rainfall make this area well suited to raising corn. In parts of the corn belt that receive less rain, many farmers irrigate their land to grow this crop.

Farmers in Nebraska also raise large crops of wheat, sorghum,* hay, and sugar beets. Golden fields of wheat cover large areas of southeastern, central, and western Nebraska. Sorghum is grown mainly in the corn belt and is used to fatten cattle and hogs. In western Nebraska and along the Platte, farmers grow sugar beets on irrigated land. Nebraska ranks third in the production of hay, which is used as winter feed for cattle.

Natural resources. Nebraska's most important natural resources are soil and water. The rich, brown soil that covers the eastern and southern parts of the state is excellent for growing crops. Although much of Nebraska receives only light rainfall, water is supplied by many rivers and streams that flow across the state. In addition, a vast reserve of groundwater* lies below the surface of the earth. This groundwater can be brought to the surface by drilling wells.

The people of Nebraska have made good use of the soil and water resources of their state. As early as the 1890's, farmers began using irrigation and dry-farming* methods to improve their land. Today, prosperous farms and ranches cover land that was once too dry for farming. Dams have been built on the Platte, the North Platte, and other rivers to store water for irrigation and to prevent floods. Along the Platte and in the Sand Hills, thousands of wells have been drilled to supply water for crops and livestock. (See map on page 172.) To protect their soil against Nebraska's strong winds, farmers have planted long rows of trees along the edges of their fields. These rows of trees, called shelterbelts, are sometimes many miles long.

Power plants located near dams on the Platte, the Missouri, and other rivers produce hydroelectricity. About one fifth of Nebraska's electric power is produced in hydroelectric plants.

Nebraska is not rich in other natural resources. Petroleum is the state's leading mineral resource. However, Nebraska does not rank high among the oil-producing states. Sand, gravel, and limestone are also produced in Nebraska. These minerals are used in constructing roads and in building and repairing dams and irrigation canals.

Industry. Nebraska is not a highly industrialized state. It ranks thirty-sixth among all our states in the value of manufactured products. There are several reasons for the lack of industry in Nebraska. This state has almost none of the raw materials needed by modern industry. Steel, copper, and other materials must be shipped in from

*See Glossary

Union Stockyards at Omaha. Omaha is the world's largest livestock market and meat-packing center. Food processing is the leading industry in Nebraska. In addition to meat, other food products of the state include breakfast cereal, flour, spaghetti, and sugar.

other states. Nebraska lies far from markets in the large cities of the Midwest and the Northeast. It is also far from most important waterways and therefore does not benefit greatly from cheap water transportation. However, Nebraska is trying to overcome these disadvantages. It offers low tax rates and cheap electric power to businessmen who will start new factories here. In recent years, several hundred new plants have opened in Nebraska.

Food processing is Nebraska's leading industry. Almost half of all the industrial workers in this state are employed in plants that prepare farm products for market.

The most important type of food processing in Nebraska is meat-packing. Each year, millions of beef cattle, hogs,

and sheep are brought to stockyards in Omaha. They come not only from farms and ranches in Nebraska but also from the neighboring states of Iowa, Missouri, Wyoming, and Kansas. After being weighed and inspected, the animals are sold to meat-packing plants located near the stockyards. Here they are slaughtered, and the meat is prepared for sale to supermarkets and butcher shops all over the United States.

Parts of the animals that cannot be used as meat, such as the horns, bones, and hides, are sold to other plants. They are used in making many useful products such as buttons, fertilizer, and leather goods.

Mills and factories in Nebraska process large quantities of corn, wheat, and other crops. Corn is made into cereals and livestock feed. A large chemical plant in Omaha uses corncobs to make furfural,* a substance used in the manufacture of nylon and in the refining of petroleum products. In many Nebraska cities, there are mills in which wheat is ground into flour. Factories in Omaha make products such as spaghetti and macaroni from wheat. In the western part of the state, where large crops of sugar beets are harvested, many people work in sugar refineries.

Nebraska has few important industries besides food processing. Factory owners here specialize in making products, such as electronic equipment, that require only small amounts of raw materials. One of the state's largest factories is an electronics plant in Omaha that makes telephone parts. This plant employs about four thousand people. Chemicals, scientific instruments, and farm machinery are other leading products of Nebraska's factories.

People and cities. About half the people of Nebraska live on farms or in small towns and villages. There are few large towns or cities here. Omaha and Lincoln are the only cities with populations of more than 100,000. Grand Island, the state's third largest city, has a population of only about 26,000.

Omaha (population 340,000; altitude 1,040 feet) is Nebraska's largest city. It is located in the eastern part of the state, directly across the Missouri River from Council Bluffs, Iowa. (See map on page 229.)

Omaha was founded in 1854 by settlers from Council Bluffs. In the early

Omaha is Nebraska's largest city. It is located on the Missouri River, in the eastern part of the state. Omaha grew up as a supply point for pioneers traveling westward across the plains. Today, Omaha is an important transportation center and a great food-processing city.

years of the settlement, merchants did a thriving business selling food, farm tools, and other supplies to pioneers passing through Omaha on their way westward. At Omaha, these pioneers had their last opportunity to buy supplies before starting across the plains.

After the first transcontinental railroad was completed, in 1869, Omaha began to grow rapidly. (See pages 92 and 93.) Farmers on the plains shipped cattle, hogs, corn, wheat, and other farm products to Omaha by rail. To process these products, businessmen established stockyards, meat-packing plants, grain elevators, and flour mills.

Today, Omaha is a great food-processing city. Its stockyards are the largest in the nation. More than four and one-half million head of livestock are slaughtered in Omaha's meat-packing plants each year. Grain is stored in twenty-two huge elevators. This grain is made into breakfast cereals, corn-starch, flour, and other products.

The people of Omaha earn their living in various other ways. Many of them work in factories that produce electronic equipment, chemicals, farm machinery, and clothing. One of the world's largest lead refineries is located in Omaha. This refinery processes lead ore received from several nearby states. Many people work in the insurance business. About forty insurance companies have their headquarters or branch offices in this city. South of Omaha is Offutt Air Force Base, the headquarters of the Strategic Air Command.

Omaha is an important transportation center. It lies on the main east-west route between Chicago and the west coast of the United States. Nine railroads and five national highways pass through the city. Large railway shops, which build and repair railway cars and equipment, are located in Omaha. In recent years, the Missouri River has been deepened, and barges now carry freight between Omaha and St. Louis, Missouri.

Lincoln (population 149,000; altitude 1,148 feet) is the capital of Nebraska. It is located about fifty-five miles southwest of Omaha, in a fertile farming area. Farmers come to Lincoln to sell their livestock, grain, and other farm products and to buy the things they need. The University of Nebraska and several other colleges are located in Lincoln. Many people here are employed by these schools or by the state government.

Although Lincoln is not mainly a manufacturing city, industry is growing. Meat, flour, telephone equipment, rubber tires, and motor scooters are among its most important products. Like Omaha, Lincoln is the headquarters for many insurance companies.

Discover Important Facts About Nebraska

1. Why is the Central Lowland in Nebraska well suited to farming?
2. How is the Platte River helpful to farmers in Nebraska?
3. How were the Sand Hills formed? Why do farmers not grow crops in the Sand Hills?
4. Why is rainfall lighter in western Nebraska than in eastern Nebraska?
5. Why is the eastern part of Nebraska especially well suited for growing corn?
6. What are shelterbelts? Why are they needed in Nebraska?
7. What are some of the different food products made in Nebraska?

23 North Dakota

Facts About North Dakota		
	Number or Value	Rank
Area (square miles)	70,665	17
Population	650,000	45
Capital — Bismarck		
Admission Date:		
November 2, 1889		39
Colleges and Universities	14	37
Farm Products	$633,095,000	23
Wheat	252,480,000	2
Cattle and calves	131,581,000	17
Barley	60,208,000	2
Fish	$ 33,000	40
Forest Products	$ 800,000	48
Minerals	$ 92,866,000	30
Petroleum	63,813,000	14
Sand and gravel	10,142,000	33
Natural gas	7,634,000	17
Manufactures	$ 72,484,000	50
Food and kindred products	34,285,000	46
Printing and publishing	11,089,000	48
Stone, clay, and glass products	5,221,000	48

Land. North Dakota is the northernmost Great Plains state. (See map on page 293.) Here farms and ranches cover the land as far as the eye can see. There are only a few cities and large towns in this sparsely populated state.

During the Great Ice Age, glaciers covered all of North Dakota except the southwestern part of the state. (See page 36.) As these great ice sheets advanced, they smoothed the land. When they retreated, they left large deposits of drift.* Over the years, this has developed into rich soil.

Late in the Great Ice Age, the easternmost part of North Dakota was covered by a huge glacial lake, called Lake Agassiz.* This lake was formed when water filled a vast depression that had

*See Glossary

A farm in the Red River Valley of North Dakota. About half of North Dakota lies in the Central Lowland. The Red River of the North flows along the eastern boundary of North Dakota's Central Lowland. The fertile valley of this river is the state's richest farming area.

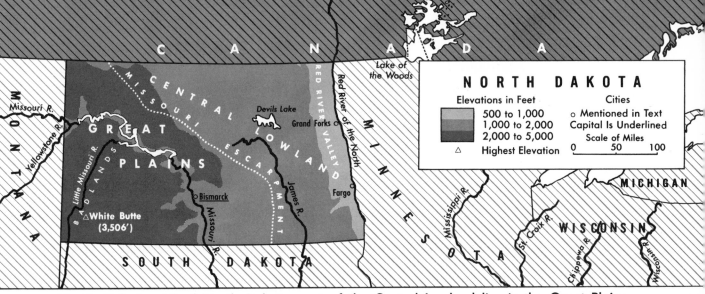

North Dakota. All of North Dakota west of the Central Lowland lies in the Great Plains. This part of the state is a high, rolling plateau. Cattle ranches and wheat farms cover most of the land. This is the most thinly populated part of North Dakota.

been gouged in the surface of the earth by a glacier. Gradually the waters of Lake Agassiz drained away, uncovering the rich silt* of the lake bottom. Today, the Red River of the North flows through the ancient lake bed. (See map above.)

North Dakota lies in the Central Lowland and the Great Plains. (See map on pages 28 and 29.) A line of steep cliffs called the Missouri Escarpment separates these two sections of the state.

The Central Lowland. About half of North Dakota lies in the Central Lowland section of our country. The lowest part of the Central Lowland in this state is the Red River Valley. (See map above.) This broad, level valley is the state's richest farming area. Farms cover 98 percent of the land here. The Red River Valley is especially noted for its crops of spring* wheat, but farmers here also raise such crops as barley, potatoes, and flax. North Dakota's two largest cities—Fargo and Grand Forks—are located in the Red River Valley.

West of the Red River Valley, the Central Lowland of North Dakota is

level or gently rolling, with low hills and many marshes and small lakes. Much of the soil in this part of the state is very fertile. Farmers here grow wheat, barley, and other crops. In areas where the soil is not fertile or the land is too hilly for growing crops, livestock raising is an important type of farming.

The Great Plains. Rising abruptly from the Central Lowland is the Great Plains section of North Dakota. (See map above.) In North Dakota, the Great Plains is a high, rolling plateau, interrupted by many flat-topped hills called buttes. Cattle ranches and wheat farms spread over most of the land. The Great Plains is the most thinly populated part of North Dakota. Only a few towns here have populations of more than five thousand. One of these is Bismarck, the state capital.

The Missouri River winds through the Great Plains section of North Dakota. (See map above.) In 1954, the federal government completed Garrison Dam on the Missouri. Before this dam was built, the river often overflowed its banks, flooding the land nearby and causing serious damage. Flood control is only one benefit of the dam, however. Garrison Dam created a reservoir 178 miles long. This reservoir provides water for irrigation and for the production of electricity. In addition, many people come to the reservoir each year to swim, water ski, and fish.

Near the western border of North Dakota, the Little Missouri River flows through an area of badlands. (See page 40.) Here are buttes and jagged pinnacles formed by uneven erosion of the land. These strange formations are beautifully colored. Bands of yellow, orange, and red contrast with bands of gray, black, and brown.

About seventy thousand acres of land in the badlands have been set aside by the federal government as a national memorial park. This park is named for President Theodore Roosevelt, who once operated two ranches along the Little Missouri River. Every year, thousands of visitors come to the park to view the beautiful scenery.

Climate. North Dakota has no sheltering mountains or large bodies of water to moderate its climate. Winters are long and cold throughout the state. The temperature often drops below zero. Summers are short, with hot days and cool nights. Sometimes, the temperature rises above one hundred degrees during the daytime. Because North Dakota's climate is dry, however, extremes of heat and cold are easier to bear here than in more humid areas.

In North Dakota, rainfall is light and the growing season is short. Farmers here have less than five months in which to grow crops. (See map on page 60.) Frosts may occur as late as May and as early as September. Fortunately, in North Dakota there are more than fifteen hours of daylight each day between the middle of May and the end of July. The long hours of warm sunshine help crops to ripen quickly. Most of North Dakota receives less than twenty inches of rainfall each year. In many areas, farmers must use dry-farming methods in order to grow crops. (See page 151.)

Strong winds and fierce storms often sweep across the plains of North Dakota. Hailstorms are frequent in summer. The hail sometimes beats down entire fields of ripening wheat. Occasionally, tornadoes swirl across the land. (See page 59.) In winter, cattle often freeze to death in raging blizzards.

Farming. Farming is the most important occupation in North Dakota. About four out of every ten workers here are farmers. This is a larger percentage than that of any other state in our country.

Wheat is grown in nearly every part of North Dakota. (See map on page 157.) This is the state's most valuable farm product. Each year, the sale of wheat provides about two fifths of the state's total farm income. North Dakota leads the nation in the raising of spring wheat and ranks second only to Kansas in total wheat production.

In the western part of North Dakota, where rainfall is especially light, the average wheat farm covers more than one thousand acres. Except in areas where there is water for irrigation, farmers must use dry-farming methods. As a result, they can plant wheat on only about half of their land each year. Also, the lack of moisture prevents farmers from getting large yields of wheat from

Harvesting barley on a farm in North Dakota. Farming is the most important way of earning a living in North Dakota. Wheat is the state's leading farm product. Other important products of North Dakota's farms include cattle and calves, barley, and flax.

each acre. Therefore, they must plant hundreds of acres of wheat in order to earn a profit.

North Dakota is also a leading producer of both barley and flax. The barley is used mainly as livestock feed. In the United States, flax is grown chiefly for its seed. An oil pressed from flaxseed, called linseed oil, is used in making products such as paints, varnishes, and linoleum. The material that remains after the oil is removed is used as livestock feed.

Farmers in North Dakota earn more money from the sale of cattle and calves than from any other farm product except wheat. Beef cattle graze on grasslands throughout the state. Most of the cattle are shipped to feedlots* to be fattened for market.

Natural resources. Fertile soil is one of North Dakota's most important natural resources. Farmers here must take good care of their soil to prevent it from being carried away by wind. Many farmers in North Dakota practice strip-cropping. (See page 151.) People here have also planted shelterbelts* of trees to conserve soil.

North Dakota has deposits of several minerals. At the present time, however, most of these mineral resources have not been developed. The state's income from mineral production is less than one fifth the amount earned from the sale of farm products.

Petroleum is the leading mineral produced in North Dakota. It provides about two thirds of the state's income from mineral production. Petroleum was discovered in the northwestern part of the state in 1951. Today, North Dakota's oil wells produce more than 25 million barrels of crude oil each year. Most of the petroleum is piped to refineries in the state, where it is made into gasoline, fuel oil, and other products. Some is sent to refineries in Minnesota and Wyoming.

Vast deposits of coal underlie most of western North Dakota. (See map on page 166.) However, the type of coal found here, called lignite, is less valuable than other types of coal. Because lignite contains large amounts of water, it produces less heat than other kinds of coal when it is burned. Recently, new ways of removing the moisture have been discovered, and more lignite is now being mined. Most of the lignite is used as fuel in plants that produce electricity.

North Dakota produces several other minerals. Among these are sand and

An oil refinery near Bismarck. Petroleum is the leading mineral produced in North Dakota. Most of the petroleum is piped to refineries in the state, where it is made into gasoline and other products.

EMPLOYMENT IN NORTH DAKOTA

AVERAGE YEARLY NUMBER OF WORKERS 221,900

Agriculture	40 %
Wholesale & Retail Trade	17 %
Government	15 %
Services	10 %
Construction	6 %
Transportation & Public Utilities	5 %
Manufacturing	3 %
Finance, Insurance, & Real Estate	3 %
Mining	1 %

gravel, which are used mainly for building and repairing roads. Natural gas is also produced here. It is used for heating homes, for cooking, and for many other purposes.

Industry. North Dakota ranks lowest among our states in manufacturing. There are several reasons for this. North Dakota's small population and its location far from large markets have held back industrial development. The state's lack of water for industry has discouraged manufacturers from establishing plants here. Also, except for farm products, there are few raw materials readily available for factories in North Dakota. Today, people in North Dakota are trying to attract new industries to their state.

North Dakota's most important industry by far is food processing. (See fact table on page 310.) This industry employs nearly half of the state's industrial workers. The farms and ranches of North Dakota provide food-processing plants with the raw materials they need. Mills in several cities and towns process wheat to make flour. Meat-packing is also an important type of food processing. Butter and candy are among the other food products of North Dakota.

People and cities. North Dakota is one of our country's most thinly populated states. This state has only about nine people for every square mile of land, compared with an average of fifty people per square mile for our country as a whole. North Dakota has the lowest percentage of city dwellers of any state in the nation. Only about one third of the people live in cities. The population of Fargo, the state's largest city, is only about 50,000.

Fargo (population 49,500; altitude 900 feet) is located on the Red River of the North, in the fertile Red River Valley. It is an important trading city, where farmers come to sell their products and do their shopping. Factories in Fargo make silos, farm machinery, canvas, and other goods. Processing meat and other foods is also important in the Fargo area.

Grand Forks (population 38,000; altitude 830 feet) is also located on the Red River of the North, about seventy miles north of Fargo. It is mainly a trading and food-processing city. An enormous state-owned flour mill is located here.

Bismarck (population 30,500; altitude 1,670 feet) is the capital of North Dakota. This city is located on the

Bismarck is the capital of North Dakota. About thirty thousand people live in this city. North Dakota has a lower percentage of city dwellers than any other state in our country.

Missouri River. It was founded by German settlers in 1872, at a place where the river could be easily crossed. Bismarck is the leading trading and manufacturing city for the western part of North Dakota. Plants here make flour and farm machinery. Near Bismarck is a large oil refinery.

Learn by Making Comparisons

How does North Dakota compare with the state in which you live? To find out, you will need to do some research. This chapter contains much useful information about North Dakota. The suggestions on pages 346-348 will help you locate information about your own state. Some of the things you might want to compare are listed in the next column. Perhaps you can think of others.

1. area
2. population
3. climate
4. natural resources
5. leading farm products
6. important industries
7. facilities for sports and recreation

Take notes on your research, and then organize your findings in the form of a chart or an oral report to present to your class.

24 Oklahoma

Facts About Oklahoma		
	Number or Value	Rank
Area (square miles)	69,919	18
Population	2,458,000	27
Capital — Oklahoma City		
Admission Date:		
November 16, 1907		46
Colleges and Universities	34	25
Farm Products	$624,075,000	24
Cattle and calves	274,935,000	11
Wheat	132,181,000	4
Dairy products	55,039,000	23
Fish	$ 87,000	37
Forest Products	$ 12,550,000	34
Minerals	$881,270,000	5
Petroleum	587,320,000	4
Natural gas	166,747,000	4
Natural-gas liquids	62,066,000	4
Manufactures	$965,305,000	32
Food and kindred products	148,586,000	32
Petroleum and coal products	112,267,000	9
Electrical machinery	106,702,000	22

Land. Oklahoma is shaped somewhat like a saucepan. (See map on opposite page.) The handle of the pan is formed by a long, narrow strip of land that extends westward from the rest of the state. This part of Oklahoma is called the Panhandle. The bottom of the pan is formed by the Red River, which flows along Oklahoma's southern border.

<u>The Central Lowland</u>. About three fourths of Oklahoma lies in the Central Lowland section of our country. (See map on opposite page.) The Central Lowland in Oklahoma consists mainly of level plains, broken by hills and low mountains. Here and there, water and wind have worn away the land, leaving steep cliffs and other rock formations.

Herding beef cattle in Oklahoma's Central Lowland. About three fourths of Oklahoma lies in the Central Lowland section of our country. This part of the state consists mainly of level plains, broken by hills and low mountains. In some areas, beef cattle graze on tall, thick grass.

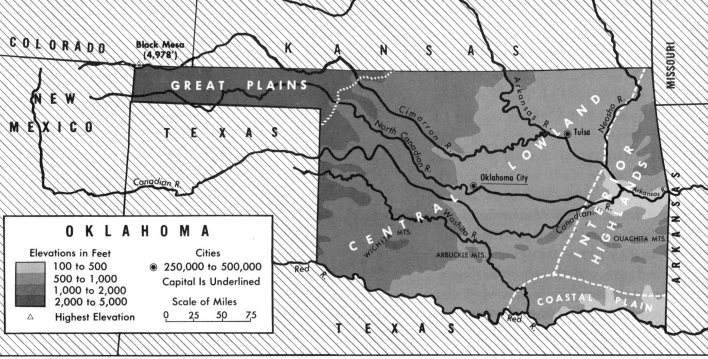

Oklahoma is shaped somewhat like a saucepan. The bottom of the pan is formed by the Red River, which flows along Oklahoma's southern border. The Oklahoma Panhandle lies in the Great Plains. This part of the state is a level grassland that rises gradually from east to west.

In some places, fields of golden wheat stretch to the horizon. In other places, herds of beef cattle graze on tall, thick grass. Oklahoma's two largest cities, Oklahoma City and Tulsa, are located in the Central Lowland.

Several rivers flow southeastward across the Central Lowland in Oklahoma. The largest of these is the Arkansas. Many dams have been built on Oklahoma's rivers to prevent flood-waters from washing away soil and to hold back water for irrigation. Water is stored in artificial lakes behind these dams. Canals and irrigation ditches carry water from the lakes to fields of growing crops.

In the southern part of the Central Lowland, two groups of low mountains rise above the surrounding plain. These are the Arbuckle Mountains and the Wichita Mountains. Millions of years ago, these mountains were much higher. Through the centuries, however, wind and water have gradually worn them down. Large herds of beef cattle graze on the grassy slopes of the Arbuckle Mountains. In the Wichita Mountains, the federal government has established a wildlife refuge. Animals such as elk, longhorn* cattle, and buffalo graze here.

The Great Plains. All of Oklahoma west of the Central Lowland lies in the Great Plains section of our country. (See map above.) This section includes Oklahoma's Panhandle. The Panhandle is a narrow strip of land about 166 miles long and 34 miles wide. Most of the Great Plains section of Oklahoma is a level grassland with very few trees. The land here rises from about two thousand feet at the eastern edge to nearly five thousand feet in the west. In the far northwestern corner of the Panhandle, a flat-topped hill called Black Mesa rises sharply above the plain to 4,978 feet above sea level. This is the highest point in Oklahoma. If you were to fly across the Panhandle, you would see vast cattle ranches and huge wheat

*See Glossary

317

Harvesting peanuts on the Coastal Plain of Oklahoma. A small part of southeastern Oklahoma lies in the Coastal Plain region of our country. Farmers in this area grow crops such as peanuts and cotton. About half the land here is used for grazing.

farms. Because ranches and farms here are so large, houses are often miles apart. This is the least densely populated part of the state.

The Interior Highlands. Part of the Interior Highlands region of our country extends into eastern Oklahoma. (See map on page 317.) Most of this highland region in Oklahoma is made up of narrow valleys, steep ridges, rolling hills, and wooded mountains. Much of the land here is too rugged for farming. However, forests of oak, pine, and other trees supply logs for making lumber and other wood products. The Arkansas River flows southeastward through this region. In the broad valley of this river are fields of spinach, carrots, and other

vegetables. South of this valley rise the wooded Ouachita Mountains.

The Coastal Plain. A small part of southeastern Oklahoma lies in our country's Coastal Plain region. (See map on page 317.) The land here is generally low and rolling. Farmers grow crops such as cotton, peanuts, and hay in the sandy soil of Oklahoma's Coastal Plain. About half of the land here is used for grazing.

Climate. Changes in temperature between winter and summer are less extreme in Oklahoma than in most other states of the Midwest and Great Plains. Winters are mild, and summers are warm.

Rainfall varies greatly from east to west in Oklahoma. (See map on page

49.)　It ranges from forty inches or more near the eastern border to less than twenty inches in the western part of the Panhandle. Much of Oklahoma's rain is brought by moist winds from the Gulf of Mexico. These moisture-bearing winds seldom reach the Panhandle of Oklahoma, however. (See page 53.) Parts of the Panhandle receive less than fifteen inches of rain.

Oklahoma does not receive the same amount of rainfall each year. When less rain falls than usual, streams dry up and crops wither. Crop failures bring great hardships to farmers.

Although most of the western half of Oklahoma receives twenty to thirty inches of rain each year, summers here are often very dry. This is mainly because much of the rainfall is lost through evaporation* before it can run off into streams or sink into the ground.

Nearly all of Oklahoma has a growing season of six months or more. This makes it possible for farmers here to grow crops that need a long time to ripen, such as cotton.

Farming. About two out of every ten workers in Oklahoma earn their living by farming. Although farming is an important occupation in Oklahoma, the state ranks only twenty-fourth in the nation in the amount of money received for farm products.

Harvesting wheat with combines. Large crops of wheat are grown in western Oklahoma, where rainfall is too light for growing most other crops. The state ranks fourth in the nation in wheat production. Cattle and calves are Oklahoma's most important source of farm income.

The most important type of farming in Oklahoma is cattle raising. The sale of cattle and calves supplies nearly one half of the state's total income from farm products. (See fact table on page 316.) Cattle raising first became important in Oklahoma in the late 1800's, when large herds were driven here from Texas to graze on the tall grass that grew in the central part of the state. Today, cattle and calves are raised throughout Oklahoma. (See map on page 157.)

There are several reasons why cattle raising is so important in Oklahoma. In the hilly and mountainous parts of the state, cattle can graze on slopes that are too rugged or steep for growing crops. In the eastern half of Oklahoma, much of the soil is infertile or thin and stony. However, the grass that grows here provides good grazing for cattle. In the western half of Oklahoma, rainfall is inadequate or too undependable for growing most crops. There is enough moisture, though, for grass to grow here. Much of this area is used as pastureland. Another advantage for raising livestock in Oklahoma is the mild winter weather. Ranchers here can graze their cattle outdoors for most of the year.

Wheat is Oklahoma's second most important source of farm income. This state ranks fourth in our nation in wheat production. Wheat is grown mainly in the western half of Oklahoma. (See map on page 157.) The eastern half of the state is generally too moist and hot for growing wheat. Since much of western Oklahoma is level, large farm machines can move easily over the land to plant and harvest the wheat. Most of this area receives enough rain for growing wheat, although not enough for growing most other crops. Many farmers here use dry-farming* methods.

Oklahoma's third leading farm product is milk. Some of the people who have small farms here keep dairy cattle and sell milk to add to their income from other farm products. Dairying is especially important near Oklahoma's big cities, where large quantities of fresh milk are needed daily.

Cotton ranks fourth as a source of income for farmers in Oklahoma. This crop is grown mainly in the southwestern part of the state. (See map on page 157.) Sixty years ago, farmers in Oklahoma grew cotton only in the humid, eastern part of the state. Gradually, however, cotton growing wore out the soil there. Also, boll* weevils often ruined much of the cotton crop. Eventually, a new variety of cotton was developed that would grow well in a drier climate, where boll weevils could not thrive. After this, farmers in the southwestern part of Oklahoma began to grow cotton. Today, this state ranks fourteenth in the nation in cotton production.

In the 1930's, farming in Oklahoma was affected by a severe drought. Over

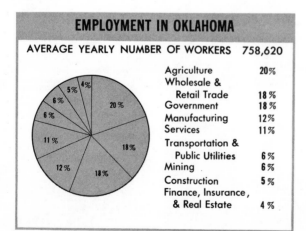

EMPLOYMENT IN OKLAHOMA

AVERAGE YEARLY NUMBER OF WORKERS   758,620

Agriculture	20%
Wholesale & Retail Trade	18%
Government	18%
Manufacturing	12%
Services	11%
Transportation & Public Utilities	6%
Mining	6%
Construction	5%
Finance, Insurance, & Real Estate	4%

Drilling an oil well. Oklahoma is rich in mineral resources. The most important of these is petroleum. Oklahoma ranks fourth in the nation in the production of this valuable mineral.

a period of several years, there was less rainfall than usual. Crops shriveled and died, and pastures turned brown. Because grass and water were scarce, entire herds of cattle died of starvation and thirst. Strong winds carried away the dry, dusty topsoil, causing violent dust storms. As a result, western Oklahoma became part of the barren area known as the Dust Bowl.* Many people had to leave their farms and look for work in other states. Today, many farmers in Oklahoma practice soil and water conservation to protect their land from drought and dust storms.

Natural resources. Oklahoma is rich in mineral resources. The most important of these is petroleum. Among all the states of our country, Oklahoma ranks fourth in the production of this valuable mineral. Huge deposits of petroleum lie deep within the earth in many parts of this state. The tall derricks of thousands of oil wells dot Oklahoma's plains. They are located in cornfields, next to farmhouses, and even in cities. Some of Oklahoma's crude* oil is pumped through pipelines to refineries within the state. Large amounts are also sent to other states. Some of the petroleum produced in Oklahoma is piped to refineries as far away as New Jersey.

Oklahoma also has valuable deposits of natural gas. Before the gas is distributed for use as a fuel, natural-gas* liquids are separated from it. Then the gas is piped to homes and factories. Large amounts of helium* are also obtained from natural gas found in Oklahoma.

A gas-processing plant. At this plant, natural gas is processed before being piped to homes and factories. Natural gas is Oklahoma's second most valuable mineral resource.

Several other minerals are also produced in Oklahoma. In the Wichita and Arbuckle mountains, workers quarry granite and other kinds of stone. These are used in the construction of buildings and roads. Another mineral produced in Oklahoma is gypsum. It is used in making building materials, such as plaster and wallboard. Although Oklahoma has deposits of high-grade soft coal, little is mined. The oil and natural gas produced in the state are less expensive to use as fuel.

Industry. Oklahoma is not an important manufacturing state. It ranks only thirty-second in the nation in the total income received from manufacturing. Several facts help explain why industry has not grown more rapidly in Oklahoma. This state is located far from many of the big cities of our country, which provide large markets for manufactured goods. Oklahoma lacks the advantage of low-cost water transportation available in states that lie along the Great Lakes or on the ocean. Also, certain industries use enormous amounts of water, and water is not always plentiful in Oklahoma. In addition, Oklahoma does not have a large labor force. Today, business leaders in Oklahoma are working to attract industries here from other parts of our country.

Food processing is the most important industry in Oklahoma. Farms in the state supply beef cattle, milk, wheat, and other farm products to plants and mills for processing. Many of the state's industrial workers are employed in meat-packing plants, dairies, bakeries, and cereal mills.

Petroleum products rank second among Oklahoma's manufactures. There are large oil refineries in Oklahoma City and Tulsa. At these refineries, crude oil is processed to provide gasoline, motor oil, and other products. Although people in Oklahoma use some of the gasoline and motor oil produced here, large amounts are shipped to other states of our country.

Many of Oklahoma's industrial workers are employed in factories that make machinery. Some of these factories make electrical machinery, such as electric motors. Electronic products are also made here. Other factories make machinery used in drilling oil wells. Many manufacturers of oil-field supplies and drilling equipment have established factories and warehouses in Oklahoma near the oil fields.

People and cities. About two thirds of Oklahoma's people live in cities and towns. However, only two cities here have populations of more than 100,000. The rest of Oklahoma's urban* population lives in small cities and towns scattered throughout the state. These serve mainly as trading and supply centers for nearby farming and oil-drilling areas. Many of the people who live in these cities and towns work in the oil fields or for companies that provide drilling services and equipment.

A large part of Oklahoma was once called Indian Territory. This was an area of land reserved for Indians by our federal government. Today, there are still many Indians living in Oklahoma. About one tenth of all the Indians in our country make their homes here.

Oklahoma City (population 380,000; altitude 1,195 feet) is the capital and largest city of Oklahoma. It is located on the North Canadian River, in the central part of the state.

Oklahoma City has an interesting history. It grew into a community of about ten thousand people in a single day. On April 22, 1889, part of the Territory of Oklahoma was opened for settlement. On the same day, thousands of eager settlers rushed into this area to claim land. Many of them stopped at the site of what is now Oklahoma City. By nightfall, approximately ten thousand people had settled here.

Petroleum was discovered near Oklahoma City in 1928. Since that time, large deposits of oil and natural gas have been found here. Today, oil derricks can be seen in many parts of

Oklahoma City is located on the North Canadian River, in the central part of Oklahoma. This is the state's capital and largest city. Deposits of oil and natural gas lie under much of Oklahoma City. Many people who live here work in oil fields or in plants that make oil-field equipment.

the city, even on the grounds of the state capitol. Within Oklahoma City's metropolitan* area are about 1,800 oil wells.

Oklahoma City is an important manufacturing and trading city. Some of the people who live here work in retail* shops and stores. Others have jobs with companies that pack meat, mill flour, or manufacture oil-field equipment. Still others work in the oil fields. Many people from Oklahoma City are employed at our government's huge Tinker Air Force Base, located outside the city.

Tulsa (population 280,000; altitude 804 feet) is the second largest city in Oklahoma. It is located on the Arkansas River in the northeastern part of the state.

Tulsa is often called the "Oil Capital of the World." This is because so many oil companies and suppliers of drilling services or equipment have offices here. Oil refining is the most important industry in Tulsa. Refineries here produce gasoline, motor oil, and other petroleum products. Many of the people who live in Tulsa have jobs that are connected with the transportation, sale, and distribution of petroleum and petroleum products.

In addition to oil refining, there are several other important industries in Tulsa. Plants here make aircraft parts, scientific instruments, and chemicals. Many workers are employed in the food-processing industry. Most of these people work in meat-packing plants and dairies.

Learn About Oklahoma With Maps

Study the maps on pages 293 and 317, and then answer the following questions:

1. What Great Plains states border Oklahoma?
2. What is the capital of Oklahoma?
3. Name three groups of mountains in Oklahoma.
4. What river forms Oklahoma's southern boundary?

Questions To Guide Your Reading

1. Why does the Panhandle of Oklahoma receive little rainfall?
2. Why is cattle raising the most important type of farming in Oklahoma?
3. Why did many people in Oklahoma leave their farms in the 1930's?
4. What is Oklahoma's most important mineral resource? How does Oklahoma rank in the nation in the production of this mineral?
5. What facts help to explain why Oklahoma

has not become an important manufacturing state?

Explore Oklahoma's History

Do some research about the history of Oklahoma and then write a report about it to share with your class. The following questions will help you carry on your research and decide what to include in your report.

1. Who were some of the first explorers to travel into the area that is now Oklahoma?
2. How did the United States gain possession of this area?
3. How did Indians gain ownership of much land in this area? Where did these Indians come from?
4. Why did the Indians lose their rights to this land?
5. How did white settlers gain ownership of land in what is now Oklahoma?

For help in locating information and in writing your report, refer to the suggestions on pages 346-351.

25 South Dakota

Facts About South Dakota		
	Number or Value	**Rank**
Area (square miles)	77,047	16
Population	682,000	43
Capital — Pierre		
Admission Date:		
November 2, 1889		40
Colleges and Universities	15	36
Farm Products	$675,412,000	21
Cattle and calves	285,681,000	10
Hogs	111,081,000	8
Wheat	58,322,000	12
Fish	$ 188,000	33
Forest Products	$ 3,150,000	41
Minerals	$ 52,824,000	41
Gold	21,592,000	1
Sand and gravel	13,641,000	25
Cement	7,073,000	14
Manufactures	$142,230,000	46
Food and kindred products	96,459,000	38
Printing and publishing	12,474,000	45
Stone, clay, and glass products	7,714,000	46

Land. South Dakota is a land of great contrasts. In this state are fertile farmlands, rugged mountains, and barren badlands. The eastern third of South Dakota lies in the Central Lowland section of our country. The rest of the state is in the Great Plains. (See map on page 326.)

The Central Lowland. The part of South Dakota that lies in the Central Lowland is a flat or gently rolling plain. During the Great Ice Age, glaciers moved across South Dakota's Central Lowland. They rounded off hills and filled in valleys. The deposits of sand, clay, and finely ground rock left by melting glaciers helped to form fertile soil in this part of South Dakota.

Much of the Central Lowland in South Dakota lies in the corn belt. (Compare

Oahe Dam on the Missouri River in South Dakota. The land in much of South Dakota is flat or gently rolling. The Missouri River flows southeastward through the state. Dams on this river hold back water for irrigation and the production of electricity, and also help to prevent floods.

map on page 153 with map below.) If you were to travel through this section of the state in summertime, you would see fields of corn and oats stretching for miles across the plains. Nearly two thirds of South Dakota's people live in the Central Lowland. The largest city in the state, Sioux Falls, is located in this section.

The Great Plains. The western two thirds of South Dakota lies in the Great Plains. The land here rises gradually upward toward the west. The Missouri River flows southeastward through the Great Plains in South Dakota.

East of the Missouri, the Great Plains section of the state was also once covered by glaciers. The land here is generally level. Because rainfall is too light for growing most crops, farmers use the land mainly for raising wheat and livestock.

West of the Missouri River, the Great Plains section is more rugged. Deep canyons have been cut into the land by rivers flowing into the Missouri. In many places,

there are flat-topped hills called buttes. Some of these rise as high as six hundred feet above the surrounding plains. Few people live in this dry, almost treeless part of South Dakota. Much of the land is used for grazing cattle and sheep.

In the southwestern part of South Dakota's Great Plains is a barren area called the Badlands. (See map below.) Over the centuries, rainwater has worn away soil and rock here, forming strangely shaped peaks and pinnacles.* (See page 40.) Bare gullies and ravines lie between the rock formations. Millions of years ago, dinosaurs and other prehistoric animals lived in the Badlands of South Dakota. Scientists have found many fossils* of these animals here. Today, few plants or animals can live in this desolate area. However, the interesting rock formations attract thousands of tourists each year.

West of the Badlands is a group of very old mountains called the Black Hills. They received this name because the dense pine forests that cover their

*See Glossary

South Dakota. About one third of South Dakota lies in the Central Lowland. The rest of the state is in the Great Plains. The most rugged parts of South Dakota are the Black Hills and the Badlands, both located in the Great Plains section of the state.

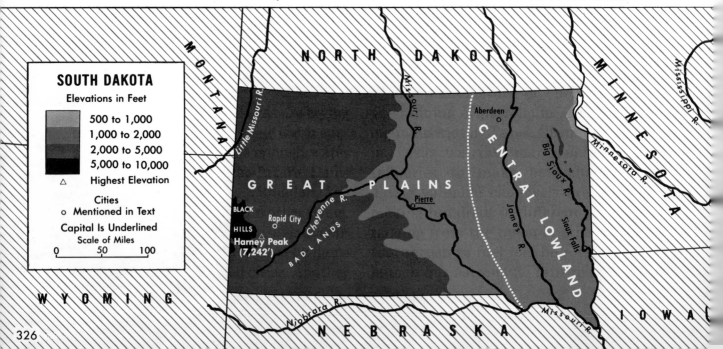

Mount Rushmore, in the Black Hills. Carved out of this granite peak are the faces of four American presidents: George Washington, Thomas Jefferson, Theodore Roosevelt, and Abraham Lincoln.

slopes make them appear black from a distance. One high granite peak here rises to 7,242 feet above sea level. This is Harney Peak, the highest point in South Dakota. The Black Hills are a favorite vacation spot for people from all over our country. Many people come here to see Mount Rushmore. Carved out of this granite peak is a giant sculpture of the faces of four presidents of the United States: George Washington, Thomas Jefferson, Theodore Roosevelt, and Abraham Lincoln.

Climate. Summers are warm and winters are cold in South Dakota. There are no large bodies of water nearby to help moderate the temperature. Because there are few trees, cold winter winds and hot summer winds can sweep easily over the plains here. However, since the climate is generally dry, extreme

temperatures are not as uncomfortable here as they are in more humid areas.

South Dakota's location helps to explain why the climate here is generally dry. This state lies far in the interior of the North American continent. Moisture-bearing winds from the Gulf of Mexico seldom reach South Dakota. By the time winds from the Pacific coast reach South Dakota, they have lost most of their moisture. (See pages 53 and 55.) As a result, rainfall is light in much of South Dakota. Fortunately, most of the rain that does fall comes in spring and summer, when it is needed by growing crops. However, South Dakota's rainfall is often undependable. In some years, less rain falls than usual, and farmers suffer great losses from crop failures.

Most of the Great Plains section of South Dakota receives only about ten to twenty inches of rain each year. (Compare maps on pages 49 and 326.) Because it is risky to grow most crops in areas that receive less than twenty inches of rain, much of the land here is used for grazing. Some farmers also grow wheat, which requires less moisture than many other crops.

In the Central Lowland section of South Dakota, the annual rainfall is about twenty to thirty inches. In most years, enough rain falls for growing corn and other crops.

Winds often bring sudden changes in the weather in South Dakota. Although snowfall is not heavy, winter winds sometimes sweep in from the northwest and cause violent storms called blizzards.* The winds pile snow into huge drifts, blocking roads and highways. Livestock must be rounded up and brought to shelter, or they might starve or freeze to death. Sometimes, a warm wind called a chinook* blows into South Dakota during winter or early spring and causes the temperature to rise as much as fifty degrees in one hour. In summer, strong winds swirl dry topsoil into the air, causing dust storms.

In most of South Dakota, the growing season lasts from four to five months. This is long enough for growing crops such as corn and spring* wheat. A small area in the southeastern part of South Dakota has five to six months of frost-free weather. Parts of western South Dakota have less than four months. (See map on page 60.)

Farming. In South Dakota, farming is much more important than industry. The amount of money received from the sale of farm products is more than four times the amount received from manufacturing. (See fact table on page 325.)

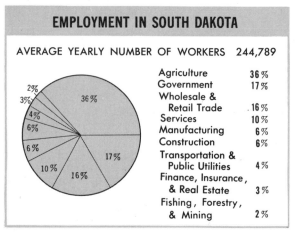

EMPLOYMENT IN SOUTH DAKOTA

AVERAGE YEARLY NUMBER OF WORKERS   244,789

Agriculture	36%
Government	17%
Wholesale & Retail Trade	16%
Services	10%
Manufacturing	6%
Construction	6%
Transportation & Public Utilities	4%
Finance, Insurance, & Real Estate	3%
Fishing, Forestry, & Mining	2%

Farms are large in South Dakota. The size of the average farm is about eight hundred acres. Many ranches* in the western part of the state cover more than three thousand acres. In recent years, the number of farms in South

Beef cattle on a ranch in South Dakota. Although most of the Great Plains section of South Dakota is very dry, the short grass that grows here is good for grazing cattle. Farmers in the state earn more money from cattle and calves than from any other farm product.

Dakota has grown smaller, while the size of the average farm has grown larger. Many people who owned small farms here have sold their farms and moved to cities in other states to find jobs in industry. This is because they often found it difficult to earn a living. For example, during drought years, some of them suffered great losses due to crop failures. Other reasons for people leaving their farms are discussed on pages 125-127.

Farmers in South Dakota earn more money from cattle and calves than from any other farm product. More than half of the state is used for pastureland. Although most of the Great Plains section of the state is very dry, the short grass that grows here is well suited for grazing. Many of the cattle raised here are shipped to feedlots* in the eastern part of the state. Here they are fattened on corn and other grains. Then they are sent to stockyards in Sioux Falls and other cities, where they are bought by meat-packing plants.

In addition to beef cattle, several other kinds of livestock are raised in South Dakota. Sheep graze on farms and ranches in many parts of the state. Some ranchers in the Great Plains section of the state prefer to raise sheep instead of cattle. Sheep do not require as much water or as rich grass as cattle do. South Dakota ranks fourth among the states of our country in wool production. In the eastern part of the state, hogs and poultry are raised. Some farmers here also keep herds of dairy cattle and sell fresh milk to nearby towns and cities.

South Dakota's two leading crops are corn and wheat. Corn is grown mainly

The Homestake Gold Mine, in the Black Hills. Although South Dakota is not rich in mineral resources, it does have deposits of gold and several other very important minerals.

in the Central Lowland, where rainfall is heaviest. Most of it is used to fatten cattle and hogs. In the Great Plains, where rainfall is lighter, wheat is the main crop. This crop needs less moisture than corn. Because winters are very cold in South Dakota, most farmers here grow spring wheat.

Natural resources. South Dakota is not rich in mineral resources. The total value of minerals produced here is less than that of any other state in the Midwest and Great Plains. However, South Dakota does have deposits of several minerals that are not found in great quantity elsewhere in our country.

South Dakota is our country's leading producer of gold. Most of the gold mined here comes from the Homestake Gold Mine, located in the Black Hills. This is the largest producing gold mine in North America.

329

In addition to gold, South Dakota produces several other metallic minerals. These include beryllium and uranium ores. Beryllium is a highly heat-resistant metal that is very important to our nation's space program. For example, it is used to make the heat shields on spacecraft.

The leading nonmetallic* minerals produced in South Dakota are sand and gravel. These are used mainly in the construction of roads. South Dakota also has deposits of limestone, which is mixed with shale and several other minerals to make cement.

The fertile soil in South Dakota is an important resource to farmers in the state. To protect their soil and keep it fertile, farmers here use scientific farming methods. For example, many of them practice dry* farming in order to conserve moisture in the soil. To prevent strong winds from blowing away valuable topsoil, farmers have planted shelterbelts* of trees along their fields. Page 151 discusses some of the other methods that farmers use to conserve soil.

Water is a very valuable resource to the people of South Dakota, especially since rainfall here is light and often undependable. In recent years, several huge dams have been built on the Missouri River to hold back water for irrigation and the production of electricity, and also to help prevent floods. The hydroelectric plants at these dams supply about seven tenths of the electricity used by the people of South Dakota. The artificial lakes formed by the dams provide recreation areas where

Sioux Falls is located in the southeastern part of South Dakota, on the Big Sioux River. Although it is the largest city in the state, only about seventy-six thousand people live here. Sioux Falls is the chief trading city for people living in the surrounding farming area.

people can enjoy boating, swimming, and other water sports.

Industry. South Dakota is not an important industrial state. It ranks forty-sixth in our nation in manufacturing. Only about six out of every one hundred workers in South Dakota are employed in manufacturing. (See chart on page 328.)

Food processing is the leading industry in South Dakota. The raw materials for this industry come mainly from farms and ranches in the state. Beef cattle and hogs are bought by meat-packing plants in Sioux Falls and other cities. There, they are slaughtered and their meat is prepared for sale. Milk is sent to dairy plants, where it is pasteurized and put into containers. Some milk is made into butter and other dairy products. Feed mills in the state make livestock feed from barley and other grains. Mills in several towns grind wheat into flour.

People and cities. Less than half of South Dakota's people live in cities or towns. The largest city in the state, Sioux Falls, has fewer than eighty thousand people. Only two other cities in South Dakota have populations of more than twenty thousand. These are Rapid City and Aberdeen. The capital of South Dakota, Pierre, has only about eleven thousand people.

More than 25,000 Indians live in South Dakota. Most of them live on reservations set aside by the government. Nearly all of South Dakota's Indians are members of the Sioux* nation. The state received its name from these Indians, who are also called the Dakota.

Sioux Falls (population 76,000; altitude 1,400 feet) is South Dakota's largest city. It is located on the Big Sioux River in the southeastern part of the state. (See map on page 326.) Sioux Falls is the chief trading city for the people who live in the surrounding farming area. Among the leading industries are meat-packing and flour milling.

Rapid City (population 47,500; altitude 3,229 feet), in the far western part of South Dakota, is the state's second largest city. Many tourists traveling to the Black Hills pass through Rapid City. People from the surrounding area come to Rapid City to buy the things they need and to sell their farm products. Plants in the city process poultry and make dairy products. Limestone and other minerals from the Black Hills are made into cement in Rapid City. Forests in the Black Hills also supply timber for lumber mills here.

Discover Important Facts About South Dakota

1. Describe the land in the Central Lowland section of South Dakota. What is the land like in the Great Plains section?
2. What are some of the ways in which winds affect the weather in South Dakota?
3. Why is much of the land in South Dakota used for grazing or for growing wheat?
4. Name some of South Dakota's important natural resources. How does this state rank in mineral production among the states of the Midwest and Great Plains?
5. What is South Dakota's leading industry? Name some of the raw materials that are used by this industry.
6. Name South Dakota's largest city. What is its population?
7. What resources from the Black Hills are useful to people in Rapid City?

26 Texas

Facts About Texas		
	Number or Value	Rank
Area (square miles)	267,339	2
Population	10,752,000	4
Capital — Austin		
Admission Date:		
December 29, 1845		28
Colleges and Universities	98	5
Farm Products	$2,304,411,000	3
Cotton	642,203,000	1
Cattle and calves	603,207,000	3
Sorghum	217,681,000	1
Fish	$ 29,651,000	6
Forest Products	$ 68,650,000	12
Minerals	$4,533,078,000	1
Petroleum	2,928,994,000	1
Natural gas	809,180,000	1
Natural-gas liquids	399,737,000	1
Manufactures	$7,053,797,000	9
Chemicals and allied products	1,653,810,000	2
Petroleum and coal products	956,140,000	1
Food and kindred products	923,362,000	7

Land. Texas is our country's second largest state. Only Alaska is larger. Texas extends farther south than any other state in the Midwest and Great Plains. (See map on page 21.) The blue waters of the Gulf of Mexico border the state on the southeast. On the southwest, the Rio Grande forms the boundary between Texas and the country of Mexico.

If you took a helicopter trip over the entire state of Texas, you would find that the land differs greatly from place to place. Along the Gulf of Mexico is a low, level coastal plain. In central Texas there are vast, rolling grasslands. High, rugged mountains rise in the far western part of the state.

Citrus groves on the Coastal Plain of Texas. Our country's Coastal Plain region extends across much of eastern and southern Texas. The land here is level or gently rolling. In this part of the state are large manufacturing cities, fertile farmlands, and rich mineral deposits.

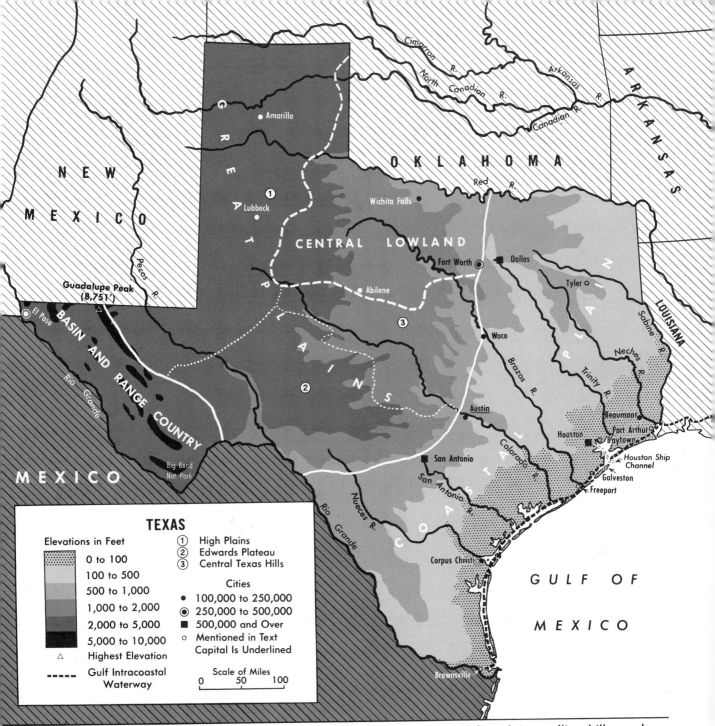

TEXAS

Elevations in Feet
- 0 to 100
- 100 to 500
- 500 to 1,000
- 1,000 to 2,000
- 2,000 to 5,000
- 5,000 to 10,000
- △ Highest Elevation
- - - - Gulf Intracoastal Waterway

① High Plains
② Edwards Plateau
③ Central Texas Hills

Cities
- ● 100,000 to 250,000
- ◉ 250,000 to 500,000
- ■ 500,000 and Over
- ○ Mentioned in Text Capital Is Underlined

Scale of Miles
0   50   100

Texas, the second largest state in our country, is made up of flat plains, rolling hills, and rugged mountains. The Gulf of Mexico borders the state on the southeast. On the southwest, the Rio Grande forms the border between Texas and the country of Mexico.

<u>The Coastal Plain.</u> Much of southern and eastern Texas lies in our country's great Coastal Plain region. (See map on pages 28 and 29.) In Texas, the Coastal Plain extends inland from the Gulf of Mexico for 150 to 350 miles.

Near the Gulf, the Coastal Plain is low and level, with large areas of marshy land. Farther inland, the land is higher and gently rolling. Many slow-moving rivers wind their way across the plain and empty into bays that indent the coast.

333

A few miles off the Texas coast is a long string of narrow, sandy islands. (See map on page 333.) These islands help to protect the coast from storms that blow in from the sea. The waterway between the islands and the Texas coast is used by barges and other vessels traveling between Gulf ports. This waterway is part of the Gulf Intracoastal Waterway. (See page 187.)

The Coastal Plain is a very important part of Texas. More than half of the state's population lives in this region, and several of Texas' largest manufacturing cities are located here. In the Coastal Plain are rich deposits of petroleum, natural gas, and other minerals. Fruits, vegetables, beef cattle, and many other products come from the farms and ranches here. In the northern part of the Coastal Plain are valuable forests of oak and pine. Raw materials and manufactured products are shipped from ports along the Gulf coast of Texas to customers in many parts of the world.

The Central Lowland. The north central part of Texas lies in the Central Lowland. Most of this area is level or gently rolling. However, steep hills and mesas* rise in some places. The land slopes gradually upward from about 500 feet in the east to about 2,500 feet in the west.

Farming is an important occupation in the Central Lowland. In the eastern part, where much of the soil is thin, many farmers raise dairy cows, poultry, or fruits and vegetables. There is a large market for milk, eggs, and fresh fruits and vegetables in nearby cities. In the western part of the Central Lowland, there are areas of deep, fertile soil

where such crops as cotton, wheat, and oats are grown. Beef cattle graze on hilly grasslands that are not well suited to growing crops.

The Great Plains. About two fifths of Texas lies in the Great Plains section of our country. This part of the state extends from the northern border of the Texas Panhandle* southward to the Rio Grande. (See map on page 333.) The Great Plains section of Texas may be divided into three parts. These are the High Plains, the Edwards Plateau, and the Central Texas Hills.

The High Plains make up the northern part of the Great Plains section of Texas. (See map on page 333.) Here, the land slopes gradually upward from the Central Lowland to an elevation of about 4,500 feet along the New Mexico border. The High Plains are generally level. In some places, however, streams and rivers have cut deep canyons into the land. Although rainfall is light on the High Plains, deep wells provide water for irrigation. Cotton, sorghum, wheat, and other crops grow well in the fertile soil here.

Extending southeastward from the High Plains is an area known as the Edwards Plateau. Although some of the land here is level, much of the Edwards Plateau is hilly or rugged. The soil is much less fertile here than in the High Plains. A combination of poor soil, light rainfall, and hilly land makes it very difficult to raise crops in many parts of the Edwards Plateau. However, the short grasses and the mesquite* growing here provide food for beef cattle, sheep, and goats.

Northeast of the Edwards Plateau is the part of the Great Plains called the

*See Glossary

The Basin and Range Country of Texas is made up of rugged mountain ranges separated by wide, flat basins. This area is the most thinly populated section of the state.

Central Texas Hills. (See map on page 333.) Here, several rivers and streams have carved deep valleys in the surface of the land. Cattle and sheep graze on hillside pastures in this part of Texas. In areas where the land is fairly level, farmers grow cotton, peanuts, and other crops. Many Texans come to the Central Texas Hills to fish in the lakes and streams, to hunt deer, and to enjoy other forms of recreation.

The Basin and Range Country. The westernmost part of Texas lies in the Basin and Range Country. (See map on page 333.) This section of the state is made up of rugged mountain ranges separated by wide, flat basins.* The basins, which receive very little rainfall, are dotted with cactus and other desert plants. More rain falls on the mountains than in the basins. Pine, oak, and other trees grow on the higher mountain slopes.

The Rio Grande flows through beautiful gorges along the southern border of Texas' Basin and Range Country. At one point, the river makes a big U-shaped turn. Here the federal government has established Big Bend National Park. Many people come to this park to view the spectacular scenery.

The Basin and Range Country is the most thinly populated part of Texas. (Compare maps on pages 117 and 333.)

Cattle and sheep graze on most of the land. Only the westernmost tip of the Basin and Range Country is heavily populated. The city of El Paso is located here. Elephant Butte Dam, on the Rio Grande in New Mexico, provides water for irrigating farmland in this area.

Climate. It is the fifteenth of January. In Brownsville, on the Gulf coast of Texas, the sun is shining brightly. The temperature is seventy degrees. People dressed in lightweight clothing are strolling through a park where bougainvillea and other flowering plants are in bloom. On a truck* farm outside the city, workers are harvesting cabbages.

In Amarillo, about seven hundred miles northwest of Brownsville, the weather on this day is very different. The sky is gray, and snow is falling. A cold wind whips the coats of shoppers as they hurry down the sidewalk.

As you can see, January weather in Brownsville differs greatly from January weather in Amarillo. There are several reasons for this. One reason is the nearness of Brownsville to the Gulf of Mexico. As page 57 explains, winds are warmed as they blow over the Gulf in winter. These winds bring very mild temperatures to the coast of Texas. Amarillo, however, is too far from the Gulf to be warmed by these winds. Also, Amarillo lies in the path of cold north winds that sweep over the plains. Sometimes these winds, which Texans call "northers," reach as far south as Brownsville. They may bring brief periods of freezing temperatures.

There are other reasons, too, why winter weather is colder in Amarillo than in Brownsville. Amarillo lies much farther north of the equator. The feature on pages 50 and 51 helps to explain how distance from the equator affects temperature. The elevation of these two cities also affects their temperatures. Brownsville lies almost at sea level, while Amarillo's elevation is more than 3,600 feet. Temperature decreases one degree for every three to four hundred feet of altitude.

Temperature differences from one part of Texas to another are not as great in summer as in winter. Summers are warm or hot throughout the state. In nearly every part of Texas, the growing season lasts more than six months. (See map on page 60.) On many summer days, the temperature rises higher than one hundred degrees. Areas along the coast get some relief from the heat when cooling breezes blow in from the Gulf. Summer weather is coolest in the mountains of the Basin and Range Country.

Rainfall varies greatly from east to west in Texas. (See map on page 49.) Moist winds from the Gulf of Mexico bring abundant rainfall to eastern Texas. Houston, for example, receives an average of forty-five inches of rainfall a year. However, only about eight inches fall in El Paso, in western Texas.

Severe storms sometimes sweep over Texas. Strong winds often blow across the plains in the western part of the state. In winter, these winds may pile snow into deep drifts. If the weather has been very dry, strong winds can create dust storms. Many parts of Texas are hit by tornadoes each year. (See page 59.) During summer and early autumn, hurricanes may strike coastal areas. These violent storms often cause great destruction of property and sometimes kill many people.

Cultivating young cotton plants. Each year, Texas produces about one tenth of the world's cotton crop. Farmers here also raise sorghum, vegetables, and many other crops. Texas is outranked only by California and Iowa in yearly income from the sale of farm products.

Farming. Texas is one of our country's leading farming states. Only California and Iowa earn more money from the sale of farm products. Texas has many advantages for farming. In nearly all parts of the state, the growing season is more than six months long. In addition, there are large areas of level land with deep, fertile soil.

Farmers and ranchers in Texas use efficient methods to keep production high. In parts of the state where rainfall is light, farmers make good use of the water that is available to them. In many dry areas, farmers are able to irrigate their crops with water from streams or from deep wells. Where there is not enough water for irrigation, many farmers raise crops by using dry-farming* methods. Farmers in Texas sometimes use airplanes to spray their crops with insecticides. On the large ranches, helicopters are used to round up cattle.

The most valuable crop grown in Texas is cotton. Texas leads the entire nation in cotton production. Each year, this state grows about one tenth of the world's cotton crop. The most important cotton-growing area in Texas is in the western part of the state, near New Mexico. (See map on page 157.) Here there is plenty of water for irrigating the cotton plants. The soil in this area is very fertile, and the land is generally level. The growing season here lasts about two hundred days, which is long enough for cotton to ripen.

Several grain crops are grown in Texas. The most important of these is sorghum. This crop is raised mainly in northwestern Texas, in the Great Plains. Both the grain and the stalks of sorghum are used as livestock feed. Large amounts of wheat are also grown in the Great Plains of Texas. Along the Gulf coast, rice is an important crop. Texas leads the nation in rice production. Other grain crops grown in the state include corn and oats.

Texas farmers raise many other crops. Large amounts of vegetables and fruits are grown on the Coastal Plain, especially in the lower Rio Grande Valley. Frost seldom occurs here, so farmers can grow crops all year long. The leading fruit crops of the lower Rio Grande Valley are grapefruit and oranges. Cabbages and carrots are among the main vegetable crops. During the winter, there is a large market for fresh fruits and vegetables in states that lie farther north. Other important crops in Texas are pecans and peanuts. Many farmers plant groves of pecan trees along the streams on their land. Large amounts of peanuts are grown in the central part of the state.

Texas ranks third in the nation in the sale of cattle and calves. (See fact table on page 332.) Only Iowa and Nebraska receive more money from the sale of these animals. There are cattle ranches in nearly every part of Texas. Many ranches cover more than 100,000 acres. Where grass is sparse, it may take as many as fifty acres of rangeland to feed each animal. In most parts of Texas, cattle can graze outdoors all year long. However, cattle that eat only grass may be too lean to slaughter

Beef cattle grazing on the High Plains of western Texas. There are cattle ranches in nearly every part of Texas. Many of the ranches are larger than 100,000 acres. The sale of cattle and calves provides more than one fourth of Texas' total farm income each year.

for meat. Therefore, large numbers of Texas cattle are fattened on grain in feedlots* before they are sold.

Natural resources. Since 1935, Texas has been our nation's leading mineral-producing state. The most valuable mineral resource of Texas is petroleum. The state leads the nation in the production of this important mineral. Petroleum accounts for more than half of the total value of the state's yearly mineral production.

Oil derricks rise in almost every part of Texas. Much of the petroleum pumped from wells in Texas is used by industries here. In addition, pipelines, railroad tank cars, and oceangoing tankers transport oil to other states and to foreign countries. (See pages 162-164 for more information about petroleum.)

Texas also leads the nation in the production of natural gas and natural-gas* liquids. Natural gas is found wherever petroleum deposits exist, but it is also found alone. This fuel is used for cooking, for heating, and in the production of electric power. Natural-gas liquids are used as raw materials in the chemical industry.

Many other minerals are also produced in Texas. Large amounts of limestone quarried here are used to make cement. The state supplies about half of our country's sulfur. There are also deposits of salt in Texas. The chemical industry here uses large quantities of this mineral. In the northwestern part of the state, helium* is produced from natural gas. Our federal government uses large amounts of helium in its defense and space programs.

Texas is the leading fishing state in the Midwest and Great Plains. Each

Drilling for oil in the Gulf of Mexico, off the coast of Texas. Texas is our nation's leading mineral-producing state. The state's most valuable mineral by far is petroleum.

year, fishermen bring to port about thirty million dollars' worth of fish from the Gulf of Mexico. The sale of shrimp provides about nine tenths of the state's income from fishing. Texas fishermen also bring to port thousands of tons of menhaden.*

Forests are another important natural resource of Texas. This is the leading lumber-producing state in the Midwest and Great Plains. Texas' most important lumbering area is in the northeastern part of the Coastal Plain. Here, forests of pine, oak, and other trees cover several million acres of land. Not all of the timber cut here is used to make lumber, however. Large numbers of trees are cut for making wood pulp. Mills in Texas use pulp in the manufacture of such products as paper and cardboard.

Texas needs more water. The western two thirds of the state receives less than thirty inches of rainfall each year. (See map on page 49.) Some areas receive only about ten inches. Much of the rain that falls evaporates* before it can be used. In some areas, there is not enough moisture to grow crops.

Fortunately, in some parts of western Texas there are large supplies of water under the ground. In the High Plains, for example, farmers can pump water from wells to irrigate their crops. Water for irrigation is very important to farmers in Texas. Each year, the sale of crops grown on irrigated farmlands provides about one fourth of the state's total farm income.

The eastern third of Texas has an adequate supply of water. Each year, this area receives thirty or more inches of rainfall. There are many rivers here to provide water for homes, farms, and industries. People in eastern Texas also use huge quantities of water from underground sources. This good supply of water is one reason why there are great cities and thriving industries in the eastern part of the state.

The underground water supplies of Texas are not limitless, however. Farms, homes, and cities are using up these supplies faster than rainfall can replace them.

Today, the people of Texas are trying to preserve and increase their water supplies so that there will be enough water to meet their needs in the future. Dams have been built on the Canadian, the Trinity, the Rio Grande, and other rivers, and more dams are now being constructed. The reservoirs created by dams store water for farms and cities. Another possible source of water for Texas is the Gulf of Mexico. The federal government operates a plant at Freeport that produces fresh water from salt water. However, removing the salt from seawater is still a very costly process.

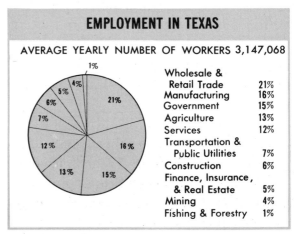

EMPLOYMENT IN TEXAS

AVERAGE YEARLY NUMBER OF WORKERS 3,147,068

Wholesale & Retail Trade	21%
Manufacturing	16%
Government	15%
Agriculture	13%
Services	12%
Transportation & Public Utilities	7%
Construction	6%
Finance, Insurance, & Real Estate	5%
Mining	4%
Fishing & Forestry	1%

Industry. Texas is the most industrialized of the Great Plains states. It is one of the ten leading manufacturing states in our nation. The great oil and natural-gas fields of Texas, as well as the state's farms, forests, and mines, provide an abundance of raw materials for manufacturing. Natural gas is also used to produce electric power for factories. Manufactured goods can be shipped easily by water or by land to customers in other states and other countries. The large population of Texas provides skilled workers for industry and a market for manufactured goods.

The manufacture of chemicals and the refining of petroleum are the leading industries in Texas. Chemical plants in Texas use raw materials from oil refineries to make petrochemicals.* These valuable chemicals are used in making hundreds of different products, ranging from the nylon bristles of your toothbrush to fuel for the rockets that launch our astronauts into space.

Petroleum products and chemicals are made in this huge plant at Baytown, on the Texas coast. The manufacture of chemicals and the refining of petroleum are Texas' leading industries. These industries are located mainly along the Gulf coast, where cheap water transportation, good water supplies, and raw materials are readily available.

If you were to visit Houston, Corpus Christi, and other port cities along the Gulf of Mexico, you would see many scenes like the one shown in the picture above. The state's chemical and petroleum industries are located mainly along the Texas coast. There are several reasons for this. First, petroleum products and chemicals that are manufactured here can be shipped easily and cheaply by water to customers in other parts of the United States and in foreign countries. Second, refineries and chemical plants need huge amounts of water, which they can get from rivers that flow into the Gulf of Mexico and from the Gulf itself. In addition, raw materials

that these industries need are readily available on the Gulf coast. The refineries use petroleum that is brought through pipelines. Chemical plants use products from the refineries and other raw materials produced in the area, such as salt, sulfur and natural-gas liquids.

Food processing is the third most important industry in Texas. There are large meat-packing plants in Fort Worth, Amarillo, and other cities. Along the Gulf of Mexico are mills where rice from nearby farms is cleaned, polished, and packaged. Here, too, are plants where shrimp are packaged and frozen. Shrimp from Texas are sold in stores

Houston is the largest city in the Great Plains states. It is located in southeastern Texas, about fifty miles from the Gulf of Mexico. The Houston Ship Channel connects the city with the Gulf. Houston is one of our nation's leading port cities.

throughout our country. Some factories in the state process cottonseed, peanuts, and soybeans for their oil.

Texas has many other industries. In the Dallas and Fort Worth areas are large automobile-assembly and aircraft plants. Many factories make oil-field equipment and other kinds of machinery. One of the fastest-growing industries in Texas is the manufacture of radio and television equipment and other electronic products.

People and cities. Nearly all of the people who live in Texas are native-born Americans. Many of them are descended from immigrants who came here from Germany, Czechoslovakia, and

other parts of Europe in the 1800's. Texas also has many people of Mexican descent. (See pages 121 and 122.)

About three fourths of the people of Texas live in urban areas. Thirteen cities in the state have populations of 100,000 or more. (See map on page 333.) No other state in the Midwest and Great Plains has as many cities this large.

Houston (population 1,100,000; altitude 57 feet) is the largest city in Texas, as well as the largest in the Great Plains states. It was named for General Sam Houston, who led Texas to victory over Mexico in the Battle of San Jacinto. Houston is located in southeastern Texas, about fifty miles from the Gulf of Mexico. The Houston Ship Channel connects the city with the Gulf. (See map on page 333.)

Houston is our country's third leading port city, outranked only by New York and New Orleans. Ships from all over the world load and unload goods at wharves along the Houston Ship Channel. Many of the city's factories are located along this waterway. Among Houston's leading exports are crude oil, petroleum products, and wheat. Imports include iron ore and steel products.

Houston is the central city of one of our country's major industrial areas. (See map on pages 194 and 195.) Chemicals and petroleum products are by far the leading products manufactured here.

However, several other industries are also important in the Houston area. Many people work in factories that make construction machinery or other metal products. The food processing industry also employs a large number of Houston's workers.

In the Houston metropolitan* area is the huge Manned Spacecraft Center of the National Aeronautics and Space Administration (NASA). Here, NASA trains astronauts and controls flights into space. Spacecraft are also developed at the Manned Spacecraft Center.

Dallas (population 790,000; altitude 500 feet) is located on the Trinity River, in the northeastern part of Texas. This is the state's second largest city.

Dallas is located on the Trinity River, in the northeastern part of Texas. This is the state's second largest city. Many large oil companies have their headquarters here. Aircraft manufacturing and automobile assembling are important industries in the Dallas area.

The first settlers came to Dallas in the 1840's. In the 1870's, railroads were built through the city, connecting it with other parts of our country. Railroads helped Dallas to grow rapidly.

Today, Dallas is an important trading, transportation, and manufacturing city. It is one of the nation's leading cotton markets. Also, many large oil companies have their headquarters here. The city is served by several railroad lines. Love Field, at Dallas, is one of the busiest airports in our country. In the Dallas metropolitan area are automobile-assembly and aircraft plants. Factories here also manufacture machinery, such as oil-field equipment and electronic products.

Many people from other parts of Texas and from other states visit Dallas each year. Some come to shop in the city's fine stores. In October, thousands of people come to Dallas to attend the

Fort Worth is located about thirty miles west of Dallas. It is an important market for livestock, oil, and grain. Among Fort Worth's industries are aircraft manufacturing and meat-packing.

Texas State Fair. This is the largest state fair in our country.

San Antonio (population 645,000; altitude 650 feet) lies in the south central part of Texas. The shallow San Antonio River winds its way through the heart of the city. Here, beautiful parks line the riverbanks.

San Antonio is a mixture of the old and the new. Some parts of the city have a colorful Spanish atmosphere. In the downtown business district, tall hotels and office buildings tower above La Villita, "the little village." Here, the people of San Antonio have restored homes and other buildings that were constructed by Spanish settlers more than two hundred years ago. Near La Villita is the historic Alamo.*

Although there are many factories here, San Antonio is mainly a trading center for southern Texas. It is a market for wool, livestock, and other farm products. Among the goods manufactured here are clothing and furniture. Many people in San Antonio work for the United States government, which operates four air force bases and an army base in and near the city.

Fort Worth (population 360,000; altitude 670 feet) is located about thirty miles west of Dallas. In 1849, an army post was established here to protect settlers against Indian attacks. Today, Fort Worth is a bustling city. It is an important market for livestock, oil, and grain. Several million head of cattle move through the city's stockyards each year. The city also has large meat-packing plants. During World War II, the aircraft industry became important here. Now, huge plants in Fort Worth build jet airplanes and helicopters.

344

El Paso (population 309,000; altitude 3,762 feet) is located along the Rio Grande, in the westernmost tip of Texas. (See map on page 333.) El Paso is a Spanish term that means "the pass." The city received this name because it is situated at the entrance to a pass through the mountains of the Basin and Range Country. Across the Rio Grande from El Paso is the Mexican city of Juarez. About half of the people who live in El Paso are of Mexican descent.

Trade, transportation, and manufacturing are important in El Paso. Many of the crops grown on irrigated farmlands nearby are sold and processed here. Because there is a natural passageway through the mountains at El Paso, several major highways and railroads pass through the city. Processing copper ore, refining petroleum, and manufacturing clothing are among the leading industries here.

Austin (population 220,000; altitude 650 feet) is the capital of Texas. It is built on bluffs along the Colorado River, about 160 miles northwest of Houston. Austin has been the capital since 1839, when Texas was an independent republic. (See page 89.) Many of the people in Austin are employed in government offices. The city is also a marketing center for products from nearby farms. Among the goods manufactured here are food products, furniture, bricks, and tiles. Austin is also the home of the University of Texas.

Learn About Texas With Maps

Study the map on page 333, and then answer the following questions:
1. What body of water borders Texas on the southeast?
2. What country borders Texas on the southwest?
3. What is the capital of Texas?
4. How many cities in Texas have a population of 100,000 or more?

Learn About Texas With Fact Tables

Fact tables are important sources of information. Study the one on page 332, and then answer the questions below.
1. How does Texas rank in the nation in area? How does it rank in population?
2. What is Texas' leading farm product?
3. Which brings more money to Texas — fish or forest products?
4. The value of manufactures in Texas is about how much more than the value of farm products?
5. What mineral produced in Texas accounts for more than half the value of the state's total mineral production?

Use Your Reasoning Ability

Listed below are the four main land regions or sections of our country in which Texas is located.

Central Lowland

Basin and Range Country

Great Plains   Coastal Plain

The people who live in these different parts of Texas earn their living in various ways. Do some reading about these areas. Then decide in which area each of the following workers might be employed. You may decide in some cases that there is more than one correct answer. List facts to support or explain each decision you make.

cowboy	shrimp fisherman
wheat farmer	forest ranger
dock worker	cotton farmer
logger	grapefruit rancher

As a class, discuss the following question:

How do the physical features of Texas influence the ways in which the people here earn their living?

The suggestions on pages 352 and 353 will help you hold a successful discussion.

Mastering mental skills, such as reading, will help you to have a more satisfying life.

Learning Social Studies Skills

What is a skill? A skill is something that you have learned to do well. To learn some skills, such as swimming, you must train the muscles of your arms and legs. To learn others, such as typing, you must train your fingers. Still other skills require you to train your mind. For example, reading with understanding is a skill that requires much mental training. The skills that you use in the social studies are largely mental skills.

Why are skills important? Mastering different skills will help you to have a more satisfying life. You will be healthier and enjoy your leisure time more if you develop skills needed to take part in various sports. By developing artistic skills, you will be able to express your feelings more fully. It is even more important for you to develop skills of the mind. These skills are the tools that you will use in obtaining and using the knowledge you need to live successfully in today's world.

To develop a skill, you must practice it correctly. If you ask a fine athlete or musician how he gained his skill, he will say, "Through practice." To develop skills of the mind, you must practice also. Remember, however, that a person cannot become a good ballplayer if he keeps throwing the ball incorrectly. The same thing is true of mental skills. To master them, you must practice them correctly.

The following pages contain suggestions about how to perform correctly several important skills needed in the social studies. Study these skills carefully, and use them.

HOW TO FIND INFORMATION YOU NEED

Each day of your life you seek information. Sometimes you want to know certain facts just because you are curious. Most of the time, however, you want information for some special purpose. If your hobby is baseball, for example, you may want to know how to figure batting averages. If you collect stamps, you need to know how to identify the countries they come from. As a student in today's world, you need information for many purposes. As an adult, you will need even more knowledge to live successfully in tomorrow's world.

You may wonder how you can possibly learn all the facts you are going to need during your lifetime. The answer is that you can't. Therefore, knowing how to find information when you need it is of vital importance to you. Below are suggestions for locating good sources of information and for using these sources to find the facts that you need.

Written Sources of Information

1. Books. You may be able to find the information you need in books that you have at home or in your classroom. To see if a textbook or other nonfiction book has the information you need, look at the table of contents and the index.

Sometimes, you will need to go to your school or community library to locate books that contain the information you want. To make the best use of a library, you should learn to use the card catalog. This is a file that contains information about the books in the library. Each nonfiction book has at least three cards, filed in alphabetical order. One is for the title, one is for the author, and one is for the subject of the book. Each card gives the book's special number. This number will help you to find the book, since all the nonfiction books in the library are arranged on the shelves in numerical order. If you cannot find a book you want, the librarian will be glad to help you.

2. Reference volumes. You will find much useful information in special books known as reference volumes. These include dictionaries, encyclopedias, atlases, and other special books. Some companies publish a book each year with statistics and general information about the events of the preceding year. Such books are usually called yearbooks, annuals, or almanacs.

3. Newspapers and magazines. These are an important source of up-to-date information. Sometimes you will want to look for information in papers or magazines that you do not have at home. You can usually find the ones you want at the library.

The *Readers' Guide to Periodical Literature,* which is available in most libraries, will direct you to magazine articles about the subject you are investigating. This is a series of volumes that list articles by title, author, and subject. In the front of each volume is an explanation of the abbreviations used to indicate the different magazines and their dates.

4. Booklets, pamphlets, and bulletins. Many materials of this type are available from local and state governments, as well as from our federal government. Chambers of commerce, travel bureaus, trade organizations, private companies, and embassies of foreign countries publish materials that contain a wealth of information.

Many booklets and bulletins give accurate information. You should remember, however, that some of them are intended to promote certain products or ideas. Information obtained from such sources should be checked carefully.

Reading for Information

The following suggestions will help you to save time and effort when you are looking for information in books and other written materials.

1. Use the table of contents and the index. The table of contents appears at the beginning of the book and generally is a list of the chapters in the book. By looking at this list, you can usually tell whether the book has the type of information you need.

The index is a more detailed list of the topics that are discussed in the book. It will help you locate the pages on which specific facts are discussed. In most books, the index is at the back. Encyclopedias often include the index in a separate volume, however.

At the beginning of an index, you will usually find an explanation that makes it easier to use. For example, the explanation at the beginning of the Index for this book tells you that *p* means picture, *m* means map, and *t* means table.

The topics, or entries, in the index are arranged in alphabetical order. To locate all the information you need, you may have to look under more than one entry. For example, to find out what pages in this book discuss climate, look up the entry for climate, and also see if climate is listed under the entries for the individual states.

2. Skim the written material to see if it contains the information you need. Before you begin reading a chapter or a page, skim it to see if it has the information you need. In this way you will not run the risk of wasting time reading something that is of little or no value to you. When you skim, you look mainly for topic headings, topic sentences, and key words. For example, imagine you are looking for the answer to the question: "What kinds of goods are transported on the Mississippi River?" You might look for a topic heading that mentions the Mississippi River. When you find this topic heading, you might look for a key term such as "transportation."

3. Read carefully when you think you have located the information you need. When you think you have found the page that contains the information you are looking for, read it carefully. Does it really tell you what you want to know? If not, you will need to look further.

Other Ways of Obtaining Information

1. Direct experience. What you observe or experience for yourself may be a good source of information if you have observed carefully and remembered accurately. First-hand information can often be obtained by visiting places in your community or nearby, such as museums, factories, or government offices.

2. Radio and television. Use the listings in your local newspaper to find programs about the subjects in which you are interested.

3. Movies, filmstrips, recordings, and slides. Materials on a great variety of subjects are available. They can be obtained from schools, libraries, museums, and private companies.

4. Resource people. Sometimes, you will be able to obtain information by interviewing a person who has special knowledge. On occasion, you may wish to invite someone to speak to your class and answer questions.

EVALUATING INFORMATION

During your lifetime, you will constantly need to evaluate what you see, hear, and read. Information is not true or significant simply because it is presented on television or is written in a book, magazine, or newspaper. The following suggestions will help you in evaluating information.

Learn to tell the difference between primary and secondary sources of information. A primary source of information is a first-hand record. For example, a photograph taken of an event while it is happening is a primary source. So is the report you write about a field trip you take. Original documents, such as the Constitution of the United States, are primary sources, also.

A secondary source is a secondhand report. For example, if you write a report about what someone else told you he saw, your report will be a secondary source of information. Another example of a secondary source is a history book.

Advanced scholars like to use primary sources whenever possible. However, these sources are often difficult to obtain. Most students in elementary and high school use secondary sources. You should always be aware that you are using secondhand information when you use a secondary source.

Find out who said it and when it was said. The next step in evaluating information is to ask, "Who said it?" Was he a scholar with special training in the subject about which he wrote? Was he a newsman with a reputation for careful reporting of the facts?

Another question you should ask is, "When was it said?" Changes take place rapidly in our world, and the information you are using may be out of date. For example, many nations in Africa have won independence in recent years, so a political map of this continent that is five years old is no longer accurate.

Find out if it is mainly fact or opinion. The next step in evaluating information is to decide whether it is based on facts or whether it mainly consists of unsupported opinions. You can do this best if you are aware of these three types of statements.

1. Statements of fact that can be checked. For example, "Voters in the United States choose their representatives by secret ballot," is a statement of fact that can be checked by observing how voting is carried on in different parts of our country.

2. Inferences, or conclusions that are based on facts. The statement, "The people of the United States live in a democracy," is an inference. This inference is based on the fact that the citizens choose their representatives by secret ballot, and on other facts that can be proved. It is important to remember that inferences can be false or only partly true.

3. Value judgments, or opinions. The statement, "It is always wrong for a country to go to war," is a value judgment. Since a value judgment is an opinion, you need to examine it very critically. On what facts and inferences is it based? For example, what facts and conclusions do you think form the basis of the opinion: "It is always wrong for a country to go to war"? Do you agree or disagree with these conclusions? A reliable writer or reporter is careful to let his reader know which statements in his writing are his own opinions. He also tries to base his opinions as much as possible on facts that can be proved.

Find out why it was said. The next step in evaluating information is to find out the purpose for which it was prepared. Many books and articles are prepared in an honest effort to give you accurate information. For example, a scientist writing about a new scientific discovery will usually try to report his findings as accurately as possible, and he will be careful to distinguish between what he has actually observed and the conclusions he has drawn from these facts.

Some information, however, is prepared mainly to persuade people to believe or act a certain way. Information of this kind is called propaganda.

Some propaganda is used to promote causes that are generally considered good. A United States Army recruiting poster with a big picture of Uncle Sam and the words, "Uncle Sam needs *you*," is an example of this type of propaganda.

Propaganda is also used to make people support causes they would not agree with if they knew more about them. This kind of propaganda may consist of information that is true, partly true, or false. Even when it is true, however, the information may be presented in such a way as to mislead you.

Propaganda generally appeals to people's emotions rather than to their reasoning ability. For this reason, you should learn to identify information that is propaganda. Then you can think about it calmly and clearly, and evaluate it intelligently.

Seven Propaganda Tricks

People who use propaganda have learned many ways of presenting information to influence you in the direction they wish. Seven propaganda tricks to watch for are listed below.

Name Calling. Giving a label that is disliked or feared, such as "un-American," to an organization, a person, or an idea. This trick often persuades people to reject something they know nothing about.

Glittering Generalities. Trying to win support by using fine-sounding phrases, such as "the best deal in town" or "the American way." These phrases have no clear meaning when you stop to think about them.

Transfer. Connecting a person, product, or idea with something that people already feel strongly about. For example, displaying a picture of a church next to a speaker to give the impression that he is honest and trustworthy.

Testimonial. Getting well-known persons or organizations to announce in public their support of a person, product, or idea.

Plain Folks. Trying to win support by giving the impression of being just an ordinary person who can be trusted. For example, a political candidate may try to win people's confidence by giving the impression that he is a good father who loves children and dogs.

Card Stacking. Giving the wrong impression by giving only part of the facts about a person, product, or idea. For example, giving favorable facts and leaving out unfavorable ones.

Bandwagon. Trying to win support by saying that "everybody knows that" or "everyone is doing this."

MAKING REPORTS

There are many occasions when you need to share information or ideas with others. Sometimes you will need to do this in writing. Other times you will need to do it orally. One of the best ways to develop your writing and speaking skills is by making oral and written reports. The success of your report will depend on how well you have organized your material. It will also depend on your skill in presenting it. Here are some guidelines that will help you in preparing a good report.

Decide upon a goal. Have your purpose clearly in mind. Are you mainly interested in communicating information? Do you want to give your own viewpoint on a subject, or are you trying to persuade other people to agree with you?

Find the information you need. Be sure to use more than one source. If you are not sure how to locate information about your topic, read the suggestions on pages 346-348.

Take good notes. To remember what you have read, you must take notes. Before you begin taking notes, however, you will need to make a list of the questions you want your report to answer. As you do research, write down the facts that answer these questions. You may find some interesting and important facts that do not answer any of your questions. If you feel that they might be useful in your report, write them down, too. Your notes should be brief and in your own words except when you want to use exact quotations. When you use a quotation, be sure to put quotation marks around it.

You will be able to make the best use of your notes if you write them on file cards. Use a separate card for each statement or group of statements that answers one of your questions. To remember where your information came from, write on each card the title, author, and date of the source. When you have finished taking notes, group the cards according to the questions they answer. This will help you arrange your material in logical order.

Make an outline. After you have reviewed your notes, make an outline. This is a general plan that shows the order and the relationship of the ideas you want to include in your report. The first step in making an outline is to pick out the main ideas. These will be the main headings in your outline. (See sample outline below.) Next, list under each of these headings the ideas and facts that support it. These supporting ideas are called subheadings. As you arrange your information, ask yourself the following questions:

a. Is there one main idea that I must put first because everything else depends on it?

b. Have I arranged my facts in such a way as to show relationships among them?

c. Are there some ideas that will be clearer if they are discussed after other ideas have been explained?

d. Have I included enough facts so that I can complete my outline with a summary statement or a logical conclusion?

When you have completed your first outline, you may find that some parts of it are skimpy. If so, you may wish to do more research. When you are satisfied that you have enough information, make your final outline. Remember that this outline will serve as the basis of your finished report.

Example of an outline. The author of this feature prepared the following outline before writing this section.

I. Introduction
II. Deciding upon a goal
III. Finding information
IV. Taking notes
    A. List main ideas to be researched
    B. Write supporting facts on file cards
    C. Group cards according to main ideas
V. Making an outline
    A. Purpose of an outline
    B. Guidelines for arranging information
    C. Sample outline of this feature
VI. Preparing a written report
VII. Presenting an oral report

Special guidelines for a written report. Using your outline as a guide, write your report. The following suggestions will help you to make your report interesting and clear.

Create word pictures that your readers can see in their minds. Before you begin to write, imagine that you are going to make a movie of the subject you plan to write about. What scenes would you like to show on the screen? Next, think of the words that will create these same pictures in your readers' minds.

Group your sentences into good paragraphs. It is usually best to begin a paragraph with a topic sentence that says to the reader, "This is what you will learn about in this paragraph." The other sentences in the paragraph should help to support or explain the topic sentence.

Other guidelines. There are two other things to remember in writing a good report. First, use the dictionary to find the spelling of words you are doubtful about. Second, make a list of the sources of information you used, and include it at the beginning or end of your report. This list is called a bibliography.

A sample paragraph. Below is a sample paragraph from this book. The topic sentence has been underlined. Notice how clear it is and how well the other sentences support it. Also notice how many pictures the paragraph puts in your mind.

There are several reasons why farming is so important in the Midwest and Great Plains. Nowhere else in the world are there such large areas of fertile soil. Most of the land in the Midwest and Great Plains is level enough to be cultivated with modern farm machinery. The long, warm summers in most of this area are very good for growing crops. Rainfall is plentiful in the Midwest. Although many parts of the Great Plains states receive little rainfall, farmers here can earn a good living if they use the soil and water wisely.

Special guidelines for an oral report. When you are going to give a report orally, you will also want to organize your information in a logical order by making an outline. Prepare notes to guide you during your talk. These notes should be complete enough to help you remember all the points you want to make. You may even write out portions of your report that you prefer to read.

When you present your report, speak directly to your audience. Pronounce your words correctly and distinctly. Remember to speak slowly enough for your listeners to follow what you are saying, and use a tone of voice that will hold their interest. Stand up straight, but try not to be too stiff. The only way to improve your speaking skills is to practice them correctly.

HOLDING A GROUP DISCUSSION

One of the important ways in which you learn is by exchanging ideas with other people. You do this frequently in informal conversation. You are likely to learn more, however, when you take part in the special kind of group conversation that we call a discussion. A discussion is more orderly than a conversation, and it usually has a definite, serious purpose. This purpose may be the sharing of information or the solving of a problem. In order to reach its goal, the discussion group must arrive at a conclusion or make a decision of some kind.

A discussion is more likely to be successful when those who take part in it observe the following guidelines:

1. Be prepared. Think about the topic to be discussed ahead of time. Prepare for the discussion by reading and taking notes. You may also want to make an outline of the ideas you want to share with the group.

2. Take part. Contribute to the discussion; express your ideas clearly and concisely. Be sure that the statements you make and the questions you ask deal with the topic being discussed.

3. Listen and think. Listen thoughtfully to others. Encourage all of the members of the discussion group to express their ideas.

How to Listen

Listening is one of our most valuable communication skills. Each day, we spend a large part of our time listening and speaking to other people face to face. Often, we understand more when we listen to another person speak than we do when we read something he has written. When we listen, we have the advantage of being able to watch his facial expressions and gestures. The following suggestions will help you develop your listening skill.

Watch the speaker. As you listen, look directly at the person who is speaking. If you take a sincere interest in what he is saying, you will hear more and learn more. Showing a sincere interest in what the speaker is saying is also an act of courtesy.

Think about the speaker's message. Consider carefully what the speaker is saying.

Good listening depends mainly on the amount of thinking you do as you listen. Even when you are listening to a well-known lecturer, think about his message as though you were carrying on a personal conversation. If you disagree with something he says, remember the point for later discussion.

Learn to "picture-listen." One of the best ways to understand what a speaker is saying is to "picture-listen." When you picture-listen, you see, hear, taste, and smell in your mind the things that the speaker's words describe. These mental images make the words more meaningful.

Make a list of main images. As you listen, try to decide which images are the most important. Often, you will want to take notes. Your notes should include all of the main images and facts you wish to remember for a report, a discussion, or some other project.

Do not make up your mind about a question or a problem until all of the facts have been given.

4. Be courteous. When you speak, address the entire group. Ask and answer questions politely. When you disagree with someone, point out your reasons calmly and in a friendly way.

WORKING WITH OTHERS

In school and throughout life, you will find that there are many projects that can be done better by a group than by one person working alone. Some of these projects would take too long to finish if they were done by a single individual. Others have different parts that can be done best by people with different talents.

Before your group begins a project, you should decide several matters. First, determine exactly what you are trying to accomplish. Second, decide what part of the project each person should do. Third, schedule when the project is to be completed.

The group will do a better job and reach its goals more quickly if each person follows these suggestions:

1. Do your part. Remember that the success of your project depends on every member of the group. Be willing to do your share of the work and to accept your share of the responsibility.

2. Follow the rules. Help the group decide on sensible rules, and then follow them. When a difference of opinion cannot be settled by discussion, make a decision by majority vote.

3. Share your ideas. Be willing to share your ideas and talents with the group. When you submit an idea for discussion, be prepared to see it criticized or even rejected. At the same time, have the courage to stick up for a principle or a belief that is really important to you.

4. Respect others. Remember that every person is an individual with different beliefs and talents. Give the other members of the group a chance to be heard, and be ready to appreciate their work and ideas.

5. Be friendly, thoughtful, helpful, and cheerful. Try to express your opinions seriously and sincerely without hurting others or losing their respect. Listen politely to the ideas of others.

6. Learn from your mistakes. Look for ways in which you can be a better group member the next time you work with others on a project.

BUILDING YOUR VOCABULARY

When you do research in many different types of reading materials, you are likely to find several words you have never seen before. If you skip over these words, the chances are that you will not fully understand what you are reading. The following suggestions will help you to discover the meanings of new words and build your vocabulary.

1. See how the word is used in the sentence. When you come to a new word, don't stop reading. Read on beyond the new word to see if you can discover any clues to what its meaning might be. Trying to figure out the meaning of a word from the way it is used may not give you the exact definition. However, it will give you a general idea of what the word means.

2. Sound out the word. Break the word up into syllables, and try to pronounce it. When you say the word aloud, you may find that you know it after all but have simply never seen it in print.

3. Look in the dictionary. When you think you have figured out what a word means and how it is pronounced, check with the dictionary. Have you pronounced it correctly? Did you decide upon the right definition? Remember, most words have several meanings. Do you know which meaning should be used?

4. Make a list of the new words you learn. In your own words, write a definition of each word you include in your list. Review this list from time to time.

LEARNING MAP SKILLS

The earth is a sphere. Our earth is round like a ball. We call any object with this shape a sphere. The earth is, of course, a very large sphere. Its diameter* is about 8,000 miles. Its circumference* is about 25,000 miles. The earth is not quite a perfect sphere, however, for it is slightly flattened at the North and South poles.

Globes and maps. The globe in your classroom is also a sphere. It is a model of the earth. The surface of the globe shows the shapes of the landmasses and bodies of water on the earth. By looking at the globe, you can see exactly where the continents, islands, and oceans are located. Globes are made with the North Pole at the top, but they are usually tilted to represent the way that the earth is tilted. Maps are flat drawings that represent part or all of the earth's surface.

Scale. Globes and maps give information about distance. When you use them, you need to know how many miles on the earth are represented by a given distance on the globe or map. This relationship is called the scale. The scale of a globe or map may be expressed in several different ways.

On most maps, the scale is shown by a small drawing. For example:

Scale of Miles   0   200   400

Sometimes, the scale is expressed in this way: 1 inch = 400 miles.

Scale is often shown in another way, especially on globes and large maps. For example: 1:10,000,000. These numbers mean that any given distance on the globe or map represents a distance on the earth that is ten million times as large. When the scale is shown in this way, you may use any kind of measuring unit you wish. If you choose the inch, then one inch on the globe or map equals ten million inches on the earth, or about 158 miles. You might, however, prefer to use the centimeter,* another measuring unit. In that case, one centimeter on the globe or map would represent ten million centimeters on the earth, or 100 kilometers.

*See Glossary

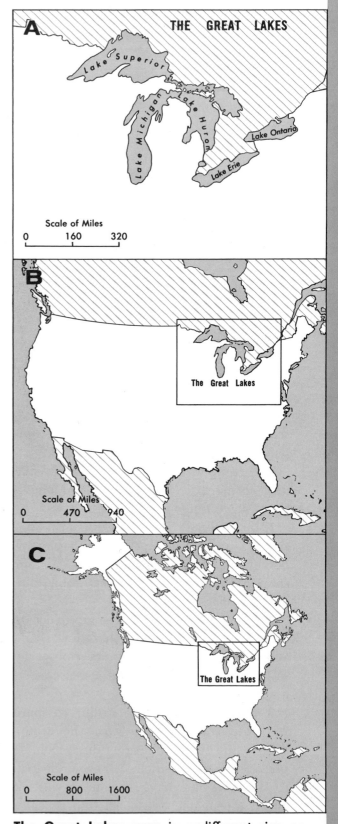

The Great Lakes area is a different size on each of the three maps above. This is because one inch on each of these maps represents a different distance on the earth.

Locating places on the earth. Map makers, travelers, and other curious people have always wanted to know just where certain places are located. Over the years, a very accurate way of giving such information has been worked out. This system is used all over the world.

In order to work out a system for locating anything, you need starting points and a measuring unit. The North and South poles and the equator are the starting points for the system we use to locate places on the earth. The measuring unit for our system is called the degree (°).

Parallels show latitude. When we want to locate a place on the earth, we first find out how far it is north or south of the equator. This distance measured in degrees is called north or south latitude. The equator represents zero latitude. The North Pole is located at 90 degrees north latitude, and the South Pole is at 90 degrees south latitude.

All points on the earth that have the same latitude are the same distance from the equator. A line connecting such points is called a parallel. This is because it is parallel to the equator. (See illustration D, below.)

Meridians show longitude. After we know the latitude of a place, we need to know its location in an east-west direction. This is called its longitude. The lines that show longitude are called meridians. They are drawn so as to connect the North and South poles. (See illustration E, below.) Longitude is measured from the meridian that passes through Greenwich, England. This line of zero longitude is called the prime meridian. Distance east or west of this meridian measured in degrees is called east or west longitude. The meridian of 180 degrees west longitude is the same as the one of 180 degrees east longitude. This is because 180 degrees is exactly halfway around the world from the prime meridian.

Locating places on a globe. The location of a certain place might be given to you like this: 30°N 90°W. This means that this place is located 30 degrees north of the equator, and 90 degrees west of the prime meridian. See if you can find this place on the globe in your classroom. It is helpful to remember that parallels and meridians are drawn every ten or fifteen degrees on most globes.

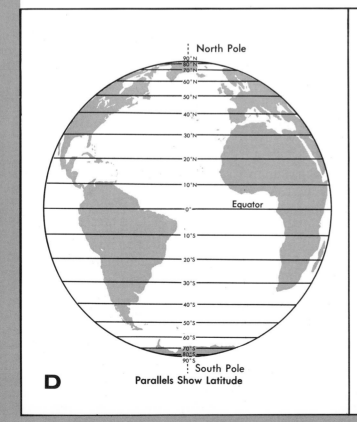

D Parallels Show Latitude

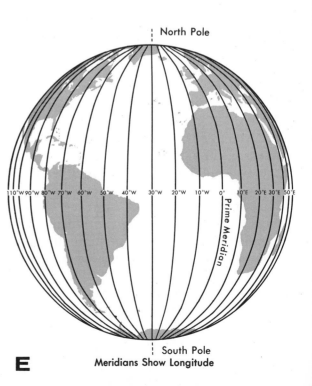

E Meridians Show Longitude

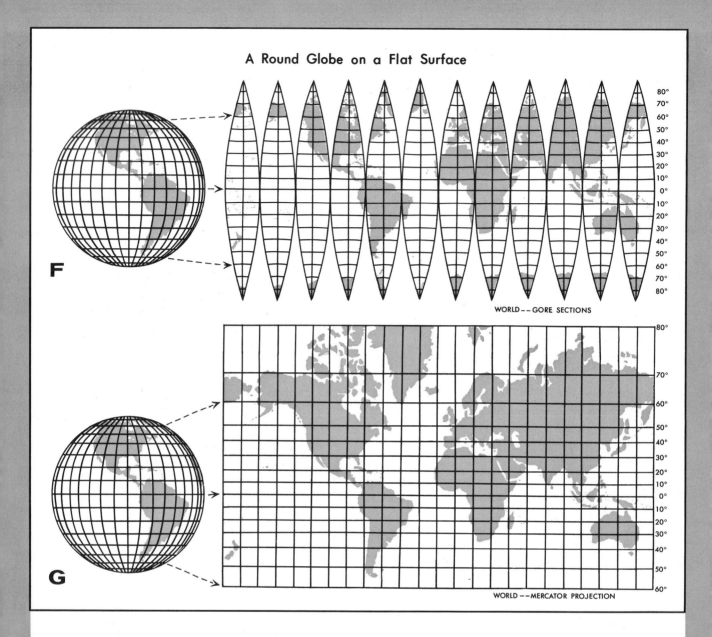

A Round Globe on a Flat Surface

WORLD – – GORE SECTIONS

WORLD – – MERCATOR PROJECTION

The round earth on a flat map. An important fact about a sphere is that you cannot flatten out its surface perfectly. To prove this, you might perform an experiment. Cut an orange in half and scrape away the fruit. You will not be able to press either piece of orange peel flat without crushing it. If you cut one piece in half, however, you can press these smaller pieces nearly flat. Next, cut one of these pieces of peel into three sections, or gores, shaped like those in illustration F, above. You will be able to press these small sections quite flat.

A map like the one shown in illustration F can be made by cutting the surface of a globe into twelve pieces shaped like the smallest sections of your orange peel. Such

a map would be fairly accurate. However, an "orange-peel" map is not an easy map to use, because the continents and oceans are split apart.

A flat map can never show the earth's surface as truthfully as a globe can. On globes, shape, size, distance, and direction are all accurate. Although a single flat map of the world cannot be drawn to show all four of these things correctly, flat maps can be made that show some of these things accurately. The various ways of drawing maps of the world to show different things correctly are called map projections.

The Mercator* projection. Illustration G, above, shows a world map called a Mercator projection. When you compare this map

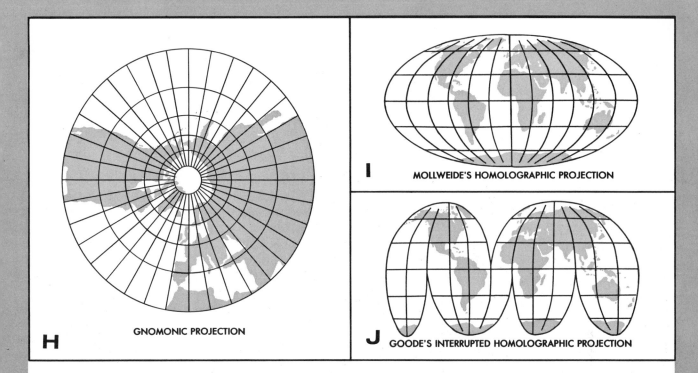

GNOMONIC PROJECTION

I MOLLWEIDE'S HOMOLOGRAPHIC PROJECTION

J GOODE'S INTERRUPTED HOMOLOGRAPHIC PROJECTION

with a globe, you can see that continents, islands, and oceans have almost the right shape. On this kind of map, however, North America seems larger than Africa, which is not true. On Mercator maps, lands far from the equator appear larger than they are.

Because they show true directions, Mercator maps are especially useful to navigators. For instance, the city of Lisbon, Portugal, lies almost exactly east of Baltimore, Maryland. A Mercator map shows that a ship could reach Lisbon by sailing from Baltimore straight east across the Atlantic Ocean.

The shortest route. Strangely enough, the best way to reach Lisbon from Baltimore is not by traveling straight east. There is a shorter route. In order to understand why this is so, you might like to perform the following experiment.

On your classroom globe, locate Lisbon and Baltimore. Both cities lie just south of the 40th parallel. Take a piece of string and connect the two cities. Let the string follow the true east-west direction of the 40th parallel. Now, draw the string tight. Notice that it passes far to the north of the 40th parallel. The path of the tightened string is the shortest route between Baltimore and Lisbon. The shortest route between any two points on the earth is called the great* circle route.

The gnomonic (nō mon′ ik) projection. Using a globe and a piece of string is not a very handy or accurate way of finding great circle routes. Instead, sailors and fliers use a special kind of map called the gnomonic projection. (See illustration H, above.) On this kind of map, the great circle route between any two places can be found simply by drawing a straight line between them.

Equal-area projections. Mercator and gnomonic maps are both very useful, but they do not show true areas. They cannot be used when you want to compare areas in different parts of the world. This is because sections of these maps that are the same size do not always represent the same amounts of the earth's surface.

Maps that do show true areas are called equal-area projections. If one square* inch of such a map represents a certain number of square miles on the earth's surface, then every other square inch of the map will represent an equal number of square miles on the earth. In order to draw an equal-area map of the world on a flat surface, the shapes of the landmasses and bodies of water must be distorted. (See illustration I, above.) To avoid this, some equal-area maps are broken, or interrupted. The breaks are arranged to fall at places that are not important. (See illustration J, above.)

SPECIAL-PURPOSE MAPS

Maps that show part of the earth. For some purposes, we prefer maps that do not show the entire surface of the earth. A map of a very small area can be drawn more accurately than a map of a large area. It can also include more details.

Illustration K, below, shows a photograph and a map of the same small part of the earth. The drawings on the map that show the shape and location of things on the earth are called symbols. The small drawing that shows directions is called a compass* rose.

Maps for special purposes. Maps can show the location of many different kinds of things. For instance, a map can show what minerals are found in certain places, or what crops are grown. A small chart that lists the symbols and their meanings is usually included on a map. This is called the legend, or key. (See map M, below.)

Symbols on some geography maps stand for the amounts of things in different places. For instance, map L, below, gives information about the number of people in the western part of the United States. The key tells the meaning of the symbols, which in this case are dots and circles.

On different maps, the same symbol may stand for different things and amounts. For example, each dot on map L stands for 10,000 persons. On other maps, a dot might represent 5,000 sheep or 1,000 bushels of wheat.

There are other ways of giving information about quantity. For example, various designs or patterns may be used on a rainfall map to indicate the areas that receive different amounts of rain each year.

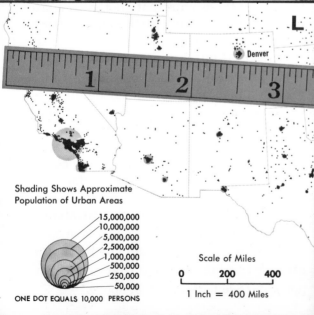

358

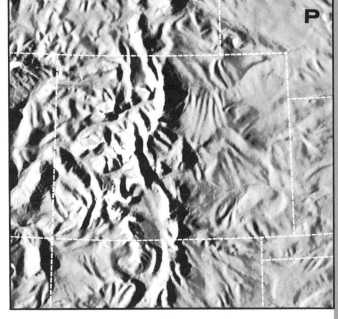

RELIEF MAPS

Some globes and maps show the roughness of the earth's surface. From a jet plane, you can see that the earth's surface is irregular. You can see mountains and valleys, hills and plains. For some purposes, globes and maps that show these things are needed. They are called relief globes and maps.

Since globes are three-dimensional models of the earth, you may wonder why most globes do not show the roughness of the earth's surface. The reason for this is that the highest mountain on the earth is not very large when it is compared with the earth's diameter. Even a very large globe would be almost perfectly smooth.

In order to make a relief globe or map, you must use a different scale for the height of the land. For example, you might start with a large flat map. One inch on your flat map represents a distance of one hundred miles on the earth. Now you are going to make a model of a mountain on your map. On the earth, this mountain is two miles high. If you let one inch represent a height of two miles on the earth, your mountain should rise one inch above the flat surface of

your map. Other mountains and hills should be modeled on this same scale.

By photographing relief globes and maps, flat maps can be made that show the earth much as it looks from an airplane. Maps N and O, at the top of this page, are photographs of a relief globe. Map P is a photograph of a relief map.

Topographic maps. Another kind of map that shows the roughness of the earth's surface is called a topographic, or contour, map. On this kind of map, lines are drawn to show

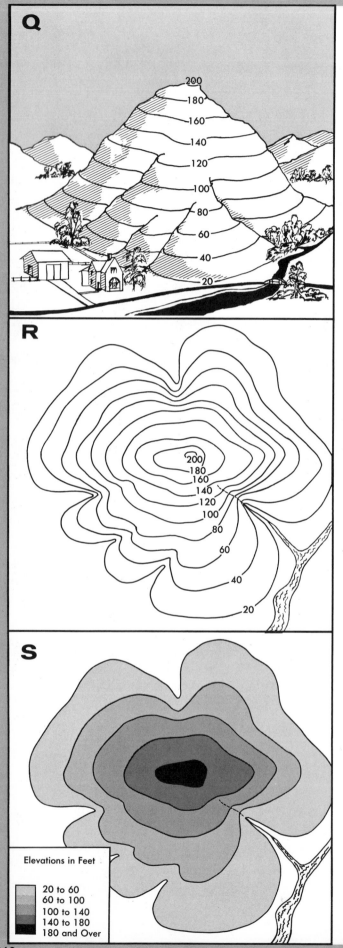

Q

R

S

Elevations in Feet

20 to 60
60 to 100
100 to 140
140 to 180
180 and Over

different heights of the earth's surface. These are called contour lines. The illustrations on this page help to explain how topographic maps are made.

Illustration Q is a drawing of a hill. Around the bottom of the hill is our first contour line. This line connects all the points at the base of the hill that are exactly twenty feet above sea level. Higher up the hill, another contour line is drawn, connecting all the points that are exactly forty feet above sea level. A line is also drawn at a height of sixty feet. Other lines are drawn every twenty feet until the top of the hill is reached. Since the hill is shaped somewhat like a cone, each contour line is shorter than the one just below it.

Illustration R shows how the contour lines in the drawing of the hill (Q) can be used to make a topographic map. This map gives us a great deal of information about the hill. Since each line is labeled with the height it represents, you can tell how high the different parts of the hill are. It is important to remember that land does not really rise in layers, as you might think when you look at a topographic map. Wherever the contour lines are far apart, you can be sure that the land slopes gently. Where they are close together, the slope is steep. With practice, you can picture the land in your mind as you look at such a map. Topographic maps are especially useful to men who design such things as roads and buildings.

On a topographic map, the spaces between the contour lines may be filled in with different shades of gray. If a different shade of gray were used for each different height of land shown in map R, there would be ten shades. It would be very hard for you to tell these different shades of gray apart. Therefore on map S, at left, black and four shades of gray were used to show differences in height of forty feet. The key box shows the height of the land represented by the different shades. On some topographic maps, colors are used to represent different heights of land.

GLOSSARY
Complete Pronunciation Key

The pronunciation of each word is shown just after the word, in this way: **equator** (i kwā′tər). The letters and signs used are pronounced as in the words below. The mark ′ is placed after a syllable with a primary or strong accent, as in the example above. The mark ′ after a syllable shows a secondary or lighter accent, as in **hydroelectric** (hī′ drō i lek′ trik).

a	hat, cap	j	jam, enjoy	u	cup, butter
ā	age, face	k	kind, seek	u̇	full, put
ã	care, air	l	land, coal	ü	rule, move
ä	father, far	m	me, am	ū	use, music
		n	no, in		
b	bad, rob	ng	long, bring		
ch	child, much			v	very, save
d	did, red	o	hot, rock	w	will, woman
		ō	open, go	y	young, yet
e	let, best	ô	order, all	z	zero, breeze
ē	equal, see	oi	oil, voice	zh	measure, seizure
ėr	term, learn	ou	house, out		
		p	paper, cup		
f	fat, if	r	run, try	ə	represents:
g	go, bag	s	say, yes	a	in about
h	he, how	sh	she, rush	e	in taken
		t	tell, it	i	in pencil
i	it, pin	th	thin, both	o	in lemon
ī	ice, five	ŦH	then, smooth	u	in circus

---

acre. A unit of area. A football field covers about one and one-third acres.

Alamo. A former Spanish mission in San Antonio, Texas. In 1836, the Alamo was the scene of the most famous battle in Texas' struggle for independence from Mexico. Beginning on February 23, a force of fewer than 200 Texans used the Alamo as a fort to resist an army of more than 4,000 Mexicans. The Mexicans finally captured the Alamo on March 6. The entire force of Texans was killed in the battle. "Remember the Alamo" became a famous battle cry of the Texas movement for independence.

alumina. (ə lü′ mə nə). A substance from which aluminum is made. Alumina is usually obtained by processing an ore called bauxite.

American Samoa. A United States possession in the South Pacific Ocean about 2,600 miles southwest of Hawaii. American Samoa consists of seven small islands.

annex. To make one territory part of another.

Appalachian (ap′ə lā′chən) **Mountains.** A name often used to refer to mountainous sections of the Appalachian Highlands. (Compare maps, pages 19 and 29.)

Appalachian (ap′ə lā′chən) **Plateau.** The westernmost section of the Appalachian Highlands region. (See map, pages 28 and 29.)

arctic. Refers to the region near the North Pole or the Arctic Circle. See **Arctic Circle**.

Arctic Circle. An imaginary line around the earth, about 1,600 miles south of the North Pole. (See top chart, page 50.)

Arkansas River. An important tributary of the Mississippi River. It begins in central Colorado and flows through Kansas, Oklahoma, and Arkansas. (See map, pages 18 and 19.)

Asia. The eastern part of the continent of Eurasia. Sometimes Asia itself is considered to be a continent. See **Eurasia**.

asphalt. A dark-colored, gummy substance used for paving roads and for making roofing materials. Deposits of natural asphalt are found in some parts of the world. Most asphalt, however, is obtained from petroleum.

atmosphere (at′ mə sfir). The name given to the layer of air that surrounds the earth.

automation. The development and use of machinery that requires few, if any, human operators.

axis of the earth. An imaginary straight line that passes through the earth, joining the North and South poles. It takes the earth about twenty-four hours to rotate, or turn around, once on its axis.

Aztec. Refers to a group of Indian tribes in Mexico. The Aztecs created a great empire, which fell to the Spanish in 1521.

badlands. The name given to any area that has been eroded in the same way as the Badlands of South Dakota. (See page 40.)

barge. A flat-bottomed boat used mainly to carry freight on rivers and canals. Barges are usually pushed by towboats. (See picture, page 32.)

barite (bãr′ īt). A heavy mineral that may be white, yellow, or colorless. It is used in drilling oil wells and in the manufacture of various paints and chemicals.

barley. A plant that looks somewhat like wheat. Its grain, also called barley, is used mainly in making beverages and animal feed.

basic chemicals. Common chemicals that are produced in large quantities for use in industry. (See **chemicals.**) Sulfuric acid is an example of a basic chemical. It is used in the manufacture of products such as fertilizers, explosives, and rayon. It is also used in refining petroleum.

basin. An area of land that is largely surrounded by higher land. Also, the total area of land that is drained by a river and its tributaries.

Basin and Range Country. One of three main sections of the Plateau Country. (See map, pages 28 and 29.) The Basin and Range Country is made up of short mountain ranges separated by wide basins.

Battle of San Jacinto. See **San Jacinto, Battle of.**

bauxite (bôk′sīt). An ore that is the chief source of aluminum. Bauxite may occur as a rocklike or claylike material. It may be red, yellow, or brown in color. Bauxite is processed to obtain alumina, from which aluminum is made.

beryllium (bə ril′i əm). A grayish-white metal, similar to aluminum, but stronger and lighter in weight. Beryllium is often combined with other metals to make them harder. Because beryllium is heat resistant, it is used to make heat shields for spacecraft.

Bessemer process. A process by which steel is made by forcing a current of air through hot, melted iron.

bituminous (bə tü′ mə nəs) **coal.** Another name for high-grade soft coal, the most plentiful and important type of coal. (See pages 166 and 167.)

Black Hills. A group of very old mountains in western South Dakota and northeastern Wyoming. (See map, page 326.)

blast furnace. A cylinder-shaped furnace in which iron is made from iron ore. It is called a blast furnace because a strong blast of air is blown into the bottom of the furnace. The air, which rises through a mixture of iron ore, coke, and limestone, helps the coke to burn at the high temperature needed for producing iron.

blizzard. A severe snowstorm in which powdery snow is driven by extremely strong, cold winds.

boll weevil. A small beetle that lays its eggs in the buds or bolls of cotton plants. The grubs that hatch from the eggs, as well as the adult beetles, cause much damage by eating the buds and bolls.

brine. Water that contains large amounts of salt, such as seawater. In some places, brines occur deep beneath the surface of the earth. In addition to salt, brines usually contain other chemical substances.

bromine (brō′ mēn). A poisonous, dark-red liquid with a disagreeable odor. It is obtained from chemical substances that occur in brines or in salt deposits. Bromine is used in making dyes, medicines, and many other chemical products.

butte (būt). A steep-sided, flat-topped hill that rises abruptly from the surrounding land. A butte is similar to a mesa, but smaller. See **mesa.**

cactus. A family of plants with soft stems and branches covered with thorns or scales. Because they store water in their stems and branches, cactus plants can live in very dry places.

Cadillac (kad' əl ak'), **Antoine de la Mothe,** 1658-1730. A French colonial governor in North America. He came to America from France in 1683. In 1694, Cadillac was put in charge of a French trading post at the Straits of Mackinac. Several years later, he established a fort and colony at the place that is now Detroit. In 1711, Cadillac was appointed governor of the French territory of Louisiana.

canyon. A valley with high, steep sides.

capitol. A building in which a lawmaking body meets. When spelled with a capital *C*, this word refers to the building in Washington, D.C., where Congress meets.

carbon. A common substance found in nature in many different forms. A diamond is pure carbon and so is graphite, the black writing material in your pencil. Anthracite, a high-quality coal, is composed almost entirely of carbon. In combination with other substances, carbon is found in all living things, in many kinds of rock, and in petroleum.

cash crop. A crop that a farmer raises to be sold, rather than to be used by himself and his family.

Catholic. See **Roman Catholic.**

centimeter. A unit for measuring length. It is equal to slightly less than half an inch. The centimeter is a unit of the metric system of measurement. The metric system is used in most countries and by scientists throughout the world. In this system, 100 centimeters equal one meter, and 1000 meters equal one kilometer. A meter is about 39 inches in length, and a kilometer is equal to about two thirds of a mile.

central city. The main city, or one of the main cities, of a metropolitan area. See **metropolitan area.**

Central Lowland. One of the two main sections of the Interior Plains region of our country. (See map, pages 28 and 29.)

chemicals. Substances that are used in or obtained from chemical processes. These are processes that produce new materials by changing the composition of the original substances. Many chemicals are complicated substances with strange-sounding names. Others, such as salt, soda, and ammonia, are simple and familiar household items.

Chicago River. A small river in Chicago that is part of the Illinois Waterway. (See **Illinois Waterway**.) Until 1900, the river flowed into Lake Michigan. Then, engineers reversed the flow of the river to prevent waste materials that were being dumped into it from entering Lake Michigan. Today, the Chicago River flows into the Sanitary and Ship Canal.

chinook (chə nük'). A warm, dry wind that sweeps down the eastern slopes of the Rocky Mountains and onto the plains nearby. The wind becomes warmer as it moves down the mountain slopes. It raises temperatures rapidly, sometimes as much as forty degrees in fifteen minutes. Chinooks usually occur during winter or early spring.

Christianity (kris' chi an' ə ti). The religion that takes its beliefs and practices from the life and teachings of Jesus Christ.

chub. Any one of several different kinds of fish. The kind of chub caught in the Great Lakes is a small food fish similar to the lake herring.

circumference (sər kum'fər əns). The distance around an object or a geometric figure, especially a circle or a sphere.

Civil War, 1861-1865. The war that resulted when a group of states in the southern part of our country broke away from the Union and formed a separate nation known as the Confederacy. The war began on April 12, 1861, when Confederate soldiers fired on Union troops stationed at Fort Sumter, in South Carolina. After four years of fighting, the Union forces won the war. (See page 91.)

Clark, William, 1770-1838. An American soldier and explorer. He helped Meriwether Lewis lead the expedition that traveled through the Louisiana Territory and westward to the Pacific coast.

Coastal Plain. A large region of the United States that borders the Atlantic Ocean and the Gulf of Mexico. (See map, pages 28 and 29.) The land in this region is level or gently rolling.

PRONUNCIATION KEY: hat, āge, cāre, fär; let, ēqual, tėrm; it, īce; hot, ōpen, ôrder; oil, out; cup, put, rüle, ūse; child; long; thin; ŦHen; zh, measure; ə represents a in about, e in taken, i in pencil, o in lemon, u in circus. For the complete key, see page 361.

363

coke. A fuel made by roasting coal in special airtight ovens. It is one of the three main raw materials used in the production of iron. Coke, together with iron ore and limestone, is loaded into a blast furnace. (See **blast furnace.**) The coke serves as a fuel, burning at a very high temperature, to melt the other materials. The burning coke also provides gases that react with the molten ore to separate the iron from waste materials.

coking coal. Bituminous coal that is suitable for making coke. Most of the good coking coal mined in our country comes from the Appalachian Plateau. See **coke.**

combine. A machine that cuts and threshes grain as it moves across a field. See **thresh.**

Communist. Refers to an economic system known as communism. (See **economic system.**) Under communism, the government controls industry, farming, trade, education, and most other activities. The term Communist also refers to political parties, governments, and individuals who promote communism. The governments of the Soviet Union, China, and various other countries are controlled by Communist parties.

commuters. People who travel back and forth regularly between one place and another, especially between a home in the suburbs and a place of work in the city.

compass rose. A small drawing included on a map to show directions. A compass rose is often used as a decoration. Here are three examples of compass roses:

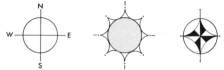

computer. An automatic machine that solves complicated mathematical problems very rapidly, usually by means of electronic devices.

Confederacy (kən fed′ ər ə si). Common name for the Confederate States of America. This was a nation made up of eleven states that withdrew from and fought against the Union in the Civil War. The Confederacy included Texas and all of the states that now make up the South except Kentucky. See **South.**

Confederate (kən fed′ər it). Of or relating to the Confederacy. See **Confederacy.**

Congress. The lawmaking, or legislative, branch of the United States government. It consists of the Senate and the House of Representatives.

consumer. A person who buys and uses goods, such as food and clothing, to meet his needs.

contagious disease. A disease that is spread by contact. The common cold and measles are contagious diseases.

conterminous (kən tėr′mə nəs) **United States.** The forty-eight states of the United States that are enclosed by an unbroken boundary. The word conterminous means "having the same boundary."

continent. One of the main landmasses on the earth. There are six continents—Eurasia, Africa, North America, South America, Australia, and Antarctica. Some people consider Eurasia to be two continents—Europe and Asia.

continental climate. The type of climate found in the interior of large continents, especially in the Northern Hemisphere. Most parts of the Midwest and Great Plains have a continental climate. (See pages 46-48.)

contour plowing. Plowing rows that curve around hillsides instead of plowing up-and-down rows. (See page 151.)

conveyor belt. A moving belt, usually made of canvas, rubber, or metal, that carries things from one place to another.

corn belt. An area of the United States that is especially well suited for growing corn. (See pages 153-155.)

cotton boll. The seedpod of the cotton plant. The cotton boll is nearly round and about as large as a golf ball. It contains from thirty to fifty seeds covered with cotton fibers.

crop rotation. A farming procedure in which various crops are raised on the same land in different years. (See page 151.)

crude oil. Petroleum as it comes from the ground, before it has been refined.

crust. The outer layer of the earth.

cultivate. To break up the soil around the roots of growing plants, mainly for the purpose of killing weeds. Also, to prepare and use land for growing crops.

dairy belt. An area in which the raising of cows for milk is the main type of farming. (See pages 152 and 153.)

depression. In economics, a period of decreased business activity and widespread unemployment.

diameter (dī am′ ə tər). The length of a straight line that extends from one side of a circle or a sphere to the other. This line must pass through the exact center of the circle or sphere.

diesel (dē′zəl) **engine.** A type of engine used mainly for heavy-duty work. The diesel engine burns a petroleum product called diesel fuel. Diesel engines are used in trucks and other heavy vehicles. They are also used to operate electric generators.

discrimination. The act of withholding rights or freedoms from people because they belong to minority groups. (See page 133.)

District of Columbia. An area that serves as the seat of the federal government of the United States. The District of Columbia lies along the Potomac River, between Maryland and Virginia. (See map, page 19.) It is not part of any state. Washington, our national capital city, has the same boundaries as the District of Columbia.

drift. Loose materials, such as sand, clay, or finely ground rock, that were moved from one place to another by glaciers during the Great Ice Age. The term drift also refers to loose materials deposited by streams, winds, and waves.

Driftless Area. An area of the United States that was surrounded but not covered by glaciers during the Great Ice Age. (See page 36.) The Driftless Area includes a large part of Wisconsin and smaller parts of Minnesota, Illinois, and Iowa. It is called the Driftless Area because it was not covered by glacial drift. See **drift.**

drought (drout). A long period of dry weather.

dry farming. A farming method used in dry areas where the land is not irrigated. Farmers raise crops that need little moisture. They leave part of their land idle, or fallow, each year to let the soil store moisture. (See page 151.)

Dust Bowl. An area of the Great Plains where many severe dust storms took place during the 1930's. This area included southwestern Kansas and the panhandles of Texas and Oklahoma. Poor farming methods and a severe drought helped create the Dust Bowl. Farmers in this area plowed up the tough prairie grass in order to plant crops. They did not realize that the roots of the grass had helped to protect the dry soil from erosion by strong winds. In the 1930's, rainfall was far below normal for several years, and the soil became very dry and powdery. Strong winds carried away millions of tons of rich topsoil. In places where large amounts of topsoil were lost, farmers could no longer grow crops. Thousands of people had to leave their farms and find work elsewhere. Toward the end of the 1930's, rainfall increased in the Great Plains. The additional rain helped to control dust storms.

economic system. The system followed by the people of a country in deciding what goods and services shall be produced, how they shall be produced, and to whom they shall be distributed. There are several different economic systems in the world today. For example, the economic system of the United States is known as capitalism or free enterprise. The economic system of the Soviet Union is called communism.

electronic (i lek′tron′ik). Refers to certain devices, such as vacuum tubes and transistors, or to products that make use of such devices. Radios, television sets, computers, and X-ray machines are examples of electronic products.

England. A division of the United Kingdom. England occupies most of southern Great Britain. See **Great Britain** and **United Kingdom.**

environment. The conditions surrounding a person, which affect his growth and development.

equator (i kwā′tər). An imaginary line around the middle of the earth, halfway between the North and South poles.

equinox (ē′kwə noks). Either of two times of the year when the sun shines directly on the equator. These occur about March 21 and September 22. At these two times, day and night are of equal length everywhere on earth.

PRONUNCIATION KEY: hat, āge, cãre, fär; let, ēqual, tèrm; it, īce; hot, ōpen, ôrder; oil, out; cup, pùt, rüle, ūse; child; long; thin; ᴛʜen; zh, measure; ə represents a in about, e in taken, i in pencil, o in lemon, u in circus. For the complete key, see page 361.

Erie Canal. A canal in New York that connected the Hudson River, near Albany, with the port city of Buffalo, on Lake Erie. It was completed in 1825. In the early 1900's, the Erie Canal became part of a system of canals called the New York State Barge Canal.

erosion. The process by which the rock and soil of the earth's surface are worn away by the forces of nature. Erosion includes wearing away by the action of rainfall, running water, ice, wind, and waves. Erosion may benefit man, as when soil is formed from rocks, or it may be harmful, as when fertile soil is washed away.

Eurasia (ūr ā' zhə). The largest continent on the earth. Some people consider Eurasia to be two separate continents—Europe and Asia.

Europe. The western part of the continent of Eurasia. Sometimes Europe itself is considered to be a separate continent. See **Eurasia.**

evaporate (i vap' ə rāt). To change from a liquid to a gas or vapor. When water evaporates, it mixes with the air as water vapor.

evaporation. See **evaporate.**

export (ek spôrt'). To send goods to another country or region for the purpose of selling them. These goods are called exports (eks' pôrts).

fallow. Farmland on which no crop is being grown is said to be fallow. In dry farming, the fallow land is cultivated to kill weeds and store moisture. See **dry farming.**

feedlots. Places where cattle are kept while being fattened for market.

ferry. To transport people or goods by boat back and forth across a body of water such as a river or a lake. A boat used for this purpose is also called a ferry.

fertilizer. A substance that is added to soil to make it produce larger yields or better-quality crops.

fiberboard. A building material that is made by pressing tiny threads of wood or other substances together to form stiff sheets. Fiberboard is used in building houses and making furniture.

fiber glass. Very fine, flexible threads of glass that are used in the manufacture of a variety of products, including textiles, automobile bodies, and fishing rods.

fishery. A place where fish are caught.

flax. A tall, slender plant with long, narrow leaves and, usually, blue flowers. The fibers of the stem are used to make products such as linen cloth, thread, and rope. Oil pressed from the seeds is used in paint, linoleum, and many other products. The meal left after the seeds have been pressed is used as food for livestock.

fodder. Coarse food for livestock. Hay and cornstalks are examples of fodder.

fossil. Any remains or trace of an animal or plant of a past age, preserved in rock or clay.

foundry. A place where founding is carried on. Founding is the process of pouring melted metal or glass into hollow forms called molds. When the metal or glass cools, it hardens into the desired shape, and the mold is removed.

Fox River. A river about 175 miles long that begins in south central Wisconsin. It flows into the west side of Lake Winnebago. The Fox then flows out of the north end of the lake and northward to Green Bay. (See map, page 285.)

French and Indian War, 1754-1763. A war in North America in which the French and their Indian allies fought the British. (See page 79.)

fuel oil. A petroleum product that is burned as a fuel for heating buildings and for producing electric power.

furfural (fėr'fə ral). An oily yellow or brown liquid made by treating plant materials, such as corncobs, with sulfuric acid. Furfural is used in refining petroleum products and in making drugs and synthetic fibers.

generator. A machine that changes mechanical energy into electrical energy. In an automobile, a small generator uses mechanical force from the drive shaft to produce the electricity needed to run the lights and starter. In large power plants, huge generators produce electricity from mechanical force provided by engines called turbines.

gin. A machine that separates seeds and other materials from cotton fibers. Teeth on a revolving drum hook the cotton fibers and pull them through openings that are too small to allow the seeds and other materials to pass through. The building in which such a machine is operated may also be called a gin.

glaciated. Covered with a glacier or changed by the action of a glacier.

glacier (glā' shər). A mass of slowly moving ice. (See page 36.)

gondola (gon' də lə) **car.** A railroad freight car that has a flat bottom and low sides but no top. Gondola cars are used mainly for carrying bulky goods such as coal.

gorge. A deep, narrow valley with steep, rocky walls.

Great Britain. The largest island of the British Isles, a group of islands off the western coast of Europe. Great Britain includes three divisions of the United Kingdom—England, Scotland, and Wales. At one time these areas had separate rulers. However, Wales has been joined to England since the sixteenth century, and Scotland and England were officially united in 1707. Today, the name Great Britain is often used to mean the United Kingdom. See **United Kingdom.**

great circle. Any imaginary circle around the earth that divides its surface exactly in half. The equator, for example, is a great circle. The shortest route between any two points on the earth always lies on a great circle.

Great Ice Age. A period during which glaciers spread over large areas of the earth. (See feature, page 36.)

Great Lakes. Five huge lakes in the central part of North America. These are Lakes Superior, Michigan, Huron, Erie, and Ontario. (See map, pages 18 and 19.)

Great Lakes–St. Lawrence Waterway. A great inland waterway that consists of the St. Lawrence River, the five Great Lakes, and several smaller connecting waterways. The system of canals, dams, and locks on the St. Lawrence between Lake Ontario and the city of Montreal, Canada, is known as the St. Lawrence Seaway. (See map, pages 184 and 185.)

Great Plains. One of the two main sections of the Interior Plains region of our country. (See map, pages 28 and 29.) The land in the Great Plains is generally flat.

Great Plains states. The part of our country that is made up of the states of Kansas, Nebraska, North Dakota, Oklahoma, South Dakota, and Texas. (See map, page 21.)

Green Bay. An arm of Lake Michigan, on the northwestern side of the lake. Green Bay is about 120 miles long and 20 miles wide. Green Bay is also the name of a city in Wisconsin at the southern end of the bay.

groundwater. Water that seeps into the ground and collects in layers of soil and rock. This is the water that supplies wells and springs.

growing season. The period of time when crops can be grown outdoors without danger of being killed by frost.

Gulf Intracoastal Waterway. A waterway that extends along the Gulf coast of our country from Texas to Florida. In some places, the waterway is protected by offshore islands. In other places, it lies inland. A similar waterway extends along the Atlantic coast.

Gulf of Mexico. A great arm of the Atlantic Ocean. (See map, page 20.)

gypsum. A chalky mineral used in making plaster and other construction materials.

helium (hē' li əm). A very light, colorless gas that will not burn or explode. Most of the world's helium is obtained from natural gas found in the Great Plains states. Helium is used mainly to keep the fuel supply in missiles and rockets under pressure. It is also used in welding, in many kinds of research, and to fill weather balloons.

homestead. The house and nearby land belonging to a family. Also refers to land acquired under the Homestead Act of 1862 or other homestead laws. See **Homestead Act of 1862.**

Homestead Act of 1862. A law passed by Congress in 1862. This law offered 160 acres of land to the head of a family if he was 21 years of age or over and would live on the land and cultivate it.

Houston Ship Channel. A waterway that connects Houston, Texas, with the Gulf of Mexico. (See map, page 333.) This waterway was formed by dredging a channel through Buffalo Bayou, the San Jacinto River, and Galveston Bay. The channel

---

PRONUNCIATION KEY: hat, āge, cãre, fär; let, ēqual, tèrm; it, īce; hot, ōpen, ôrder; oil, out; cup, pùt, rüle, ūse; child; long; thin; ᴛʜen; zh, measure; ə represents a in about, e in taken, i in pencil, o in lemon, u in circus. For the complete key, see page 361.

is deep and wide enough for oceangoing ships to sail to Houston.

humid (hū′mid). Moist. When used in connection with weather or climate, refers to air that contains a large amount of moisture.

hurricane. A violent storm that forms over large bodies of warm water. The winds of a hurricane whirl around a calm center called the eye. The eye is usually about fifteen miles in diameter, but the entire storm may be as much as five hundred miles across. In a hurricane, the whirling winds blow at a speed of more than seventy-five miles an hour. The storm itself, however, travels rather slowly, at about fifteen or twenty miles an hour.

hybrid. Usually, the offspring of two different plants or animals. For example, a mule is the hybrid offspring of a donkey and a horse. Scientists have also developed many hybrid plants that are the offspring of two different varieties of the same plant. Often these plants are hardier and produce better crops than the parent plants.

hydroelectric (hī′drō i lek′trik). Refers to hydroelectricity. See **hydroelectricity.**

hydroelectricity (hī′drō i lek′tris′ə ti). Electricity produced by waterpower. The force of rushing water is used to run machines called generators, which produce electricity. (See pages 173 and 174.)

Illinois Waterway. A waterway that extends from Lake Michigan at Chicago, to the point at which the Illinois River empties into the Mississippi. (See map, page 205.) The Illinois Waterway is made up of the Chicago River, the Sanitary and Ship Canal, the Des Plaines River, and the Illinois River. The Illinois Waterway is part of a great water highway that connects the Great Lakes with the Gulf of Mexico.

immigrant. A person of foreign nationality who enters a country to make it his permanent home.

Inca Indians. A group of Indians who ruled over a large area of South America. The Incas were highly skilled craftsmen who developed a great civilization. From mines in their empire they obtained rich stores of gold and silver. In the 1530's, the Spanish explorer Francisco

Pizzaro and his men conquered the Inca empire.

India. A country in southern Asia. See **Asia.**

Indian summer. A short period of warm, sunny weather that often follows the first cold spell in autumn. Indian summer usually comes in late October or early November.

industrialized. Refers to a country or area where industry is highly developed.

Interior Highlands. A region of the United States. (See map, pages 28 and 29.)

Interior Plains. A large region in the central part of the United States. (See map, pages 28 and 29.) Most of the land in this region is level or gently rolling.

interstate commerce. Trade or transportation that crosses one or more of the state borders in the United States. The Constitution gives Congress the power to regulate trade, or commerce, among the states. Congress does not, however, generally have any control over commerce within each state. Congress controls interstate commerce through various agencies such as the Interstate Commerce Commission. Through these agencies, Congress is able to regulate rates, trade practices, and employment policies of companies engaged in interstate commerce.

Ireland. The second largest island of the British Isles, a group of islands off the western coast of Europe. Also, the country that occupies most of this island.

irrigate. To supply land with water by artificial rather than natural means. Ditches, canals, pipelines, and sprinklers are common means of irrigation.

jaspilite. A low-grade iron ore mined in northern Michigan. It is a hard, dark-colored rock that contains about 30 percent iron.

kiln. (kil). A furnace or oven in which a substance is processed by burning, baking, or drying.

Lake Agassiz (ag′ə sē). A lake formed late in the Great Ice Age. (See page 36.) Lake Agassiz was larger than all the present Great Lakes combined. It covered parts of what are now the states of North Dakota and Minnesota and the Canadian provinces of Manitoba, Saskatchewan, and Ontario. During the last part of the Great Ice Age, a glacier covered this area. When the ice sheet retreated, it left behind a huge basin. This basin filled with rainwater, river water, and water from melting ice, forming Lake Agassiz. Gradually, most of the lake waters drained away into rivers. Some present-day lakes, such as Lake of the Woods and Lake Winnipeg, were once part of Lake Agassiz. The Red River of the North flows through the ancient lake bed. Lake Agassiz was named for the scientist Louis Agassiz, a pioneer in the study of glaciers.

lamprey (lam′pri). An eel-like water animal that has a large, round mouth. Lampreys are destructive animals that attach themselves to valuable food fish and suck their body fluids.

latitude. Distance north or south of the equator, measured in degrees. (See page 355.)

lead. A soft, heavy metal. It is used to make pipes, storage batteries, and many other products.

Lewis, Meriwether, 1774-1809. Commander of the famous exploring expedition that traveled through the Louisiana Territory and westward to the Pacific coast. Before taking this command, he served as a captain in the United States Army and as private secretary to President Jefferson. After the expedition, Lewis served as governor of the Louisiana Territory.

Lewis and Clark. See **Clark, William,** and **Lewis, Meriwether.**

lignite. A low-grade coal that is about half carbon and half water. (See **carbon.**) When lignite is burned, it gives off less heat than coal that contains more carbon. Most of the coal found in the Great Plains states is lignite. (See map, page 166.)

lime. A white substance made by burning limestone, bones, or shells in an oven called a kiln. Lime is used in manufacturing fertilizer, glass, and many other products.

limestone. A common rock that occurs in various colors, from white to dark gray or brown. Light-colored limestone that can be cut into blocks is valued as building stone. Crushed limestone is widely used in road building and other kinds of construction. Limestone is also used as a raw material in making cement, lime, soda ash, and many other products. In addition, limestone is used in making iron and steel.

literacy test. A test of a person's ability to read and write, used in some states to determine whether a citizen is qualified to vote. In the past, literacy tests were sometimes used to prevent certain people from voting even though they could read and write. For example, election boards sometimes denied the right to vote to Negroes who could read and write, just because their answers to certain questions were "unsatisfactory" to the board. The Voting Rights Act of 1965 forbids using literacy tests in this way.

lock. A section of a canal or river that is used to raise or lower ships from one water level to another. Gates at each end permit ships to enter or leave the lock. When a ship is in the lock, the gates are closed. The water level in the lock is raised or lowered to the level of the part of the canal or river toward which the ship is bound. Then the gates in front of the ship are opened, and the ship passes out of the lock.

longhorn cattle. A breed of cattle with very long horns. Huge herds of longhorn cattle were once raised on the rangelands in Texas and other parts of the Great Plains. However, cattlemen stopped raising longhorns because these cattle do not produce as much beef as other breeds. Today, longhorns are nearly extinct, but some are being preserved on wildlife refuges.

loom. A frame or machine for weaving two or more sets of threads into cloth.

Louis XIV, 1638-1715. The King of France from 1643 to 1715.

Louisiana Purchase. The purchase of the territory called Louisiana. See **Louisiana Territory.**

Louisiana Territory. An area between the Mississippi River and the Rocky Mountains. The United States bought this land from France in 1803. (See map, page 85.)

lumberjack. A man who earns his living by lumbering. This includes cutting down trees, sawing them into logs, and taking the logs to the place where they are sold.

PRONUNCIATION KEY: hat, āge, cāre, fär; let, ēqual, tėrm; it, īce; hot, ōpen, ôrder; oil, out; cup, pu̇t; rüle, ūse; child; long; thin; ᴛʜen; zh, measure; ə represents a in about, e in taken, i in pencil, o in lemon, u in circus. For the complete key, see page 361.

machine tools. Power-driven machines that cut, grind, and shape metal to produce parts needed in making other machines.

magnesium. A grayish-white metal that is very lightweight. It is used in processing other metals, and in making equipment such as skis and cameras.

Mandan. A tribe of Indians who lived in what is now North Dakota. The Mandan built villages of earth-covered houses, and farmed nearby. They also traded with wandering Indian tribes. In 1837 most of the Mandan died from a disease called smallpox.

McCormick reaper. A grain-harvesting machine patented in 1834 by an inventor named Cyrus McCormick. Before reapers were available, grain had to be cut by hand. The first McCormick reaper, which was pulled by horses, included cutter blades and a platform. The machine cut the grain and piled it on the platform. A man who followed the reaper raked the grain off the platform into piles on the ground. In 1847, McCormick built a factory in Chicago to manufacture these reapers. Later in the 1800's, better reapers were made. Today, most farmers in the United States harvest wheat and other grains with combines. See **combine**.

menhaden (men hā'dən). A fish of the herring family. Menhaden are found in abundance along the Atlantic and Gulf coasts of the United States. They are chiefly used to make fertilizer, livestock feed, and oil.

Mercator (mer kā' tər) **projection.** One of many possible arrangements of meridians and parallels on which a map of the world may be drawn. It was devised by Gerhardus Mercator, a Flemish geographer who lived from 1512 to 1594. On a Mercator map, all meridians are drawn straight up and down, with north at the top. The parallels are drawn straight across, but increasingly farther apart toward the poles. If you will compare the first section, or gore, of the "orange-peel" map on page 356 with the section of the Mercator map directly below it, you will see how the Mercator map straightens out the meridians. Because the earth features have been stretched in an east-west direction, except at the equator, they appear wider in the Mercator section than they do in the "orange-

peel" section. To make up for this east-west stretching, earth features on the Mercator map are also stretched in a north-south direction. Therefore, on Mercator maps the shapes of landmasses and bodies of water are fairly accurate, but their sizes are not.

mesa (mā' sə). A small plateau that rises abruptly from the surrounding land. A mesa has a flat top and steep sides. Mesa is a Spanish word that means table.

mesquite (mes kēt'). A spiny, shrublike tree with long roots. It grows in the southwestern part of the United States and in other dry lands. The seed pods of mesquite provide good fodder for livestock.

metropolitan (met' rə pol' ə tən) **area.** A densely populated area that includes at least one large central city. In addition to the central city, a metropolitan area usually includes several neighboring towns and settled sections.

Mexico. The country that borders the United States along its southwestern land boundary. (See map, page 17.)

Midwest. A part of the United States. The Midwest includes the states of Illinois, Indiana, Iowa, Michigan, Minnesota, Missouri, Ohio, and Wisconsin. (See map, page 21.)

mineral. Any of various substances found in the earth that have a definite chemical composition. Diamonds and salt are examples of minerals.

mission. A place where missionaries live and work. See **missionaries**.

missionaries. People who are sent out by a religious group to persuade other people to follow the same religion.

Mississippi River. A large river in the central part of the United States. It begins in northern Minnesota and flows southward into the Gulf of Mexico. (See map, pages 18 and 19.)

Missouri River. A river about 2,500 miles long that flows from southwestern Montana to the Mississippi River. (See map, pages 18 and 19.)

mohair. The long, silky hair of the Angora goat. Also, yarn or cloth made of mohair.

Mongolian. Refers to people of Asia who generally have yellowish skin, straight hair, and eyes that appear to be slanted.

moon. Usually refers to the natural satellite that revolves around the earth about once every twenty-eight days. The moon has a diameter of 2,160 miles. It is located about 239,000 miles from the earth. The word moon may also refer to a heavenly body that circles any other planet, or to a man-made satellite of the earth. See **satellite**.

muck. A dark, heavy soil containing large amounts of decayed plant materials.

mural. A picture, usually very large, that is painted on a wall.

national forests. Areas of forest land owned and managed by the government of the United States.

National Forest Service. The agency of the United States government that manages national forests. See **national forests**.

National Road. For many years, the main American road leading westward from the Atlantic coast. The first section of this road, completed in 1818, connected Cumberland, Maryland, with Wheeling, in what is now West Virginia. This section was known as the Cumberland Road. Later, the road was extended westward to Vandalia, Illinois. It was then known as the National Road.

natural gas. A gas found in layers of sand or rock beneath the surface of the earth. Natural gas is used as a fuel. It also provides raw materials for the manufacture of many chemicals.

natural-gas liquids. Valuable liquids obtained from natural gas. The liquids are separated from the gas before it is piped to homes and factories.

New England. One of the two groups of states into which the Northeast may be divided. (See **Northeast.**) New England is made up of Maine, New Hampshire, Vermont, Massachusetts, Connecticut, and Rhode Island.

newsprint. An inexpensive, coarse paper made mostly from wood pulp. It is mainly used for newspapers.

nonmetallic minerals. Minerals that are used by man for purposes other than the production of metals.

nonporous. Not porous. See **porous**.

North. In American history, refers to the states and territories that supported the Union during the Civil War period. See **Civil War**.

Northeast. A part of the United States. (See map, page 21.) It includes Connecticut, Delaware, the District of Columbia, Maine, Maryland, Massachusetts, New Hampshire, New Jersey, New York, Pennsylvania, Rhode Island, Vermont, and West Virginia.

Northern Hemisphere (hem′ ə sfir). The half of the earth that is north of the equator. See **equator**.

Northwest. A name once used for the land included in the Northwest Territory. See **Northwest Territory**.

Northwest Territory. An area of land that became part of the United States by the terms of the treaty that ended the Revolutionary War. This territory extended northward from the Ohio River to Canada and westward from Pennsylvania to the Mississippi River.

Ohio River. A river, nearly one thousand miles long, that flows generally southwestward from Pittsburgh, Pennsylvania, to the Mississippi River. (See map, page 19.)

open range. Unfenced land that is used for grazing livestock.

Ordinance of 1785. A law that provided for the division and sale of land in the Northwest Territory. (See pages 83 and 84.)

Ordinance of 1787. A law that set up the way in which the Northwest Territory was to be governed. (See pages 83 and 84.) It also outlawed slavery in the territory and promised public education.

ore. Rock or other material that contains enough of some valuable substance, such as a metal, to make it worth mining.

Ouachita (wäsh′ ə tô) **Mountains.** An area of low, rugged mountains in the Interior Highlands region. (See map, page 29.)

Ozark Plateau. A hilly area in the Interior Highlands region. (See map, page 29.)

Pacific Ocean. The largest ocean on the earth. It extends from the western coasts of North and South America to eastern Asia and Australia.

Panama Canal. An artificial waterway built across the Isthmus of Panama to connect the Atlantic Ocean with the Pacific Ocean. It was completed in 1914.

PRONUNCIATION KEY: hat, āge, cāre, fär; let, ēqual, tėrm; it, īce; hot, ōpen, ôrder; oil, out; cup, pùt, rüle, ūse; child; long; thin; ᴛнen; zh, measure; ə represents a in about, e in taken, i in pencil, o in lemon, u in circus. For the complete key, see page 361.

Panama Canal Zone. A strip of land ten miles wide in the country of Panama. (See map, page 17.) The Panama Canal extends through the center of the Canal Zone. The Canal Zone is controlled by the United States.

panhandle. A relatively narrow strip of territory that extends into another area. The western extension of Oklahoma and the northern extension of Texas are panhandles. (See maps, pages 317 and 333.)

parallel. Any imaginary circle drawn east and west around the earth, connecting all points of the same latitude. Also, such a line drawn on a map or globe. Lines of latitude are called parallels because they are always parallel to the equator. (See page 355.)

patented. Refers to an invention that has received an official government grant, called a patent. A patent guarantees that no one except the owner can make or sell the invention for a certain number of years.

penicillin. A powerful germ-killing substance used in curing pneumonia and many other infectious diseases. Penicillin is produced from certain molds similar to the mold that forms on damp bread.

peninsula (pə nin′ sə lə). An area of land that is almost surrounded by water and is connected to a larger body of land.

Peru. A country in western South America. It is bordered on the west by the Pacific Ocean.

petrochemicals (pet′ rō kem′ ə kəlz). Chemicals obtained from petroleum or natural gas. Petrochemicals are used in making hundreds of products, such as paint, fertilizer, and synthetic rubber.

petroleum. A thick, oily liquid obtained from the earth. It is usually dark brown or greenish black in color. Gasoline, kerosene, and many other products are made from petroleum. (See page 163.)

pinnacle. A high, slender, pointed tower on a building, such as the steeple on a church. A land formation having a similar appearance is also called a pinnacle.

Plateau Country. A large region in the western part of the United States. (See map, page 28.) Within this region are many plateaus. Some of these plateaus are more than one mile above sea level. There are also rugged mountains, low basins, and deep canyons in this region.

pollute. To make something dirty or impure.

population density. The average number of people per square mile, or some other unit of area, in a given place. Density of population may be figured by dividing the total number of people in an area by the area's total number of square miles or other units.

porous. Full of tiny holes, or pores. Able to absorb liquids.

portage. The carrying of boats or goods overland between two bodies of water, as between a lake and a river. Also, the route followed by people making a portage.

port of entry. A place through which people or goods from a foreign country may legally enter another country.

prairie. A large area of level or rolling land covered with grass and generally treeless.

prehistoric. Relating to the period before written history began.

prejudice. The dislike of a person just because he happens to belong to a minority group. (See page 133.)

primary metals. Metals produced by smelting or refining natural ores, concentrates, or other mineral materials. For example, iron and steel produced from either natural ores or concentrated pellets are referred to as primary metals.

Proclamation of 1763. An order by the British King that prohibited the American colonists from settling west of the Appalachian Mountains.

pulp. A soft, damp material usually made from wood or rags. It consists of many tiny threads, or fibers. Pulp is used in making paper and other products.

pulpwood. Wood that is used to make pulp. (See **pulp.**) Trees commonly cut for pulpwood include pine, hemlock, and spruce.

quarry. An open pit in the earth from which stone is taken. (See picture, page 222.)

rain shadow. An area is said to lie in a rain shadow if mountains shelter it from moisture-bearing winds. When moist winds rise to cross mountains, they are cooled and lose moisture in the form of rain or snow. By the time they have crossed the mountains, they are drier. As the winds descend to the lower land on the other side of the mountains, they become warmer. This causes them to take up moisture instead of releasing it. Thus the land in the "rain shadow" is drier than the land on the other side of the mountains.

ranch. The land and buildings of a large farm where cattle, sheep, or horses are raised. Also, a farm devoted to a particular specialty, such as poultry or wheat.

rangeland. Large areas of open land where cattle or other livestock may graze. Also referred to as range.

ravine (rə vēn'). A small, narrow valley.

raw materials. Substances that can be manufactured into useful products. For example, flax is the raw material used to make linen cloth.

reaper. See **McCormick reaper.**

Red River of the North. A river, about 300 miles long, that begins in Minnesota and flows northward into Lake Winnipeg in Canada. The Red River of the North forms most of the border between Minnesota and North Dakota. (See map, page 252.)

Red River Valley. The valley of the Red River of the North. See **Red River of the North.**

refinery. A place where something is refined. Usually, the building and equipment used for refining metals, sugar, or petroleum. In a petroleum refinery, crude oil is separated into gasoline, kerosene, and other useful products.

reformatory. An institution to which young lawbreakers are sent. Generally, the purpose of a reformatory is not to punish these young people but to train and guide them.

reservoir (rez' ər vwär). A lake, either natural or man-made, that stores large quantities of water until it is needed. The water may be used in homes, in manufacturing, or for irrigating dry land.

retail (rē' tāl). Refers to stores that sell goods directly to the person who will use them. Grocery stores and department stores are examples of retail stores.

Revolutionary War, 1775-1783. The war in which thirteen British colonies in America won their independence from Great Britain. (See page 83.) Although fighting began in 1775, it was not until July of 1776 that the colonies declared their independence. The fighting continued until late in 1781. The Treaty of Paris, which ended the war, was signed in 1783.

Riley, James Whitcomb, 1849-1916. A popular midwestern poet who lived in Indiana. (See page 118.)

Rio Grande. A river that begins in Colorado, flows southward through New Mexico to the Mexican border, and then flows southeastward to the Gulf of Mexico. The Rio Grande is 1,800 miles long. (See map, page 18.)

rock salt. Salt in the form of large crystals.

Rocky Mountains. A long chain of mountains in the western part of Canada and the conterminous United States. (See map, pages 18 and 19.) Many peaks in the Rockies reach more than 14,000 feet above sea level.

roller bearings. Cylinder-shaped objects that enable one part of a machine or a mechanical device to slide smoothly over or around another part. For example, roller bearings are often used in car wheels. They allow wheels to turn easily.

Roman Catholic. Refers to a church that is one of the three main branches of Christianity, or to members of this church. The pope is the head of the Roman Catholic Church.

rosin. A hard, brittle substance that is prepared, along with turpentine, from the sap of living pine trees or from dead pinewood. Rosin is used in products such as paints, varnishes, and soaps.

rotation crop. Any crop, such as clover, alfalfa, or soybeans, that is grown as part of the procedure of crop rotation. See **crop rotation.**

St. Lawrence River. A river about 750 miles long that flows northeastward from Lake Ontario to the Gulf of St. Lawrence, a bay of the Atlantic Ocean. The St. Lawrence is the main outlet of the Great Lakes. See **Great Lakes–St. Lawrence Waterway.**

St. Lawrence Seaway. See **Great Lakes–St. Lawrence Waterway.**

Sand Hills. A vast area of grass-covered sand dunes in central Nebraska. (See map, page 303.)

PRONUNCIATION KEY: hat, āge, cāre, fär; let, ēqual, tėrm; it, īce; hot, ōpen, ôrder; oil, out; cup, pu̇t, rüle, ūse; child; long; thin; ᴛʜen; zh, measure; ə represents a in about, e in taken, i in pencil, o in lemon, u in circus. For the complete key, see page 361.

San Jacinto (jə sin′ tō), **Battle of.** The final battle in Texas' war for independence from Mexico. (See page 89.) This battle took place on April 21, 1836, near what is now the city of Houston. A force of about 800 Texans, led by General Sam Houston, defeated a Mexican army of about 1,500 men. Nearly all the Mexicans were killed or captured. The Mexican general, Santa Anna, was captured the next day. After gaining its independence, Texas became a republic. In October, 1836, Sam Houston was elected the first president of the Republic of Texas.

satellite. A body in space that revolves around a larger body. For example, the moon is a satellite of our planet, earth. Any man-made object that is sent into orbit around the earth or some other heavenly body is also called a satellite.

Scandinavian (skan′ də nā′ vi ən). Refers to the people of Scandinavia, a region in northwestern Europe. Scandinavia includes the countries of Norway, Sweden, and Denmark. Finland and Iceland are also sometimes considered Scandinavian countries.

scholarship. An award of money or other benefits to a student to help him continue his education.

sea level. The level of the surface of the sea. All surfaces on land are measured according to their distance above or below sea level.

secede (si sēd′). To withdraw from an organization, or to declare oneself no longer part of it.

second growth. Refers to a forest that has grown naturally after the original forest was cut down or burned.

segregation (seg′ rə gā′ shən). In the United States, the separation of a minority group from other people, either by law or by custom. For example, under segregation, Negroes generally attend separate schools, eat in separate restaurants, and sit in separate sections of buses. They also live in separate sections of cities.

shale. A fine-grained rock that was probably formed from clay.

shelterbelt. A row of trees planted close together to help prevent soil erosion. (See page 151.)

shrimp. A small, slender sea animal that has a shell, long feelers, and five pairs of legs. There are many kinds of shrimp, several of which are used for food.

silage (sī′ lij). Livestock feed consisting of chopped cornstalks or other green fodder that has been stored in an airtight structure called a silo. In the silo, part of the green material ferments. This helps to preserve the silage as a feed for cattle and other animals in winter.

silt. Material consisting of soil particles that are finer than grains of sand. Silt may be transported by wind or by running water. In lakes, rivers, and other bodies of water, large amounts of silt settle to the bottom. Flooding rivers often deposit silt along their banks. Soil that contains a large amount of silt is usually very fertile.

Sioux (sü) **nation.** A group of Indians, made up of many tribes. The Sioux Indians are also known as the Dakota, which means "allies."

skim milk. Milk from which the cream has been removed.

slum. A crowded section of a town or city, where the houses and other buildings are old, dirty, and run-down, and most of the people are very poor.

smelt. Any of various small, slender food fish with silvery sides and greenish backs.

smelting. The process by which metal is obtained from ore.

sod. A layer of soil held together by the matted roots of grass.

soda ash. An important basic chemical used in the manufacture of products such as glass and paper. It is also used in the manufacture of various chemicals and chemical products. Soda ash is usually made from salt and limestone.

solar system. Our sun and the planets and smaller heavenly bodies that revolve around it. (See page 14.)

solstice (sol′ stis). Either of two times of the year when the direct rays of the sun are farthest from the equator. This occurs about June 21, when the sun shines directly on the Tropic of Cancer, and about December 22, when the sun shines directly on the Tropic of Capricorn. See **Tropic of Cancer** and **Tropic of Capricorn.**

Soo Canals. Canals on the St. Marys River that make it possible for ships to travel between Lake Huron and Lake Superior.

(See map, pages 184 and 185.) More information about these canals is provided on page 244.

sorghum (sôr′ gəm). A plant that resembles corn. There are many varieties of sorghum. In the Great Plains states, many farmers grow grain sorghums. The seeds, leaves, and stalks of grain sorghums are all used as feed for livestock. Sometimes the entire plant is made into silage. (See **silage**.) Grain sorghums grow well even where the weather is very dry.

South. A part of the United States. It includes the states of Alabama, Arkansas, Florida, Georgia, Kentucky, Louisiana, Mississippi, North Carolina, South Carolina, Tennessee, and Virginia. "South" also refers to the states that opposed the Union in the Civil War. See **Civil War**.

soybean. A bushy plant of the pea family. It has hairy stems, leaves, and pods. Soybeans are raised as a farm crop in many parts of our country. The beans and oil pressed from the beans are used to make foods, paint, and many other products. The green plants are sometimes used as feed for livestock. They may also be plowed into a field to enrich the soil.

spring wheat. Wheat that is planted in the spring and harvested in late summer or early fall. See **winter wheat**.

square inch. A unit for measuring area, equal to the area of a square that measures one inch on each side.

standard of living. The average level of conditions in a community or a country, or the level of conditions that people consider necessary for a happy, satisfying life. Among the factors considered in determining standard of living are the general living and working conditions of the people, and the amount and kind of things they possess. In countries with a high standard of living, many different goods and services are generally considered to be necessities. In countries with a low standard of living, many of these same items are luxuries enjoyed by only a few people.

stockyard. A place with pens and sheds where cattle, sheep, hogs, or horses are kept before being sold, slaughtered, or shipped to market.

strip mine. A type of mine in which a mineral is dug from huge open trenches. (See pages 164 and 165.)

suburb. An outer part of a city, or a smaller community near a city.

sulfur. A pale-yellow substance found in large quantities in nature, either pure or combined with other substances. It is used to make fertilizer, paper, medicine, and many chemicals.

Superior Upland. A region of rugged land in the northern part of the United States. (See map, pages 28 and 29.)

surplus. An excess of something. The amount that remains when all uses and needs have been filled.

synthetic (sin thet′ ik). Refers to certain man-made substances, such as plastics and nylon, developed to replace similar natural materials.

taconite. A low-grade iron ore. (See page 167.)

taxes. Money that must be paid to a government. Taxes are used to pay for government operations and public services, such as schools and roads.

telegraph. Refers to an electrical system for communicating over long distances by wire. Telegraph messages, called telegrams, are sent by transmitting coded signals.

tenement. An apartment building occupied by many families. Usually, a tenement is in a run-down condition and is occupied by families that do not have much money.

terminus. The end of a transportation route.

Territory of Wisconsin. A territory, organized in 1836, that included all of what are now the states of Wisconsin, Minnesota, and Iowa, as well as parts of North Dakota and South Dakota.

Texas Panhandle. See **panhandle**.

textile. Refers to woven cloth or the yarn used to weave cloth.

thresh. To separate the grain from the husks and stems of the plant.

topsoil. The top layer of soil on the earth's surface. It is seldom much more than one foot deep. Normally, topsoil is more fertile than the soil beneath it, because

---

PRONUNCIATION KEY: hat, āge, cãre, fär; let, ēqual, tėrm; it, īce; hot, ōpen, ôrder; oil, out; cup, pùt, rüle, ūse; child; long; thin; ᴛнen; zh, measure; ə represents a in about, e in taken, i in pencil, o in lemon, u in circus. For the complete key, see page 361.

it contains a larger amount of decayed plant material.

treadle (tred′ əl). A lever pressed by the foot to run a machine.

treaty. An agreement, usually written, between two or more independent governments.

Tropic of Cancer. An imaginary line around the earth, about 1,600 miles north of the equator. (See top chart, page 50.)

Tropic of Capricorn. An imaginary line around the earth, about 1,600 miles south of the equator. (See top chart, page 50.)

truck farm. A farm on which vegetables are raised to be sold. One meaning of the word "truck" is to trade things. Formerly, vegetables often were traded for other products.

turbine. An engine commonly run by the force of water or steam striking against blades fitted on a drive shaft. Turbines are used to run electric generators. (See pages 167 and 174.)

turpentine. An oily liquid prepared from the sap of living pine trees or from dead pinewood. It is often used for thinning paints and varnishes.

Union. The United States. When used in referring to the Civil War, it means the states that did not secede. See **Civil War.**

United Kingdom. Short name for the United Kingdom of Great Britain and Northern Ireland. A country in western Europe made up of England, Scotland, Wales, and Northern Ireland. See **Great Britain.**

uranium (yù rā′ ni əm). An extremely heavy, silvery-white metal. It is important as the source of certain materials used to produce atomic energy. This energy can be used for many purposes, including the production of electricity.

urban. Refers to cities or other heavily populated areas as opposed to small towns or thinly settled areas.

valve. A device used to control the flow of liquid or gas. A water faucet is a type of valve.

vineyard (vin′ yərd). A place where grapevines have been planted.

wallboard. A building material made in large sheets and used to make or cover inside walls. Fiberboard is one of various kinds of wallboard. See **fiberboard.**

Wayne, Anthony, 1745-1796. An American army officer, known for his reckless courage. Wayne served during the Revolutionary War. In the 1790's, he was appointed commander in chief of the troops sent to the Northwest Territory to halt Indian attacks on pioneer settlements there. (See **Northwest Territory.**) Wayne defeated a large force of Indians in Ohio in 1794 and signed a peace treaty with them the following year. About this time, he also built a fort at the place where Fort Wayne, Indiana, stands today.

weather satellite. A man-made satellite carrying instruments that transmit information about weather to scientists on the earth. See **satellite.**

West Indies. A group of islands located between North America and South America. (See map, page 75.)

wharf. A platform at which ships dock to load and unload passengers or cargo.

wildlife refuge. An area that is set aside for the protection of wild animals or birds.

windbreak. A row of trees or shrubs that serves as a shelter against the force of the wind. Windbreaks are often called shelterbelts.

winter wheat. Wheat that is planted in late summer or early fall and harvested early the following summer.

Wisconsin River. A river about four hundred miles long that flows southwestward from northern Wisconsin into the Mississippi River.

World War I, 1914-1918. The first war in history that involved nearly every part of the world. (See feature, page 111.)

World War II, 1939-1945. The second war in history that involved nearly every part of the world. (See feature, page 111.)

yield. Amount produced. In farming, yield is often expressed as the average number of bushels of a crop produced per acre of land.

zinc. A silvery, bluish-white metal. Zinc resists rust and is used chiefly as a protective coating over other metals, especially iron and steel.

INDEX

Explanation of abbreviations used in this Index:
p — picture   *m* — map   *t* — table

PRONUNCIATION KEY: hat, āge, cãre, fär; let, ēqual, tėrm; it, īce; hot, ōpen, ôrder; oil, out; cup, pùt, rüle, ūse; child; long; thin; ᴛHen; zh, measure; ə represents a in about, e in taken, i in pencil, o in lemon, u in circus. For the complete key, see page 361.

PRONUNCIATION KEY: hat, āge, cãre; fär; let, ēqual, tėrm; it, īce; hot, ōpen, ôrder; oil, out; cup, pùt, rüle, ūse; child; long; thin; ᴛʜen; zh, measure; ə represents a in about, e in taken, i in pencil, o in lemon, u in circus. For the complete key, see page 361.

Rio Grande Valley, 160
roads, *see* transportation
Rockford, Illinois, 217; *m* 205
rock salt, 243, 373

Saginaw, Michigan, 245; *m* 239
St. Lawrence Seaway, 185, 187, 244, 291; *m* 185
St. Louis, Missouri, 97-98, 120, 268-269; *p* 268; *m* 262
St. Marys River, 244; *m* 184
St. Paul, Minnesota, 253, 257-259; *p* 259; *m* 252
salt, *see* minerals
San Antonio, Texas, 344; *m* 333
sand and gravel, *see* minerals
Sand Hills, 40, 304, 305, 306, 373; *p* 305; *m* 303
San Jacinto (jə sin′ tō), Battle of, 342, 374
satellites, 110, 112, 374; *p* 110
scientific attitude, 98-99
seasons, *see* climate
segregation, 131, 133, 134, 135, 374. *See also* discrimination *and* prejudice
settlers, *see* history
sheep, *see* farm products
shipping, *see* transportation, waterways
Sioux (sü) City, Iowa, 237; *m* 229
Sioux Falls, South Dakota, 329, 331; *p* 330; *m* 326
slavery, 90-91, 122; *m* 91
slums, 139, 141-143, 374; *p* 124
social problems, 108, 131-137; *p* 132, 133. *See also* unemployment
social studies skills, 346-353
soil erosion, 150, 151
solar system, 13-15; *p* 13, 14
Soo Canals, 99, 244, 277, 374-375; *p* 186; *m* 184
sorghum, *see* farm products
South Bend, Indiana, 227; *p* 227; *m* 219
South Dakota, 325-331; *p* 325, 327-330; *m* 326
  admission date, *t* 325
  area, *t* 325
  capital, 331; *m* 326
  cities, 331; *p* 330; *m* 326

  climate, 327-328
  colleges and universities, *t* 325
  farming, 328-329, 330; *p* 328; *chart* 328
  farm products, 329; *t* 325
  fisheries, *t* 325
  forest products, *t* 325
  history, 120
  industry, 331; *t* 325; *chart* 328
  land, 39-40, 325-327; *p* 39, 40, 325, 327; *m* 326
  minerals, 329-330; *p* 329; *t* 325
  people, 331
  population, *t* 325
  waterpower, 330; *p* 325
Southern Hills and Valleys, 219-220; *m* 219
South Platte River, 303; *m* 303
South St. Paul, Minnesota, 256; *m* 252
soybeans, *see* farm products
spacecraft, 15; *p* 12
spring, *see* climate
Springfield, Illinois, 217; *m* 205
Springfield, Missouri, 267, 270; *m* 262
spring wheat, 156, 375
standard of living, 107, 375
Straits of Mackinac (mak′ ə nô), 238, 240, 243; *p* 238; *m* 239
strikes, 131
strip-cropping, 151
sugar beets, *see* farm products
sulfur, *see* minerals
summer, *see* climate
Superior Upland, 34-35, 37, 239, 241, 252-253, 285-286; *p* 35; *m* 29

taconite, 167-168
Taum Sauk Mountain, 262; *m* 262
temperatures, *see* climate
Texas, 332-345; *p* 332, 335, 337-339, 341-344; *m* 333
  admission date, *t* 332
  area, *t* 332
  capital, 345; *m* 333
  cities, 342-345; *p* 342-344; *m* 333
  climate, 53, 57, 336
  colleges and universities, *t* 332

  farming, 42, 44, 156, 158, 159, 160, 337-339; *p* 44, 332, 337, 338; *chart* 340
  farm products, 42, 44, 158, 159, 160, 337-339; *p* 44, 61, 337, 338; *t* 332
  fisheries, 339; *t* 332
  forest products, 177, 339; *t* 332
  forests, 176, 339
  history, 85, 89, 93, 342, 344, 345; *p* 74
  industry, 197, 202, 340-342; *p* 129, 197, 200, 341; *t* 332; *chart* 340
  land, 41-42, 43-44, 332-336; *p* 43, 44, 332, 335; *m* 333
  minerals, 164, 170, 339; *p* 339; *t* 332
  people, 116, 121-122, 342
  population, 116; *t* 332
  ports, 187, 343
  waterpower, 340
Texas Annexation, 85; *m* 85
Texas Panhandle, 41-42, 156, 334
Texas State Fair, 344
thunderstorms, *see* climate
Toledo, Ohio, 282; *m* 272
toll roads, 182
Topeka (tə pē′ kə), Kansas, 301; *m* 295
tornadoes, *see* climate
transportation, 109-110, 179-187; *p* 179, 181-183, 186
  airways, 181, 183, 186, 215; *p* 183
  problems of, 138
  railroads, 91-93, 179-180, 181, 183, 198, 243, 301; *p* 92, 179; *m* 94
  roads, 181, 182, 243; *p* 182
  waterways, 31-32, 33, 37, 181, 186-187, 198, 215-216, 243-244, 256, 277; *p* 32, 87, 186, 244; *m* 184-185
transportation equipment, *see* industry
Tropic of Cancer, 50, 376; *chart* 50
Tropic of Capricorn, 50, 376; *chart* 50
truck farms, 160, 376
Tulsa, Oklahoma, 324; *p* 51; *m* 317
Twin Cities, 257-259

---

unemployment, 128-130
Union Pacific Railroad, 92-93;
    m 94
United States, 20; *m* 18-20
uranium, 330, 376

Van Wert, Ohio, 279; *m* 272
vegetables, *see* farm products

Wabash River, 218; *m* 219
War of 1812, 86
wars, 111
Waterloo, Iowa, 237; *m* 229
water resources, 33, 170-174;
    p 171, 173; *m* 172. *See also*
    names of states, waterpower
waterways, *see* transportation
Watt, James, 102; *p* 102

wells, 174
wheat, *see* farm products
wheat belts, 155-157
Whiting, Indiana, 226; *m* 219
Wichita (wich′ ə tô′), Kansas,
    201, 299-300, 301; *p* 300; *m*
    295
Wichita Mountains, 317, 322;
    m 317
winds, *see* climate
winter, *see* climate
winter wheat, 156, 376
Wisconsin, 284-292; *p* 284, 287-
    289, 291; *m* 285
  admission date, *t* 284
  area, *t* 284
  capital, 292; *m* 285
  cities, 290-292; *p* 291; *m* 285
  climate, 286; *p* 57
  colleges and universities, 292;
    t 284
  farming, 152, 285, 286-288; *p*
    284, 287; *chart* 286

  farm products, 153, 285, 287,
    288; *p* 287; *t* 284
  fisheries, 289; *t* 284
  forest products, 288; *p* 288; *t*
    284
  forests, 288; *p* 176, 288
  history, 120, 287, 288, 290, 292
  industry, 200, 201, 289-290; *p*
    289; *t* 284; *chart* 286
  land, 284-286; *p* 284; *m* 285
  minerals, 288; *t* 284
  people, 290
  population, *t* 284
  ports, 291
  transportation, 289, 291
Wright brothers, 283
writers, 118-119

Youngstown, Ohio, 272, 278;
    m 272

PRONUNCIATION KEY: hat, āge, cãre, fär; let, ēqual, tėrm; it, īce; hot, ōpen, ôrder; oil, out; cup, pu̇t, rüle, ūse; child; long; thin; ᴛHen; zh, measure; ə represents a in about, e in taken, i in pencil, o in lemon, u in circus. For the complete key, see page 361.